Meanings of
Occupational Work

Issues in Organization and Management Series

Arthur P. Brief and Benjamin Schneider, *Editors*

Meanings of Occupational Work

A Collection of Essays

Edited by

Arthur P. Brief

A.B. Freeman School of Business
Tulane University

and

Walter R. Nord

College of Business Administration
University of South Florida

Lexington Books
D.C. Heath and Company/Lexington, Massachusetts/Toronto

Library of Congress Cataloging-in-Publication Data

Meanings of occupational work / edited by Arthur P. Brief and Walter
    R. Nord.
        p.   cm. — (Issues in organization and management series)
    ISBN 0–669–12341–2 (alk. paper)
    1. Work. I. Brief, Arthur P., 1946–   . II. Nord, Walter R.
III. Series.
HD4904.M398   1990
306.3'6—dc20   90–33706
                                                                    CIP

Published simultaneously in Canada
Printed in the United States of America
Casebound International Standard Book Number: 0–669–12341–2
Library of Congress Catalog Card Number: 90–33706

The paper used in this publication meets the minimum requirements of
American National Standard for Information Sciences—Permanence of
Paper for Printed Library Materials, ANSI Z39.48–1984. ∞™

Year and number of this printing:

90 91 92 93 94 8 7 6 5 4 3 2 1

To workers—past, present, and future—whose labor was, is, and will be toil and little more.

Contents

Unless otherwise noted, chapters are coauthored by the editors.

Figures and Tables

Figures

Tables

Foreword

Benjamin Schneider
University of Maryland

Academics and business people of many kinds make assumptions about what work means to people. These assumptions lead them to conduct research on and manage people in ways that fit the underlying assumptions they make about the meaning of work to people. In addition, and perhaps more interestingly, academics and business people make assumptions about what *work* means to people. Thus, above and beyond the *meaning* of work to people is the question of what it means to work.

Of interest is the fact that scholars and practitioners make assumptions about these issues and behave in accordance with those assumptions. The fact that the assumptions may be bounded by historical happenstance or time, may be dictated by larger politico-economico-social contextual conditions, and may be clearly differentiated on the basis of a person's familial attachments and current psychological state (e.g., feeling stress), have not been issues receiving great attention in the study of work and work organizations.

Brief, Nord, and their colleagues have clarified for us what some of the assumptions may be under which we view work and the meaning of work. They have done this by reviewing a very broad range of historically focused and contemporary literatures on these issues. Indeed, their review points out the historical, psychological, social, and politico-economico issues that may influence the meaning of work for persons at any one point in time. In other words, the meaning of work is a variable not an absolute both for individuals and societies over time.

This is a very interesting book because the chapters deal with issues usually left unaddressed by others. For this reason, the book presents no definitive answers; the chapters, however, serve to bound the issues. The chapters serve an orienting function: they focus attention on previously unidentified assumptions that guide, and thus, influence, research and practice.

I can only begin to empathize with the effort these scholars have put into identifying the cosmologies with which we approach the study and management of work. It is as if they have begun to clarify in which forests we have been studying the trees of interest. I am delighted they put in the effort and delighted to have the book in the Brief/Schneider series.

Preface

Arthur P. Brief
Walter R. Nord

T his is a book about the meaning of work in people's lives, its origins and consequences. It grew out of a paper we coauthored with Jennifer Atieh and Elizabeth Doherty. That paper, which appeared in Barry Staw and Larry Cummings' (1988) *Research in Organizational Behavior,* primarily was a critique of how organizational psychologists had approached the study of work values. We felt, however, that we had considerably more to say about the values individuals attach to their work. Indeed, we envisioned this book as a thorough review *and* integration of the various literatures that have dealt with the meaning of work. As you will find, difficulties surfaced in trying to write the very first chapter where our goals were merely to define the terms *work* and *meaning.* Very quickly, therefore, it became apparent that the task we had defined for ourselves was a formidable one.

The difficulty in comprehensively treating the meaning of work stems from several related factors. First and foremost, what work means to people cannot be disentangled from what their lives mean to them. Academically, it is interesting to consider an individual's life as an integrated set of identifiable domains which can be separated from one another for purposes of examination; but, in fact, life is a gestalt. Thus, to study the meaning of work entails studying the meaning of life.

Even if one were to approach the meaning of work as if it could be isolated from life as a whole, difficulties in constructing a comprehensive treatment still abound. The learned literatures, presumably pertinent just to the domain of work, are so voluminous as to seem unmeasurable and so diverse as to be unaccessible to even the most Renaissance person. Not only are facets of each of the social sciences concerned with the work domain; it also appears as subject matter in the areas of literary criticism, philosophy, religion, social history, and, in fact, most of the disciplines which comprise the humanities. The size and diversity of the salient literatures are not the only obstacles one confronts in trying to treat the work domain comprehensively. Upon first encountering a discipline with which we generally were unfamiliar, it seemed we had found a conclusive body of evidence; but, not surprisingly, upon further examination we saw matters, in fact, were provisional and tentative. Simply, we wanted to find agareement about what is known but we often found the work domain to be ill-understood.

While this book is not a comprehensive treatment of the meaning of work, we have collected a set of related (not integrated) essays which hopefully will prove to be of value to those who study what people think and feel about their work and how they act at work. This anticipated value might materialize in a number of different ways. For example, much of the study of work attitudes and behavior is microspherical in nature such that investigators rarely look beyond the boundaries of the workplace for explanations of what occurs at work. Several of the essays, however, suggest that by adopting a more macro-level perspective (e.g., one which explicitly embeds a person's work into the economic, political, and social fabric of his/her life away from work), alternative explanations for observed work attitudes and behaviors will be generated and, thereby, enhance our current level of understanding.

The essays may also prove to be of value to students of work attitudes and behaviors in ways other than supplying rival answers to currently addressed questions. They might, perhaps more importantly, be suggestive of questions not now posed. Those expert in what happens at work often do not meaningfully consider how these happenings may affect individuals when they are away from their place of work. Simply, the essays, by examinig the meaning of work *in life,* may stimulate some to contemplate seriously the effects of specific features of work (both intrinsic and extrinsic) on, for instance, families, communities, or even larger units of society. For now, this mostly is the subject matter of humanists and those social scientists having no particular expertise in the content and conditions of work. Again, it is our hope that the current collection of essays may help alter this state of affairs, and lead to a broader approach to studying the effects of work on society.

As the collection's contents page indicates, we are contributors to the volume, not the authors of it. We are the primary authors of chapters 1 and 2, chapters 6 through 9, as well as the epilogue and this preface. Several highly regarded colleagues contributed to the other essays or were their sole authors: Elizabeth Doherty, George W. (Bill) England, Jennifer Atieh, Ed Locke, Loriann Roberson, Susan Taylor, and William Whitely. One aim of engaging this talent was to help ensure that somewhat of a balanced perspective on the meaning of work was approached in the collection. We are reasonably confident this aim was achieved, and for this we are grateful to our collaborators. We are also appreciative of their patience. This expression of gratitude is due to the regrettable fact their essays were completed months and months prior to ours.

Thanks is also due to two other groups. First, when we shared the ideas contained in our essays with our doctoral students, they always seemed to find a point where the logic of our arguments broke down or where our position could be enhanced through recognizing a stream of reasoning we had neglected. Secondly, we are appreciative of the excellent secretarial staffs at New York University and Washington University who not only typed our essays but also managed to keep track of the seemingly endless number of revisions we wrote. In addition, for their continued intellectual stimulation of and social support for our efforts to understand the meaning of work we owe a particular debt of gratitude to a number of colleagues and friends: Ray Aldag, Larry Cummings, Elizabeth Doherty, Jenner Atieh, and Barry Staw. Finally, we extend our appreciation to Bob Bovenschulte, former vice president of Lexington Books, for his willingness to take the risk on the rather esoteric nature of this collection.

We close with a very brief preview of each of the essays which follows. As we indicated earlier, the goal of chapter 1 was to bound our subject of interest by attempting to define the terms *work* and *meanings*. The chapter explicates the particular difficulty in defining the term *work* and concedes it is perhaps best to qualify the phenomenon of interest by labeling it *occupational work*.

Chapter 2 is a case study which focuses on how one group of social scientists—organizational psychologists—have approached the study of the meaning of work. The essay is primarily concerned with the argument that the efforts of organizational psychologists are not only overly narrow but are also based on a false interpretation of Max Weber's view of the Protestant ethic. The chapter concludes on a positive note by suggesting a more catholic approach to the study of the meaning of work.

Chapter 3 by Bill England and William Whitely is a summary of a mammoth cross-national research project. As such, it provides empirically derived alternative construals of the meaning of work and shows the extent to which each alternative is adhered to within and across six countries.

Chapter 4 by Loriann Roberson attempts to demonstrate the usefulness of the meaning of the work construct for understanding behavior in the workplace. Essentially, it is a conceptual analysis of the ways in which work motivation might be affected by varying meanings of work.

Chapter 5 by Ed Locke and Susan Taylor is concerned with job-related distress and its association with the meaning people attached to their work. The authors present a heuristic discourse which explicitly ties the meaning of work to stress and coping.

Chapter 6 essentially provides a brief review of the literature that addresses the relationship between job satisfaction and life satisfaction. From this review and other evidence, the authors attempt to define the roles that work plays in people's lives.

Chapter 7 is concerned with the impact of work on the family and what that impact implies about the meaning of work. The authors provide a framework for thinking about the various ways work may affect different sorts of family units.

Chapter 8 is also concerned with inferring the meaning of work and does so by examining empirical evidence. The research reviewed in this essay, however, addresses involuntary job loss and a more "legitimate" form of unemployment—retirement.

Chapter 9 adopts perhaps the broadest view of the meaning of work. In this essay, the meaning of work is treated as a dependent variable with the forces shaping it seen as stemming from the social, political, and economic context. In effect, much of the chapter focuses on the role of consumption in society.

The epilogue is an attempt to draw a set of conclusions about the meaning of occupational work. The conclusions presented say more about what was left unsaid in the collection of essays than they do about the arguments contained in the essays themselves. In this way, the epilogue represents an agenda for future explorations.

As can be seen, the collected esssays *selectively* examine the questions: What is the meaning of work? and What are its origins and consequences? But again, the collection is eclectic and in no way meant to be viewed as comprehensive. Such completeness remains an elusive goal.

1

Work and Meaning: Definitions and Interpretations

Arthur P. Brief
Walter R. Nord

Job, trade, profession. Produce, create, serve. Drudge, toil, grind. Succeed, advance, satisfy. Words—words people attach to their work. Each reflects a different meaning. These are the sort of meanings of work we had in mind when we began this book.

We did not set out to examine the meaning of life, but found it difficult to keep our study of the meaning of work from growing to include such an examination. In fact, given the American preoccupation with work (see Triandis, 1973), if we had assumed work and life are one, the assumption might not have even been challenged by many readers. However, while our research moved us to recognize the deep interrelationships of work with the rest of life, we stopped far short of treating them as one.

We view the fabric of life as imprinted with a pattern and attempt to describe the position of work in this pattern. Are working, loving, and playing experienced as concentric circles with the former at their core? Alternatively, are they seen as disjoint spheres of existence? These questions represent two extreme positions, neither of which we choose to identify with a priori. The answers to both may be affirmative; more likely, the answers depend on the circumstances. When we set out to learn if and when work has meaning in and of itself, the nature of such meaning, *and* relationships between the meaning of work and other domains emerged as important parts of this pattern. Moreover, it became apparent that the pattern itself is discernible only when work is viewed together with economic, historical, political, and social institutions and processes.

Our research questions are not purely academic. It will be shown that meanings attached to work spill over and help to create the economic, political, and social texture of society. Moreover, work has real personal and social consequences. For the worker who finds dignity and pride in his work and for the one who sees her work only as a means of sustaining her family, the nature of work and its ramifications are obvious.

Our treatment of these issues revolves around these terms: *work, meaning,* and *values.* The remainder of this chapter reports the results of our attempts to define these words. As will be made clear, arriving at acceptable definitions of these words is surprisingly difficult.

Work

As Neff (1985) noted, *Webster's International Dictionary* contains twenty different definitions of the noun *work* and over thirty of the verb. Take, for example, the following common usages: the student working on an assignment at home, the weekend gardener at work in her yard, the church member volunteering his time to work at the annual bazar, a couple trying to work out their relationship, and a carpenter at work raising the roof. It appears that the only element these usages share is some notion of *purposeful activity.* To define work only as a purposeful activity, however, leaves one with a concept so broad in scope as to be almost useless; components of almost all human activity including loving and playing seem to consist of purposeful activities. Thus, it is necessary to bound our use of the term *work.* Neff bounded the word by stating that the purpose of work is to procure the means of subsistence in order to maintain life. Polanyi (1957) referred to the various ways people attain their livelihoods as *work,* and in a similar vein Wallman (1979) observed: "The primeval purpose of work is the human need to control nature, to wrest a living from it and to impose culture in it" (p. 1).

In recent times, wresting a living has come to have a rather special connotation. Historically, the introduction of cash crops and wage labor into a society has often been associated with the emergence of money as "the means of subsistence" produced by working (Schwimmer, 1980). As a result, in modern society, work frequently refers to activities that one receives financial (or some tangible) remuneration for doing. However, this economic definition of work is not without its problems (see Nosow and Form, 1962; Salz, 1944). In particular, Pence (1978–79) feared dangerous political implications from such economic definitions, noting that housework, for instance, does not fit the economic definition and, in our society, such an exclusion entails loss of status and privileges for those who perform it. Again, the answer to the question, "What is work?" has more than merely academic significance.

Defining Work—One Meaning Out of Many

Most contemporary writers employ the economic definition of work; it is what people do for financial compensation in order to earn a living. Ultimately, although reluctantly, so do we. We use this definition because it is what the word appears to mean most often when it is used at the present time by the people we hope will benefit from this book—social scientists, businessmen and -women, and policy makers.

Our reason for using this definition reluctantly, comes from our belief, as we will describe below, that this definition partially obscures the understanding of the personal and institutional consequences of work. The word *work* or its equivalent has different meanings in different societies. Moreover, just as the dictionary indicated, within a society of even moderate complexity, the word has many meanings simultaneously. We attempt to be sensitive to these various meanings by stressing that the word *work,* like other words, has no absolute meaning; its meaning is given in the context of a particular language community.[1]

Our approach is to acknowledge the multiple meanings of work but focus more heavily on one than on the others. This compromise may appear to be an "easy out" of the problem we faced in defining work. It may be an "out," but we did not come to it easily. Our training as social scientists drove us to feel that the only place to begin inquiry is with a meaningful conceptual definition. We had been taught that if we are to talk about a phenomenon such as work, we should at least be able to distinguish clearly what *is* work from what *is not* work in some more psychologically or sociologically meaningful way than that it is an activity one is paid for doing. For a long time, we attempted to arrive at such a definition. Although this struggle did not lead to where we had expected it would, the process did lead us to recognize serious problems with the conventional economic definition and to recognize that the meaning of work changes with shifting patterns of social existence. In short, we came to a relativistic view. The argument for relativity and its importance can be shown by a brief look at work in Western economic history.

History and Work

Peter Kelvin (1984) observed that a critical distinction between social and physical scientists is the degree to which the latter are able to state the conditions of theoretically pure cases. For example, while the velocities of falling objects vary greatly depending on the conditions under which they fall, the student of physics is able to explicate all (or at least the most important) conditions that may influence the rate of descent and, thereby, establish a theoretical template to use as a basis for measuring and calculating real phenomena. Kelvin wrote: "The natural sciences have reached this stage precisely because they came to distinguish between particular occurrences and the general ('universal') processes which underlie them" (p. 406). Social scientists have been less successful.

In some ways, social scientists have devoted a great deal of effort to distinguishing the universal from the particular. The extensive array of contingency theories, and efforts to control for alternative explanations of results in empirical research, are evidence of this concern. Often, however, this sensitivity is manifested almost exclusively through attention to events that are spatially and temporally proximate to the research itself. For example, events or conditions that existed shortly before or during the collection of data are the subject of diligent search and careful explication and control. This search and control constitute the heart of accepted research methodology and reduce the chances that the particular will be mistaken for the universal.

Of course, physical scientists are concerned with controlling concomitant events as well. However, at least for many problems the physical scientist studies, the more distant histories of the elements under investigation are either not very important or their effects can be easily eliminated (e.g., by sterilizing or demagnetizing a piece of material) or measured.

The social scientist cannot control for history so easily. As a result, if attempts to discover and control for variables that affect a particular phenomena are concentrated in such close proximity to data collection itself, the social scientist is quite likely to mistake the *historically* particular for the universal. To illustrate, consider two social variables that are related to the nature of work—technology and forms of social organization. As major changes in technology and forms of social organization take place, it becomes extremely difficult to argue that relationships between two social entities (e.g., labor and capital), observed at one point in time (e.g., Time 2) provide much information about relationships at Time 3 or at Time 1. In other words, the contextual variables are changing. However, the problem is even more complex because one or both of the entities themselves may change with time.

Consider the example noted above—labor and capital. In discussing the economic history of Europe between 1000 and 1700, Cipolla (1980) noted the difficulty we in the present have in comprehending the nature of what these entities (or phenomena) were "really" like in the past. One of the major difficulties in historical reconstruction is that, in order to express ourselves, we must use current language. Unfortunately, the words we use today evoke mental images of the contemporary world. Expressions such as *labor* and *capital,* for instance, automatically evoke pictures of the factory, with its high concentration of managers, wage laborers, and complex machinery. Cipolla observed that imagination is required to recapture "the very different reality of the past." On the other hand, imagination introduces new problems. Cipolla added, "In this attempt, one must be careful not to go to the other extreme, to fall victim to stereotyped, fanciful typologies" (pp. 64–65).

Social scientists have made both errors in their studies of work. On the one hand, students from Marx through modern organizational behaviorists have accepted a stereotype of work prior to the industrial revolution. In this view, the industrial revolution robbed people of intrinsically interesting work and the opportunity to develop and apply a wide variety of skills. On the other hand, students have failed to give adequate attention to factors that have changed the social relationships that surround how people make a living. These changes have been so dramatic that working cannot be assumed to involve similar experiences now as at earlier points in time. Consider some of Cipolla's observations.

- Even before the industrial revolution child labor was common.
- In the manorial form of organization that dominated Europe early in the current millennium, money and the division of labor were almost unknown.
- Certain occupations were far more prominent than today; for example, a large percentage of the population, often nearly twenty percent, in European cities was domestic servants (although the statistics are not systematically available and are subject to considerable error). The ecclesiastical population was large and prostitution played a significant role in the economy. (Cipolla reported that in 1600, census data put the number of prostitutes at two percent of the adult female population.)
- Preindustrial craftsmen typically owned some or all of the capital and worked on a commission basis for merchants who provided the raw materials and disposed of the output.
- Guilds played a major role in the European economy for the centuries preceding the seventeenth and performed a variety of protective, social, economic, charitable, and religious functions.

In view of these differences alone (to say nothing of the more widely recognized changes in technology, the physical and social nature of the workplace, and so forth), it is hard to believe work had anything close to contemporary meaning. The meaning of work is historically relative.

Once the historical relativity is recognized, a number of dimensions of social organization come into view that have changed dramatically over time and seem likely to have altered the nature and meaning of work. Obviously, the degrees and forms of coercion and choice that govern who works, what they do, and when, where, why, and how they do it vary over time. There is wide variety in the modes of organizing labor in the Western world—slavery, feudalism, sharecropping (both coerced and noncoerced), wage labor, and self-employment. Each of these forms became concentrated in different regions at different points in time because, at least from the perspective of functional theory, each mode was better suited for a particular type of production.

The implications of such analysis for present purposes are several. First the structures used to control people while they have "made a living," have varied widely. Clearly, for example, it cannot be assumed that the experience of making a living under slavery is the same as that of a modern American executive. While this is an extreme example, it demonstrates the absurdity of assuming that some essential meaning of work exists given the variety of structures. If there is a common essence, it must be discovered, not assumed. Simply subsuming so many diverse human experiences under the same label undoubtedly obscures more than it illuminates. Second, Wallerstein (1974) concluded that not only have the various forms of control served particular production requirements better than others, but they also affected the political system and the nature of the state. In other words, the nature of the work process affects the way societies are ruled (and, as we will show, vice versa). Third, the nature of work at a particular point in time has been influenced by demographic factors, such as the scarcity of labor. Universal statements about the nature and experience of work which do not factor these elements into the equation are apt to be misleading.

Taken together, these ideas make it clear that the nature of work and the conditions under which people do it vary widely on a number of dimensions. Analysis of work (in order to capture these differences), must include the impact of historical, social, political, and economic perspectives which will reveal how these changes are imprinted on the patterns of human experience from which the meaning of work is derived. Approaches that attempt to understand work and its meaning at a particular point in space and time without recognizing the broader patterns will lead to us mistaking the particular for the general. In short, work and the meanings people derive from and give to it, cannot be isolated from the fabric of the society in which they exist.

In our view, the study of work by most modern social scientists has failed to recognize the importance of this rich context. This failure has meant that we have not produced a universal understanding of the meaning of work. Perhaps even worse, however, we have mistaken the particular understanding of work that we have provided for a universal one. Investigation of how people make a living under the conditions of the "free" labor market in the Western world of the late twentieth century is indeed the study of the particular.

To a degree the problem is unavoidable. There seems to be no way of preventing scholars of a particular era from verifying the present. [Geertz's (1988) recent book would certainly give strong support for this position.] Certainly, we make no pretense of being immune to this problem; in fact by accepting the economic definition of work, we demonstrate that we are infected. Throughout, however, by pointing to the larger pattern, we hope to protect the reader and ourselves from mistaking the particulars for the universal.

Work and the Present

The failure to appreciate the historical and social relativity of work and the meanings people give to it is only one of two basic ways that the particular has been mistaken for the universal in the social science of work. A related error is to assume a common essence across the work of people *within* a particular era. The problems of doing so are obvious from a simple extension of the view we have just developed—right now, hundreds of millions of people are earning a living by doing millions of different things, under a wide variety of control systems and demographic conditions.

In response to this assertion, it might be argued that current treatments never really sought to develop a worldwide understanding, but instead only one for industrially advanced societies or even more specifically for the Western world, the United States in particular. However, even such a bold retreat does not solve the problem. Within the United States, people earn a living doing a wide variety of things under a wide variety of conditions. These conditions vary as a function of both macro-level (societal) and micro-level (local, individual) factors.

Variations in macro-level conditions can be illustrated by considering economic cycles. Sometimes work is done during a period of prosperity and growth and at other times during periods of recession and decline. During prosperity, people may focus on alternative opportunities and the negative aspects of their jobs; during a recession, they may be apt to be thankful for any job. International events also can affect the meaning of work within a society. Sometimes, for instance, people work while their nation is at peace, but at other times their society may be involved in a war that threatens its existence. The meaning of work changes as a result. Support for this assertion comes from Turner and Miclette's (1962) report that the way workers for a defense contractor approached their tasks was affected by their awareness of the importance of quality products for national defense.

Variations in conditions at micro-levels include that people may be: working in rising or declining industries; directing the work of others or having others direct them; working as principals (owners) or agents of principals; temporary or part-time employees; rewarded according to their output, the output of their group, or independently of their output; and so forth. Moreover, the nature of their work may vary along a number of well-known dimensions, such as those described by Hackman and Oldham (1980): skill variety, task indentity, task significance, autonomy, and feedback from the job. In addition, as Salancik and Pfeffer (1978) have suggested, people work under a wide variety of social conditions which will influence the interpretation they give to any objective set of job characteristics. Finally, some people experience more choice about having to work in general or to continue on a particular job. A number of psychological theories (e.g., what Brehm (1966) labeled *psychological reactance*) predict that the degree of coercion or choice will influence the meaning that people give to any situation.

This range of conditions is not intended to be exhaustive. We believe it is sufficient, however, to substantiate our claim: namely that the objective characteristics of what people do to earn a living, and the conditions under which they do so, vary greatly within a given society. These variations are introduced by forces operating at all levels of society. Therefore, the study of what work is and what meaning it has to people must be based on a framework that incorporates a broad spectrum of individual, social, political, and economic factors. The meaning of work cannot be studied adequately within the confines of workplaces as most contemporary social scientists have attempted to do.

Hopefully, we have made it clear that we do not believe that work has any ultimate essence that can give it universal meaning. In fact, this is true of most words—words have meaning in the language community that uses them at a particular place and time in history. In our verbal community, *work* is viewed as something one does to earn a living or is paid for—we use this requirement as a major component in our definition because of its frequent use by the audience we address. Still, some problems in definition need attention.

Remaining Definitional Problems

Even with the extreme simplification of limiting work to activity done for pay, problems remain. While operationally the distinction between paid and unpaid activity is relatively unambiguous, the distinction leads one into such difficult positions as having to rationalize why a professional golfer who in a seemingly effortless manner drives a ball three hundred yards is "working," but one of us taking three mighty swings and traversing a less direct route to achieve approximately the same physical displacement is "playing." Similarly, it seems to make little sense to argue that my neighbor and I (who have identical lawns) are not "working" when we each cut our own lawn, but that if we agreed to cut each other's lawn for equal pay, we would be working.

In view of this last example, it is tempting to use the domain within which an activity takes place to distinguish what is work from what is not. However, this distinction breaks down also because a number of activities take place within any given domain. For example, people may play or love at a place where they are being paid for some other activity. To put it somewhat differently, certain activities are shared across the domains of life. Neither the activity, the place, nor the interaction of the two allows us to distinguish work from nonwork.

Moreover, even if the activity and the context are the same, the meaning that the activity has can be affected by whether one does something for pay or does it because it provides "the means of subsistence" for one's livelihood. Doing something for a living implies greater coercion than doing it for pay; some people do not need the money they earn to live and, in fact, the money they earn may be so small a proportion of their total wealth that it contributes little to even maintaining the standard of living to which they are accustomed.

Some examples may help clarify this distinction: the working wealthy whose investment income could adequately maintain their lifestyles, working spouses whose husbands' or wives' income is more than ample for the family unit, and persons with comfortable retirement incomes who choose to continue working.

These examples point to two issues that must be considered in assessing the meaning of work. First, since some individuals work when the income they earn is inconsequential, it seems that the definition of work we employ does not provide a complete understanding of the various motives of people who do activities for which they are paid. Put in different words, the meaning of work to an individual is apt to be a function of his/her perceived economic need. In short, one's wealth affects the meaning of one's work. Second, this effect is moderated by the level of economic need. Unfortunately, the factors that influence the level of economic need a person experiences are largely unknown (Brief and Aldag, in press), although objective conditions such as the number of dependents the person supports, the state of the economy, and the host of subjective factors that collectively can be labelled as *expectations* are apt to play major roles. Economic expectations are difficult to measure and may be greater for adults reared in affluent families than those from more impoverished backgrounds, for people with a college degree than those less educated, and for persons working in prestigious occupations than those engaged in lower status work. But, again, we simply do not know. In fact, as we will discuss in a later chapter, what constitutes "a living" varies greatly across historical eras, societies, and even stages of a person's life.

In suggesting that economic need (both objective and subjective) affects the meaning people attach to their work, we are asserting that the two key elements of conventional definitions of work—doing something to make a living, and being paid to do it—may not necessarily go together. However, both are widely included by our verbal community; and most people in the social system we are writing about achieve both through work. Therefore, we will not bother further with this distinction.

We also largely ignore one other possible distinction. Some social scientists (e.g., Dubin, 1959), and a number of labor leaders (see Tyler, 1983) have argued that working is an involuntary behavior because it is performed out of economic necessity. However, the distinction between such "coerced" work and "voluntary" work is not made in the data currently available on work. While excluding the extremes of slavery and hobbies, the existing literature lumps together many states of economic necessity in studying work. Although the degree of perceived coercion may be a crucial variable to consider in future research, the existing literature does not provide any guidance about the role such a variable plays. We therefore are compelled to define work as something done for pay and to make a living, and ignore the degree of coercion that is perceived.

Work = Occupational Work

Even by narrowing concepts as we have, the term *pay* itself introduces still other problems in distinguishing work from nonwork. Most discussions of activities done for pay are concerned with the social role Miller (1980) termed *occupational work*. The defining attributes of an occupational work role are: "(1) its existence as a role discrete and separate from the other roles occupied by the individual, and (2) the primary use of such direct financial rewards as salaries or wages to obtain a minimal level of involvement in the role by the worker" (p. 382).

The idea of occupational work helps us move closer to what we think most people today have in mind when they use the word *work*. However, even here certain ambiguities remain. Neither the requirement of financial compensation nor separation of roles allows us to carve up reality in a fully satisfactory manner. For example, using this definition, should the activities of members of an Israeli kibbutz (see Criden and Gelb, 1974) be considered work? Other activities within contemporary alternative communities and movements, including the Hutterite (Hostettler, 1974), "The Form" (Hall, 1978), and the Hare Krishna (Judah, 1974), raise similar issues. Members of these systems earn their livelihoods through activities that are often labeled as *work*, but they do not receive direct financial compensation. These people also do not have role separation, and so they would appear to fall outside of Miller's definition of occupational work.

By the same logic, housework would seem to be nonoccupational work. Here again, we see clearly the difficulties with the definition of work we are using. The activities of housework involve toil, drudgery, management, planning, decision-making, and other components of occupational work. Moreover, by excluding housework from work (especially in a culture that values work in the way ours does), one risks degrading and potentially disempowering those who perform it. By using Miller's notion of occupational work, we de-emphasize but do not exclude such activities, for reasons that will become apparent below.

There are at least two other problems in using Miller's criteria. First, the term *financial* does not describe all possible compensation arrangements. Second, if role separation is required, many activities which seem to be generally understood as *work* would be excluded.

A major problem with defining work as activities performed for financial compensation is that it implies that work tends to be denoted by the payment of money. But, what is money? If money is held to refer to a medium of exchange that has no value in itself besides acceptance by the members of defined groups, then something such as gold that has other uses would not qualify. Once gold is included, then where can the line be drawn? Payment in all commodities would seem to qualify as well. So too would what Ferman

(1983) called *informal work*—that is, work activity which occurs outside of the traditional marketplace of economic activities, including: bartering, stealing, and the social exchange of services. Persons engaged in these activities do not receive wages or salaries and are not self-employed in the traditional sense. Yet they too, at least in part, earn their livelihoods from activities that under other circumstances would be classified as working. Clearly, the definition of work we have chosen does not emphasize nonoccupational or informal work; however, it also does not explicitly exclude them.

The second problem in using Miller's notion is that role separation is almost always partial. Most occupations involve an occupant in a number of interlocking roles. Role obligations can even extend to one's family members—say, for example, the social obligations of an executive's spouse. Moreover, some occupations (such as priest or nun) make it very difficult to separate any aspect of one's self from one's occupation.

Nevertheless, we define work as an activity for which one receives financial remuneration and is separated from other roles. We have shown why this is not a fully satisfactory solution and also why no such solution exists. We must, however, begin some place and the usage of the term in the verbal community we address seems a reasonable place to start. It is a pragmatic choice and, as with most pragmatic choices, certain aesthetics are sacrificed.[2]

Some Dimensions of Work

Even though we have attempted to narrow our scope considerably through our definition of work, we are still left with an enormous task. Jobs vary widely in terms of their content; that is the kinds of tasks which comprise them. The U.S. Department of Labor's (1965) *Dictionary of Occupational Titles* described more than thirty thousand jobs. These work forms vary in several different ways, each of which might influence the meaning of work.

A number of dimensions for distinguising among forms of work have been proposed. For example, Wallman (1979) listed ten dimensions that might be used for comparing work across cultures: energy, incentive, resources, value, time, place, person, technology, identity, and alienation. Likewise, industrial psychologists have devised various taxonomies to characterize the configurations of mental, physical, and interpersonal tasks which, in terms of content, describe alternative forms of work (e.g., Fleishman and Quaintance, 1984). It is expected that as jobs differ on one or more of these dimensions or as one moves from one cell to another of such taxonomies, the meaning a person attaches to work will somehow be different. For example, contrast the activities of a lawyer who, after years of training, performs a variety of mentally and interpersonally demanding tasks, with those of a freight handler, whose work primarily involves the use of a few simple but physically taxing actions. Although it is an empirical matter, it seems likely that, given the different inputs they make, the lawyer will find a different sort of meaning in her tasks than will the freight handler.

Outputs as well as inputs influence the meaning of one's work. The outputs of the tasks a worker performs constitute a contribution to the production of some good or service (Vroom, 1964) and the nature of a product or service affects meaning (Turner and Miclette, 1962). For example, even though both are practicing law, a lawyer engaged in public service law to the poor may attach very different meaning to his work than a lawyer supplying tax advice to corporate clients. Viewed from the side of outputs, one may view a particular job as a way to make certain social statements. (In view of this possibility, both the lawyer for the poor and the tax attorney may feel they are making social statements.) In addition, work places one in certain social relationships. As Marx (1967) recognized in the *German Ideology,* part of the meaning of work stems from these social relationships, such as those between the producer and the consumer.

The potential meaning of work is also apt to be influenced by the location at which it is performed. As Baran and Sweezey (1966) noted some time ago, the physical surroundings of modern corporations send off a variety of ego-enhancing or ego-degrading signals. [See Eric Sundstrom's (1986) *Work Places* for an informative discussion of the symbolic properties of location and characteristics of work-space.] Similarly, if one works for an organization, its reputation is apt to affect the meaning one attaches to a job.

The identified ways in which work varies—content, product, location—do not represent an exhaustive list of the elements that affect meaning. They simply illustrate, once again, the complexity of the meaning of work even within our heavily constrained definition of work.

Meaning of Meaning

There are two key words in the subject of this book: *work* and *meaning.* So far we have focused on the complexities introduced in attempting to define the former. Unfortunately, defining *meaning* is no easier.

Two of the definitions of *meaning* that are given in *Webster's New Twentieth-Century Dictionary* are pertinent to our treatment of the meaning of work. The first is: "that which exists in the mind, view, or contemplation as a settled aim or purpose; that which is meant or intended to be done." The second definition is: "sense, understanding; knowledge."

Viewing the meaning of work from the perspective of the first definition, we focus on why people work—what they intend to accomplish by working. Most people who have written on the subject, at least in Western cultures, have adopted this perspective. Implicit in this perspective is the assumption that an individual's behavior stems from purposes (or decisions) that precede their actions. More recently, however, the idea that purpose is a retrospective process (Weick, 1979) is congruent with another interpretation of this definition. In this view the aim or purpose is not known to a person until after he/she has acted in some way. In other words, purpose is the aim that the individual constructs to be congruent with something that he/she is doing or has already done. Meaning comes after the fact. The second definition of meaning is also compatible with both a prospective and a retrospective perspective. Sense, understanding, and knowledge could both precede and/or follow action.

In our view, both the prospective and retrospective senses of the two definitions are necessary to capture the meaning of work. Whereas both definitions suggest that meaning involves a cognitive process, each leads us to consider quite different features. The prospective sense of the former definition reminds us that often people do work to accomplish one or more ends. Its retrospective sense reminds us that the reasons people give for working change as a result of what they do. The prospective sense of the second definition reminds us that people may have an understanding of work that is based on information they have received without any direct experience with a particular job or even with work in general. The retrospective sense alerts us to the fact that meaning changes as a result of direct experience and that much of the experience of work comes from "incidentials"—events and thoughts that take place while one is working or that only exist when people reflect on what they have done or have had done to them. It is important to note that the content of all of these processes can be quite unique to a particular individual. Hence, the meaning of any type of work may be highly idiosyncratic.

Taken together, these perspectives indicate that work can be viewed as a purposeful activity; but understanding the meaning of work as only intentional, purposeful activity runs the risk of missing many aspects that are experienced by the worker but do not explain why one works. Our use of the word meaning includes both one's purpose and one's sense or knowledge about the experience of work and recognizes that both of these have prospective and retrospective dimensions.

What Determines Meaning?

We postulate that the meaning of all human activities is derived from two basic sources—intent and understanding. Therefore, comprehension of how meaning of any given activity comes about requires knowledge of the acquisition of purpose and the acquisition of understanding. Both of these matters would require volumes in themselves. Here, we will only describe briefly some of the factors we believe are affected by the meaning of work to an individual.

We view the acquisition of one's purpose(s) for working as a combination of personal development and of one's perception of past, present, and future events and needs. Clearly, some of the factors that contribute to one's purpose for working are biological. Such factors as the need to acquire the elements of subsistence and the use of skills and energies would seem to fall under a biological heading. Also, some reasons for working are acquired in the process of socialization through which a person acquires norms and values about work itself and one's role in society that makes work an end in itself or a means to other things that are expected of the individual. Thus, treatment of the meaning of work must include analysis of both biological and social processes.

In addition, to say that the meaning of work is developmental is to recognize that the purpose of work can change over time for the same individual. The same person may perform the same activity or job under the very same social, technological, and other conditions for very different reasons at age twenty-five than at age sixty. Thus, changes in purpose are part of the meaning of work.

What one intends to accomplish and one's interpretation of what he/she has done are also affected by past, present, and expected future events. People's intentions and understandings about what they will get and have gotten from work are shaped through socialization, social norms, and their own and others' experience. Also, people learn from past experiences what they are apt to be able to accomplish through specified activities and often they adjust these expectations on the basis of current events. For example, as we suggested earlier, economic conditions affect the experience of work. People may give up hope of advancement on their jobs due to an economic downturn but develop new goals for success when the industry they are in suddenly prospers. Expectations about the future may change for any number of reasons and as they change, so do people's intentions. Moreover, as individuals reflect back, the purposes they attribute to their actions and their sense of what they did will be influenced by events that they associated with their behavior.

At a more abstract level, one's purposes and understandings are influenced by the general state of human development at any given point in time. For example, it is generally agreed that one of the reasons people work in modern industrial societies is to earn money so that they can consume. While biologically a minimal level of consumption of certain basics seems essential, above that level one's desire to consume is quite probably a function of what is available for purchase. This is, of course, influenced by the level of invention and technological development at any given point in time. Moreover, the desire to consume is quite likely influenced by what people know other individuals are consuming. Again, we are driven to recognize the elements of context that affect the meaning of work.

Finally, meaning is influenced by the verbal community in which one exists. The words associated with a phenomenon play a major role in how one experiences it. White and Mitchell (1979), in a clever experiment, revealed how the words of co-workers can affect the reported experience of a task. More generally, Berger and Luckmann's (1966) discussion of the social construction of reality and Edelman's (1977) treatment of political language have shown how language generates meaning. In this vein, it is worth noting how words such as *toil, burden,* and *pain* which were often used to refer to work in earlier times (see *Encyclopedic Dictionary of the Bible*, 1963) have been replaced, almost totally, in contemporary discussions by less evocative terms such as *work* and career. Undoubtedly changes in the physical demands of jobs have been associated with these lexical changes. Nevertheless, it is interesting to contemplate the effects these different words may have on how people perceive their work.

In sum, the meaning of a socially embedded process such as work is affected by a complex and dynamic social context. While the concrete realities operate directly on one's senses, one's understanding of them is influenced by these data and the intentions and expectations one holds for work. These in turn are influenced by the complex set of forces we describe as the social system. Thus, the meaning of work is not simply the purposes plus the concrete conditions. Rather the meaning of work reflects both of these, and their dynamic interrelationships. One's sense and understanding of the concrete aspects of work are affected by one's purposes. One's purposes for doing something are affected by concrete experiences as well as by what one has learned vicariously through observing or listening to others. And, to repeat a major point, both the purposes and the concrete realities are themselves dynamically interrelated with past social and economic events and institutions.

Individual as Focus of Meaning

In order to understand the meaning of work, we must be prepared to investigate a broad spectrum of human history and the concrete experiences of people in and around work at any particular point in history. The dynamic nature of the interrelationships makes the puzzle even more complex. However, ultimately all of these factors impact on the individual—it is the individual to whom we attribute understanding and purpose.

Because we focus on the individual, our use of the term *meaning* will usually be psychological in nature. Essentially, we use *meaning* as a catchall to refer to people's beliefs, values, and attitudes which are generated by processes analyzed in numerous other disciplines such as anthropology, economics, history, philosophy, political science, psychiatry, and, most of all, sociology. The beliefs, values, and attitudes, however, are our central concerns.

Our view of what defines beliefs, values, and attitudes is strongly influenced by Rokeach (e.g., 1973; 1979). His writings focus on the concept of values and thus we begin with his definition: "A *value* is an enduring belief that a specific mode of conduct or end state of existence is personally or socially preferable to an opposite or converse mode of conduct or end state of existence" (Rokeach, 1973, p. 5). Complete stability is not implied by use of the word *enduring*. Individual and social change would be impossible if values were completely stable; but, if they were completely unstable, then continuity of human affairs would be impossible. Thus, *enduring* implies relative stability. Indeed, changes in values will be a subject of concern.

Not all beliefs are values. A value is a prescriptive or proscriptive belief, "a belief on which a man acts by preference" (Allport, 1961, p. 454). Rokeach (1968) identifies two other types of beliefs: those capable of being true or false, descriptive or existential beliefs; and, evaluative beliefs, wherein the objective belief is judged to be good or bad. As Feather (1975) has noted, judgments about what is good or bad are expected to be highly correlated with views about what is desirable or undesirable. This entwining makes the distinction between evaluative and prescriptive or proscriptive beliefs less than a sharp one.

Attitudes are a function of values (e.g., Allport, 1961) but they differ from values. Attitudes refer to an organization of several beliefs about a specific object or situation; values refer to a single belief of a very special kind (Rokeach 1968; 1973). Like values, attitudes have cognitive, affective, and behavioral components. They involve knowledge about likes/dislikes or desirables/undesirables; feelings generated when they are challenged; and, potentially an action when they are activated.

Beliefs, values, and attitudes have overlapping domains and, together, serve the individual in giving meaning to ongoing events (Feather, 1985). However, following Rokeach, we treat values as the core concept. To Rokeach, values are the products of cultural, institutional, and personal forces acting upon the individual that in turn have consequences of their own—"values are guides and determinants of social attitudes and ideologies on the one hand and of social behavior on the other" (Rokeach, 1973, p. 24).

Importantly, Rokeach's views on the antecedents and consequences of values are far from pure conjecture. He has developed a Value Survey from which the importance of eighteen instrumental and eighteen terminal values as guiding principles in a person's life can be measured. Instrumental values refer to modes of conduct—the qualities of being ambitious, capable, responsible, and self-controlled. Terminal values refer to end-states of existence. Some examples of these are a comfortable life, an exciting life, a sense of accomplishment, and salvation. Using the Value Survey, Rokeach has found that social class, religiousness, political affiliation, and nationality are predictive of people's values. Moreover, it has been shown that these values are systematically associated with attitudes toward blacks, poor people, student protests, and communism, and with behaviors such as joining the NAACP, attending church, returning borrowed pencils, and choosing an academic major (see Rokeach, 1973).

But what does all this have to do with the meaning of work? A great deal, we argue. The way we have framed our use of the term *meaning* leads us to ask questions addressing beliefs about work, attitudes toward work, and most of all, values attached to work. Rokeach's program of research tells us that these work-related beliefs, attitudes, and values are linked to a person's total belief system; are culturally, institutionally, and experientially conditioned; and are behaviorally relevant. Thus, we expect to find the meaning of work to be tied to the person's beliefs, attitudes, and values he/she evidences in other spheres of his/her life; to vary as a function of the social context in which the person is embedded; to be affected by his/her personal experiences with work; and to stand behind the ways in which the person acts toward work.

Conclusion

Work has no ultimate essence that can give it universal meaning. Its meaning is a function of its use in particular verbal communities. In the community we seek to speak to, work generally is viewed as something one does to earn a living or is paid for. While this pragmatic definition conveys some sense of purpose, the meaning of work is not simply this purpose. Rather, the meaning of work an individual experiences reflects his/her purposes (that is, intentions and expectations), the concrete realities which operate on those purposes, and their dynamic relationships. In the process of arriving at this perspective, we learned that the conventional economic definition of work we have chosen to use has serious problems; but, we realize, no definition of work is problem free. Moreover, our journey taught us that the meaning of work changes with shifting patterns of social existence. Thus, as a particular verbal community evolves politically and economically, for instance, so do the meanings individuals within that community attach to their work.

Now we can move forward with at least some guidance to explore the meaning of work in people's lives. More specifically, our aims are to better understand: (a) the nature of people's beliefs about, attitudes toward, and values attached to the purposeful activities for which they receive financial remuneration; (b) how these beliefs, attitudes, and values arise; and (c) in what ways they influence behaviors and the cultural, institutional, and work contexts of society.

Notes

1. Although the essence of this idea is that of Ludwig Wittgenstein, we owe a great deal to Joanne Ciulla for showing us the relevance of it to what we were doing and getting us out of the morass our efforts to define work in some more absolute sense kept us in for a long time.

2. Other students of work have reported the need to make similar pragmatic decisions. For example, Wallman (1979) defined work as "the production, management, and conversion of the resources necessary to livelihood" (p. 20), but quickly demonstrated that even this definition could not adequately serve all the writers in her volume devoted to comparative anthropology of work. She observed that given the definitional problems one might opt to simply stop the discussion or to prolong it until a general all-purpose definition is found. Finding neither approach acceptable, Wallman suggested proceeding by compromise.

References

Allport, G.W. (1961). *Pattern and growth in personality.* New York: Holt, Rinehart and Winston.

Baran, P.A., and Sweezey, P. (1966). *Monopoly capital.* New York: Monthly Review Press.

Berger, P.L., and Luckmann, T. (1966). *The social construction of reality.* New York: Anchor.

Brehm, J.W. (1966). *A theory of psychological reactance.* New York: Academic Press.

Brief, A.P., and Aldag, R.J. (In press). The economic function of work. In K. Rowland and G. Ferris (eds.), *Research in personnel and human resources management.* Greenwich, CT: JAI Press.

Cipolla, C.M. (1980). Before the industrial revolution. *European society and economy, 1000–1700,* 2nd edition. New York: Norton.

Criden, Y., and Gelb, S. (1974). *The kibbutz experience.* New York: Schocken Books.

Dubin, R. (1958). Industrial research and the discipline of sociology. In *Proceedings of the 11th Annual Meeting.* Madison, WI: Industrial Relations Research Association, pp. 134–72.

Edelman, M. (1977). *Political language: words that succeed and policies that fail.* New York: Academic Press.

Feather, N.T. (1975). *Values in education and society.* New York: Free Press.

———. (1985). Attitudes, values, and attributions: Explanations of unemployment. *Journal of Personality and Social Psychology, 48,* pp. 876–89.

Ferman, L.A. (1983). The work ethic in the world of informal work. In J. Barbash, R.J. Lampman, S.A. Levitan, and G. Tyler (eds.), *The work ethic—A critical analysis.* Madison, WI: Industrial Relations Research Association, pp. 211–29.

Fleishman, E.A., and Quaintance, M.K. (1984). *Taxonomies of human performance.* Orlando, FL: Academic Press.

Geertz, C. (1988). *Works and lives: The anthropologist as author.* Stanford, CA: Stanford University Press.

Hackman, J.R., and Oldham, G.R. (1980). *Work redesign.* Reading, MA: Addison-Wesley.

Hall, J. (1978). *The ways out.* London: Routledge and Kegan Paul.

Hartman, L.F. (1963). *Encyclopedic dictionary of the Bible.* New York: McGraw-Hill.

Hostettler, J.A. (1974). *Hutterite society.* Baltimore: Johns Hopkins Press.

Judah, J.S. (1974). *Hare Krishna and the counterculture.* New York: Wiley.

Kelvin, P. (1984). The historical dimension of social psychology: the case of unemployment. In H. Tajfel (ed.), *The social dimension,* vol. 2. Cambridge, England: Cambridge University Press, pp. 405–24.

Marx, K. (1967). *The German ideology.* In L.D. Easton, and K.H. Guddat (eds.), *Writings of the young Marx on philosophy and society.* New York: Anchor, pp. 403–73.

Miller, G. (1980). The interpretation of nonoccupational work in modern society: A preliminary discussion and typology. *Social Problems, 27,* pp. 381–91.

Neff, W.S. (1985). *Work and human behavior.* New York: Aldine.

Nosow, S., and Form, W.H. (1962). *Man, work, and society.* New York: Basic Books.

Pence, G.E. (1978–79). Towards a theory of work. *The Philosophical Forum, 10,* pp. 306–20.

Polanyi, K. (1957). The economy as instituted process. In K. Polanyi, C.M. Arensberg, and H.W. Pearson (eds.), *Trade and market in early empires.* Glencoe, IL: The Free Press.

Rokeach, M. (1968). *Beliefs, attitudes, and values.* San Francisco: Jossey-Bass.

———. (1973). *The nature of human values.* New York: Free Press.

———. (1979). *Understanding human values.* New York: Free Press.

Salancik, G.R., and Pfeffer, J. (1978). A social information processing approach to job attitudes and task design. *Administrative Science Quarterly, 23,* pp. 224–53.

Salz, A. (1944). Occupations: Theory and history. In E.B.A. Seligman, and A. Johnson (eds.), *Encyclopedia of the Social Sciences,* vols. 11–12. New York: Macmillan.

Schwimmer, E. (1980). The limits of economic ideology: A comparative anthropological study of work concept. *International Social Science Journal, 32.* pp. 517–31.

Sundstrom, E. (1986). *Work places.* Cambridge: Cambridge University Press.

Triandis, H.C. (1973). Work and nonwork: Intercultural perspectives. In M.D. Dunnette (ed.), *Work and nonwork in the Year 2000.* Monterey, CA: Brooks/Cole, pp. 29–52.

Turner, A.N. and Miclette, A.L. (1962). Sources of satisfaction in repetitive work. *Occupational Psychology, 36,* pp. 215–31.

Tyler, G. (1983). The work ethic: A union view. In J. Barbash, R.J. Lampman, S.A. Leviton, and G. Tyler (eds.), *The work ethic—A critical Analysis.* Madison, WI: Industrial Relations Research Association, pp. 197–210.

Vroom, V. (1964). *Work and motivation.* New York: Wiley.

Wallerstein, I. (1974). *The modern world—system I.* New York: Academic Press.

Wallman, S. (1979). *Social anthropology of work.* London: Academic Press.

Weick, K.E. (1979). *The social psychology of organizing,* 2nd edition. Reading, MA: Addison-Wesley.

White, S.F. and Mitchell, T.R. (1979). Job enrichment versus social cues: A comparison and competitive test. *Journal of Applied Psychology, 64,* pp. 1–9.

2

Studying Meanings of Work: The Case of Work Values

Walter R. Nord,
Arthur P. Brief
Jennifer M. Atieh
Elizabeth M. Doherty

W hat is the meaning of work? is a question which has intrigued humanists and social scientists alike. The aim of this essay, however, is not to provide yet another answer to the question. Rather, the intent is to examine how answers to the question have been sought. Underlying this intent is the goal of identifying alternative approaches to the meaning of work question. The need for scholars in one camp or another to recognize a variety of approaches is established in the text which follows.

The analytic strategy chosen for our examination essentially is that of the case study; that is, we examine the attempts of only one group of scholars to construct knowledge about the meaning of work. The group whose efforts are to be examined is applied social scientists who primarily study the thoughts, feelings, and actions of people at work. We will refer to this group as organizational behaviorists, although other terms—especially organizational psychologists—could be used as well. Organizational behaviorists borrow heavily from whatever social science discipline appears may be helpful in understanding a particular applied problem or phenomenon.

In organizational behavior, the meaning of work question has been principally addressed through focusing on so-called work values. *Work values* are defined broadly as the end states people desire and feel they ought to be able to realize through working. These feelings and desires can be acquired in a variety of ways, such as through: reading, conversation, observation, and actually doing work. However acquired, work values are of great practical importance because they affect the means that can be used to manage a society's economic activities. For example, work values may influence what people believe to be legitimate and hence define what they will tolerate. These outcomes will in turn affect what costs elites may pay in directing various forms of work activity and how easily people can be induced to change their ways

This essay has been adapted from a paper by Walter R. Nord, Arthur P. Brief, Jennifer M. Atieh, and Elizabeth M. Doherty (1988), in B.M. Staw and L.L. Cummings (eds.): *Research in Organizational Behavior*. Greenwich, CT: JAI Press.

to satisfy imperatives of technology. Thus, at least indirectly, values affect the flexibility and productivity of a given work force.

Work values have a mutually causal relationship with the meanings that individuals attach to their work. On the one hand, over time, work values are a consequence of the meanings that individuals collectively attach to work. On the other hand, at any given point in time, these collective meanings can be viewed as given and, hence, be a cause of the meanings that individuals attach to a given activity. This causal role suggests that work values are of considerable practical importance. As shared interpretations of what people want and expect, work values are an important component of social reality which influences their actions and the nature of society, including: the type of work people design for others to do, how people are socialized for work, and how people can successfully relate work to other aspects of their lives. The latter, the role that work values play in helping people create what Culbert and McDonough (1985) termed *effective alignments,* may have a significant impact on overall psychological well-being. For example, the easier it is for individuals to perceive a positive relationship between what they do to earn a living and achieving other valued ends, the better they are apt to feel about the quality of their lives in general. Clearly, organizational behaviorists who study work values are dealing with a matter of considerable practical import.

The close relationship between work values and ongoing human experience raises two challenges that need to be addressed in the study of work values. First, inquiry about work values must be historically grounded and sensitive to changes in work over time. Work values represent efforts to come to terms with particular arrangements of work under particular social conditions. As the arrangements and/or the conditions change, so will, in all probability, the work values. Moreover, it is likely that work values of one era will influence the work values, work arrangements, and social conditions of the next era. Consequently, students of work values need to be historically informed.

Second, as Gergen (1982) has argued so persuasively, the close association of applied scientists with practitioners often has dysfunctional effects on the development of science, because often scientists are overly influenced by the perspectives of the practitioners. We know of no reason to expect that the scientific study of work values will be immune to such influence. Organizational behaviorists are vulnerable to accepting unconsciously the assumptions, beliefs, goals, and definitions of reality about work that are fashionable among their contemporaries, including various interest groups (see Baritz, 1960; Dubin, 1976a; Gordon, Kleiman, and Hanie, 1978; Nord, 1977). As Gordon, et al. noted, industrial-organizational psychology is uncomfortably close to common sense; as Dubin observed, applied scientists often pass a market test where passing is a function of sharing common definitions of problems and symptoms with practitioners. Consequently, conventional approaches in applied social science often ignore a variety of alternative sets of beliefs and social constructions.

In part, the failure to recognize alternative possibilities stems from what seems to be a tendency of organizational behaviorists to see the present state of social organization as overdetermined, or, in other words, to see it only from *their* historical perspective. We believe that contemporary organizational behaviorists suffer from lack of historical perspective on the evolution of work and from an overly close tie to certain aspects of the conventional wisdom. (In fact, if, as we have argued, work values are a major component of collective understanding, work values *are* a major part of the conventional wisdom of those who share them.) Below we analyze the conventional approach to work values, show the intellectual and practical reasons for organizational behaviorists to reexamine and explain their assumptions about work, and point to some of the new perspectives that reexamination might produce.

Framing the "Case"

The study of work values has had a central place in Western intellectual thought for several centuries. At first, philosophers, theologians, poets, and fiction writers played dominant roles; it was not until early in the twentieth century that social scientists began to play a role. Currently, however, social scientists in general and organizational behaviorists in particular have come to be some of the most important contributors on the topic. But even though social scientists have framed their efforts as positive science, their inquiry remains linked in important ways to the intellectual zeitgeist, especially to the assumptions about the evolution of work in modern society.

It is commonly taken as given that at some point in the evolution of modern industrial society production activities of individuals became severed from other aspects of their daily lives. Implicit in this assumption, of course, is the belief that at some earlier point—usually prior to the industrial revolution—the work of individuals was harmoniously integrated with their total existence, and that after the industrial revolution, work ceased to be meaningfully related to other aspects of life. Often, this assumed change is seen as the source of major social problems, including alienation from work. As Zuboff (1983) observed: "The context of meanings that held people together could no longer be counted upon to provide what we now think of as 'intrinsic work motivation'" (p. 153). This perspective has spawned an interest in work values in order to support the meanings of work assumed to have existed in an earlier idyllic state.

In this case study, we examine the intellectual assumptions that have guided contemporary organizational behaviorists and the larger intellectual tradition of which they are a part. Stimulated by Anthony (1977), Rodgers (1974), and others, we begin with a somewhat radical perspective—one that views the assumed harmonious relations between work and the rest of life as a prelapsarian myth, not as accurate history. As a consequence, the intellectual history of the study of work values becomes problematic—especially upon examination of the process through which the dominant perspective emerged and the alternative possibilities that may have been obscured.

We approach this task in four parts. First, we review the history of work and what we term the *conventional* view of modern work values. We also suggest that while the conventional view seems to have been built upon Max Weber's description of the Protestant ethic, it has ignored important components of his analysis. Second, we present an alternative perspective on the evolution of work values. This *alternative* view reveals certain latent aspects of the conventional view and highlights distinctions that frequently have gone unrecognized. Third, we present a framework for examining these differences and for classifying various orientations to work values. This framework reveals lacunae in various contemporary treatments of work and important distinctions between what we call the *neoconventional* view and more traditional perspective. Finally, we use this framework and the alternative perspective to raise "new" questions and approaches to work—new at least to organizational behavior—and suggest the intellectual and practical value of this broadened perspective.

Work Values: The Conventional View

Although work values are developed and transmitted through historical processes (see Aldag and Brief, 1979), this history is often ignored or misunderstood. An ahistorical stance, however, leads one to overlook the interests, values, and ideologies that influenced ultimate outcomes. In other words, it misleads us by failing to recognize the alternative courses that history may have taken; instead, the course of history appears to have been inevitable. For example, we often see modern technology as a product of the application of objective scientific methods to meet human needs in an environment dictated by the laws of nature. This view makes modern technology appear to be, if not the "one best" way, very close to it. However, as Noble (1984) has shown so well, historical analysis reveals that the evolution of technology could have been very different. Its development was influenced by more than the physical laws of nature. Had certain social and institutional arrangements been other than they were, different forms of technology (for example, ones that gave more power to lower-level workers) might have thrived. Conventional accounts have overlooked these other forms and, with them, the political and economic forces that contributed to their demise.

We hypothesize, with considerable support from scholars such as Braverman (1974), Clawson (1980), Gutman (1976), Nelson (1975), and others, that a similar process has operated in our understanding of the history of organizations and management. A number of scholars (Dubin, 1976b; George, 1968; Heneman, 1973; Parker and Smith, 1976) have argued that the way historical events have been reported and interpreted in the management literature provides only a partially valid picture. As a result, the conventional view is based on a distorted and incomplete understanding of history. Here, too, what has been accepted as historical fact has been influenced by a complex interaction of values, interests, and ideologies. Moreover, by ignoring any depth analysis of the historical process, those who hold the conventional view see the unfolding of history to be a far more linear process than it was. In actuality, the evolution of work and beliefs about it emerged out of conflicting interests, and the conventional view reflects the ideologies of those who were successful in promoting their particular interests. When history is ignored or simplified, the ideological components are obscured, and people become subject to what Bem and Bem (1970) spoke of as an *unconscious ideology*. An unconscious ideology contains attitudes and beliefs which an individual accepts without awareness. These beliefs constrain a person's ability to conceive of alternative possibilities and tend to go unrecognized until confronted by a fundamentally different perspective. The more widely shared a given perspective, the less likely alternative perspectives are to be influential.

The conventional view of work values, so widely shared by managers, organizational psychologists, politicians, and even trade union leaders, embodies an unconscious ideology. Managers frequently respond to problems with workers by lamenting the decay of the work ethic. Organizational psychologists have built much of their theory, research, and advice to managers on the premise that work is somehow noble, and that psychologically engaging work is a necessary condition for human development. Politicians appear to find it useful to attach their comments to an assumed set of work values. In celebrating Labor Day, 1971, for example, the president of the United States saluted "the dignity of work, the value of achievement, and the morality of self-reliance. None of these is going out of style" (In Gutman, 1976, p. 4). In fact, the work ethic is so widely shared that Rodgers (1974) observed that trade unionists, radicals, and conservatives of the past often attempted to rally support for their causes through an appeal to the premises of the work ethic. Even today, it is popular to appeal to the need to rekindle the work ethic to solve a variety of social and economic problems. Clearly, the conventional view represents a major feature of American society.

In this section we examine the conventional view. We summarize its history, its substance, and its lacunae. We begin with a very cursory look at the concept of work in the history of Western civilization. [For a fuller description see Tilgher (1931); de Grazia (1964); and Neff (1985).]

A Sketch of the History of the Conventional View

Ancient Greek philosophers saw work as a waste of a citizen's time and as a corrupting activity that made the pursuit of truth and virtue more difficult. Leisure time provided the vehicle for the attainment of truth and virtue; it was reserved for the exercise of the mind and spirit. For example, Aristotle (1912) maintained that leisure itself was a source of intrinsic pleasure, happiness, and felicity. In his view, happiness did not arise from an occupation; it was a property of those who had leisure. Through the writings of Aristotle as well as Plato and Epicurus, these work values spread to Rome and were largely embraced. Of course, in both societies this classical ideology of work was dependent on slavery: slaves were viewed more as instruments than as people. As Grant (1960) observed, the Roman writer Cato the Elder offered the following advice: "The best principle of management is to treat both slaves and animals well enough to give them the strength to work hard" (p. 112). Thus, work was a curse which could be separated from the good life, but the separation required a class of persons to whom one could assign, without feeling remorse, vulgar or degrading activities.

Ancient Hebrew philosophers and theologians shared the Greco-Roman system of work values, but with one principal exception. While they saw work as a form of punishment, the ancient Hebrews also valued it as a means of atonement. In other words, work was seen by them *both* as drudgery and as a way of redeeming oneself in the eyes of God. Work, therefore, as a way of cooperating with God in bettering the world, began to emerge in a positive light.

These more positive feelings about work became part of the very early Christian teachings and continued to be evident through the Middle Ages. Work was viewed as a route to goodness; it was a path for accumulating a surplus of goods and services to be shared with the needy. The hoarding of riches, however, was considered a transgression of the law of God, the sin of avarice. But work itself (that is, the activities of work *per se*), as seen for example by Thomas Aquinas, was a morally neutral, natural condition of Christian life.

With Luther, the moral neutrality of work itself started to wane. He advocated the concept of a *calling,* a life-task set by God. According to Weber (1930), Luther believed that a calling was "something which man has to accept as a Divine ordinance to which he must adapt himself" (p. 85). Failure to accept one's calling, whatever type of work may constitute it, was seen as immoral. Weber argued that interpretations of Luther's concept of a *calling* by Calvin and his followers symbolized the *Protestant ethic* of work and played a major role in the development of capitalism. Weber's analysis of the role of work values and the Protestant ethic in the development of capitalism is a key component of the conventional wisdom of modern organizational behavior.

Weber saw the development of Calvinism as adding the value of proving one's faith through "good works" to the ideology of work. Furthermore, he saw other Christian movements contributing to the religious foundations of a worldly asceticism, of a secular belief in the practice of strict self-denial as a measure of personal discipline. For example, in discussing the contributions of Richard Baxter (a writer on Puritan ethics whom Weber used to represent the major tenets of the doctrine), Weber (1930) noted that wastage of time became, in principle, "the deadliest of sins" (p. 157), and that hard, continuous bodily or mental labor was "the specific defense against all those temptations which Puritanism united under the name of the unclean life" (p. 158). Although the avoidance of such temptations through the pursuit of a calling to work was viewed as an important contribution to production, Weber argued that this emphasis was directed toward maximizing activities that would increase the glory of God—a nonsecular motive. In this way, work became "in itself the end of life, ordained as such by God" (p. 159). The Protestant ethic of work justified diligence and frugality for nonsecular reasons, but in so doing supported economic growth by motivating hard work and encouraging savings.

Over time, much of the religious content (serving the glory of God) of the work ethic disappeared. Maccoby (1981) and others have proposed that a secularized version of the work ethic, heavily influenced by Benjamin Franklin, then emerged. Hard work and thrift were still important, but for oneself, not for God. Maccoby called this newer ethic the *craft ethic*. Throughout the nineteenth century, some combination of the religiously based work ethic described by Weber and the more secular emphasis present in the craft ethic heralded the importance of work for the development of the individual and society. This emphasis continued forward. It is reflected in statements like those of the president of the United States quoted above. Moreover, it is embedded in the thinking of influential organizational behaviorists and managers.

Hulin and Blood (1968), for example, described the work norms of the middle class as follows: "Positive affect for occupational achievement, a belief in the intrinsic value of hard work, a striving for the attainment of responsible positions, and a belief in the work-related aspects of Calvinism and the Protestant ethic" (p. 48). They added that the dominance of these values can be explained by children learning in school and at home those values

> brought by the Anglo-Saxon Protestants from Europe in the seventeenth and eighteenth centuries. The values have become the standard in middle-class society. Children are taught these values in school by their middle-class teachers and attempt to reach goals defined in terms of these values by means of behavior consistent with these values. (p. 52)

The potential of this view to influence social policy and managerial action can be seen in Blood's (1969) description of efforts to assimilate hard core unemployed into the industrial work force. These efforts attempted to instill Protestant work values in members of the targeted underclass. Other examples evident in the literature include McClelland's (1961) treatment of the Protestant values and the motives presumed to be required for success in management, and Aldag and Brief's (1979) view that commitment to Protestant ethic values directly moderates the relationships between job characteristics and various outcome measures.

So ingrained is the work ethic as an explanation for the success of the U.S. economy that managers reflexively attribute declines in productivity and increases in worker recalcitrance and discontent to the decline of the work ethic. For example, in analyzing unrest in the workplace in the early 1970s, Deans (1973) observed: "Corporation executives seem no less puzzled than many other Americans as to why young people entering the labor force—even in a time of job scarcity—are less enchanted with the so-called Protestant ethic of hard work and upward striving than their parents and grandparents" (pp. 8–9). The recent success of Japanese manufacturers is often attributed simply to a combination of a strong work ethic in Japan and a declining one in the United States. Thus, it is evident that the tenets of the Protestant work ethic and its secularized derivatives are still taken seriously by managers, scholars, and policy makers. They are viewed as central to the development and functioning of capitalism.

Aspects of Protestantism Not Emphasized in the Conventional View

Weber discussed two other aspects of Protestantism that contributed to the success of capitalism that are often ignored in contemporary discussions. First, the Protestant ethic was like the earlier Christian teachings in treating *all* work as potentially worthy. This suggests that the nature of work itself was not an issue. In other words, the Protestant ethic can be said to have held a content free view of work. Second, Weber saw the nature of social relationships promoted by early Protestant thinkers as important in the development of capitalism. The conventional view has not recognized these two points and their implications sufficiently.

Content-Free View of Work. At least two features of an ideological system contribute to its impact. First, the acceptance of an ideology is influenced by its explicit substance—what issues it is perceived to address and what it appears to say about these matters. Second, dissemination is affected by what the system is silent on—what issues it *does not* address and what it *does not* say about those matters it does treat (Gouldner, 1970). These two features are closely linked, in the same manner as figure and ground are related to each other. However, like figure and ground, they tend to affect perception and thought in qualitatively different ways. The presence of something (figure) tends to draw attention to it and to things associated with it. It heightens awareness about a somewhat finite set of things or ideas. In contrast, the aspects of a situation that are not focused on (that is, that are treated as ground) tend to be taken as given and their effects go unnoticed.

The conventional view has focused mainly on what the Protestant ethic and its derivatives said about work—it has centered attention on the figure. It has not considered what the ethic did not deal with and how its silence on certain matters influenced its impact on society.

The Protestant ethic was not concerned with either the content of work or the nature of the product/service produced. According to Weber, the spirit of capitalism focused attention on earning and accumulating money as an outward sign of salvation. Although Weber (1930) personally lamented the fact that the ethic's ascetic character spawned modern machine production, his description of the Protestant ethic made no mention of the intrinsic outcomes of work itself. Weber maintained that an individual's calling in early Protestantism was "an obligation which the individual is supposed to feel and does feel towards the content of his professional activity, *no matter in what it consists*" (p. 54; italics added). Wealth is what mattered for salvation, and it could be contingent on any type of work.

Weber also viewed the Protestant ethic as consistent with work on almost any kind of product. The only constraint was a very loose and general one: the product was to have some value to the community. Weber (1930) wrote: "the usefulness of a calling, and thus its favour in the sight of God, is measured primarily in moral terms, and thus in terms of the importance of the goods produced in it for the community" (p. 162). But he added in the next sentence: "Further, and, above all, in practice the most important criterion is found in private profitableness" (p. 162). Thus, although the value of the goods to the community was one constraint, it was subsidiary to larger, nonsecular purposes.

The relative unimportance of the content and products of work allowed economic activities to proceed free from a variety of traditional concerns, moral issues, and social values that could have retarded economic progress by reducing flexibility. Efficient markets require capital and labor to be highly mobile. If wealth is the end and the means are unimportant, then investors and workers can concentrate on their economic activities and be unconstrained by noneconomic concerns. For example, as Hirschman (1977) suggested, if lending money in return for interest had not been freed from moral prohibitions, then capitalist economic development would have been retarded. Similarly, if workers were unwilling to work in a certain way or produce particular products because of religious or other noneconomic reasons, then degrees of freedom would have been removed from economic activity. Had the Protestant ethic emphasized intrinsically meaningful activity or placed conditions on the achievement of wealth (for example, the production of only those goods which are consistent with some narrowly defined moral standard), it would have introduced constraints. Since the Protestant ethic was generally free of such content—all work was equally good—it imposed few limitations on how to gain wealth.

While the conventional view, too, is generally silent on the products of work (Nord, 1977), it is often concerned with the content of work, as evidenced by the emphasis it gives to redesigning jobs. For example, the authors of *Work in America* (1973) argued that it was a mistake to assume that the recalcitrance of young people in the workplace during the late 1960s and early 1970s represented any real change in traditional work values; instead, the problem was a decrease in "their willingness to take on meaningless work in authoritarian settings that offers only extrinsic rewards" (p. 47). Often the traditional work values referred to in such statements are assumed to have some relationship to the Protestant ethic. We, in contrast, suggest that the emphasis on content represents a sharp departure from the traditional values of the Protestant ethic (as described by Weber) in at least three ways. First, there is no reference to the religious basis for the importance of work. As Pence (1978–79) observed, the modern notion of a calling is entirely absent. Second, it is different from the Protestant ethic which saw all work as potentially worthy: the calling came from God, not from the secular world. Likewise, Spence (1985) observed that the modern-day form of the work ethic "has been watered down to the belief that work is inherently good in and of itself. . . . Any sense of a larger purpose has been largely lost" (p. 1292). Third, extrinsic rewards were the only secular rewards the work ethic stressed.

Modern discussions of job design (e.g., Argyris, 1957; 1973) that center on the importance of the content and process of work go well beyond the contents of the Protestant ethic described by Weber. The central outcomes advanced in Protestant teachings were extrinsic: they were contingent upon results of work, not work itself. In short, viewing recent work on job redesign by organizational behaviorists and others as being consistent with the tradition of the Protestant ethic is misleading.

Social Relations and the Protestant Ethic.   Users of the conventional perspective have misrepresented the Protestant ethic in a second way: they have virtually ignored the nature of social relationships implied in many of the major teachings of Protestantism. Although the conventional view does recognize the strong individualism advanced by the Protestant ethic, it tends to ignore certain sociological implications of individualism. For one thing, the Puritan stance against the spontaneous enjoyment of life did more than remove distractions from work, help to standardize production, and restrain consumption; Weber argued, it achieved these results by promoting uniformity through certain prohibitions, such as those against differences in dress. Second, Calvinism discouraged social bonds among people and legitimated class differences and economic inequality. Weber (1930) observed that the Calvinist's intercourse with God was focused on the *individual's own* salvation and "was carried on in deep spiritual isolation" (p. 107). Further, the achievement of worldly success by an individual was conducive to a rather asocial elitism. In Weber's words:

> This consciousness of divine grace of the elect and holy was accompanied by an attitude toward the sin of one's neighbor, not of sympathetic understanding based on consciousness of one's own weakness, but of hatred and contempt for him as an enemy of God bearing the sign of eternal damnation. (p. 122)

In fact, the "bourgeois businessman," according to Weber, received "comforting assurance that the unequal distribution of the goods of this world was a special dispensation of Divine Providence" (p. 177).

According to Weber, the Calvinist doctrine splintered social relationships in yet another way: it promoted distrust of others. Weber observed that a major consequence of Calvinism "was a feeling of unprecedented inner loneliness of the single individual. In what was for the man of the age of the Reformation the most important thing in life, his eternal salvation, he was forced to follow his path alone. . . . No one could help him" (p. 104). Puritanism was a source of "disillusioned and pessimistically inclined individualism" (p. 105). Its doctrines warned against trusting in the aid of friendship—"Even the amiable Baxter counsels deep distrust of even one's closest friend, and Bailey directly exhorts to trust no one and to say nothing compromising to anyone. Only God should be your confidant" (p. 106).

Clearly, to the degree this doctrine influenced sociological relations, its direct effects would have been to divide people. It fostered elitism. Not only did it legitimate inequalities in wealth, but the way it did so spawned dehumanizing views of one's social inferiors (somewhat reminiscent of those underlying Cato the Elder's advice on treating slaves and animals). Moreover, by centering attention on people's own individual outcomes and fostering distrust of others, it ran counter to the development of close social relations and organizing for collective interests.

With the major exception of Spence (1985), who pointed to the dangers of a work ethic that is driven by narrow self-interest in the absence of further justification, most psychologists and organizational behaviorists have emphasized the values pertaining to individuals qua individuals and have failed to recognize the latent social implications noted above. Little attention has been given to desires for community and other collective outcomes that are affected by work. As we will show, alternative views about the role of collective action in and around the workplace are possible. For example, the Roman Catholic church (see Pope Leo XIII, 1936) has been explicit about the benefits to be derived from worker collectivities.

Impact of the Protestant Ethic. So far our discussion has centered on the formal statements of the Protestant ethic. We have assumed, with Weber and the conventional view, that somehow these formal statements were related to the work experiences of individuals. Although some influence seems likely, how much these statements influenced the day-to-day behavior of people is open to question. It seems likely that such statements affected the content of social norms and institutions (for example, churches) and thus had some impact on behavior. Similarly, a person's feelings about his/her own worth on earth almost surely influenced behavior. Some leading scholars (Clayre, 1974; Rodgers, 1974), however, question whether the work ethic itself had much influence upon the working classes. While the ethic undoubtedly had a *de facto* secular impact, how much and through what processes it influenced the behavior of the bulk of the population remains to be documented.

Summary

We have discussed how work—something despised by the Greeks—took on a positive value when it came to be viewed as a means of atonement by the ancient Hebrew philosophers, a route to goodness in early Christian teachings, and a calling with the rise of Protestantism. We have examined the Protestant ethic and its role in the development of capitalism, and we have explored discontinuities between the conventional view of work and the Protestant ethic.

These discontinuities provide the stimulus for the remainder of the chapter. We believe that the failure to recognize these discontinuities reflects basic problems in how contemporary organizational behaviorists view work. The nonsecular aspects emphasized by Weber that are not present in the conventional view, and the secular emphasis in the conventional view that are not included in Weber's account are important differences. The fact that organizational behaviorists have not recognized them is noteworthy to say the least. Similarly, the inattention given to the sociological implications of Calvinism and many of its related Protestant sects by users of the conventional view merits attention. Finally, the ease with which the conventional view has accepted the belief that the ethic affected the day-to-day behavior of the masses, in the absence of evidence, is revealing.

What does it reveal? We believe it reveals that the conventional view contains a limiting unconscious ideology that induces people to misinterpret the past and present and err in their efforts to predict the future. The conventional view is built on an incomplete and problematic understanding of history. It fails to consider contradictory ethical and historical views about the nature of work and its relationship to individuals and society. Consequently, it fails to provide important insights into the past, present, and future. A deeper understanding of these assertions can be gained from the study of an alternative perspective, which we explore in the next section.

Work Values: An Alternative Perspective

During the 1970s, a very different interpretation of the social history of modern work values came into vogue. Major contributors have been: Anthony (1977), Bowles and Gintis (1976), Braverman (1974), Burawoy (1979), Clawson (1980), Edwards (1978), Gutman (1976), Jackall (1978), Marglin (1974), Nelson (1975), Rodgers (1974), Stone (1974), and Watson (1977). Although others had crossed this terrain previously (for example, Hays, 1957; Pollard 1963; Thompson, 1963), it was during the 1970s that this very different view of the emergence of work forms and values became prominent. This view, which we call the *alternative* perspective, is useful in uncovering the unconscious ideology of the conventional view because it is built on different assumptions. (Of course, the conventional view can serve the same function for the alternative perspective.) One should not be misled by the word *alternative*. In reality, this perspective (like the conventional view) is a loose collection of ideas which, taken together, provide a new perspective.

Among the tenets of the alternative view is the idea that members of the working class did not share in the Protestant ethic work values. In particular, during the period of industrialization (1850–1920) in the United States when these values are assumed to have had their effect on motivating economic activity, it is unlikely that they did so by motivating members of the working classes. To the degree the alternative view is correct, Weber (1930) was wrong when he described the United States of this period as the highest developed offspring of the wedding of the Protestant ethic and the spirit of capitalism. If Weber was wrong, if during this period strict adherence to Protestant work values by working class Americans was a myth, a number of important questions arise. What, for example, can account for the growth in American productivity during this era? What explains the behavior of the working classes of this time? What explains why the work ethic has received so much attention? Whose interests might it have served? Does the work ethic play any role in contemporary society? These questions have led to a series of challenges to the conventional view.

The alternative perspective is a label we have placed on a complex, diverse, and voluminous body of work which is difficult to summarize. In comparison with the traditional view, the alternative perspective tends to be built more on efforts to understand history by looking at the experiences of the "ordinary" person. Moreover, it tends to stress the coercive aspects of work and to see a greater amount of class conflict in and around the work-place. Given this conflict, the alternative perspective examines how it is managed. Of particular importance to the present discussion, this perspective sees the work ethic as a substitute for more direct forms of coercion.

Since several themes of this perspective are central to the current analysis, a brief characterization of it is needed. To provide this overview, we present a summary of one of the most perceptive contributors to this perspective—Daniel Rogers. We have chosen Rodgers (1974) because his work has had the greatest impact on us, it has been widely acclaimed by historians, it deals explicitly with the work ethic, it has received so little attention in the organizational behavior literature, and it captures the essence of the alternative perspective.

Rodgers (1974) asserted that "the work ethic as it stood in the middle of the nineteenth century [in the United States], at the threshold of industrialization, was not a single conviction but a complex of ideas with roots and branches" (p. 7). In fact, Rodgers observed that there were serious tensions among its components:

> The clearest of the tensions lie between the idea of work as ascetic exercise and work as art. The one looked toward system, discipline, and the emerging factory order; the other towards spontaneity, self-expression, and a narrowing of the gulf between work and play. (pp. 13–14)

Work was supposed to be a creative act, yet it demanded self-expression; it was a social duty, but its payoffs were private rewards. Moreover, Rodgers added, there was a nagging contradiction between the ideals of duty and of success—between the dignity of all labor, even the humblest, and the equally universal counsel to work one's way as quickly as possible out of manual toil (p. 14).

In addition to these contradictions within the Protestant work ethic, Rodgers saw tensions between the classes:

> Praise of work in the mid-nineteenth century was strongest among the mid-dling, largely Protestant, property-owning classes: farmers, merchants, ministers and professional men, independent craftsmen, and nascent industrial-ists. . . . The ascetic injunctions of Puritanism never penetrated very far into the urban working classes. (pp. 14–15)

In fact, Rodgers suggested that the work ethic became important to the moralists during industrialization in the United States because it helped to paper over some basic social contradictions—namely, "the unsettling presence of the factories in a society committed to the Free Labor ideal" (p. 40).

Rodgers (1974) began by observing that to many members of the middle class of the post-Civil War North, life in the factory seemed uncomfortably close to slavery. He argued that the work ethic was in large measure a creation of middle-class writers to reduce this discomfort. A product of middle-class thought, the work ethic became increasingly less related to the realities of most workers as the industrial revolution took hold. Wage employment and the mechanization of labor widened the gap between Protestant work ideals and the realities of work. Under wage employment, for example, the assumption of the keepers of the mid-nineteenth-century Protestant work ethic that "the worker owned his own toil—that a man's efforts were his to exert and the successes his to be reaped" (p. 30), began to crumble. Likewise the growing routinization of work weakened the foundation for the view that work was a creative activity.

The writers who attempted to help the middle class respond to these dilemmas developed a wide array of approaches. In response to the institutionalization of wage employment, for instance, moralists promised upward mobility, launched the cooperative movement, experimented with profit sharing, advocated piecework, and crusaded for worker democracy. In response to the lack of opportunities for advancement through work, writers of children's stories promoted the work ethic in a more abstract form that was not rooted in the realities of the factory. For example, the Horatio Alger stories, so widely assumed to be part of the American ethic, showed success coming when the heroes were at leisure or after they had lost their jobs or after they had performed a major act of kindness.

We have not told all of Rodger's story. Nevertheless, the theme is evident: Prior to the industrial revolution, Protestant work values did not represent a wholly consistent statement. The revolution itself sharpened these inconsistencies and made the differences more apparent between the spokespersons for Protestant work values and the masses who were supposed to adhere to them. As far as the holders of the alternative view are concerned, the work ethic in the United States has functioned to conceal the coercive forces that made people work. As Rodgers (1974) said in concluding his discussion of industrial workers:

> But even for those who chafed at labor, the appeal to the moral centrality of work was too useful to resist. Pitched in the abstract, it turned necessity into pride and servitude into honor; it offered a lever upon the moral sentiments of those whose power mattered. (p. 181)

Other creators of the alternative view (such as Clawson, 1980; Nelson, 1975) concur with Rodgers about the role of coercion in the workplace. An indepth look at their ideas would show that many elements of modern management (such as scientific management, certain aspects of technology, personnel management, and supervisory training) had been, in part, a response to the desire by managers to exercise the control needed to operate factories efficiently while preserving the image of the ideal of free labor.

In general, holders of the alternative view have proceeded from a critical—often Marxist—orientation. As a result, rather than finding harmony, they have found struggle. Typically they have seen large discrepancies between the actual work values of participants and those assumed in the conventional view.

Scholars of the alternative view also differ from most modern organizational behaviorists in the sources of their data. These scholars focus on the experiences of the working classes of the past and present. Their descriptions of the concrete experiences of workers have drawn heavily on literature from American history, political science, participant observation, and oral history. When these sources are used for study, coercion emerges as a frequent explanation for the "motivation" to work.

Although we have oversimplified, we have presented enough of the alternative view for our purposes in this chapter. While we recognize that much work is required to validate this perspective, in our judgment it is already sufficiently documented to be taken seriously.

Of course, to take it seriously does not mean to accept it uncritically. The alternative view, too, may suffer from an unconscious ideology. By focusing on the urban centers of the Northeast, as Rodgers did, opportunities and sentiments of other sectors of the nation are ignored. Similarly, the focus on the coercive aspects of work misses the substantial improvements in working conditions introduced over the last century, and tends to treat those who behaved in ways congruent with tenets of the Protestant ethic and achieved great success as "flukes" and therefore not requiring explanation. Thus, we perceive the alternative view as just that—another perspective. However, like many "other" perspectives, it is useful for stimulating analysis of the blind spots of the conventional view.

It was this stimulation that led us to consider a wide variety of treatments of work values. In doing so, we developed a framework for classifying the perspectives. The framework highlights some of the contradictions observed by Rodgers and makes it even more clear that the Protestant work ethic and contemporary approaches to enriching work—which are often lumped together in the conventional view—are based on very different premises. The framework and some of these implications are developed in the next section.

A Framework for Work Values

Pespectives on work values can be compared through a two-dimensional framework. One dimension assumes two possible loci of benefits from work—a secular outcome and a nonsecular outcome (for example, salvation). The second dimension concerns the relationship between work itself and out-

	Intrinsic	Extrinsic
Secular	**1** Neoconventional view (Argyris, Maslow, McGregor, Hertzberg), Classical Marxism	**2** Roman Catholic church[a] Economic theory, Maoist China, Organizational behaviorists such as Goldthorpe, et al., Fein
Locus of Benefits Nonsecular	**3** Monasteries/communities (where work develops person spiritually for communion with God), Hindu religion	**4** Protestant ethic (as described by Weber)

[a] The classification of the Roman Catholic church as secular is based on the contents of two major papal encyclicals on work. Obviously the teachings of the church are linked to nonsecular outcomes. However, the contents of the encyclicals about the role of work have a secular focus.

Figure 2–1. Possible Stances on Work Values: Relationship of Preferred State and Work Activity

come(s). On the one hand, outcomes can be intrinsic to work—that is, they occur through work. On the other hand, outcomes can be extrinsic—that is, they follow or are contingent upon work. While the terms *intrinsic* and *extrinsic* are difficult to define unambiguously (see, e.g., Brief and Aldag, 1977; Dyer and Parker, 1975), their use here is rather specific. *Intrinsic* refers to the content of activities of the work itself (that is, what people do at work) and *extrinsic* explicitly denotes independence from the content of work. In figure 2–1, these two dimensions are used to show four possible ways to classify treatments of work values. We have classified some of the major approaches to work values in the figure; our rationale for the classifications is in the text. The contrasts shown so boldly in the figure are, of course, less clear in reality. Nevertheless, the figure is helpful in pointing out a number of useful distinctions.

Extrinsic Values

While most treatments of work give at least some attention to extrinsic outcomes, there is great variation in the type of outcomes considered. One is salvation, others are economic, and still others are social (for instance, achieving equity). These outcomes are extrinsic in that while they are contingent upon work, they do not depend on the substance of work itself. Figure 2–1 reveals two sets of extrinsic outcomes.

Extrinsic/Nonsecular Outcomes (Cell 4). Some approaches view outcomes of work as contingent upon work, make no mention of the specific content of the work, and view the outcomes as taking place in a nonsecular arena. The classic statement of Protestant ethic, stressing the extrinsic outcome of salvation, is the prime example. Unlike money or status or other extrinsic outcomes which are reaped in this world, salvation is nonsecular. Of course, the Protestant ethic did stress secular outcomes as well; but in its pure form, these secular results were not ends in themselves, but were merely indicators of ultimate states.

Extrinsic/Secular (Cell 2). Many approaches which view outcomes of work as contingent upon work make no mention of the specific content of work, but view the outcomes as occurring in the secular world. Obviously those who have focused on money and other material rewards belong in this cell. Interestingly, so do the treatments of other major religions and political doctrines.

The Roman Catholic church, in its teachings about work (see Pope Leo XIII, 1891; Pope John Paul, 1981), has for some time centered on extrinsic/ secular outcomes. Although the linkages of worldly activity to salvation are so strong in the teachings of the Catholic church that perhaps they are assumed to be present in any particular document, the papal encyclicals of 1891 and 1981 focused primarily on secular outcomes of work. This secularism was associated with a quite different sociological stance than early Protestantism.

The worldly focus of the Roman Catholic church near the end of the industrial revolution can be seen clearly in the papal encyclical of 1891, *Rerum Novarum*. Quality of life, justice, and social harmony were major concerns. As Pope Leo XIII (1936) put it: "some opportune remedy must be found quickly for the misery and wretchedness pressing so unjustly on the majority of the working class" (p. 2). Because work was seen as a major factor in producing social tensions, work relationships needed to be changed to promote social harmony. In the words of Pope Leo XIII: "The church . . . tries to bind class to class in friendliness and good feeling" (p. 13).

This concern contrasts sharply with the views of the early Protestant theologians who justified class differences as part of God's order and who encouraged the individuals to ignore their economic inferiors. As a result, the Catholic church dealt with a number of issues that were of little explicit concern to many Protestant churches, including: a just wage, rights of workers, property rights, an equitable division of property, and "Workingmen's unions" for mutual benefit. Moreover, contrary to the emphasis on the accumulation of wealth and the splintering of social elites from the masses implicit in Protestant theology, Pope Leo XIII had special praise for affluent Catholics who have "cast in their lot with the wage earners, and who have spent large sums in founding and widely spreading benefit and insurance societies." (pp. 31–32). Similarly, he wrote against greed and thirst for pleasure "which too often make a man who is void of self-restraint miserable in the midst of abundance." (p. 17). In short, Pope Leo XIII focused on extrinsic/secular outcomes, including a wide spectrum of social conditions—justice, harmony, and equality.

Jewish teachings are even more difficult to classify unambiguously in figure 2–1 because they appear to emphasize both secular and nonsecular extrinsic outcomes relatively equally. Sombart (1913), seeking to exemplify the teachings of the Old Testament and the Talmud on the issue, tells the following story:

> Let us imagine old Amschel Rothschild after having "earned" a million on the Stock Exchange, turning to his Bible for edification. What will he find there touching his earnings and their effect on the refinement of his soul, an effect which the pious old Jew most certainly desired on the eve of the Sabbath? Will the million burn his conscience? Or will he not be able to say, and rightly say, "God's blessings rested upon me this week. I thank Thee, Lord, for having graciously rested upon me this week. I thank Thee, Lord, for having graciously granted the light of Thy countenance to Thy servant. In order to find favor in Thy sight I shall give much to charity, and keep Thy commandments even more strictly than hitherto"? Such would be his words if he knew his Bible, and he did know it. (p. 217)

Like at least early Protestantism, traditional Jewish moral theology teaches that prosperity in work is at one and the same time the outward symbol and guarantee of God's pleasure; it also teaches that prosperity provides the means (through charity) to do God's will on earth. Thus, Judaism directs the expenditure of economic success toward the less well-off in a way more consistent with the social emphasis of the Catholic church.

The concepts of many organizational behaviorists belong in cell 2, but because they have not often linked their ideas explicitly to underlying values, classification is speculative. Studies of compensation systems (such as, Lawler, 1971), for instance, focus on extrinsic/secular outcomes without suggesting explicit justification—except for improved performance, which is presumably another secular/extrinsic outcome.

A growing amount of research has revealed the importance of extrinsic/secular concerns to workers. Goldthorpe et al. (1969) reported that work was mainly a means to consumption. More recently, Fein (1976) concluded that many people value work primarily as an activity that is instrumental for their lives outside of work—for instance, to provide means for consumption and support of one's family. Jackall (1978) arrived at a similar conclusion.

Although it is possible that these concerns are rooted in some nonsecular outcomes, social scientists have seldom considered such "ultimate" uses.

A variety of other approaches also emphasize extrinsic/secular outcomes. Modern economists, much like the social scientists we have just discussed, deal mainly with material rewards for work and ignore any specifics about how they should be consumed. The economists merely assume that rewards will be spent in ways that maximize individual utility and eschew any further value judgments. Also in cell 2 is the approach of Maoist China where, according to Whyte (1973), one works to benefit the revolutionary cause. Schwartz (1983) proposed yet another set of extrinsic/secular values. Arguing from a psychoanalytic perspective, Schwartz developed a theory of deontic work motivation in which work is instrumental for self-esteem through a feeling of moral worthiness that results from having lived up to one's responsibility to others. In short, work serves to discharge social obligation; the activity is done for others, not for the self.

As diverse as these outlooks are, they all focus on the extrinsic outcomes of work in the secular world. They are generally silent on the role that the content of work might play.

Some spokespersons for American organized labor, such as Irving Bluestone (Maccoby, 1981), have been concerned with the self-development aspects of work; but for the most part, trade union leaders have focused on extrinsic/secular outcomes. Although, as Rodgers (1974) noted, labor has often felt compelled to state its agenda in ways consistent with the work ethic, the sentiments expressed by William Haywood, a working-class leader of the late 1800s—"less work the better" (see Zuboff, 1983, p. 164)—seem to have been more central to labor's concerns than were the intrinsic benefits of work. Recently Tyler (1983) spoke of a union work ethic that takes as the prime concern "the worker, rather than the work" (p. 209). In this view, work is a necessity that does not need to be justified "with theologic overtones" (p. 198)—humans work to live, not live to work. The union work ethic is concerned with hours, working conditions, safety, wages and benefits, and psychological and physical safety. It is concerned that leisure be available, not merely as an escape from drudgery or for rejuvenation so that one can work better, but as an opportunity for people to grow and develop themselves and participate fully in a democratic society.

A comparison of the approaches of the social scientists with those of the theologians reveals an interesting difference within the extrinsic focus represented by cell 2. The social scientists stop their considerations of what people want from work at the attainment of the rewards; they pay little attention to how the rewards are spent. Similarly, Tyler's union work ethic asserts no ultimate purpose. In contrast, theological approaches are more apt to be concerned with how the fruits of labor are consumed. In general, though, the cell 2 writers, like the developers of the Protestant ethic, are not especially concerned about the content of work.

Intrinsic Values

Some organizational psychologists have drawn attention to the positive outcomes that can be gained through work itself. The content of work and the relationship of that content to human development and/or psychological well-being are central to these treatments. For the most part, social scientists assume that intrinsic values are realized in the secular world; however, other perspectives have introduced nonsecular outcomes.

Intrinsic/Nonsecular (Cell 3). Sometimes work is valued as a means to develop the human spirit, and/or to prepare people to communicate with God or for some other postworldy experience. Since the nature of work matters, these approaches are intrinsic; because the outcomes occur in an afterlife, they are nonsecular. Such views may characterize certain monastic orders or spiritually-oriented communities. Service to the poor, work that requires a special form of discipline, and activities that promote contemplation, may be assumed to develop the character of the individual's spirit in some desirable way. For instance, one of the Vedas, the holy books of the Hindu religion, treats working as a process of purifying one's spirit. The ultimate purpose of this process is to transmigrate to Nirvana. Overall, however, organizational behaviorists and social scientists have given little attention to work values indicated in cell 3.

Intrinsic/Secular (Cell 1). Most writers who have used secular criteria and who have focused explicitly on values that are achieved through the work itself have been concerned primarily with human development. Within this category there seem to be two subgroups: writers who treat human development as a collective or social process (for example, Marx); and writers who treat human development as an individual outcome (for example, Maslow). Although the similarities that do exist between Marx and modern behavioral scientists have been documented by a variety of writers (viz., Clayre, 1974; Nord, 1974; Anthony, 1977), these views have not drawn on each other.

Marx glorified work. Work was a major way that humans differed from other animals: "as soon as [they begin] to produce their means of subsistence, [they] are indirectly producing their material life" (Marx and Engels, 1965, p. 33). Marx's philosophical position was that "Man created his world, and therefore himself, through work" (Anthony, 1977, p. 140). Thus, he saw work as an essential human activity. Fromm (1961) interpreted Marx as asserting: "Labor is the self-expression of his [man's] individual physical and mental powers. In this process of genuine activity man develops himself, becomes himself; work is not only a means to an end—the product—but an end in itself, the meaningful expression of human energy" (pp. 41–42). Israel (1971) came to a similar conclusion: "Through creative work man achieves self-realization; that is, he realizes the potentialities of the species and at the same time gives expression to his basic social nature" (p. 38).

The emphasis on social nature is important. Marx saw work as a means through which people related to each other; it was a way in which one could help satisfy the needs of others. Thus it appears that work content was important in a double sense—both the nature of the process and the product make a difference for human development.

Another intrinsic/secular view assumes that individual psychological development results from specific types of work. This view has been so important in contemporary organizational behavior that we call it the *neoconventional* view. Most recent treatments of job redesign, quality of work life, worker participation/democracy, and organizational development seem to stem from this perspective. It is widely espoused and has affected both governmental policies and managerial practices (Zuboff, 1983).

The neoconventional writers share much of Marx's perspective about work content and the nature of control of the workplace, but omit attention to the nature of the product and tend to be more concerned with individual than with collective development (Nord, 1977). These values are at the core of the writings of McGregor (1960), Herzberg (1966), and Argyris (1957; 1973). While there are differences among these writers, for the most part there is consensus on definition of the essence of human nature and on the need for "enriched" forms of work to fully utilize and develop human capacities. Such work is necessary both for human growth, productivity, and organizational effectiveness.

We will refer primarily to early and paradigm shaping work of Argyris (1957; 1973) in describing the neoconventional perspective because he has provided one of the most influential and explicit statements of this view. His personality versus organization theory proposed a model that described the human adult as striving for such things as: independence, autonomy, development of many abilities, use of a few abilities in depth, and a longer time perspective than one had in youth. When arrangements at work suppress these ends, conflict and frustration result. According to Argyris, the social scientist needs to take a normative approach which "promulgates certain values" (p. 160). Although the focus has been mainly on individual development, Argyris (1973) noted that the nature of work can affect the social organization of society, including its ability to operate as a democracy. In this sense, Argyris went well beyond most contemporary cell 1 writers who tend, as do their social science colleagues in cell 2, to be interested only in the consequences of work *at the workplace.*

When compared to Marx and the Protestant ethic, the neoconventional view is interesting in several respects. First, when classified in terms of figure 2–1, its emphasis on the process of work and shared control in the workplace align it more closely with Marx than with the Protestant ethic. Second, both Marx and the neoconventional writers are humanistic; they focus on outcomes in this world rather than in an afterlife. If work is a calling to Marx and Argyris, it is because of human nature, not of Divine action (unless, of course, human nature is taken as an expression of Divine action). Third, unlike Marx, the neoconventional view is content free with respect to the product; it seems to make little difference what one produces as long as he or she does it in the right way (Nord, 1977).

The neoconventional view also embodies an unconscious ideology. In particular, as Anthony (1977) and Clayre (1974) have argued, its psychological growth models may lead neoconventional writers to entertain romantic notions of humanity and of the past and present. Given the wide influence of the neoconventional view, the consequences of this unconscious ideology may be substantial.

Anthony (1977), in tracing the ideology of work from the Greco-Roman period to the present, observed large costs associated with deficiencies that stem from ignoring historical evidence that contradicts an underlying ideology. Although Anthony may have overstated the case, we believe he was correct when he wrote:

> If there are methodological problems concerning the validity of behavioral science theory these problems are multiplied by the time unreliable theories have been vulgarized by consultants and then simplified by teachers in order to transmit them to managers, whose knowledge of basic behavioral science theory may be nil. Perhaps we can understand why there is no controversy. It would be hard to find another field of educational activity in which intelligent, and sometimes educated minds, were so harmoniously disposed. There may be occasional disagreement about educational methods, never about doctrine. (p. 262)

Clayre (1974) raised a related matter. Clayre sought to understand the origins of the view of work as a central life interest, concerned with more than instrumental outcomes. Study of the work of Marx, Ruskin, Morris, and others revealed that they shared a desire to return to the type of work available prior to the factory. Clayre asked: Was work better then?

The only available clues for answering this question were in the oral history of preindustrial times that he was able to trace. Analysis of songs and poems from this period revealed concerns over pay, cruelty, and injustice, but no evidence that there was any great pleasure derived from the intrinsic nature of the work. Clayre found that people wanted to combine necessary work with intrinsically rewarding activities—they desired to fuse work and play. These people saw work as a necessity that was neither fun nor consistent with things they valued, such as human rhythms and freedom. Escape from work and the control of one's own relation to work were also important, but little evidence exists that they valued intrinsically interesting work. In short, the work values assumed by Marx and the neoconventional writers to have been achieved in preindustrial times may never have existed.

In addition to the critiques by Clayre and Anthony, the neoconventional writers have been severely criticized by Strauss (1963), Fein (1976), and others for representing their own personal values as universal ones and for ignoring material, extrinsic interests. These critiques are similar to Rodgers' (1974) conclusions about the middle-class moralists who wrote on the work ethic a century ago. In essence there are conflicts between certain tenets of our important social values and the realities of workers and the workplace.

To some degree these critiques are unfair—most of the neoconventional writers do deal with the "lower-level needs" by explicitly stating the importance of satisfying them or implicitly assuming they are satisfied. Nevertheless, such statements or assumptions do seem to bypass the realities of many members of the work force. For example, we do see a tendency for the extrinsic outcomes to get more attention as social scientists base their notions empirically on data collected from workers at lower levels in the organization (cf., e.g., Harris and Locke, 1974; Jackall, 1978; Locke, 1973).

Implications

When approaches to work values are classified as they are in figure 2–1, some significant commonalities, differences, and omissions can be observed. It is important to note that we observed, but did not attempt to fully discuss, the differences among writers within specific cells. Further, it should be recognized that the framework does not permit precise classification in many cases. A number of perspectives such as Judaism and perhaps Clayre's (1974) view of work and play have components that make them difficult to classify within this typology. These ambiguities indicate that there are deficiencies in the framework for which other dimensions are needed to obtain more precise classification. Moreover, the boundaries between the cells should be viewed as permeable. As we will suggest in the next section, this permeability means that it may be very easy for one to be unaware of having moved through the different cells.

The typology does, however, in combination with the alternative view, help to frame some issues for future inquiry about work values. In addition, this combined perspective aids in our understanding of the practice of modern organizational behavior by calling attention to some subtle and not so subtle similarities and differences among theories and perspectives. Some examples of such benefits will be evident in the next section when we apply this framework to the writings of some key figures in the study of work whose contributions underlie much of the field of modern organizational behavior.

Implications for Organizational Behavior and the Study of Work Values

We have suggested a number of problems and omissions in previous perspectives on work values. In this final section we attempt to account for these problems and to explore the practical and intellectual implications of our analysis. First, we explore how organizational psychologists may have come to misunderstand the relationship between the neoconventional view and the work ethic. Second, we consider how the close ties between applied science and the language and concerns of the layperson have confused the study of work values. Third, we outline the rudiments of an expanded approach to work values.

From Weber to the Neoconventional View: A Paradigm Shift in Organizational Behavior

We have shown that the neoconventional view in cell 1 differs from the Protestant work ethic on two salient dimensions. Yet it is not unusual for applied social scientists, managers, and policy makers to view the desire of people for intrinsically interesting work as a modern statement of the *calling*. How did organizational psychologists come to tie intrinsically interesting work to the work ethic?

Although a fully defensible answer to this question would require at least another chapter, here we sketch a scenario that demonstrates how the framework we have presented might be useful in understanding the development of the neoconventional view in organizational behavior. This scenario draws on two ideas that we developed earlier—Rodgers' (1974) alternative view and the classification of work values summarized in figure 2–1. In addition, we build our discussion on three assumptions. First, we assume that the tendency for psychologists and other modern American social scientists to be ahistorical (Sarason, 1981) applies also to organizational behaviorists. Second, we assume that the nature of work and working conditions have changed markedly during the last century. Third, we assume the importance of what Zuboff (1983) described as concept of a *psychologized* work ethic.[1] In our scenario the ahistoricism is a background factor that helps to explain why organizational behaviorists reflect so little awareness of the interaction between their enterprise and events in the larger social system. Hence, in developing our scenario, we do not consider the ahistoricism further; the alternative view, figure 2–1, the changes in the nature of work, and the "psychologized" work ethic receive most of our attention.

Starting in Cell 2. In our simplified story, Rodgers' (1974) account is used to provide evidence that many people (including early industrial psychologists) were interested in finding some form of ideology and reconcile the irreconcil-able—the harsh realities of work and the belief in voluntary, free labor. We suggest that the neoconventional view has come to play this role.[2]

Rodgers' analysis stopped with 1920—a time when social scientists had just begun to examine work. Before stopping, however, he did give us the basis for classifying these early efforts in terms of figure 2–1. Rodgers noted that industrial psychologists had begun to focus attention on the surroundings of work. Drawing on the concept of *habit* from nineteenth-century psychol-ogy, early industrial psychologists argued that routine work was good for the worker—"routine emancipated the worker by wearing deep comfortable tracks in the nervous system that set his mind free for thought" (p. 88) If monotony was a problem, the answer was to change the worker's mental state, not the work. A widely advocated solution was to give the worker "something to think about" (p. 89), such as an article from the company newspaper, tasteful surroundings, or friendships made at work. Hugo Munsterberg (1913), of course, focused on individual differences in tolerance for repetitive work and the use of testing to match people to appropriate work. Thus, although born into a culture that still held the work ethic as social doctrine, industrial psy-chology was essentially secular and did not consider intrinsic benefits from work. Hence, according to the rationale underlying figure 2–1, industrial psychology began in cell 2.

In the 1920s and 1930s, a related but qualitatively different way of resolv-ing the tensions emerged from the Hawthorne studies. Like early industrial psychology, it offered the promise of a scientific base. The findings of such a science promised many benefits to result from enlightened management.

The Hawthorne studies pointed to a new way of reducing conflict over work without introducing major changes in either the nature of work or the control of the workplace or technology. The promise of cooperation made by the Hawthorne studies and Mayo's (1960) book, *The Human Problems of an Industrial Civilization* (first published in 1933), became an important part of the foundation for organizational behavior. Despite disputes over their scien-tific merit, the Hawthorne studies contributed the credibility of science to the pursuit of cooperation in the workplace. However, when viewed in terms of figure 2–1, they did more.

Zuboff (1983) observed that the Hawthorne studies "psychologized" the matter of cooperation. "If managers were to achieve . . . cooperation, they would have to become competent in deciphering the psychological map of the work force and harnessing workers' sentiments in support of the organization as a whole" (pp. 165–6). Clues for this success could be gained from scientific disciplines—especially psychology. Thus, the way had been paved for man-agers to take an interest in theories of human motivation in order to achieve cooperation. What assumptions characterized the psychological theories of the human relations movement? Where do they belong in figure 2–1?

It is somewhat difficult to be certain about how to classify the human relations writers because they were not fully explicit about the exact consequences of work for individuals. It seems clear that they assumed important individual differences in what people wanted from work—for example, Roethlisberger and Dickson (1939) wrote: "No two individuals are making exactly the same demands of their job" (p. 553). They added that "Noneconomic motives, interests, and processes, as well as economic, are fundamental in behavior in business" (p. 557). Although they considered mechanization of work as a possible cause of problems, they concluded that even though most of the jobs they studied were semi-automated, there was little evidence to suggest that repetitive work was a major source of problems. Rather, they suggested, modern industry had created many new occupations; and few of these had labels that would be recognized in the community outside the plant. The loss of such an outer symbol, they suggested, "may in part account for the worker's preoccupations over wages and wage differentials, and also may account for complaints of monotony in work" (p. 574). Whatever the cause—modern industry, the depression, or something else—the interviews in Roethlisberger and Dickson's (1939) *Management and the Worker* indicated that most of the workers' concerns were over what we would now call *hygiene factors*.

It seems reasonable to conclude from these observations, interpreted in the context of the well-known emphasis that the human relations writers placed on sentiments and needs for social integration, that their view of what people sought and expected from work did not depend on the nature of the work itself. Besides the traditional instrumental value of pay, the important outcomes of work were to be located in social relationships both inside and outside the plant. In short, we conclude that the early human relations movement appears to belong in cell 2. No intrinsic matters were involved—the nature of work itself was not taken as problematic. What was problematic were ways of managing the social relationships in the workplace to increase collaboration. As Miles (1966) summarized so well:

> If management would simply treat people as human beings, acknowledge their needs to belong and to feel important by listening to and heeding their complaints where possible and by involving them in certain decisions . . . then morale would surely improve and workers would cooperate with management in achieving good production. (p. 40)

So far we have encountered little evidence for the importance of intrinsically interesting work in the general social history we have reviewed or in the human relations movement. Yet, the importance of intrinsically interesting work has for some time been a major theme in organizational behavior. How did this view develop? In short, how did organizational behaviorists move from the stances in cell 2 to those in cell 1?

The move from the portion of cell 2 we have been discussing to cell 1 involved several background developments. First, after the depression and World War II, working conditions and the economic well-being of much (but not all) of the work force appeared much improved from the past. Second, the managerial, professional, and white-collar components of the work force grew rapidly, and the nature of work and the social relationships surrounding it were different for many of these people than for the factory worker. For example, coercive aspects of mechanized work were less visible and the potential for upward mobility in management appeared to be more realistic. Research on human responses to this type of work could be expected to yield different results than from blue-collar work.

In this context several key studies and their integration by Argyris (and probably others) provided the path from cell 2 to cell 1. We speculate that the work of Walker (1950), Walker and Guest (1952), and Turner (1955) played a major role in this transition. Certainly they played a key role in Argyris' (1957) influential formulation.

In Walker's (1950) paper he reported a job enlargement effort conducted by IBM in 1943. Although the jobs were indeed enlarged (in fact *enriched* in modern terminology), the success might equally well have been attributed to changes in status, compensation, patterns of interaction, or a Hawthorne effect, as to any intrinsic desire to work. Interestingly, Walker himself *did not* interpret these results as evidence of a need for intrinsically interesting work. Although he did lament the "overspecialization" of modern industry, he provided no clear psychological explanation for any problems. Moreover, he explicitly denied the generalizability of the experiment, "in precisely this form at least" (p. 58), to the assembly line.

Walker and Guest's (1952) *Man on the Assembly Line* potentially provided a basis for attributing a desire for intrinsically interesting work to blue-collar workers. However, the authors stopped far short of doing so. In fact, the respondents reported that the extrinsic aspects of pay and security were the most liked things about the job, and that social and group relationships were very important. Walker and Guest nevertheless did begin to emphasize the importance of job content. They pointed to the importance of variety and a relationship to the "*whole* product" (p. 149). Moreover, they noted that the jobs of utility men are more satisfactory because they involved greater variety. Given this context, their suggestion of job rotation and enlargement is not surprising; but it is far from clear that either they or the workers were calling for intrinsically meaningful work.

Part of the ambiguity stems from the fact that Walker and Guest discussed job rotation and enlargement in their treatment of workers' complaints about pacing and repetitiveness. Workers sought to escape from pacing and repetition and aversive conditions through including: rest periods, opportunities to vary the pace and to have "breathers" through such activities as building "banks" (that is, accumulating a supply of output or "working up the line"), job rotation and enlargement, and freedom to plan their work and choose their own tools. While all of these alternatives are means to escape repetitiveness and machine pacing, only a few seem to indicate a desire for more intrinsically rewarding work.

Workers' comments on their mental activity at work also provided mixed support for the view that they wanted challenging work. Although some reported disliking the surface mental attention required by their work, this did not necessarily imply they wanted more demanding jobs. Rather, what seemed to bother many of them was having to pay so much attention to their work that they could not daydream even while the job was not complicated enough to "absorb their mental faculties to any depth" (Walker and Guest, 1952, p. 155). Perhaps either less demanding jobs or more demanding ones (that is, *enriched* work) would have resolved their concerns. In short, the data Walker and Guest reported stop far short of providing a compelling case that the workers sought more meaningful tasks.

In fact, in their final conclusions, Walker and Guest de-emphasized even the role of pacing and repetitiveness. Instead, they turned to the lack of opportunities for promotion as a source of problems. The short progression ladder was, in their words, "one of the most important effects of mass production methods. . . . By all but obliterating job progression among production workers, it strikes at one of the strongest human incentives. It also strikes at a cultural tradition closely interwoven with American ideas and ideals—the belief in the desirability and possibility of 'rising in the world'" (p. 160). Finally, they concluded that the real problem did not directly stem from either the machine pacing or repetition, but rather from the fact that technology makes people interchangeable. *Depersonalization* was the core of the problem. They wrote:

> The sense of becoming *de*personalized, or becoming anonymous as against remaining one's self, is for those who feel it a psychologically more disturbing result of the work environment than either the boredom or the tension that arise from repetitive and mechanically paced work. This appeared to be the basis of such bitterly critical comments as were made against Company x as such. (p. 161)

The degree to which these matters represent a desire for work characterized by intrinsic aspects that promote human growth or represent extrinsic matters is open to debate. Much like Roethlisberger and Dickson (1939) who saw the lack of clearly defined occupational labels that communicated one's identity to others, Walker and Guest saw machine-paced work as a source of anonymity—an extrinsic and secular consequence. Their work, therefore, seems to reflect the central features characterizing cell 2.

Similarly Turner (1955), drawing on research by Walker and Guest, argued that foremen who successfully reduced the negative influence of the assembly line on their people, did so in two ways. First, they reduced the pressures from mechanical pacing. Second, these supervisors counteracted the impersonality introduced by repetitiveness and the destruction of the small group by the technology through measures including: absorbing pressure themselves, trusting workers' willingness to work, recognizing individual differences, introducing variety, delegating responsibility, developing groups of workers, and establishing a personal relationship with the men as individuals.

Do these measures belong in cell 1 or cell 2? For the most part, they seem to belong in cell 2. Although some are related to job content, even these have a tone of removing negative features of work rather than indicating positive desires for intrinsically interesting work. Finally, impersonality belongs in cell 2.

On to Cell 1. We described these findings in such depth because, driven by a psychological model, Argyris (1957) gave a cell 1 interpretation to them. For example, Argyris wrote: "These findings are understandable since these requirements [of assembly line work] run counter to the needs of relatively mature human beings" (p. 73). Later he cited Walker (1950) and Walker and Guest (1952) as reporting "that one way to increase employee satisfaction *or self-actualization* is to increase the number of formal tasks assigned to an employee" (p. 178; italics added).

What we seem to observe here is a gestalt shift from the introduction of a new paradigm (Kuhn, 1970). From a cell 2 perspective, the comments of the workers in Walker and Guest's research could easily be accommodated, particularly if one included the removal of aversive stimuli (for instance, pressure) introduced by work as extrinsic factors. On the other hand, when the assembly line studies are interpreted through a paradigm of psychological growth, such as Maslow's (1943) hierarchy of needs or White's (1952) competence motive, they appear to belong in cell 1. For example, Argyris (1957), influenced by White's work, interpreted these and a number of other studies on job enlargement as demonstrating the needs of employees to use the abilities of the mature personality—"the knowing and feeling abilities" (p. 181).

The great majority of these early studies centered on blue-collar workers and foremen. Although some research has continued to focus on these groups, since the 1950s the study of work increasingly became the study of the work of white-collar and professional employees, if for no other reason than that these groups make up a much higher percentage of the work force than they did before.

The pioneering work of Herzberg, Mausner, and Snyderman (1959), more than any other research, focused attention on the intrinsic aspects of work in the white-collar arena. As Hulin and Blood (1968) and Fein (1976) noted, most of the research that came to support the importance of intrinsic components was based on this segment of the work force. The essence of this perspective appears in many contemporary systems for improving human performance, including quality of worklife (QWL), job design, various versions of organization development (OD), job enrichment, and human-resources management (Miles, 1966). So powerful is this vision in the minds of neo-conventional writers that some, such as Miles and Rosenberg (1982) have concluded: "There is no longer a meaningful debate in the United States about applicability of the human resources approach to management" (p. 40). Zuboff (1983) concluded on a similar note, suggesting that the psychological work ethic may indeed allow employees to achieve their complex psychological needs and fulfill their aspirations at work.

Not only do these cell 1 statements contrast sharply with a cell 2 perspective, but they are far removed from cell 4. Unfortunately, these distinctions have gone unrecognized. Contemporary managers and social scientists, while lacking a full understanding of history and the nature of the Protestant ethic and acting seemingly unaware of alternative perspectives, have diagnosed problems in the modern workplace as being due to the decay of the traditional work ethic (Bernstein, 1980; Kopelman, 1986) and the loss of the opportunity for craft work (Maccoby, 1981). Cell 1 solutions are advanced to restore both. As we have shown, even if the models in cell 1 do describe the reality of many members of today's professional work force, their focus on secular outcomes of intrinsically meaningful work bears little logical relationship to the Protestant work ethic as described by Weber. Moreover, in view of the work of Clayre, Anthony, and Rodgers, the assumption that today's emphasis on cell 1 is an effort to restore work to its preindustrial state is suspect as well.

Whether in fact cell 1 even represents current reality is also problematic. It is important to note that Miles and Rosenberg's (1982) conclusion was published at a time when leading contributors to the field (such as, Salancik and Pfeffer, 1978; White and Mitchell, 1979) were concluding that the actual design of jobs was far less important than is the socially constructed reality of the workplace in determining a worker's satisfaction. Also, at about that time, based on a major survey of a wide spectrum of the American work force, Schiemann and Morgan (1983) concluded that while most employees were satisfied with the work itself, a number of extrinsic matters (for example, pay, benefits, supervision, security, and responsiveness of the company to employee concerns) were of major importance in evaluating a company as a place to work. Despite these results it is possible that, as some organizational behaviorists have suggested, intrinsically satisfying work is universally desired but that failure to find convincing empirical support for this cell 1 position is due to individual differences—such as growth need strength (Hackman and Oldham, 1980), achievement motivation (Steers and Spencer, 1977), and place of early socialization (Martinson and Wilkening, 1984)—that obscure the expected relationships. However, there is a great deal of research evidence (Aldag, Barr, and Brief, 1981; Cummings, 1980; and White, 1978) that runs counter to this view.

In sum, what the neoconventional view and the psychological work ethic appear to share with the Protestant ethic is a result more of process than of substance. Both the traditional and the psychological work ethic are the creations of middle-class writers. Both concepts seem to ignore the concrete experiences of work advanced by the alternative view. Both seem oriented to reducing conflict at the organizational level without considering causes that may be at a more sociological level. Overall, they appear to be linked more by the common social concerns they address than by what they have to say about work.

It should be clear by now that we view the neoconventional view as seriously flawed. Most important, we believe it blinds its adherents to conflicts surrounding experiences of work that are inherent in modern society. Closely related, it binds its adherents (and those they influence) to a misinformed perspective of what was, what is, and what could be. While some of the problems may be particular to the study of work values, we think the "case study" we have described of how work has been defined and interpreted has several implications for applied social science more generally. In the next section we move tangentially to sketch these thoughts. After this brief detour, we will conclude by suggesting where we think the study of work values should be headed.

Some Costs of Being Relevant: Problems Arising from Mixing Scientific and Lay Constructs

Because applied social science tends to be tightly coupled with ongoing social processes, it seems more difficult to conduct inquiry and develop constructs without incurring significant contamination from the "real world." The study of work and work values is no exception. Bias, overgeneralization, and construct deficiency are three types of contamination that appear to have played a role in the study of work values.

Bias. The problem of bias in organizational behavior has been so widely discussed (see, for example, Baritz, 1960; Nord, 1977; Bramel and Friend, 1981), that all we need do here is acknowledge the fact that undoubtedly the interests of those who have controlled resources that are valued by organizational behaviorists have affected the conduct of some research and, hence, the content of knowledge in ways favorable to themselves. Such bias can affect the choice and framing of research questions, research design decisions, and the interpretation of results (see Kaplan, 1964; Weber, 1949). We have seen how in the study of work values, focusing on the interests of the working class leads exponents of the alternative view to conclusions different from those who have adopted some other stance. For present purposes we are not concerned with the direction or amount of bias; our major objective in mentioning it here is to reemphasize this generic problem in applied social science.

We know of no ways to eliminate the bias; we suggest that at present the best we can do is recognize the influence of values in interpreting every piece of research. Procedurally, two ways to stimulate this awareness are: encouraging disclosure and acknowledging diversity.

In regards to disclosure, Mills (1961) reasoned that studying society and publishing the results constitutes a political and moral act; researchers who conceal this condition from themselves and from their audiences are morally adrift. Moreover, Keniston (1965) observed that when the writer's biases are disclosed "the reader is at least allowed to challenge these assumptions as stated and not required to ferret them out as embedded in 'objective' reporting and interpretation" (pp. 11–12). Of course, merely listing biases and values does not guarantee that the researcher is willing and/or able to give his/her true ones. The problems of a truly "reflexive" social science are difficult ones—disclosure is only a start.

Our second suggestion, diversity, merely recognizes that no one set of biases is apt to be the universally best set on which to conduct all inquiry. As Feyerabend (1975) has argued so well, the quest for knowledge may be best advanced when it employs a wide variety of perspectives.

Overgeneralization. A second set of problems in the study of work values and other areas of applied social science seems to stem from the effort to aggregate research findings. A good example of the process can be found in the study of performance.

Campbell and Pritchard (1976) observed how constructs such as performance subsume such a diverse set of elements that they lack construct validity. What seems to happen is that one research project investigates some outcome that is valued by a given organization and measures success in ways that make sense in that specific context. Other researchers do the same—each in a specific setting with a context specific measure. When we attempt to combine the various findings, we use some general word such as *performance,* but because the aggregation embodies so many different interpretations, definitions, tasks, and specific contexts, all hope of obtaining a unitary construct is lost. Employing the result as if it were a construct is dysfunctional because it leads users to overlook important distinctions across these studies. We submit that the term *work* raises similar problems that to date have not been considered sufficiently by organizational behaviorists.

Our inquiry into the history of work and work values sensitized us to the changes in work over time. Ultimately, we realized that organizational behaviorists, ourselves included, have a very poor concept of what work really means. Pence (1978–79) observed:

> A surprisingly common error in thinking about work is to think of it as having some common essence. . . . The basic error is a classic "category mistake." An activity which is complex, highly variable, and meaning-dependent on the individual, is erroneously made into a simple, invariable activity of universal meaning. (p. 310)

Does it make sense to use the same word to talk about what people did to earn a living in the Middle Ages with what they did in the industrial revolution and what they do today? Does the same word apply equally well to what professionals, managers, and laborers do? Okrent (1978–79), for example, argued it does not. To illustrate his point, he suggested that if we carefully analyze the words *play* and *work,* it makes more sense to characterize members of the managerial class as playing for a living. In short, one consequence of using an everyday word such as *work* as if it were a construct suitable for scientific discourse is overgeneralization. Our answers to such questions as: What should result from work? and What can result from work? may change substantially once we recognize the coarseness of the concept of work. Discussions of work values would benefit from greater attention to the construct of work itself.

Clearly such discussions require that the nature of work as experienced by members of society at one point in time is not taken to be universal. Finer discriminations about work are required, although how much finer is difficult to say. To date, organizational behaviorists seem to have taken an extreme view—work is work whether it was done in 1600 or 1985; whether it is managerial or blue-collar; whether it is done during a depression or an economic boom. The latter example may be particularly poignant in revealing the contents of the unconscious ideology of contemporary students of organizational behavior. Economic conditions appear to be irrelevant to organizational behaviorists. Seldom do they report the economic conditions of the industry and local labor market at the time of data collection or even the dates when they collected their data. We assert that work must be understood in the context of human experience in its full complexity. To do otherwise runs the risk of overgeneralization. A simple first step in this direction would be for journal editors to insist on the reporting of macro-data necessary for understanding the context of the phenomena investigated.

Construct Deficiency. The constructs that have guided research on work values are deficient in the sense that they do not subsume all the end states people might desire. According to Schwab (1980), a measure is deficient if it omits part of the construct it purports to measure. We suggest that concepts about work values are deficient because they fail to encompass a number of components individuals might want from work. For example, it is somewhat paradoxical that, in view of the religious origins of the work ethic, spiritual dimensions have received so little attention. Likewise, the relationships between producers and customers and the nature of the product relative to its ability to satisfy important human needs have received little attention in the study of work values.

The consequences of deficiency may be more subtle than those of bias. Following Anthony (1977), we believe the consequences of deficiency are negative for *all* people who seek to use the work of organizational behaviorists, including those we are presumed to favor—managers! Anthony observed that because our assumptions about work are so narrow, we do not provide a body of knowledge rich enough to capture reality. He wrote: "On the very rare occasions when a manager, or come to that one of his teachers, meets someone carrying another set of doctrines based upon different values, he reacts with bewilderment" (p. 262).

Anthony's (1977) observations introduce a paradoxical result concerning the role of a managerial bias among organizational behaviorists. If our constructs are deficient, the solutions we formulate will be relevant to only a portion of the problem or phenomenon we purport to address. Thus, even if we are biased in the sense that these are the matters managers explicitly seek to have investigated, we may not be serving their needs. As consultants and educators—because our models and constructs omit a variety of possible inputs and outcomes—organizational behaviorists may be perpetuating a false doctrine through deficient knowledge. As a result, any group attempting to apply the knowledge we offer will often be disappointed. With respect to work values specifically, solutions predicated on a particular dogma of work, when applied to individuals who do not believe in that dogma, are unlikely to solve the problems to which they were addressed. Broader, alternative perspectives are needed.

Perspectives for the Study of Work Values in the Future

We have suggested that unconscious ideology, ahistoricism, bias, overgeneralization, and construct deficiency have contributed to the misunderstanding of work values in the past and present. Our suggestions for the future are in the spirit of Gergen's (1982) sociorationalism. Among other things, Gergen suggested that social scientists need to recognize: the historical embeddedness of knowledge, the social construction of knowledge, the dynamic interaction of social theory and practice, and the roles of values, ideologies, and visions in "knowledge making." The sociorationalist perspective urges investigators to take their own values as a serious component of their professional work—to be motivated by "intellectual expression in the service of his or her vision of the good" (p. 208). In light of this framework and our analysis of work values, we suggest a number of directions for future thought.

First, work values must be treated as socially constructed notions. We should not expect to find uniformity across time, place, and people. Instead, effort must be devoted to discovering a rich array of alternative values. Data from a variety of workers and nonworkers are needed. These data must be interpreted in the genres of the providers instead of being quickly transformed into abstract frameworks. Such interpretation, more than anything else, would protect us from unconscious ideology, bias, overgeneralization, and construct deficiency.

Second, the question, "Why do we hear so much about the work ethic and work values from managers, politicians, unionists, social scientists, and others?" needs to be considered repeatedly. Iaffaldano and Muchinsky (1985), for example, speculated that the incessant research on the relationship between job satisfaction and performance, in the face of a body of evidence indicating that the two are only slightly correlated, reveals an illusory correlation in the minds of organizational behaviorists. Such an account is closely aligned with our view of the role of an unconscious ideology in the study of work values: we continue, in the intellectual tradition of the moralists, of the writers, and the intellectuals described by Rodgers (1974) and of our predecessors in social science, to find a way to think of work so that it appears to be a less coercive activity than it is for many people. In other words, work values have received so much attention because they have reduced the need to confront the potentially disquieting realities of work in our society.

Third, we need to emphasize the distinction between work beliefs and work values, and to give more attention to the former than we have to date. Beliefs refer to what people view as possible; values refer to desires or wants (see Scheibe, 1970). While there has been considerable discussion of work values and also of how people experience their particular jobs, to our knowledge little study has been applied to the area between the extreme abstraction of values and the extreme concreteness of daily experiences. We suggest that there be greater inquiry into what people believe is possible from work and what their expectations are of the costs, benefits, and probabilities of such work. One reason for studying beliefs is that they may be empirically more potent than values. For example, the relationship between beliefs and concrete experience may exert a greater influence on the quality of experience than do the end-states the worker desires. Knowledge about what people believe that work can realistically provide may supply useful guidance in contemplating work redesign. Among other things, knowledge of these beliefs may help provide people with accurate information about what is possible, what the necessary trade offs are, and the accuracy of their beliefs. In addition, inquiry should be directed to the causes of beliefs people hold about what work can provide. If we know these causes, we might be able to expand and/or contract people's horizons to develop more realistic beliefs.

Fourth, organizational behaviorists need to consider the relationship between work and other social institutions, and investigate the philosophical and religious aspects of work values. We have suggested some of the alternative values that have been considered and others that have been ignored, and also the lack of solid intellectual or moral justification for either outcome. More inquiry, such as Keeley's (1978; 1983), which revealed how social, ethical, and scientific interests complement each other in the study of organizations, is an example of what we have in mind.

Such study would call attention to latent value judgments in our research. In particular, we would quickly see how truncated our thinking about work has been. For example, most recent treatments of work focus within the bounds of the workplace. We suggest that limiting analysis of work to the confines of the workplace is an arbitrary decision (common both to cell 1 and cell 2 writers), that reduces their ability to understand important aspects of the psychological, social, and political meanings of work. If work is viewed as instrumental for some other outcome (as in cell 2), the value of that other outcome ought to influence the assessment of the instrumental activity. For example, the value of working for money is likely to be affected by the attractiveness of what one can buy with money. (This issue is addressed more fully in chapter 9.) Likewise, the value of psychological growth from work (cell 1) will be affected by the value of the payoffs for psychological growth possible both inside and outside the workplace.

Similarly, the recognition of the need to study work values beyond the bounds of the workplace, raises the possibility of reintroducing nonsecular values into our study of work. As Cox (1984) noted, recently religion has come to play an increasingly important role in the secular world. What, for example, are the implications of the heightened influence of Fundamentalist Protestantism for work? Also, the encyclical of Pope John Paul II (1981), *Laborem Exercens,* raises many important issues about work values in modern society. Perhaps the scientific positivism and the humanistic orientations embedded in our treatments of work values have led us to ignore an important part of human experience—the association of spiritual values and work. The most recent effort in the organizational behavior literature to attempt such a linkage that we know of was Purcell's (1967) discussion of an industrial theology. Perhaps it is time for a deeper consideration of the relationship between work and nonsecular concerns. Many people seem to be seeking some framework for relating their existence to some larger purpose. Since work is such a major part of the existence of most of us, some attention to the existing perceptions and possible alternatives that might foster such a linkage would seem to be an essential part of understanding the human condition.

Fifth, we need to consider work values of other cultures seriously and prudently. If the rapid growth of the global economy continues, increasingly we will be dealing with work values of other cultures. On the one hand, the contrasts between these cultures and our own may help us understand ourselves better. On the other hand, we will need a richer framework for understanding their work values. Such an understanding of work—both in our own and other cultures—will require serious attention to the history of work and of work and society. Inquiry into the origins, functions, nonfunctions, and dysfunctions of particular work values in individual cultures is needed. Indeed, we are apt to find that stated values about work may be equally as misleading about reality in other cultures as in our own.

Finally, we suggest the need to recognize that espoused work values in a society may often be a result of work activity rather than a cause of it. Rodgers' (1974) argument about the work ethic seems to show this quite well. We suggest the same approach be considered at the individual level. Jackall's (1978) research suggests, for example, that what might appear to be statements about work values are actually responses by individuals to legitimize to themselves the ambiguities and tensions about work and its relationship to the rest of their lives. Clearly, this perspective has much in common with the retrospective sense-making view championed by Weick (1979) and the political scientist Edelman's (1977) treatment of political language. Viewing work values as personal and social constructions may be more productive than viewing them as ideals to achieve. Among other things, this would move students of work values toward understanding *how* contemporary individuals come to terms with an important aspect of their total lives.

Concluding Remarks

Our critique has been sweeping, although probably we have been hardest on the neoconventional writers. Because we share so much with them, however, we cannot conclude without acknowledging their important contributions. Argyris and the other neoconventional writers have done much of what Gergen's (1982) sociorationalist view asks. They have had the courage to step beyond "normal science" and ask: What *should* and what *can* work be? Long before it was fashionable, they did what Howard (1985) suggested—they explicitly incorporated nonepistemic values into their work to envision what is possible, instead of merely reporting what is.

Our quarrel with the neoconventional writers concerns their tendency to treat work values as psychological phenomena only, while often ignoring major historical, sociological, philosophical, and economic processes. We suggest that this inattention is embedded in an unconscious ideology and that the nature of the unconscious ideology is revealed by consideration of alternative perspectives. What people desire and expect from work is relative to particular historical and social conditions. There has been and will continue to be great variation in work values. Study of them demands an intellectual framework sufficiently rich to capture this variety.

Our examination of how organizational behaviorists study work values was intended as a case study of the ways in which just one camp of scholars approaches the meaning of work question. To what degree our findings might generalize other camps is unknown. Given the extent to which organizational behaviorists were shown to borrow from various facets of the psychological and sociological literatures, we speculate that organizational behaviorists, in their approach to the study of meanings of work, are not unlike other camps of social scientists.

What our findings do indicate is that those social scientists interested in the meaning of work would do well to turn to various branches of the humanities. In doing so, the social scientist, of course, will not find scientific knowledge but, rather, knowledge of a different sort. Although the humanities are apt to have their own unconscious ideologies, they can provide an important source of perspectives that will be new and different from those that dominate modern social science. Social scientists are apt to find in the humanities questions, as well as answers, about the meanings of work not previously conceived by them. Simply, we believe that the intellectual richness required to address meaning-of-work issues adequately will be found by those investigators willing to risk the hazards of camping out in the sparsely populated territory between the social sciences and the humanities.

Notes

This paper has benefited from conversations with many people, including: Chris Argyris, John Clancy, Larry Cummings, Steven Feldman, Peter Frost, Stanley Mellish, Ann Nord, Russell Johnson, Barry Staw, Howard Schwartz, Sterling Schoen, Ralph Stablein, and John Zipp. Their thoughts and criticisms are gratefully acknowledged.

1. It is interesting to note that the work became "psychologized" rather than "physiologized." This shift would of course support Rodgers' (1974) thesis stating that work values have played a primary role of turning attention away from the concrete toward the abstract. Of course, organizational and other types of psychologists have given some attention to the physiological aspects of work. The reasons for and consequences of the lack of integration among these various approaches is also worthy of investigation.

2. Most likely the notion of free choice in a free labor market provided by liberal economics played a parallel role, but this is a subject for another time.

References

Aldag, R., Barr, S., and Brief, A.P. (1981). Measurement of perceived task characteristics. *Psychological Bulletin, 90,* pp. 415–31.

Aldag, R.J., and Brief, A.P. (1979). *Task design and employee motivation.* Glenview, IL: Scott, Foresman.

Anthony, P.D. (1977). *The ideology of work.* London: Tavistock.

Argyris, C. (1957). *Personality and organization.* New York: Harper.

———. (1973). Personality and organization theory revisited. *Administrative Science Quarterly, 18,* pp. 141–67.

Aristotle (1912). *Politics.* London: J.M. Dent and Sons.

Baritz, L. (1960). *The servants of power.* New York: Wiley.

Bem, S.L., and Bem, D.J. (1970). Case study of a nonconscious ideology: Training the woman to know her place. In D.J. Bem, *Beliefs, attitudes, and human affairs.* Belmont, CA: Brooks/Cole, pp. 89–99.

Bernstein, P. (1980). The work ethic that never was. *Wharton Magazine, 4*(3), pp. 19–25.

Blood, M.R. (1969). Work values and job satisfaction. *Journal of Applied Psychology, 53,* pp. 456–59.

Bowles, S., and Gintis, H. (1976). *Schooling in capitalist America.* New York: Basic Books.

Bramel, D, and Friend, R. (1981). Hawthorne, the myth of the docile worker, and class bias in psychology. *American Psychologist, 36,* pp. 867–78.

Braverman, H. (1974). *Labor and monopoly capital.* New York: Monthly Review Press.

Brief, A.P., and Aldag, R.J. (1975). Employee reactions to job characteristics: A constructive replication. *Journal of Applied Psychology, 60,* pp. 182–86.

———. (1977). The intrinsic-extrinsic dichotomy: Toward conceptual clarity. *Academy of Management Review, 2,* pp. 496–99.

Burawoy, M. (1979). *Manufacturing consent. Changes in the labor process under monopoly capitalism.* Chicago: University of Chicago Press.

Campbell, J.P., and Pritchard, R.D. (1976). Motivation theory in industrial and organizational psychology. In M.D. Dunnette (ed.), *Handbook of industrial and organizational psychology.* Chicago: Rand McNally, pp. 60–130.

Clawson, D. (1980). *Bureaucracy and the labor process. The transformation of U.S. industry, 1860–1920.* New York: Monthly Review Press.

Clayre, A. (1974). *Work and play. Ideas and experience of work and leisure.* New York: Harper and Row.

Cox, H. (1984). *Religion in the secular city: Toward a postmodern theology.* New York: Simon and Schuster.

Culbert, S.A., and McDonough, J.J. (1985). *Radical management: Power politics and the pursuit of trust.* New York: Free Press.

Cummings, L.L. (1980). Task design. In B. Karmel (ed.), *Point and counterpoint in organizational behavior.* Hinsdale, IL: Dryden Press, pp. 95–107.

Deans, R.C. (1973). Productivity and the new work ethic. In *Editorial research reports on the American work ethic.* Washington, DC: Congressional Quarterly, pp. 1–20.

de Grazia, S. (1964). *Of time, work, and leisure.* Garden City, NY: Anchor Books.

Dubin, R. (1976a). Theory building in applied areas. In M.D. Dunnette (ed.), *Handbook of industrial and organizational psychology.* Chicago: Rand McNally, pp. 17–39.

———. (1976b). Work in modern society. In R. Dubin (ed.), *Handbook of work, organization, and society.* Chicago: Rand McNally, pp. 5–35.

Dyer, L., and Parker, D.F. (1975). Classifying outcomes in work motivation research: An examination of the intrinsic-extrinsic dichotomy. *Journal of Applied Psychology, 60,* pp. 455–58.

Edelman, M. (1977). *Political language. Words that succeed and policies that fail.* New York: Academic Press.

Edwards, R.C. (1978). Who fares well in the welfare state? In R.C. Edwards, R. Reigh, and T. Weisskopf (eds.), *The capitalist system.* 2nd ed. Englewood Cliffs, NJ: Prentice Hall, pp. 244–51.

Fein, M. (1976). Motivation for work. In R. Dubin (ed.), *Handbook of work, organization, and society.* Chicago: Rand McNally, pp. 465–530.

Feyerabend, P. (1975). *Against method.* London: Verso.

Fromm, E. (1961). *Marx's concept of man.* New York: Frederick Ungar.

George, C.S. (1968). *The history of management thought.* Englewood Cliffs, NJ: Prentice Hall.

Gergen, K.J. (1982). *Toward transformation in social knowledge.* New York: Springer-Verlag.

Goldthorpe, J.H., Lockwood, D., Bechhofer, F., and Platt, J. (1969). *The affluent worker in the class structure.* Cambridge: Cambridge University Press.

Gordon, M.E., Kleiman, L.S., and Hanie, C.A. (1978). Industrial-organizational psychology: Open thy ears, O'house of Israel. *American Psychologist, 33,* pp. 893–905.

Gouldner, A.W. (1970). *The coming crisis of Western sociology.* New York: Basic Books.

Grant, M. (1960). *The world of Rome.* London: Weidenfeld and Nicolson.

Gutman, H.G. (1976). *Work culture, and society in industrializing America: Essays in American working-class and social history.* New York: Alfred A. Knopf.

Hackman, J.R., and Oldham, G.R. (1980). *Work redesign.* Reading, MA: Addison-Wesley.

Harris, T.C., and Locke, E.A. (1974). A replication of white-collar differences in sources of satisfaction and dissatisfaction. *Journal of Applied Psychology, 59,* pp. 369–70.

Hays, S.P. (1957). *The response to industrialism, 1885–1914.* Chicago: University of Chicago Press.

Heneman, H.G., Jr. (1973). Work and nonwork: Historical perspectives. In M.D. Dunnette (ed.), *Work and nonwork in the year 2000.* Monterey, CA: Brooks/Cole, pp. 12–27.

Herzberg, F. (1966). *Work and the nature of man.* Cleveland, OH: World Publishing.

Herzberg, F., Mausner, B., and Snyderman, B.B. (1959). *The motivation to work.* New York: Wiley, Inc.

Hirschman, A.O. (1977). *The passions and the interests.* Princeton, N.J.: Princeton University Press.

Howard, G.S. (1985). The role of values in the science of psychology. *American Psychologist, 40,* pp. 255–65.

Hulin, C.L., and Blood, M.R. (1968). Job enlargement, individual differences, and worker responses. *Psychological Bulletin, 69,* pp. 41–55.

Iaffaldano, M.T., and Muchinsky, P.M. (1985). Job satisfaction and job performance: A meta-analysis. *Psychological Bulletin, 97,* pp. 251–73.

Israel, J. (1971). *Alienation: From Marx to modern sociology.* Boston: Allyn and Bacon.

Jackall, R. (1978). *Workers in a labyrinth.* New York: Universe Books.

Kaplan, A. (1964). *The conduct of inquiry.* Scranton, PA: Chandler Publishing.

Keeley, M. (1978). A social-justice approach to job attitudes and task design. Administrative Science Quarterly, 23, pp. 272–92.

————. (1983). Values in organizational theory and management education. *Academy of Management Review, 8,* pp. 376–86.

Keniston, K. (1965). *The uncommitted alienated youth in American society.* New York: Harcourt Brace Jovanovich.

Kopelman, R.E. (1986). *Managing productivity in organizations.* New York: McGraw-Hill.

Kuhn, T.S. (1970). *The structure of scientific revolutions.* 2nd. ed. Chicago: University of Chicago Press.

Lawler, E.E. (1971). *Pay and organizational effectiveness.* New York: McGraw-Hill.

Locke, E.A. (1973). Satisfiers and dissatisfiers among white-collar differences in sources of satisfaction and dissatisfaction. *Journal of Applied Psychology, 59,* pp. 369–70.

Maccoby, M. (1981). *The leader.* New York: Ballantine.

Marglin, S.A. (1974). What do bosses do? The origins and function of hierarchy in capitalist production. *Review of Radical Political Economics, 6,* pp. 60–112.

Martinson, O.B., and Wilkening, E.A. (1984). Rural-urban differences in job satisfaction: Further evidence. *Academy of Management Journal, 27,* pp. 199–206.

Marx, K., and Engels, F. (1965). *The German ideology.* London: Lawrence and Wishart.

Maslow, A.H. (1943). A theory of human motivation. *Psychological Review, 50,* pp. 370–96.

Mayo, E. (1960). *The human problems of an industrial civilization.* New York: Viking Press.

McClelland, P.C. (1961). *The achieving society.* Princeton, NJ: Van Nostrand.

McGregor, D. (1960). *The human side of enterprise.* New York: McGraw-Hill.

Miles, R.E. (1966). *Theories of management: Implications for organizational behavior and development.* New York: McGraw-Hill.

Miles, R.E., and Rosenberg, H.R. (1982). The human resources approach to management: Second-generation issues. *Organizational Dynamics, 10* (Winter), pp. 26–41.

Mills, C.W. (1961). The sociological imagination. New York: Grove Press.

Munsterberg, H. (1913). *Psychology and industrial efficiency.* Boston: Houghton Mifflin.

Neff, W.S. (1985). *Work and human behavior.* New York: Aldine.

Nelson, D. (1975). *Managers and workers: Origins of the new factory system in the United States, 1880–1920.* Madison, WI: University of Wisconsin Press.

Noble, D.F. (1984). *Forces of production: A social history of industrial automation.* New York: Knopf.

Nord, W.R. (1974). The failure of current applied behavioral science: A Marxian perspective. *Journal of Applied Behavioral Science, 10, 557–78.*

———. (1977). Job satisfaction reconsidered. *American Psychologist, 32,* pp. 1026–35.

Nord, W.R., Brief, A.P., Atieh, J.M., and Doherty, E.M. (1987). Work values and the conduct of organizational behavior. In B.M. Staw and L.L. Cummings (eds.), *Research in organizational behavior,* vol. 9. Greenwich, CT: JAI Press, pp. 1–42.

Okrent, M. (1978–79). Work, play, and technology. *Philosophical Forum, 10,* pp. 321–40.

Parker, S.R., and Smith, M.A. (1976). Work and leisure. In R. Dubin (ed.), *Handbook of work, organization, and society.* Chicago: Rand McNally, pp. 37–62.

Pence, G.E. (1978–79). Towards a theory of work. *Philosophical Forum, 10,* pp. 306–20.

Pollard, S. (1963). Factory discipline in the industrial revolution. *Economic History Review, 16,* pp. 254–71.

Pope, L. (1942). *Millhands and preachers: A study of Gastonia.* New Haven: Yale University Press.

Pope John Paul II. (1981). *Laborem Exercens.* In C. Carlen (ed.), *The Papal Encyclicals, 1958.* Wilmington, NC: McGrath Publishing, pp. 299–326.

Pope Leo XIII. (1936). *On the condition of the working classes. (Rerum Novarum).* New York: America Press.

Purcell, T.V. (1967). Work psychology and business values: A triad theory of work motivation. *Personnel Psychology, 20,* pp. 231–57.

Rodgers, D.T. (1974). *The work ethic in industrial America, 1850–1920.* Chicago: University of Chicago Press.

Roethlisberger, F.J., and Dickson, W.J. (1939). *Management and the worker.* Cambridge: Harvard University Press.

Salancik, G.R., and Pfeffer, J. (1978). A social information processing approach to job attitudes and task design. *Administrative Science Quarterly, 23,* pp. 224–53.

Sarason, S.B. (1981). An asocial psychology and a misdirected clinical psychology. *American Psychologist, 36,* pp. 827–36.

Scheibe, K.E. (1970). *Beliefs and values.* New York: Holt, Rinehart and Winston.

Schiemann, W.A., and Morgan, B.S. (1983). *Managing human resources: Employee discontent and declining productivity.* Princeton, NJ: Opinion Research.

Schwab, D.P. (1980). Construct validity in organizational behavior. In B.M. Staw and L.L. Cummings (eds.), *Research in organizational behavior,* vol. 2. Greenwich, CT: JAI Press, pp. 3–43.

Schwartz, H.S. (1983). A theory of deontic work motivation. *Journal of Applied Behavioral Science, 19,* pp. 203–14.

Sombart, W. (1913). *The Jews and modern capitalism.* London: T. Fisher Unwin.

Spence, J.T. (1985). Achievement American style: The rewards and costs of individualism. *American Psychologist, 40,* pp. 1285–95.

Steers, R.M., and Spencer, D.G. (1977). The role of achievement motivation in job design. *Journal of Applied Psychology, 62,* (4), pp. 472–79.

Stone, K. (1974). The origins of job structures in the steel industry. *Review of Radical Political Economy, 6,* pp. 113–73.

Strauss, G. (1963). Some notes on power equalization. In H.J. Leavitt (ed.), *The social science of organizations*. Englewood Cliffs, NJ: Prentice Hall, pp. 39–84.

Thompson, E.P. (1963). *The making of the English working class*. London: Victor Gollantz.

Tilgher, A. (1931). *Work: What it has meant to man through the ages*. London: Harrap.

Turner, A.N. (1955). Management on the assembly line. *Harvard Business Review, 33*, pp. 40–48.

Tyler, G. (1983). The work ethic: A union view. In J. Barbash, R.J. Lapman, S.A. Levitan, and G. Tyler (eds.), *The work ethic—A critical analysis*. Madison, WI: Industrial Relations Research Association, pp. 197–210.

Walker, C.R. (1950). The problem of the repetitive job. *Harvard Business Review, 28*, pp. 54–58.

Walker, C.R., and Guest, R.H. (1952). *The man on the assembly line*. Cambridge: Harvard University Press.

Watson, T.J. (1977). *The personnel managers: A study in the sociology of work and employment*. London: Routledge and Kegan Paul.

Weber, M. (1930). *The Protestant ethic and the spirit of capitalism*. (trans. T. Parsons). New York: Charles Scribner's Sons.

———. (1949). *The methodology of the social sciences*. Glenco, IL: Free Press.

Weick, K.E. (1979). *The social psychology of organizing*. 2nd ed. Reading, MA: Addison-Wesley.

White, J.K. (1978). Individual differences and the job quality worker response relationship: Review, integration, and comments. *The Academy of Management Review, 3*, pp. 267–80.

White, R.W. (1952). *Lives in progress*. New York: Dryden.

White, S.E., and Mitchell, T.R. (1979). Job enrichment versus social cues: A comparison and competitive test. *Journal of Applied Psychology, 64* (1), pp. 1–9.

Whyte, M.K. (1973). Bureaucracy and modernization in China: The Maoist critique. *American Sociological Review, 38*, pp. 149–63.

Work in America. (1973). Cambridge: MIT Press.

Zuboff, S. (1983). The work ethic and work organization. In J. Barbash, R.J. Lampman, S.A. Levitan, and G. Tyler (eds.), *The work ethic—A critical analysis*. Madison, WI: Industrial Relations Research Association, pp. 153–81.

3
Cross-National Meanings of Working

George W. England
William T. Whitely

ork and working are an integral part of the human existence. Today, there is widespread recognition that the activity of working and the outcomes flowing from working are of fundamental significance to most individuals. In most industrialized societies, the average employed person spends approximately one-third of his/her waking hours in the activities that are known as *working*. Additionally, the time one spends in preparation and training for work, seeking work, and planning for changed working situations suggests that work-related activities constitute a major utilization of time in the adult life. Related to this time-utilization feature of working, is the fact that a majority of individuals in industrial societies derive the major part of their economic well-being (and their families') from income and fringe benefits generated through their working activities.

Working and outcomes from working also provide nonfinancial or noneconomic benefits to individuals. Were this not so, it would seem difficult to understand why 65 percent to 95 percent of individuals in national labor force samples in a variety of industrialized countries, state that they would continue to work even if they had enough money to live a life of leisure (Vecchio, 1980; Warr, 1982; MOW International Research Team, 1987). This stated preference for working even when financial necessity is presumed not to be a significant consideration is undoubtedly related to the broader social value or significance attached to working by individuals. This is demonstrated in studies such as those by Morse and Weiss (1955), in which most respondents indicated that "working gives them a feeling of being tied into the larger society, of having something to do, and of having a purpose in life." (p. 191).

This chapter was written while the first author was a Fulbright fellow at the Institute of Psychology, Berlin Technical University, West Berlin, and while the second author was on sabbatical at the Laboratory for Applied Psychology, State University of Ghent, Ghent, Belgium. Our thanks are extended to our colleagues on the Meaning of Work (MOW) International Research Team and especially to Bernhard Wilpert, Antonio Ruiz Quintanilla, Pol Coetsier, and Rita Spoelders-Claes for their encouragement, comments, and facilities while we were writing this chapter.

Working situations and activities may also generate negative consequences, outcomes, and personal states for individuals. Working is sometimes experienced as boring, dull, or unchallenging at one end of the spectrum or as excessively overloaded at the other. The result can be frustration, dissatisfaction, stress, or inadequate person-job fit, all of which can impact negatively both on mental and physical health. Cooper and Payne (1978; 1980) have recently summarized much of this relevant literature.

Another indicator of the general significance of working to individuals is found in the fifty years of research concerning the impact of unemployment and retirement on people who have actively worked during their lives (see Israeli, 1935; Friedmann and Havighurst, 1954; Wilensky, 1961; Aiken, Ferman and Sheppard, 1968; Kaplan and Tausky, 1974; Parnes and King, 1977; Jahoda, 1979; Dolley and Catalano, 1980; Hepworth, 1980; Warr, 1983). If the nonworking person find other meaningful sets of activities in which to become involved, the effects of limited activity, idleness, and work outcome loss are often demoralizing and dehabilitating. Studs Terkel (1972) captures a vivid description of this loss in an interview with a 45-year-old unemployed construction worker:

> Right now I can't really describe myself because . . . I'm unemployed. . . . So, you see, I can't say who I am right now. . . . I guess a man's something else besides his work, isn't he? But what? I just don't know. (p. 44)

Working seems, then, to be of general significance to individuals because it occupies a great deal of their time, because it generates economic and sociopsychological benefits and costs, and because it is so interrelated with other important life areas such as family, leisure, religion, and community.

As documented in previous chapters, work and working have been written about and studied in most of mankind's recorded history. While the purposes, focal points, and methods of such inquiry are certainly influenced by the current zeitgeist, the unrelenting subjective significance and value of working to individuals, to organizations, and to societies seems always evident. We perceive, however, that there is an increased urgency to the study of working in the past two decades. In our judgment, this increased concern about the topic of working stems from at least six interrelated conditions:

- increased international competition in the marketplace;
- increased rates of technological change and organizational and industrial sector restructuring;
- changes in labor force composition and educational qualifications;
- trends in productivity and saving patterns in a number of economies which are viewed as disturbing;

- concern that elements of the *work ethic* seem to be changing in many countries in ways that are presumed to be undesirable;
- concern that working may not provide the type of meaning, social significance, and satisfaction to individuals that was once presumed to be the case.

This recent increased concern about work and working is not a single country phenomenon but seems relatively universal in the industrialized world, although the focal points of concern differ somewhat in various countries.

A Conceptual View of the Meaning of Work

It was out of this general mileau that the first comprehensive Meaning of Working (MOW) study, jointly designed and conducted by behavioral scientists from advanced technological nations, was articulated in the scientific literature (MOW International Research Team, 1981). The primary data collection from nearly fifteen thousand respondents in eight countries was undertaken during 1981 to 1983, and international comparative results have been published in the book, *The Meaning of Working* (MOW International Research Team, 1987).[1]

The authors of the present chapter are members of the MOW International Research Team and we wish to express sincere appreciation to our MOW colleagues for long-term cooperation on the MOW project. Without their ideas, knowledge, effort, and the resulting data, we would have much less to contribute to a chapter such as this. While responsibility for the present interpretation of the MOW data must rest solely with us, we acknowledge a great debt to our colleagues.

In the MOW project, we clearly recognized that the meaning of working is a broad and general topic analogous in many respects to other broad meanings, such as the meaning of love or the meaning of life. These broad meanings seem predominantly experiential in nature; thus a logical approach for their study (in our case, the meaning of working) was to query, observe, and study those experiencing working. Common observation and research evidence also suggest that the meaning of working can vary tremendously from one person to the next. It seemed necessary to therefore focus study on the individual and then to aggregate individual data to form relevant groups of concern such as occupational groups, age groups, gender groups, and national labor forces. All of these considerations led us to a strategy of studying the meaning of working for representative national labor force samples using carefully developed, translated, pretested, and standardized forms of questioning.

Major Components in the Meaning of Working

The conceptual framework in the MOW project posited that the meaning of working should be defined and thus assessed in terms of three major components: work centrality; work goals; and societal norms about working.

Work Centrality: was defined as the degree of general importance that working has in the life of an individual at any given point in time. Work centrality was assessed by combining an absolute measure of the importance of working in one's life and a relative measure of the importance of working in one's life as compared to the importance of other life roles. The work centrality measurement attempts to answer the question: How central or important is the role of working in one's life?

Work Goals: were defined as the relative importance of eleven work goals and values which are sought or preferred by individuals in their working lives. The work goals were:

1. A lot of opportunity to learn new things.
2. Good interpersonal relations (with supervisors, co-workers).
3. Good opportunity for upgrading or promotion.
4. Convenient work hours.
5. A lot of variety.
6. Interesting work (work that you really like).
7. Good job security.
8. A good match between your job requirements and your abilities and experience.
9. Good pay.
10. Good physical working conditions (such as light, temperature, cleanliness, low noise level).
11. A lot of autonomy (you decide how to do your work).

Societal Norms about Working: The MOW project focused on two normative views—the entitlement norm and the obligation norm—toward work and working that capture much of the historical and contemporary discussion relevant to the meaning of working. The *entitlement* norm represents the underlying rights of individuals and the work-related responsibilities of society and organizations toward all individuals. This norm includes the notions that *all members* of society are entitled to have work if they desire it; are entitled to interesting and meaningful work; are entitled to training when it is needed; and have the right to participate in work method decisions. All of these notions of entitlements or rights are derived from standards of reasoning about property rights and the psychological contract, as applied to the work setting.

The *obligation* norm represents the underlying duties of all individuals to organizations and to society with respect to working. This norm includes the notions that *everyone* has a duty to contribute to society by working; should save for the future from their work income; and should value his/her work whatever its nature. These notions of obligations or duties come from standards of reasoning about internalized personal responsibility and social or institutional commitment.

Each individual studied can show a high, medium, or low degree of agreement with each of the two norms. Additionally, an individual's responses to the two norms may be characterized as representing: a balanced orientation (similar levels of agreement to the entitlement and the obligation norms); an entitlement orientation (greater agreement with the entitlement norm than with the obligation norm); or an obligation orientation (greater agreement with the obligation norm than with the entitlement norm).

It is primarily through the assessment of these three major components (work centrality, work goal preferences, and societal norms about working) that we attempt to portray the meaning that working has for the individual.

Work Definitions: A Correlative View of Working

We also have sought to understand in some detail how individuals define the activity of working. These definitional patterns of how people view working suggest certain exchange processes occurring between an individual and his working environment. At present, we consider such information to be more a definitional attribution about working than a major variable component of the meaning of working. Thus, work definition data will be reported separately in a later section of the chapter. Theoretically, the two ways of viewing working must overlap to some extent; we have not sufficiently explored this issue as yet.

Analytical Considerations

In focusing on similarities and differences in the meaning of working between different national labor forces, we have made the significant choice of considering a wholistic view of the meaning of working to individuals as opposed to comparing individuals in countries variable by variable (e.g., first look at work centrality, then work goals, then societal norms). While both approaches have utility, we believe that more meaningful comparisons among individuals or aggregations of individuals (i.e., labor forces) can be made by treating individuals wholistically. Theoretically, the meaning of working is to some extent unique for every individual because no two individuals will share a totally similar background of characteristics and experiences which have shaped their personal meaning of working.

Thus our analytical procedures have been selected to identify *major* patterns of meanings of working *and* to compare their incidence across countries. Our expectation is that there will be no major work meaning pattern that is totally unique to any one country but that there may well be substantial differences across countries in major MOW pattern distributions. Distributions of types or patterns of meanings of working will thus provide the primary method for comparing national work meanings. The analytical procedures which we will utilize are consistent with the above rationale.

The following sections, then, will be concerned with an exploration of major work meaning patterns found in each country and across the studied countries. Work definition patterns will be treated in a similar way and we will then view the totality of our results toward understanding similarities and differences in the meaning of working among industrialized societies.

Meaning of Working Patterns in Different Nations

In the introductory chapters to this book the authors argued for the view that *the* work ethic is not, nor likely ever was, clearly observable among labor force samples. Instead, they reason for several work ethics. In this section we would like to expand on this idea and suggest that there are many work ethics, or, in our terms, *meaning of working* (MOW) patterns. There is nothing particularly novel in this view. It is entirely consistent with the recognition that MOW patterns probably have their origin in the dynamic and reciprocal influence of people and their environmental experiences on each other over one's entire life-span. The socialization that results from varied transactions between people and their successive work socializing environments is likely to result in multiple and distinct MOW patterns.

This life-span developmental view of the origin of work values, cognitions, and behaviors has received increased attention by work psychologists and sociologists as they have sought to recast and broaden the scope of basic conceptual frameworks and paradigms (see Mortimer and Simmons, 1978; Super, 1980). While we will return to this broader life-span view in the concluding section of this chapter, for the moment we would like to restrict our discussion to the idea that there are multiple MOW patterns that include significant proportions of national labor force samples in advanced industrial economies.

Adopting this view, especially in comparative research, raises several descriptive questions which form the outline for this section. What are the identifiable MOW patterns among national labor force samples in different countries? What are the personal attributes, work characteristics, and outcome variables associated with each MOW pattern? Finally, what are the national similarities and differences in MOW pattern membership and in the correlates of the profiles? After initial discussion of several procedural and methodological considerations, we will present findings that address these general questions in succession and then propose some general conclusions.

Procedures

The results of this study are based on the responses of national labor force samples in six countries. The countries and the sample sizes (in parentheses) are: Belgium (Flanders only) (442), West Germany (980), Israel (739), Japan (980), the Netherlands (941) and the United States (978). Sampling procedures used and the sample characteristics are extensively discussed in chapter 3 of the recently published book *The Meaning of Working* based on this comparative research (MOW International Research Team, 1987). The general sampling plan within each country was some form of stepwise random selection of respondents according to random household identification and random choice of labor force members within households.

We used five indices based on the three major components of the meaning of working discussed earlier in this chapter. The work centrality index (WC) is a scale of varying from 2–10 points based on responses to two questions. The absolute question asked respondents to rate work on a 7-point scale from one of the least to one of the most important things in their lives. The relative question used a forced choice format in which each respondent divided 100 points between five areas of his/her life to reflect relative importance. The five life areas were leisure, community, work, religion, and family.

The two work goal indices included here are the economic and the expressive indices. The economic index is based on the responses of individuals to the importance of good job security and good pay as personal work goals. The expressive index is based on the responses of individuals to the importance of interesting work, skill utilization, and autonomy as personal work goals. Responses to each set of goals were averaged to form the two indices.

The obligation and the entitlement indices were based on the extent of agreement of workers with normative statements regarding the duties and the rights of workers. These normative statements were discussed earlier in this chapter. The extent of agreement with each set of statements was averaged to obtain a score on each index.

To identify the MOW patterns based on responses to these five indices, cluster analysis and discriminant analysis were used. Because of program limitations, we identified the clusters based on the national labor force data from West Germany, Japan, and the United States. Then we used discriminant analysis to assign the respondents from the national labor force samples in Belgium, the Netherlands, and Israel to one of the previously identified clusters. Eight clusters were identified based on the optimal cluster solution. The percentage of correct classifications of the respondents from the three *new* countries (that resulted from one use of discriminant analysis) varied from 85 percent to 64 percent with a mean of 74 percent.

We have also sought to increase our understanding of each MOW pattern by examining some of its major demographic, work, and outcome correlates. We will examine age, gender, and education characteristics of each cluster in order to address some general questions about the workers. Are the workers who make up a particular pattern primarily young and in the early experiental portion of their work lives? Are the older workers nearing the end of their active experiences with working? Or are the workers more evenly distributed across the age groups, thus suggesting an age irrelevant pattern? Regarding gender, are there male or female differences in the patterns? Such differences may reflect particular childhood and adolescent socialization for work, differential preparation for work, and differential experiences since the respondents began working. Finally, differences in educational attainment might suggest that formal occupational preparation is related to particular MOW patterns.

We have chosen five features of the work of individuals to provide a wholistic and somewhat ecological understanding of current working experiences and conditions that are related to each MOW pattern. First, we examine the quality of work that characterizes each MOW pattern. What are the working experiences of the respondents in terms of variety, autonomy, responsibility, and skill utilization in their present work situation or job? Second, what proportion of respondents in the pattern are in nonsupervisory, supervisory, and managerial positions? Third, what is the occupational representation within each pattern? In addition to these content features of their work, we examine two contextual features: the income that workers in each pattern receive from their work, and the average length of their work week.

Finally, we include two outcomes that may be considered as correlates of the interaction between an individual's MOW pattern and his or her work experiences. First, we include occupational satisfaction, which we measure by asking the workers whether they would choose the same work if, based upon their experiences, they could begin working again. Additionally, we asked them if, based upon their experiences, they would recommend their type of work to their children. Second, we asked them the classic work commitment question alluded to early in this chapter. If they received a large enough sum of money to ensure a lifetime of financial comfort, would they stop working, continue working in the same job, or continue working but under different conditions?

Having described each MOW profile and its correlates, we attempt to summarize by placing the description in the context of an exchange process. Specifically, what is it that workers in each profile seem to exchange for the features of their work that they experience on a daily basis in their present work lives? We use salient components both of the MOW patterns and the work of respondents to describe the content of this exchange process.

Meaning of Working Patterns and their Demographic, Work, and Outcome Correlates

The eight MOW patterns are shown in table 3–1. This table shows the five index scores for each pattern, the percentage of the total sample included in the pattern, and the grand means for each index. In addition, both the percentage of pattern members endorsing each variable and the averages for the combined national samples (in parentheses) for each variable are indicated. As shown in the table, the MOW patterns vary considerably in terms of the percent of respondents, from a high of 19.4 percent (cluster 2) to a low of 5.6 percent (cluster 5). As we will see subsequently, there are large national differences in MOW pattern representation. We turn now to the task of describing and labeling the eight MOW patterns.

For purposes of description and comparison, we used the three indices that most characterize each pattern (underlined in table 3–1). We compared each index score for a pattern to the score on the same index in other patterns and to the index grand mean. The five index scores within a pattern were considered to gain a wholistic understanding for succinct labeling. In addition, we used information from table 3–2 on the demographic, work, and outcome variables for workers within each pattern.

The *apathetic workers* pattern has the second lowest work centrality scores among the eight profiles. Their economic values are considerably lower than their relative moderate expressive values. Finally, their obligation norms are the lowest among the eight patterns and considerably lower than their relatively high entitlement norms. These workers do not value working very highly and they have a relatively low normative orientation toward duty to employers or society. Additionally they have relatively low economic goals.

From table 3–2 we see that there is an above average percentage of young females with levels of education similar to the general averages with this pattern. Fifty percent (versus 32 percent) are less than thirty years of age. Forty-five (versus 36) percent are females. Thirty-eight (versus 36) percent have at least some postsecondary education.

The work quality experienced by these people is moderate. Respondents reported some variety (35 versus 32 percent), moderate decision autonomy (38 versus 35 percent), moderate responsibility (33 versus 29 percent), and utilization of some of their skills. Their average monthly net income is well below average and is the lowest among the eight groups. A high proportion

Table 3–1
MOW Patterns for Combined National Labor Force Samples from Six Countries

Patterns	Work Centrality Index	Economic Index	Expressive Index	Obligation Index	Entitlement Index	% Index
Pattern 1 N = 611 Apathetic workers	5.20	5.55	7.11	2.19	3.41	12.1
Pattern 2 N = 979 Alienated workers	5.15	6.89	5.92	3.10	3.28	19.4
Pattern 3 N = 664 Economic workers	7.32	9.27	4.76	2.72	3.22	13.1
Pattern 3 N = 422 High rights and duty economic workers	7.40	8.77	5.65	3.60	3.74	8.3
Pattern 5 N = 284 Techno-bureaucratic workers	7.19	6.07	6.52	2.70	2.39	5.6

Pattern 6 N = 613 Duty-oriented social contribution workers	<u>7.80</u>	4.07	<u>7.29</u>	<u>3.34</u>	3.29	12.1
Pattern 7 N = 550 Work-centered expressive workers	<u>8.27</u>	<u>3.98</u>	<u>8.66</u>	2.47	3.37	10.9
Pattern 8 N = 937 Work-centered and balanced values workers	<u>8.36</u>	<u>7.58</u>	<u>7.80</u>	2.93	3.19	18.5
Index averages*	7.0 (1.85)	6.6 (2.40)	6.7 (1.81)	2.90 (.57)	3.27 (.46)	N = 5060

*Standard deviation in parentheses.

Note: The three underlined indices for each pattern are those that deviate most from the index averages; thus they are generally the most salient measures in understanding the pattern.

Table 3–2
Summary of the Correlates of MOW Patterns

	Pattern 1 *Apathetic Workers*	*Pattern 2* *Alienated Workers*	*Pattern 3* *Economic Workers*	*Pattern 4* *High Rights and Duties Economic Workers*
Demographic				
Age	Younger over-represented	Similar to overall dis-tributions	Similar to overall dis-tributions	Older over-represented
Sex	Females overrepresented	Females overrepresented	Slight over-representation of males	Over-representation of males
Education	Similar to general averages	Similar to general averages	Lower educa-tional attain-ment than average	Lower educa-tional attain-ment than average
Work				
Quality	Moderate quality on all characteristics	Low on variety, autonomy, and responsibility	Relatively low variety, autonomy, and responsibility	Relatively low on all four characteristics
Occupation	Clerical jobs relatively high	Clerical, service, and construction jobs rela-tively high	Production, clerical, and service jobs relatively high	Construction and service jobs relatively high
Organization role	Nonsupervisory jobs over-represented	Nonsupervisory jobs over-represented	Nonsupervisory jobs over-represented	Nonsupervisory jobs over-represented
Length of of work week	Lowest among groups	Two hours per week less than average	Similar to average	Similar to average
Net Monthly pay	Lowest among groups	Slightly below average	Second lowest	Third highest
Outcome				
Occupational satisfaction	Low, nearly half would choose other work	Lowest among eight patterns	Low, above average would choose other work	Slightly above average
Work commitment	Below average, third highest percentage would quit working	Low, second highest percentage would quit working	Very low, highest percentage would quit working	Average percentage would quit working

Pattern 5	Pattern 6	Pattern 7	Pattern 8
Techno-Bureaucratic Workers	*Duty-Oriented Social Contribution Workers*	*Work-Centered Expressive Workers*	*Work-centered and Balanced Workers*
Middle aged overrepresented	Older workers overrepresented	Younger to middle aged overrepresented	Middle aged overrepresented
Similar to overall distributions	Slight over-representation of females	Slight over-representation of females	Sales over-represented
Higest percentage of college graduates	Similar to overall distributions	High over-representation of post-secondary education	Slightly above average percentage of college graduates
High quality on all four characteristics	High quality on all four characteristics	High quality on variety and autonomy	Moderate quality especially on variety and autonomy
Managers, professionals, and sales jobs relatively high	Proprietors, managers, and sales jobs relatively high	Highest percentage of managers and professionals	Most even distribution across jobs
High percentage of supervisors and managers	High percentage of managers supervisors	High percentage of managers relative to averages	High percentage of managers relative to averages
Slightly above average	Slightly above average	Somewhat above average	Longest work week among patterns
Similar to average, but highly variable across countries	Similar to average	Second highest	Highest among eight groups
High, nearly two-thirds would choose same work	High, high percent choose job and recommend to children	Highest among groups	High, high percentage would choose same job
Slightly above average percentage would quit working	High, lowest percentage would quit working	High, low percentage would quit, but high percentage would choose other work	High, low percentage would quit working

Table 3–2 continued.

	Pattern 1	Pattern 2	Pattern 3	Pattern 4
				High Rights and Duties
	Apathetic Workers	*Alienated Workers*	*Economic Workers*	*Economic Workers*
Work values	Family, leisure, and interpersonal contacts valued highly	Highest family and religious values	Highest economic values, lowest expressive values	Second highest economic values; norms high and balanced

(65 versus 59 percent) are in nonsupervisory positions. They are an overrepresented group in terms of clerical jobs (28 versus 22 percent).

These workers are not highly work motivated. They tend to place a high value on family, leisure, and interpersonal contacts relative to the value they place on work. They have the third highest percentage of workers among the eight patterns who would quit working if they were financially able (20 versus 15 percent). They also are relatively dissatisfied with their occupations. Nearly half (versus 40 percent) would continue working only if they could do so in another occupation. Forty-six (versus 40) percent indicate that they would choose another occupation if they could. The MOW pattern and work characteristics suggest that these people are *apathetic* about work as a significant life activity and therefore this is the label used to describe them. They exchange a below average amount of effort (thirty-nine hours per week versus forty-three)—the lowest among the eight groups—for social interaction and a low wage.

The three salient characteristics for the *alienated workers* are their low work centrality, low expressive values, and relatively high obligation norms. The work centrality score is the lowest, and expressive values are the third lowest of the eight MOW patterns. These workers agree slightly more with statements concerned with their rights than statements concerned with their duties. However, the obligation score is moderately above the grand mean and these workers have the third highest obligation score among the eight patterns.

This pattern includes slightly higher than average proportions of young female workers. Approximately 34 percent of the workers (versus 31.7 percent of the total sample) are less than thirty years of age. About 41 percent (versus 26 percent for the entire sample) are women. The levels of educational attainment of the workers within this pattern closely match that of the total sample. Fifty-five percent of the respondents are secondary school graduates.

These workers tend to be in nonsupervisory and low quality clerical, ser-

Pattern 5	Pattern 6	Pattern 7	Pattern 8
Techno-Bureaucratic Workers	*Duty-Oriented Social Contribution Workers*	*Work-Centered Expressive Workers*	*Work-centered and Balanced Workers*
Low economic and expressive values and work norms; value status and prestige; identify with products and services	High work centrality; low economic values	Lowest economic values; highest expressive values; identify with tasks, products, and services	Highest work centrality; high balanced work goals

vice, and construction jobs. Their jobs tend to be more repetitious, offer low decision autonomy, entail very limited responsibility, and offer a moderate degree of skill utilization when compared to the grand means. These workers are paid slightly below average wages. On average, they work about two hours per week less than the grand mean—suggesting modest levels of work involvement. Workers within this pattern have the highest values toward family and religion of any cluster, and also tend to have high values toward leisure. They have the lowest occupation satisfaction level of any pattern. Forty-eight percent (versus 40 percent on average) would choose a different occupation if they could.

In summary, what characterizes these workers is that they exchange a modest amount of their time for a near average wage. Their MOW pattern of low work centrality and expressive values, and above average norm of obligation, suggests that these people are *alienated* from their low quality work and instead value other facets of their lives.

Economic workers have the highest economic work goals and the lowest expressive work goals among the eight patterns. Additionally, their entitlement norms are approximately one standard deviation higher than their obligation norms. However, the entitlement and obligation scores are both relatively low in this MOW pattern, so the normative imbalance is between two relatively weak norms. Since the dominant features of this MOW pattern are the relative levels of and the imbalance between the work goals, we call these people *economic* workers.

These workers are well-distributed by age; each age group is distributed much like the percentages for the entire sample. There is a slightly higher than average male representation in this MOW pattern (67 versus 64 percent). They tend to have a lower level of educational attainment. Sixteen (versus 11) percent have a primary school education and 59 (versus 53) percent have a secondary school education.

The work quality of these people is relatively low. Their jobs are repetitious (31 versus 24 percent), with low autonomy (22 versus 10 percent), and below average responsibility (22 versus 19 percent). The proportion of nonsupervisors and the average length of the work week of these people are similar to the overall averages. There is a higher than average representation of production, clerical, and construction workers in this MOW pattern.

These workers have a relatively low level of occupational satisfaction: 46 (versus 40) percent would choose a different occupation. A relatively high percentage (23 versus 15 percent) would quit working if they were financially able to do so. In summary, these workers exchange a near average level of effort (42 hours per week versus 43 hours) which is directed by others for a below average wage.

High rights and duty economic workers have the second highest economic work goals among the eight groups. Additionally, both their obligation norms *and* their entitlement norms are the highest among the eight profiles. These two norms are also balanced or approximately equal. These dominant features of high economic work goals, and high and balanced work norms, especially characterize this MOW pattern in comparison to the other patterns. For these reasons we have labeled these people as *high rights and duty economic workers*.

There is a higher than average representation of older, male workers who have lower levels of educational attainment in this pattern. Twenty-seven (versus 19) percent are over fifty years old. Seventy-one (versus 64) percent are males. Twenty (versus 11) percent have a primary school education, while 60 (versus 53) percent have a secondary school education. These workers' jobs are of relatively low quality. They experience considerable repetitiveness (36 versus 24 percent) and low to moderate autonomy, responsibility, and skill utilization in their work. Construction (25 versus 15 percent) and service (12 versus 9 percent) jobs are overrepresented. A relatively high percentage are in nonsupervisory positions. They receive the third highest average net income among the eight groups. The length of their work week is similar to the overall average.

These workers indicate near average occupational satisfaction. They have the second highest economic values among the eight groups. The percentage who would stop working if they were able to do so is similar to the general average. In summary, these workers exchange a high and balanced normative orientation for an above average income and a feeling of belonging.

Techno-bureaucratic workers in the fifth pattern have the fifth lowest economic goals scores. Two other salient features center around their norms. Their entitlement norms are the lowest among the eight patterns. Their obligation norms are the third lowest among the patterns. Thus, workers within this pattern have weak norms regarding both rights and duties, although duties are endorsed somewhat more than rights. These workers have a particularly complex work values pattern. In addition to the three major features mentioned, they have a moderate level of work centrality and their expressive values, though higher than their economic values, are relatively moderate.

These workers tend to be primarily middle-aged with a similar gender composition to the general average. They are the most highly educated of the eight groups. Fifty-two (versus 49) percent are between thirty-one and fifty years old. Sixty-two (versus 64) percent are males. Thirty-one (versus 17) percent have college degrees.

These people work in high quality jobs characterized by high variety (45 versus 34 percent), wide decision autonomy (34 versus 26 percent), high responsibility (31 versus 24 percent), and extensive skill utilization (48 versus 32 percent). There is an overrepresentation of managers and supervisors (40 versus 33 percent), professionals (18 versus 12 percent), and sales workers (6 versus 5 percent) in this MOW profile. Their monthly net income is similar to the average in the eight groups but is highly variable. Their work week is just above the average (44 versus 43 hours). They attach a relatively high importance to status and prestige. They tend to identify most strongly in their work with the products or services they produce.

They have a moderately high level of occupational satisfaction and work commitment. Sixty-three (versus 60) percent would choose the same occupation again and 49 (versus 44) percent would continue to work in the same job even if they were financially able to quit working. Seventeen (versus 15) percent indicate that they would quit working if they were financially able.

In summary, workers in this MOW profile seem to exchange skill, knowledge, and responsibility for a mixture of economic, expressive, and status-prestige rewards. Features of their MOW pattern, their high educational attainment, and their high job quality suggests that these people are best labeled *techno-bureaucratic* workers.

Duty-oriented social contribution workers have the third highest work centrality average score among the eight groups. Other major features of this profile are the large imbalance between the expressive and economic goals, and the relatively high obligation norms score. The economic work goals score is the next to lowest among the eight patterns and is about two standard deviations below that for their expressive goals. The obligation score is the second highest among the eight MOW patterns. Thus noneconomic goals and high duty norms characterize this profile. For these reasons we call these respondents *duty-oriented social contribution* workers.

There is an overrepresentation of older workers and an underrepresentation of younger workers, with a slightly above-average education in this group. Twenty-five percent (versus 19 percent) are over fifty years of age, while 27 (versus 32) percent are thirty years old or younger. Thirty-nine percent (versus 36 percent) have some postsecondary schooling leading to a university degree.

These workers are employed in high quality jobs characterized by wide variety (41 versus 34 percent), high autonomy (32 versus 26 percent), above average responsibility (26 versus 24 percent), and high skill utilization (23 versus 12 percent). There is a slightly above average percentage of proprietors, managers, administrators, and sales occupations represented in this pattern, and a lower than average representation of production and construction occupations. The monthly net income of these workers is similar to the overall average, but they have relatively low values for money, income, or wages.

These workers strongly define the concept *work* as service to society. The occupational satisfaction of these workers is very high. Sixty-seven (versus 60) percent would choose the same occupation and two-thirds of them would recommend their occupation to their children. Only 7 percent indicate that they would stop working if financially able to do so, while 59 percent would continue to work in the same job. This last percentage is the highest among the eight MOW patterns. In summary, the workers within this MOW pattern seem to exchange skill, knowledge, and responsibility for socially generated satisfaction and average income.

Work-centered expressive workers have the second highest average work centrality score among the eight MOW patterns. Another notable feature of this pattern is the large imbalance among the work goals. There is about a two standard deviation difference between expressive work goals and economic work goals. Expressive work goals, and work being central to one's life, particularly characterize this profile. For these reasons we have called these respondents *work-centered expressive* workers.

These workers tend to be younger to middle-aged, with a slight overrepresentation of females. In addition, these workers have the highest level of educational attainment of any of the eight groups. Thirty-six (versus 32) percent are under thirty years of age, while 52 (versus 49) percent are between thirty to fifty years. Thirty-nine (versus 36) percent of these workers are female. Twenty-seven (versus 19) percent are college graduates.

These workers experience relatively high quality work in their present jobs. They perceive their work as providing wide variety (46 versus 34 percent) and high autonomy (33 versus 26 percent), but more moderate levels of responsibility and skill utilization. This pattern has the highest percentage of managers (22 versus 15 percent) and professionals (34 versus 27 percent) and the lowest representation of production, service, and clerical positions among the eight groups. These workers have the second highest monthly net income among the eight patterns, but value money and income the least. (More than the average, they tend to identify in their work with the tasks they do and the products or services they produce.)

These workers have the highest occupational satisfaction among the eight groups. Seventy-four (versus 60) percent would choose their occupation again, while 69 (versus 62) percent would recommend their occupation to their children. These workers have a high commitment to their type of work, but not necessarily to any kind of work. Only 4 percent (versus 15 percent) would quit working if they were financially able, while 41 percent would choose a different job. In summary, workers with this MOW profile appear to exchange value-adding mental effort for intrinsic satisfaction and above average income.

Work-centered and balanced values workers have high work centrality, and relatively high and balanced economic and expressive work goals. This MOW pattern has the highest average work centrality score among the eight groups. The economic and expressive work goals are the third and second highest respectively, and differ from each other only slightly. Based on these findings we have labeled this a *work-centered and balanced values* MOW pattern.

Workers within this pattern tend to be middle-aged males among whom there is a slightly above average percentage of college graduates. Approximately 54 percent are between thirty to fifty years old. Nearly 75 percent (versus 64 percent for the grand mean) are males—the highest percentage of any of the eight patterns.

These workers perceive their jobs as having slightly above average work quality. The jobs offer moderate to wide variety and decision autonomy. The levels of job responsibility and skill utilization of these workers are similar to the general averages. This pattern is the most evenly distributed of the eight across the occupational categories. There is only a slightly larger percentage of proprietors (11 versus 7 percent) and managers (17 versus 13 percent) than in the entire sample. Even given this wide distribution across occupational categories, the monthly net income of these workers is the highest among the eight groups.

Several findings indicate the high level of the work involvement of these workers. They have the longest average work week of any profile (47 versus 43 hours). Workers within this pattern have the highest level of work centrality among the eight groups. Consistent with this finding and their high behavioral involvement, we observe that they have a high level of commitment to their present work. Only 8 percent (versus 15 percent) would stop working if they were financially able to do so. Additionally, 65 percent (versus 60 percent) would continue working in the same occupation. In summary, the MOW pattern and work characteristics of this group suggest that these workers exchange mental and/or physical effort for intrinsic satisfaction and high income.

This description of MOW patterns points out the wide diversity in work value orientations of national labor force samples in six advanced industrial countries. By indicating this diversity, we have endeavored to broaden the scope of descriptive understanding of the cognitive and affective frameworks used by workers in responding to or actively seeking to influence their work environments. The eight clearly identifiable and contrasting MOW patterns provide examples of the richness of work value orientations. They suggest that overemphasis on any single work ethic is likely to inhibit discussion, inquiry, and practical understanding of working as a major life activity.

National Differences in MOW Pattern Representation

A related question we would like to address concerns the national correlates of MOW patterns. Specifically, what are the national similarities and differences in the MOW patterns between the six countries? The answers to this question are, of course, not independent of the national labor force policies in these six countries—whether these policies reflect conscious and more centralized decisions or are more implicit in the plethora of actions and goals of individual decision units. These policies will be reflected in individual, work, and outcome characteristics we have just discussed.

As one would expect, there are differences in some characteristics that likely reflect national differences in national labor market structures and processes. For example, the male composition of the samples in these countries ranges from a high of 73 percent in the Netherlands to a low of 53 percent in the United States. The educational level of the labor supply in these samples also differs considerably. Thirty and 28 percent of the samples in the United States and Japan are college graduates, while 5 and 10 percent of the Netherlands and West Germany samples have this level of educational attainment.

Similar differences can be observed on the more national labor market demand characteristics. There are differences in occupational mix that indicate some differences in structural characteristics of these national markets. Perceived qualitative features of the jobs in which people in these countries work differ considerably. For example, 71 percent of the Japanese workers and 70 percent of the West German workers indicate that they have at least a moderate level of variety in their jobs. In contrast, about 81 percent of the U.S. workers respond this way. Similarly, 83 percent of the Dutch workers indicate that their jobs require that they utilize a considerable amount of their skills. About 73 percent similarly respond in the United States. Sixty-five percent of the Japanese workers, 56 percent in the United States, and 47 percent in Israel, are in nonsupervisory positions.

From a national labor market perspective, hours of work can be thought of as an outcome variable. Occupational satisfaction and work commitment are also outcome variables. The national differences in average work week range from a high of forty-nine hours in Japan to a low of slightly under forty hours in West Germany. The U.S. work-force sample averaged nearly forty-three hours per week. Occupational satisfaction, as indicated by the percentage of workers who would choose the same occupation again, ranged from nearly 65 percent in Japan to 54 percent in the United States. Finally, the percentage of workers who would stop working if they were financially able ranges from nearly 29 percent in West Germany to under 6 percent in Japan. Twelve percent of all U.S. workers would stop working.

This background of differential characteristics, which indicates structural differences in the labor forces, labor market processes, and policy decisions, must be kept in mind as we describe national similarities and differences in MOW patterns. These background differences may represent partial explanations for the observed MOW differences. In describing the national differences, we will refer to figure 3–1, which groups the patterns according to whether they represent a positive, neutral, or negative orientation to working.

Figure 3–1 clearly shows that the positive patterns—duty-oriented social contribution, work-centered expressive, and work-centered and balanced goals—are especially prominent among Japanese workers. Among the remaining countries, with the exception of West Germany, there are only small differences in the percentage of workers with positive work value orientations. The neutral patterns—economic, high rights and duty economic, and techno-bureaucratic, tend to be especially prominent among West German workers and to some extent among U.S. workers. The remaining countries,

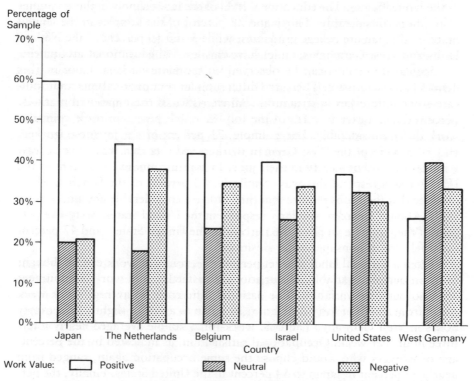

Figure 3–1. Evaluated MOW Patterns in Labor Force Samples

with the exception of the Netherlands, show only small differences. The Netherlands sample includes a relatively large percentage of workers having negative work value orientations. There are only small differences between the remaining countries on these negative orientations, with the exception of the relatively low percentage among Japanese workers.

This figure, of course, masks some notable differences in the distribution of the eight patterns among the national labor force samples within each of the six countries. The Israeli workers are overrepresented (21.1 percent of the national sample) among those in the duty-oriented social contribution group, while West German workers (6.3 percent) are notably underrepresented. Approximately 19 percent of Dutch workers are among those in the work-centered expressive group, while about 6 percent or less of the West German, Israeli, and U.S. workers were found in this group. About one-third of the Japanese sample are included among workers within the work-centered and balanced goals pattern, while only about 13–15 percent of the Israeli, Dutch, and West German workers are in this group. Approximately 21 percent of the West German workers have an economic value orientation, while about 9–10 percent of the Dutch, Israeli, and Japanese workers are in this group. About 12 percent of Israeli workers have a rights and duty economic pattern, while only about 5 percent of the Japanese, Dutch, and U.S. samples are in this group. The techno-bureaucratic workers are largely a U.S. pattern and include 13 percent of this sample. In the remaining countries this pattern includes less than 5 percent of each sample. Apathetic workers comprise from 18–21 percent of the Belgian and Dutch samples, but only 7–9 percent of the Israeli, U.S., and Japanese samples. Alienated workers comprise from 23–27 percent of the Israeli and U.S. samples, but only 12 percent of the Japanese samples. These specific country differences are important to recognize since the work and personal correlates of these national contrasts, and the consequences of pattern differences, have separate human resource policy implications.

How Working Is Defined in Different Nations[2]

As indicated in the introductory conceptual section of this chapter, the criteria and rationales used by individuals to decide when an activity is considered *working* seem more a definitional attribution about working than a major MOW variable. Such definitional information is both important and useful, however, and we present it in this section. We view work definitions as supportive of the meaning of working rather than as an intrinsic part of it.

Work Definition Measurement

A work definition measurement procedure was developed by reviewing the general literature about work definitions and work meanings in search of concepts and ideas which should be represented. Three major classes of concepts emerged from review of this voluminous and variable literature: 1) broad rationales or reasons for doing or being engaged in working activities; 2) personal outcomes or states of the individual which result directly from performing or engaging in working activities; and 3) constraints or controls which are relevant to the context or performance of working activities.

Within the category of broad rationales or reasons for working, many authors have emphasized the economic rationale for working. Firth (1948) noted that "income producing activity" covers a general definitional use of the term work. Friedman and Havighurst (1954) observed that one function of work was maintenance of a minimum sustenance level of existence. Dubin (1958) suggested that by *work* we mean continuous employment in the production of goods and services for remuneration. Anderson (1961) saw work as an "activity of some purpose" or in more direct terms as time given to a job for which one is paid. Braude (1975) noted that work may be viewed as that which a person does in order to survive; work is simply the way in which a person earns a living. Miller (1980) emphasized the various ways in which human beings attain their livelihoods in defining work. Other major rationales for working which are noneconomic in nature also have been suggested. Friedman and Havighurst (1954) and Donald and Havighurst (1959) observed that one function of work is to serve or benefit society. The authors of *Work in America* (Special Task Force, 1973) viewed work as an activity that produces something of value for other people. Salz (1955) saw work as activity one does in the execution of a task or project.

Personal outcomes or states which result directly from being engaged in the working activity include a variety of notions. Weiss and Kahn (1960), in one of the few attempts to define work empirically, found that one-fifth of the men interviewed in their samples defined work as an activity which requires physical or mental exertion. Warr (1981) also saw employment as providing outlets for the utilization of physical and mental energy. Morse and Weiss (1955) identified a sense of belonging as a personal outcome resulting from working; their interviewees noted that working gave them a feeling of being tied into a larger society. Work also has been seen as a source of identity and peer group relations (Friedmann and Havighurst, 1954; Steers and Porter, 1975). Shimmin (1966) noted that one distinguishing feature of work is that it is not enjoyable. Support for this idea was also advanced by Weiss and Kahn (1960) in defining work as activity one performs but doesn't enjoy. Firth (1948), however, warned against representing work simply as something which people do not like doing.

Finally, other authors have identified several notions which are constraints or controls relevant to the context or performance of work activities. Miller (1980) stated that the context of meaning about work that has most occupied sociologists of work in this century is that of the workplace. Anderson (1961) identified "time given to a job" as important. Thus, both where work takes place and when it takes place are possible defining elements.

Hearnshaw (1954), Weiss and Kahn (1960), and Friedman (1961) identified elements of obligation, control, and constraint when defining work. Accountability, compulsion, and being directed by others were suggested as potential defining elements of working.

It is easy to see why Firth (1948) concluded that any definition of working must to some extent be arbitrary. The MOW project formulation of work definition measurement is notable in that it attempted to include major conceptual elements identified in the literature, it relied on the views of those working, and it was done in a standardized manner based on pilot studies in all countries involved. The work definition item finally utilized in the MOW project which provides the basic data for the present section is as follows (MOW International Reserch Team, 1981 and 1987):

Not everyone means the same thing when they talk about working. When do you consider an activity as working? Choose four statements from the list below which best define when an activity is *working*.

a. You do it in a working place.
b. Someone tells you what to do.
c. It is physically strenuous.
d. It belongs to your task.
e. You do it to contribute to society.
f. By doing it, you get the feeling of belonging.
g. It is mentally strenuous.
h. You do it at a certain time (for instance, from eight until five).
i. It adds value to something.
j. It is not pleasant.
k. You get money for doing it.
l. You have to account for it.
m. You have to do it.
n. Others profit by it.

The above item resulted from pilot studies on various versions of the item involving some twenty-six defining statements. Respondents were asked to choose four statements because of the following pilot-study results. When respondents were asked to choose all of the statements that indicated when they considered an activity as working, 61 percent utilized either three or four statements. The four-statement choice occurred about three times as frequently as the three-statement choice. The other numbers of statements chosen ranged from two to ten but none was utilized by more than 6 percent of the pilot-study group. The benefits from utilization of a standardized four-statement defining task for respondents seemed to us to be greater than the relatively small amount of information lost by the standardization. It should also be noted that the definition of working item occurred rather late in the

MOW questionnaire (about two-thirds of the way through), and that the preceding context implied but never directly stated that employment served as the general referent for working.

National Responses to the Work Definition Item[3]

Table 3–3 shows what percentage of individuals in each country chose each of the fourteen statements to indicate when an activity is considered as working. The data are presented for each of the three classes of concepts identified from the literature. The percentage frequencies in the table are ranked from highest to lowest within each country to provide a second way of viewing country similarities and differences in the use of each defining statement.

While table 3–3 reveals both similarities and differences between countries in the use of the fourteen statements by their labor forces in defining working, it is strikingly clear that statements from the class of broad rationales or reasons for being engaged in an activity are the most frequently cited defining characteristics of working. The four most frequently chosen statements in each country are found among these broad rationales in twenty out of a possible twenty-four instances (four statements × six countries). Only in West Germany is the overall definitional power of broad rationales appreciably lower than in the other countries.

While it is clear, then, that the broad purposes of work are generally dominant in the ways people define working, the specific nature of these purposes differs considerably across the countries. As one might suspect from the literature, the economic rationale (getting money for doing an activity) is the most frequently cited defining characteristic of working in five of the six countries (Belgium being the exception). Belgium and Japan utilize the obligatory or expected rationale (it belongs to your task) more than do other countries and Germany utilizes it least. West Germany and Israel least utilize the value added rationale (it adds value to something), while the Netherlands and Japan are the highest utilizers. The Netherlands most uses the societal contribution rationale (you do it to contribute to society), while West Germany and Japan are lowest in this respect. Israel utilizes the social benefit rationale (others profit by it) considerably more than do the other countries (the United States falling between Israel and the other four countries).

Finally, it can be seen quite clearly from table 3–3 that working is being defined in all countries both in personal economic terms and societal value terms. There are both personal rationales and collective rationales for working. In this sense, those working do care about the nature and use made of the products/services which result from their working activity. They see their working activities as "adding value," as "contributing to society," and as "providing profit to others."

Several additional points should be observed from the data in table 3–3.

Table 3–3
Percentage Distributions and Intra-Country Frequency Ranks of Definitional Statements of Working in Six Countries

Country	Belgium (N = 450)		The Netherlands (N = 900)		West Germany (N = 900)		Israel (N = 900)		United States (N = 900)		Japan (N = 900)	
Statement	%	R	%	R	%	R	%	R	%	R	%	R
Rationales												
If you get money for doing it	58	(2)	61	(1)	66	(1)	68	(1)	53	(1)	70	(1)
If it belongs to your task	66	(1)	49	(4)	36	(4)	50	(2)	49	(3)	61	(2)
If it adds value to something	46	(3)	55	(3)	24	(8)	23	(8)	49	(2)	53	(3)
If you do it to contribute to society	33	(5)	55	(2)	15	(12)	40	(3)	36	(4)	23	(7)
If others profit by it	14	(11)	14	(10)	13	(13)	34	(4)	24	(9)	10	(11)
Mean Category Usage	43		47		31		43		42		43	
Constraints/controls												
If you have to account for it	25	(6)	37	(6)	39	(2)	12	(13)	24	(8)	50	(4)
If you do it in a working place	12	(13)	9	(11)	38	(3)	29	(5)	23	(10)	23	(6)
If you do it at a certain time (for instance from 8 to 5)	21	(7)	19	(8)	24	(7)	16	(11)	25	(7)	24	(5)

If you have to do it	20	(9)	7	(12)	18	(11)	16	(10)	15	(13)	22	(8)
If someone tells you what to do	13	(12)	6	(13)	19	(10)	14	(12)	17	(12)	7	(12)
Mean Category Usage	18		16		28		17		21		25	
Personal states												
If by doing it you get the feeling of belonging	44	(4)	41	(5)	35	(5)	24	(7)	31	(5)	7	(13)
If it is mentally strenuous	18	(10)	25	(7)	21	(9)	26	(6)	27	(6)	15	(9)
If it is physically strenuous	21	(8)	17	(9)	27	(6)	20	(9)	20	(11)	15	(10)
If it is not pleasant	6	(14)	2	(14)	4	(14)	1	(14)	8	(14)	5	(14)
Mean Category Usage	22		21		22		18		22		11	

Source: Adapted from England and Harpaz (1987).

Note: % = percentage (rounded to closest whole number) of the sample in a country that identified a given statement as one defining when an activity is considered as working.

R = frequency rank of a statement within a country

$$\text{Mean Category Usage} = \frac{\Sigma\,(\text{Item Percentage Frequencies})}{\text{Number of Items}}$$

Table 3–4
Frequency of Statement Occurrence and Binary Frequency Ratio for Each of Six Work Definition Patterns

Work Definition Patterns	A		B		C		D		E		F		TOTAL
Number of Individuals	527		1,368		871		1,075		525		584		4,950
Percent of All Individuals	10.6		27.6		17.6		21.7		10.6		11.8		
	%	BFR	%	BFR	%	BFR	%	BFR	%	BFR	%	BFR	Total % Occurrences
You do it in a working place	6.5	.28	17.3	.74	7.3	.32	**50.0**	**2.1**	13.1	.56	36.6	1.6	23.3
Someone tells you what to do	.8	.06	6.4	.51	7.6	.60	**28.6**	**2.3**	12.0	.96	16.1	1.3	12.6
It is physically strenuous	4.2	.21	12.2	.61	8.5	.42	19.6	.98	**80.6**	**4.0**	15.9	.80	20.0
It belongs to your task	72.7	1.4	54.2	1.1	34.8	.69	54.3	1.1	35.0	.70	51.7	1.0	50.4
You do it to contribute to society	29.0	.86	58.3	1.7	41.3	1.2	16.2	.48	16.4	.48	17.3	.51	33.8
By doing it, you get the feeling of belonging	13.3	.46	76.5	2.6	23.0	.79	9.1	.31	**3.4**	**.12**	**.7**	**.02**	29.0
It is mentally strenuous	40.2	1.8	18.1	.81	12.1	.54	7.6	.34	**82.9**	**3.7**	4.1	.18	22.3
You do it at a certain time (for instance from 8 to 5)	3.2	.15	15.1	.70	10.1	.47	7.7	.36	19.2	.89	**97.8**	**4.5**	21.5
It adds value to something	**89.2**	**2.2**	51.8	1.3	36.1	.88	26.0	.63	28.4	.69	19.5	.48	41.1
It is not pleasant	.4	.09	1.2	.28	5.2	1.2	**7.2**	**1.7**	**8.6**	**2.0**	3.9	.94	4.2
You get money for doing it	48.4	.76	59.1	.93	58.8	.93	71.6	1.1	55.2	.87	84.6	1.3	63.2
You have to account for it	**84.6**	**2.7**	19.4	.61	21.0	.66	39.3	1.2	17.1	.54	29.3	.92	31.9
You have to do it	4.6	.28	2.0	.13	5.6	.35	**48.6**	**3.0**	17.1	1.1	13.5	.84	16.0
Others profit by it	1.7	.092	5.9	.32	**82.1**	**4.4**	7.3	.40	3.8	.21	2.4	.13	18.5

Source: Adapted from England and Harpaz (1987).

Note: % = Percent of individuals in the pattern who utilize the statement as defining of work.
  BFR = Binary Frequency Ratio of a statement within a pattern.
  Bold face indicates the four statements in each work definition pattern, whose BFR departs most from 1.0.

The defining power of statements classified as constraints or controls related to the context or performance of working activities is utilized more by West Germany and Japan overall than is the case for the other countries. Again, one also can see differences between countries in terms of the specific content of the constraints or controls which are seen as defining working activities. Personal outcomes or states of the individual which result directly from performing or engaging in working activities are utilized as defining characteristics of working significantly less by the Japanese labor force than is the case in the other five countries. Again, the specific content of constraints/controls which defined working differ by country, particularly in the case of the statement "if by doing it you get the feeling of belonging."

Work Definition Pattern Development

Cluster analysis was conducted on the definitional statements chosen by all individuals in the total sample from the six countries. This analysis was undertaken for the purpose of empirically identifying major work definition patterns in the data set. Ward's (1963) method of hierarchical clustering was applied to the 4,950 individual respondents' choices on the fourteen statements of the work definition question. Utilizing this clustering procedure, respondents who selected similar work definition statements have been grouped together to form homogeneous definitional groups which differ as much as possible from other definitional groups. Considering the optimal ratio between loss of variance (error coefficient) and the number of clusters, identification of six work definition clusters was the optimal solution (Wishart, 1982).

To determine the relatively unique and homogeneous content of each cluster to be used for interpretation, we examined the ratio percentage of occurrence of a statement in a cluster versus the percentage of overall occurrence in the total sample. This ratio is called the *Binary Frequency Ratio (BFR)*. A general criterion for identifying statements which differentially define the content of each cluster is to select statements having the largest possible BFR deviation from 1.0. While there are several rationales for deciding how many statements to utilize in defining the content of each cluster, we used the four statements in each cluster which had the largest BFR deviation from 1.0. This solution worked well and it has a high level of similarity to the original defining task that was asked of individuals. Table 3–4 contains the basic data for the six work definition patterns which are used for pattern interpretation and for understanding the six major ways in which individuals define the activity of working.

When using the above procedures and the data contained in table 3–4 for interpretation and understanding, two important points should be kept in mind. First, the samples from each of the six countries represent the range of jobs, occupations, organizations, industries, sex distributions, educational levels, age ranges, backgrounds, and situational contexts as found in the employed labor force; in many respects, these represent a rather heterogenous group of 4,950 employed individuals. Second, the interpreted meaning of each work definition pattern can be seen as some joint function of the quality of coverage and clarity of expression of the fourteen definitional statements, the analytical procedures utilized which result in table 3–4, and the theoretical regularities existing in definitional notions in such a sample. We have attempted to handle the first two issues sufficiently well so as to obtain an adequate representation of real theoretical regularities in the ways working is defined by this large sample of individuals.

As seen from table 3–4, only two statements—"if you get money for doing it" and "if it belongs to your task"—do not indicate the differential content among the six patterns. It seems clear, however, that these are important elements of defining working because they are the two most frequently chosen statements within the total sample. However, they do not define working in a highly differentiating way across the six work definition patterns. Thus one can correctly say that both statements provide definitional content for all six patterns *or* that neither statement provides differential content among the six patterns. We have chosen the latter course for initial interpretation, but do recognize the importance of the general and high endorsement of the statement "if you get money for doing it." It is used in identifying the kind of exchange process in each pattern which occurs between a working person and his/her working environment.

Work Definition Pattern Interpretation

Utilizing the basic information in table 3–4, the six work definition patterns have been interpreted as follows. Individuals in pattern A define working as activity which adds value through its performance and for which one is accountable. The activity is not directed by others (it is generally self-directed) and there is almost no negative affect accompanying its performance. This definition of working suggests that individuals exchange value-adding accountability which is largely mental in nature for intrinsic satisfaction and monetary income. Pattern A includes 10.65 percent of the individuals from the six countries.

Pattern B individuals define working as activity through which one gains positive personal affect and identity. This activity is seen as making a contribution to society and there is very little compulsion or unpleasantness connected to its performance. This way of defining working suggests that individuals gain personal affect, identity, and income in exchange for making contributions to society through working. This concept of working includes several ideal elements of professionalism. Pattern B is the most inclusive pattern, containing 27.64 percent of the total sample from the six countries.

Pattern C individuals define working as activity which brings profit to others through its performance and which is not strictly confined to a working place. There is limited compulsion connected to the performance of the activity and it is only slightly characterized as being physically strenuous. This definition of working suggests that individuals exchange effort (largely mental in nature) which brings profit to others for monetary income and intrinsic satisfaction. Pattern C contains 17.6 percent of the individuals from the six countries.

Pattern D individuals define working as activity which one has to do, which is directed by others, and which is performed in one's working place. There is significant unpleasantness connected to the performance of the activity and it does not generally bring about positive affect. This definition of working suggests that individuals exchange effort which is directed and controlled by others for monetary income. Pattern D is the second most inclusive pattern and contains 21.72 percent of the individuals from the six countries.

Pattern E individuals define working as activity which is both physically and mentally strenuous. This activity is experienced as significantly unpleasant and does not generally bring about positive affect. All four defining statements for pattern E individuals are contained in the category of personal states or outcomes which result directly from performing or engaging in the activity. All four statements are centered on the self and it is in this sense that pattern E could be characterized as being self oriented. This definition of working suggests that individuals perform a burdensome activity (both physical and mental in character) in exchange for monetary income. Pattern E (along with pattern A) is a relatively low frequency pattern, containing 10.61 percent of the individuals from the six countries.

Pattern F individuals define working as activity which occurs during specified time periods and which does not bring about positive affect through its performance. The activity is not seen as being mentally strenuous and it is characterized as not profiting others through its performance. This definition of working suggests that individuals make a rather direct exchange of their time for monetary income. Pattern F contains 11.8 percent of the individuals from the six countries.

National Distributions of Work Definition Patterns

Table 3–5 presents the distributions of work definition patterns for each national labor force sample and the accompanying chi-square test. There is a large and statistically significant effect of national context on the work definition distributions as shown by the national frequency distributions among

Table 3–5
Percentage Frequency of Work Definition Patterns and Significance Test by Country

Work Definition Pattern	A	B	C	D	E	F
	Percentage frequency in total sample (N = 4,950)					
	10.6%	27.6%	17.6%	21.7%	10.6%	11.8%
Country						
Belgium	8.0	40.0	12.7	18.9	11.3	9.1
West Germany	7.2	26.0	13.2	28.3	11.4	13.8
Israel	3.7	21.8	33.1	23.0	9.2	9.2
Japan	20.7	10.6	12.7	29.1	10.2	16.8
The Netherlands	15.1	43.2	12.3	10.7	9.4	9.2
United States	7.9	30.4	19.1	18.9	12.3	11.3

χ^2 = 680.98 (25 df) P < .0001 *Sign.*
Source: Adapted from England and Harpaz (1987).

the six patterns and by the chi-square test. Patterns A, B, C, and D show the largest national differences with high country/low country frequency ratios ranging from slightly under 3-to-1 to more than 5-to-1. Clearly, there are large national differences in how people define working and these national differences are considerably greater and more general than those resulting from demographic status and organizational role category influences.[4]

General Observations

It seems useful to consider the empirical findings from this rather large-scale study of the defining characteristics of working in fairly general terms. We will do this by making several assertions from varying viewpoints—from the perspectives of the individual, the employing organization, and the national society at large. Recognizing that these general interpretations are both complex and value laden, we will offer our own tentative views and cite the supporting data. We trust that readers will carefully examine what we say and the relevant data in forming their own conclusions.

The two most frequently expressed rationales for working were the personal economic rationale (if you get money for doing it) and an obligatory or expected rationale (if it belongs to your task). Both of these were among the four most frequently selected statements in each country and in five of the six work definition patterns. In work definition pattern C the statement (if it belongs to your task) was the fifth most frequently selected statement (see tables 3–3 and 3–4). The economic and the obligatory expectation rationales are clearly dominant and general rationales for working.

Working is clearly *not* defined by most individuals as an activity that is experienced as unpleasant. Only 4.2 percent of the total sample selected the "unpleasantness" statement and it was the least frequently chosen statement in all six nations. When unpleasantness was found to be significantly present (patterns D and E), it was always in conjunction with controlling and constraining features of working or physically and mentally burdensome activities (see tables 3–3 and 3–4).

Analysis of the content of each of the six work definition patterns suggests to us that individuals in patterns A, B, and C generally experience working in positive terms while individuals in patterns D and E generally experience working in negative terms. The content of pattern F seems neutral or indeterminant in this respect. Thus we find that across the labor forces in the six countries nearly six of every ten individuals experience working in positive terms, slightly more than three of every ten individuals experience working in negative terms, and slightly over one in ten individuals seem neutral in this regard (as table 3–5).

Patterns A, B, and C also seem to differ from patterns D, E, and F in another important way. Individuals in patterns A, B, and C include both a personal rationale in defining work (if you get money for doing it) and a more other-oriented or collective rationale. In pattern A the collective rationale is (if it adds value to something), in pattern B it is (if you do it to contribute to society), and in pattern C it is (if others profit by it). Patterns D, E, and F utilize the personal rationale (if you get money for doing it) but none of the collective rationales in defining working (see table 3–4). Thus individuals in patterns A, B, and C seem to be both personally and collectively oriented to working while patterns D, E, and F individuals seem primarily personally oriented to working. The former orientation recognizes work and working as both a "private good" and a "public good" and in this respect is more balanced than is the case for the latter orientation. One can certainly speculate that the more balanced orientation might well have greater long-term societal utility because it is more in tune with the reality of work in advanced technological countries.

Applying the notions central to the last two points, it is evident that there are large national differences in terms of the proportion of individuals experiencing working in positive versus negative terms and in terms of utilizing both personal and collective rationales in defining working. The Netherlands clearly represents the highest level of both experiencing working in positive terms and in having balanced rationales. Belgium, Israel, and the United States represent middle levels, while West Germany and Japan represent the lowest level of experiencing working positively and in terms of having both personal and collective rationales for working (see table 3–5).

Finally, if one speculates about the ways of defining working which would seem to be most desirable as we move into the next century, we believe that having more pattern A individuals and less pattern D individuals would be movement in a positive direction. Pattern A individuals define working in terms of two rationales (adding value and obtaining income), they see working as accepting constraints (of having to account for what they do), and they almost totally reject that the experience of working is unpleasant. Such a conception of working seems to us to be near optimal. It balances the interests of individuals, organizations, and societies in a way that seems consistent with labor force developments, organizational requirements of the future, and long-term societal benefit.

Pattern D individuals, in contrast, use only a personal rationale (obtaining income) in defining working, they see working largely in terms of constraints or controls (being told what to do, having to do it, and doing it in a working place), and they have a relatively high incidence of experiencing working as unpleasant. Such a definition of working seems largely negative from the viewpoint of the individual, it hardly seems to fit the needs of most organizations of the future, and it seems of limited social value.

We clearly recognize that there may be real limits and feasibility difficulties in implementing this directional suggestion and that there would undoubtedly be different national constraints in so doing. Even allowing for such problems, we still believe the basic direction implied in our suggestion is essentially correct. It also has the distinct merit of dealing with real empirical realities of how people define working rather than with ideal or imagined patterns.

Concluding Remarks

We have sought to provide a wholistic understanding of the meaning of working in people's lives by presenting findings from responses of national labor force samples in six advanced industrial countries. In doing so we have presented two major ways of trying to understand what working means to these people. These two approaches utilize work values in the first instance and work definitions in the second. Our results clearly indicate that working is a complex phenomenon in each country and that a plurality of views about working seems to be the rule. We conclude that to unduly concentrate on one view, or to wittingly or unwittingly use it as a standard by which to evaluate other work meanings, is clearly unwarranted. Thus we view the empirical types of work meaning patterns to be more useful for many purposes rather than "ideal type" formulations which reflect biased views or ignore the vast diversity in people's cognitive and affective orientations to this major life activity.

As outlined in previous sections, we have made some judgments about the MOW patterns and work definition patterns. Applying these judgments to each of the approximately five thousand individuals who comprise the national labor force samples of the six countries, we conclude that:

- approximately one-half of these people view work positively in terms of work values or in terms of how they define working;
- slightly more than one-sixth of these people view working in relatively neutral terms based on their work values and work definitions;
- slightly less than one-third of these people view working in negative terms as expressed by their work values and by their work definitions.

While this conclusion applies to the combined sample for all six countries, we realize that it neglects some real differences between countries. We would certainly not expect nor argue that these proportions of positive, neutral, and negative views of working would be reasonably accurate for other sets of national labor force samples. They do provide an overall view for these six countries, however.

One way in which we have sought to point out these national differences has been to suggest that both the correlates of the MOW patterns *and* the patterns are likely related to differences in each country's human resource policies and practices. As noted earlier, there are large national differences in educational attainment, job quality, and percentages of managerial, supervisory, and nonsupervisory jobs. These indicators suggest that the policies and practices may affect labor force structures in each country and the cognitive and affective orientations people develop about work. Thus, one implication of these findings is that implicit or explicit human resource policy decisions may influence many labor demand and labor supply factors including not only those mentioned, but also hours devoted to work, commitment to working, and occupational satisfaction. We view these national differences in patterns and correlates as particularly important for human resources decision makers.

There are numerous specific results that we can point to that have national policy implications. For example, we find the present results that indicate that young workers in low quality, low paying jobs are overrepresented in the apathetic MOW pattern to be consistent with previous youth labor market studies conducted by sociologists and labor economists (Greenberger and Steinberg, 1981; Osterman, 1980; Andrisani, 1973). Negative work experiences and negative work values at earlier time periods have been shown to relate to later similar experiences and values (Kohn and Schooler, 1983; Appelbaum and Koppel, 1978). Younger people in the apathetic worker group may continue to experience similar negative work conditions for some time, based on these earlier findings. We would note, however, that 23 percent of the work-centered and balanced workers are also under thirty years of age and they do experience better quality work. A more positive future set of work experiences would be predicted for these younger workers.

The older male workers with lower educational attainment who comprise a large proportion of the high rights and duty economic workers may represent a cohort whose historical and educational experiences still play a significant role in influencing their present work experiences and the meaning they assign to these experiences (Elder, 1974). More generally, national labor market practices, as indicated by the differences in educational attainment and the quality of the jobs created, may provide partial explanation for the observed national differences in MOW patterns. People in the various countries seem to experience quite different work socialization processes which may affect their work value patterns.

We also view the present findings as having important implications for organizations, particularly for the design of work and reward systems. We can point out some possible design implications for each of the eight value groups. The apathetic workers are a relatively young group who seem disengaged from working whether viewed from the perspective of their work values or occupational satisfaction. These people work in low quality, low paying jobs. The organization design issue would seem to be one of maintenance rather than change. Their interest in interpersonal relations might be met by personalistic styles of supervision and placement in work groups, which provide for a more positive accommodation in their early work experiences. These practices could aid the maintenance process.

The alienated workers represent the most inclusive of the eight patterns. We believe these workers represent alienation from their own rather poor work situations, rather than alienation from working in general. A relevant organizational design issue would be to improve the quality of work for these individuals. While some success could be expected from such improvement, it must be remembered that this group has high family and religious values. Any work changes that would entail greater involvement in terms of hours of work may be antithetical to interests in other facets of their lives.

Economic workers may well represent secondary labor force participation, given their lower educational attainment, low quality work, and low pay. Their very high economic values and very low expressive values would suggest an organization design issue centered around the adequacy of wages. Greater work involvement would seem to be largely a function of greater economic rewards. Organizations with both primary and secondary jobs will find these workers more attracted by internal movements that underscore wages or job security rather than by incentives like job quality.

The high rights and duties economic workers display a somewhat less severe imbalance between economic and expressive values than do the economic workers. They also have relatively strong duty and rights normative standards. The organization design issue seems to be one of establishing clear and consistent rules of the game for allocating career rewards. This, in turn, suggests that these people may be more effectively placed in work units that approximate closed systems in their work and typical human resource practices. Economic issues, opportunities for some progression, and equitable treatment would seem to offer the most promising features of designs for these workers.

The techno-bureaucratic workers seem largely a U.S. phenomenon and are probably best understood in this context. They are a well-educated group who experience good quality, primarily supervisory and managerial jobs. Their work values, however, seem contrary to these features of their work. Their most salient work values are all below average. The high value they place on status and prestige may represent a type of bureaucratic credentialism in organizations. If this is correct, these people may occupy jobs with ambiguous criteria for measuring performance and contribution to product or service goals. We would suggest that product or service designs such as product divisions, profit and cost centers, product or service management, or quality control responsibilities may be possible designs in which these people would function well. In these situations they could effectively exchange their skill, knowledge, and responsibility for a complex mixture of economic, expressive, and status-prestige rewards.

The duty-oriented social contributions workers are rather highly committed to work and report high quality present work situations, average income, and high occupational satisfaction. They see their work as making a contribution to society and this seems to be an important value for them. The organization design issue posed by this group concerns how to best maintain the potential for social contribution through job assignments and work unit assignments which incorporate this value. Real involvement and participation in important work issues and organizational support to keep them from becoming obsolete would also seem to provide beneficial practices.

The work-centered expressive group highly values their own work and are strongly attached to it in both behavioral and value terms. They have very high expressive values and very low economic values. They report having high quality jobs, receive relatively high pay, and have high occupational satisfaction. The clear organization design issue for these workers is how to continue fulfilling their high expressive values in working. They are a group for which effective placement and jobs that allow for "self-management" would seem to be particularly effective.

The work-centered and balanced work goal group includes a relatively high percentage of workers in the combined sample. This group seems the most attached to the working role among the eight we observed. They have the highest work centrality, work the most hours, and have the highest commitment to working among these eight groups. We suspect that a major organization design issue is the latitude they have in making choices and creating opportunities. While their strong personal attachment to working in both value and behavioral terms may be sustained in many organizational contexts, optimal utilization would seem to involve considerable personal and organizational career planning and development. This planning may involve in part some retirement planning or advisory-consulting opportunities for older members of the group.

While we have adopted an organization design emphasis, we do not view workers as being passive responders to their environments. People are also producers of their own environments and experiences (see Lerner and Busch-Rossnagel, 1981). Longitudinal research on work socialization has found that earlier work attitudes and work values do affect later career outcomes such as labor market attainment (Appelbaum and Koppel, 1978), career progress (Mortimer and Lorence, 1979), and experienced job characteristics (Kohn and Schooler, 1983). The job quality characteristics correlated with the particular MOW patterns can just as well be influenced by these work values as be influences on the value patterns. National or regional differences in educational attainment and job characteristics (quality, occupational mix) may also be influenced, in part, by work values of the members of that society or by a subculture (Goldthorpe et al., 1968).

Finally, we do not view the cross-sectionally-derived MOW patterns in the present study as immutable or people's membership in a pattern as fixed. The patterns may change as a result of particular work experiences or as a result of personal choices (Mortimer, Finch, and Kumka, 1982). Workers also may move to other jobs or attain more education which results in value changes. In doing so workers may move from one MOW pattern to another. Old work values and attitudes can also be reacquired, or become manifest rather than latent as a result of subsequent reversals in career experiences (Lieberman, 1956). The process is continuous, based on reciprocal influences, and also reversible. Work life-span approaches, especially the ecological approaches proposed by Super (1980), Lerner (1985), and Vondracek, Lerner, and Schulenberg (1986), are conceptually useful when viewing working from this extended perspective.

For workers, employers, and human-resource policymakers, there are some important implications in the present findings. The MOW patterns and their personal and work correlates reflect the choices and experiences of these various parties. The patterns are both an input into this process of work socialization and an outcome of the work life courses of these people as they work out their own decisions and/or experience the influence of the decisions made by those who are significant in their working lives.

Notes

1. The eight countries participating in the MOW project were Belgium, Britain, Federal Republic of Germany (FRG), Israel, Japan, Netherlands, United States, and Yugoslavia. The MOW project members (in addition to the present authors) included: Dr. J.H.T.H. Andriessen, Institute for Social Research, Tilburg, Netherlands; Vojko

Antoncic, director of the Institute of Sociology, Ljubljana, Yugoslavia; Dr. Pol Coetsier, professor of Socio-Psychology of Work and Organization, Ghent State University, Ghent, Belgium; Dr. Pieter J.D. Drenth, professor of Work and Organizational Psychology, Free University of Amsterdam, Amsterdam, The Netherlands; Dr. Itzhak Harpaz, lecturer of Human Resources, University of Haifa, Haifa, Israel; Dr. Frank A. Heller, Director, Centre for Decision Making Studies, Tavistock Institute of Human Relations, London, Great Britain; Lic. Marnix Holvoet, research fellow for Data Analysis, Ghent State University, Ghent, Belgium; Dr. Rob N. van der Kooij, work and organizational psychologist, Netherlands Railways Ltd., Utrecht, The Netherlands; Dr. Jyuji Misumi, professor of Social Psychology, Osaka University, Osaka, Japan; Dr. S. Antonio Ruiz Quintanilla, assistant professor of Work and Organizational Psychology, Technical University Berlin, Berlin, FRG; Dr. Rie Spoelders-Claes, associate professor of Socio-Psychology of Work and Organization, Ghent State University, Ghent, Belgium; and Dr. Bernhard Wilpert, professor of Work and Organizational Psychology, Technical University of Berlin, FRG.

2. Material in this section draws extensively from an article by England and Harpaz (in press) which developed this subject matter.

3. Data for table 3–3 were collected between 1981 and 1983 from national laborforce interviews of employed individuals taken by trained interviewers using a standardized questionnaire. Interviews were typically thirty to sixty minutes in duration and covered a wide range of questions relevant to the meaning work had for the individual respondent. To represent nations equally as much as possible in the present compilation, random samples of 900 individuals were drawn from each of the national samples in West Germany, Israel, Japan, the Netherlands, and the United States. The total sample from Belgium included 450 individuals, and so it was used in its entirety. Thus, the data presented here were obtained from 4,950 workers in six countries. (Data from Yugoslavia and Great Britain could not be used in this analysis.)

4. There was no statistically significant influence of age on how people define working. There was a statistically significant gender influence on work definition pattern distributions but the differences were small and difficult to interpret. There were statistically significant influences of educational level attainment and organizational role (nonsupervisory, supervisory, managerial) on how people define working but both influences were restricted largely to patterns A and F. Work definition pattern A frequency systematically increases with more education and higher locus of organizational role while work definition pattern F frequency systematically decreases with more education and higher locus of organizational role. For detailed results, see England and Harpaz.

References

Aiken, M., Ferman, L., and Sheppard, H.L. (1968). *Economic failure, alienation, and extremism*. Ann Arbor, MI: University of Michigan Press.

Anderson, N. (1961). *Work and leisure*. London: Routledge and Kegan Paul.

Andrisani, P. (1973). An empirical analysis of dual labor market. Ph.D. diss. Columbus, OH: Ohio State University.

Appelbaum, E., and Koppel, R. (1978). The impact of work attitudes formed prior to labor market entry on the process of early labor market attainment. In P. Andrisani (ed.), *Work attitudes and labor market experience*. New York: Praeger, pp. 175–212.

Braude, Lee. (1975). *Work and wonders: A sociological analysis*. New York: Praeger.

Cooper, C.L., and Payne, R. (1978). *Stress at work*. New York: Wiley.

———. (1980). *Current concerns in occupational stress*. New York: Wiley.

Donald, M.N., and Havighurst, R.J. (1959). The meaning of leisure. *Social Forces, 37*, pp. 357–60.

Dooley, D., and Catalano, R. (1980). Economic change as a cause of behavioral disorder. *Psychological Bulletin, 87*, pp. 450–68.

Dubin, R. (1958). *The world of work*. Englewood Cliffs, NJ: Prentice Hall.

Elder, G. (1974). *Children of the great depression*. Chicago: University of Chicago Press.

England, G.W., and Harpaz, I. How working is defined: National contexts and demographic and organizational role influences. *Journal of Organizational Behavior*. In press.

Firth, R. (1948). Anthropological background to work. *Occupational Psychology, 22*, pp. 94–102.

Friedmann, E.A., and Havighurst, R.J. (1954). *The meaning of work and retirement*. Chicago: University of Chicago Press.

Friedman, G. (1961). *The anatomy of work*. London: Heinemann.

Goldthorpe, J., Lockwood, D., Bechhofer, F., and Platt, J. (1968). *The affluent worker: Industrial attitudes and behavior*. Cambridge: Cambridge University Press.

Greenberger, E., and Steinberg, L. (1981). The workplace as a context for the socialization of youth. *Journal of Youth and Adolescence, 10*, pp. 185–210.

Hearnshaw, L.S. (1954). Attitudes to work. *Occupational Psychology, 28*, pp. 129–39.

Hepworth, S.J. (1980). Moderating factors of the psychological impact of unemployment. *Journal of Occupational Psychology, 53*, pp. 139–45.

Israeli, N. (1935). Distress in the outlook of Lancashire and Scottish unemployed. *Journal of Applied Psychology, 19*, pp. 67–69.

Jahoda, M. (September 1979). The psychological meanings of unemployment. *New Society*, pp. 492–95.

Kaplan, H.R., and Tausky, C. (1974). The meaning of work among the hard core unemployed. *Pacific Sociological Review, 17*, pp. 185–98.

Kohn, M., and Schooler, C. (1983). *Work and personality: An inquiry into the impact of social stratification*. Norwood, NJ: Ablex.

Lerner, R. (1985). Individual and context in developmental psychology: Conceptual and theoretical issues. In J. Nesselroade and A. von Eye (eds.), *Individual development and social change: Explanatory analysis*. New York: Academic Press, pp. 36–67.

Lerner, R., and Busch-Rossnagel, N. (1981). Individuals as producers of their development: Conceptual and empirical bases. In R. Lerner and N. Busch-Rossnagel (eds.), *Individuals as producers of their development: A life-span perspective*. New York: Academic Press, pp. 1–36.

Lieberman, S. (1956). The effects of changes in roles on the attitudes of role occupants. *Human Relations, 9,* pp. 461–86.

Miller, G. (1980). The interpretation of nonoccupational work in modern society: A preliminary discussion and typology. *Social Problems, 27,* pp. 381–91.

Morse, N.C., and Weiss, R.C. (1955). The function and meaning of work and the job. *American Sociological Review, 20,* pp. 191–98.

Mortimer, J., Finch, M., and Kumka, D. (1982). Persistence and change in development: A multidimensional self-concept. In P. Baltes and O. Brim (eds.), *Life-span development and behavior, vol. 4.* New York: Academic Press, pp. 263–313.

Mortimer, J., and Lorence, J. (1979). Work experience and occupational value socialization: A longitudinal study. *American Journal of Sociology, 84,* pp. 1361–85.

Mortimer, J. and Simmons, R. (1978). Adult Socialization. *Annual Review of Sociology, 4,* pp. 421–54.

MOW International Research Team. (1981). The meaning of working. In G. Dlugos and K. Weiermair (eds.), *Management under differing value systems: Political, social, and economical perspectives in a changing world.* Berlin and New York: Walter de Gruyter, pp. 565–630.

MOW International Research Team. (1987). *The meaning of working.* London and New York: Academic Press.

Osterman, P. (1980). *Getting started: The youth labor market.* Cambridge: MIT Press.

Parnes, H.S., and King, R. (1977) Middle-aged job losers. *Industrial Gerontology, 4.* pp. 77–95.

Salz, B.R. (1955). The human element in industrialization. *Economic Development and Cultural Change, 4,* (October; special supplement), pp. 1–96.

Shimmin, S. (1966). Concepts of work. *Occupational Psychology, 40,* pp. 195–201.

Special Task Force. (1973). *Work in America.* Cambridge: MIT Press.

Steers, R.M., and Porter, L.W. (1975). *Motivation and work behavior.* New York: McGraw-Hill.

Super, D. (1980). A life-span, life-space approach to career development. *Journal of Vocational Behavior, 16,* pp. 282–98.

Terkel, S. (1972). *Working.* New York: Pantheon.

Vecchio, R.P. (1980). The function and meaning of work and the job: Morse and Weiss (1955) revisited. *Academy of Management Journal, 23,* pp. 361–67.

Vondracek, F., Lerner, R., and Schulenberg, J. (1986). *Career development: A life-span development approach.* Hillsdale, N.J.: Lawrence Erlbaum.

Ward, J. (1963). Hierarchical grouping to optimize an objective function. *Journal of American Statistical Association, 58,* pp. 236–44.

Warr, P. (1981). Psychological aspects of employment and unemployment. *Psychological Medium, 11,* pp. 21–33.

———. (1982). A national study of nonfinancial employment commitment. *Journal of Occupational Psychology, 55,* pp. 297–312.

———. (1984). Work and unemployment. In P. Drenth, H. Thierry, P. Willems, and C. de Wolff (eds.), *Handbook of work and organization psychology,* pp. 413–43. London: Wiley.

Weiss, R.S., and Kahn, R.L. (1960). Definitions of work and occupations. *Social Problems, 8,* pp. 142–51.

Wilensky, H.L. (1961). Orderly careers and social participation: The impact of work history on social integration in the middle mass. *American Sociological Review, 26,* pp. 521–39.

Wishart, D. (1982). *CLUSTAN User Manual, 3d ed.,* (supp.). Edinburgh: Edinburgh University Program Library Unit.

4
Functions of Work Meanings in Organizations: Work Meanings and Work Motivation

Loriann Roberson

W ork meanings influence work motivation and performance. The strength of our belief in this statement is perhaps most dramatically portrayed in writings from the 1970s. During this time period, increases in strikes and absenteeism and declines in the rate of growth of national productivity alarmed many professionals. Analyses of this distressing state of affairs often pointed to the meaning of work as a major cause. Writers argued that recent changes in social values had brought concomitant changes in the meaning of work. Thus, employees stressed the importance of autonomy, interesting work, and financial rewards over the moral importance of hard work and pride in craftsmanship (Cherrington, 1980; Korman, Greenhaus, and Badin, 1977). Decreases in the rate of growth of productivity and rising unrest were viewed as the result of this decline in the traditional work ethic (Cherrington, 1980). *autonomy—independent*

For many psychologists and sociologists, the solution to this problem was *job enrichment,* a motivational technique providing higher levels of autonomy, variety, and responsibility to employees. This new method of designing work was not advocated as a way to change employee work meanings back to those held by previous generations, but was instead proposed as a way to adjust to changes. It was widely believed that the new work meanings of employees required new methods of motivating workers (Rose, 1985).

During this same time period, more ethnic minorities moved into a traditionally white male work force. This change in the nature of the work force caused great concern on the part of management, who worried over their ability to integrate these new workers into the organization (Korman et al., 1977). Management's concern was not only with the level of job-related skills and abilities that these new workers might have. The meaning of work to these subgroups also received considerable attention. Authors suggested that the work values of minorities differed from those of the majority in ways likely to influence their performance and attendance motivation. Again, proposed solutions to the problem reflected the concern with work meanings. Most of the training and orientation programs devised for minorities sought to change their values and beliefs about work to those of the dominant group (Friedlander and Greenberg, 1971).

While national concern about work meanings has died down, beliefs about the relationship of work meaning to motivation and performance remain strong (Cherrington, 1980). However, as noted by Korman et al. (1977), statements of the importance of work meaning have been most prominent in the popular media. But what does the psychological literature have to say about the influence of work meanings on work motivation? This is the question addressed in this chapter. This chapter examines the ways in which the meaning of work has been defined and treated in the work motivation literature, and examines the motivational functions of work meanings.

Meaning of Work Defined

This review focuses on treatments of the meaning of work in the American psychological and sociological literature of the twentieth century. Certain specific questions immediately arise in attempting to review this literature. The first is: What is meant by the meaning of work? What is the nature of this construct? Another question concerns not the conceptual but the operational definition of the construct. How have researchers defined and measured the meaning of work in their attempts to study it?

An answer to the first question can be found in the many writings on work meaning. Morse and Weiss (1955) defined work meaning as its perceived function in life. This refers to beliefs about the valued outcomes that are attained from working. A similar view is taken by Friedman and Havighurst (1954). To these authors, work meaning is only partly determined by what an individual sees that the job has given to his/her life—that is, the outcomes that are actually received. Work meaning also includes the work's expected contribution toward satisfying an individual's needs. Fox (1980) views the distinction of received and expected outcomes as one of personal and social meanings. Personal work meanings refer to the outcomes that the individual perceives have been experienced from working. Social meanings reflect expected outcomes, for the culture teaches individuals what the nature of work is and what consequences will be gained from work.

Another important facet of work meanings is that they involve beliefs about both positive and negative outcomes. Most writers have stressed the positive functions of work, including status, identity, income, and social opportunities. Yet work can also bring negative outcomes: powerlessness, subordination, or frustration of one's potential. While individuals might experience such negative outcomes directly, negative outcomes may also be emphasized in social work meanings. For example, the ancient Greeks viewed work as a punishment and sign of degradation (Fox, 1980; Mills, 1973). The major consequence of working was the inability to spend time on higher pursuits such as leisure or learning. Although work was seen as preventing some aversive consequences such as starvation, the activity itself was not considered to provide any positive benefit. Thus, the meaning of work refers to the individual's beliefs about the positive and negative outcomes of work and the functions that work serves in life.

How has the meaning of work been operationally defined? It is more difficult to answer this question. Operationalizations of the meaning of work have taken many forms. Measures of values, needs, preferences, ethics, and orientations have all been developed as indicators of work meaning. Unfortunately, there have been few attempts to integrate these measures on either conceptual or empirical levels (Pryor, 1982). The relationships among the various indicators have not been systematically investigated.

A review of these measures has suggested that they, and the concepts they attempt to assess, are not completely redundant. Rather, they appear to tap different dimensions of work meaning as defined above. Three major dimensions of work meaning reflected in the measures have been identified: work centrality, work values, and work orientation.

Centrality/Importance of Work

One dimension of work meaning that has been measured and studied is the importance or *centrality* of work compared to other life roles. In earlier studies, work meaning was defined as beliefs about the outcomes of work. The centrality concept refers to the value, and not the content, of outcomes available at work relative to those available or sought from other social roles. Individuals for whom the job is a central concern believe their most highly valued outcomes are available in the work setting. The job is important because the most valued outcomes in life come from work.

This aspect of work meaning was first studied by Dubin (1956), who developed the Central Life Interest questionnaire in order to challenge the assumption that for most people work was the source of many valued rewards. *Central life interest* was operationally defined as the expressed preference for a given locale in carrying out an activity. The questionnaire allows classification of workers into job-oriented, nonjob-oriented, and undifferentiated groups. Dubin (1956) found that high proportions of workers were nonjob-oriented, and he concluded that for many, work has little importance. Rather, most people seek primary rewards away from work settings.

The centrality aspect of work meaning is also captured in the concept of *job* or *work involvement*. Lodahl and Kejner (1965) originally provided two definitions of job involvement: 1) the extent to which self esteem is affected by performance; and 2) the degree to which the individual identifies with the job, so that it is a major component of self image. It is this second definition that appears to overlap with the centrality aspect of work meaning (Kanungo, 1982). Individuals who identify with the job define themselves in terms of the work role (Rabinowitz and Hall, 1977). Positive and negative outcomes available at work are highly valued, for they influence beliefs and feelings about the self. Thus, job-involved people have a "central life interest" in the work setting, for it determines their identity.

Kanungo (1982) labels the centrality aspect of work meaning as *work* and not job involvement. For him, job involvement refers to specific beliefs regarding the potential of one's present job for satisfying salient needs. Work involvement involves more general beliefs about the importance of work in life and the outcomes that ought to be gained from working. Again, the value and not the content of work outcomes is the focus of this concept.

The emphasis on outcome value exclusive of content is illustrated in the four-item job-involvement scale of Lawler and Hall (1970): 1) "The most important things that happen to me involve my work; 2) I live, eat, and breathe my job; 3) I am very much involved personally in my work; and 4) The major satisfaction in my life comes from my job." Similar to the Central Life Interest questionnaire, these items assess the relative importance of work for gaining valued outcomes but do not identify the types of outcomes gained. Factor analytic studies have also demonstrated the overlap between such job involvement items and the Central Life Interest measure (Saleh and Hosek, 1976).

Work Values/Beliefs

Another dimension of work meaning has been studied through the concept of *work values*. Rokeach (1973) defined values as the individual's beliefs about ideal modes of conduct and ideal terminal modes. While in Rokeach's studies values were not identified with any particular object or situation, values exclusive to the work setting have been discussed by other researchers. Work values represent beliefs about ideal ways of behaving at work and ideal work outcomes (Nord et al., 1988). As are any values, work values are learned early in life and reflect cultural norms. Thus, society teaches individuals about what outcomes should be expected and desired from work, and also about what one should expect and want to give to the job situation in order to achieve those outcomes (Harpaz, 1985). This concept of work values bears most similarity to the notion of social work meaning discussed above: the outcomes expected, though not always directly experienced by the individual.

The measurement of values has focused on the content of beliefs about ideal work outcomes. In developing value scales, researchers have attempted to identify what particular end states and behaviors are desired at work. However, a perusal of the measures and the research on work values reveals that a very limited set of values has been considered (Ronen, 1978). That is, rather than examine the range of values that employees may hold, researchers have identified particular patterns of beliefs that may have relevance to the work setting, and they have then investigated workers' adherence to these systems. For example, Buchholz (1977; 1978) identified five work belief systems: Marxist, humanist, organizational, work ethic, and leisure, and examined the extent to which employees endorsed each view. These systems were chosen because they were clearly definable in literature concerning work (Buchholz, 1978). Buchholz's studies are somewhat unique in that five different belief systems were identified and defined. In contrast, the bulk of the literature on work values focuses on one particular belief system: the Protestant work ethic (Blood, 1969; Wollack et al., 1971). Although once tied to religious beliefs about salvation, the work ethic is now secularized. This value system involves a belief that hard work is good in itself. One's personal worth and integrity as an individual are judged by one's willingness to work hard (Morrow, 1983). Thus, the ideals that one should attempt to achieve through work are pride in oneself and a sense of accomplishment. However, these outcomes are gained only through effort.

The work ethic represents only one particular set of work values out of many that individuals may hold. Yet most studies of values focus exclusively on the work ethic, and ignore other possible belief systems. Indeed, for some writers, the concept of values is synonymous with the work ethic system (Ronen, 1978). Thus, the study of values has been restricted to one specific domain of valued outcomes. Because of this restriction, work values, as they are most often operationally defined, capture only one small aspect of this dimension of work meaning.

Work Orientation

A third dimension of the meaning of work to receive attention in the literature is a general *work orientation*. Two major orientations to work have been distinguished—*intrinsic* and *extrinsic*. Those with an intrinsic work orientation believe that work itself results in desired outcomes (Andrisani and Miljus, 1977). The actual content and substance of work are viewed as important sources of reward. Working, as an activity, is valued because it gives opportunities to attain valued outcomes.

In contrast, people with extrinsic orientations view work in terms of its instrumental nature. Work is seen as useful for obtaining valued outcomes that are not themselves work centered. Working as an activity is not valued for any rewards it can directly provide, but is seen only as a means to an end. Valued outcomes follow from work, but do not depend on its content or process.

The intrinsic/extrinsic dichotomy has been used by many writers and is one of the most popular ways of defining work meaning (Andrisani and Miljus, 1977). The distinction provides a way for classifying an individual's work values, not according to their content, but instead according to how work is perceived in relation to achieving values. Each category can encompass a wide range of value systems. For example, the "leisure" and "organizational" positions identified by Buchholz (1978) both are examples of extrinsic systems. These value positions specify valued outcomes (for instance, free time, or group success/survival) occurring as a result of work. However, classical Marxist and "humanist" positions would be examples of intrinsic value systems (Nord et al., 1988). In these two systems, valued outcomes result from the process of work itself. Thus, although particular theorists, cultures, or ideological systems specify the content of valued intrinsic and extrinsic rewards, the concept of orientation is not concerned with the nature of the valued outcomes, but instead focuses only on their locus in relation to work.

Although the notion of work orientation is conceptually independent from the content of work values, organizational psychologists have tended to link the two together. As noted by Nord et al. (1988), researchers have overwhelmingly adopted a theoretical position based on the work of Maslow (1943), Herzberg (1966), Herzberg, Mausner, and Snyderman, (1959), and McGregor (1973), which states that the ideal intrinsic outcomes of work are individual psychological development and growth. Intrinsic work orientation is defined as a desire for these outcomes, which supposedly satisfy higher order needs. An extrinsic orientation is defined as a desire for outcomes such as money and benefits which satisfy lower order needs for security and safety.

The definition of work orientation in terms of desire for specific outcomes is reflected in typical ways of operationalizing the concept. Orientation is measured by examining job outcome preferences or the value of various job rewards. Preferences for aspects of work such as autonomy, challenge, responsibility, and ability utilization are interpreted as reflecting an intrinsic orientation. Preferences for rewards such as good working conditions, reasonable hours, and money are called extrinsic preferences. As measured and studied, work orientation is totally redundant with a desire for outcomes important within one particular value system. The content free nature of orientation and its applicability to many other value systems and outcomes have been ignored or forgotten (Nord et al., 1988). Thus while work orientation is an interesting facet of the meaning of work conceptually, as operationally defined it provides limited information. Measures of orientation do not indicate an individual's perceptions of the relationship of work to desired outcomes; they only measure one's desire for a restricted set of rewards.

Work Meanings and Behavior

Regardless of limitations in measurement, evidence indicates that these three dimensions of work meaning are indeed related to work behavior and performance. Job involvement was positively related to performance in several studies (Cummings and Manring, 1977; Weiner and Vardi, 1980), and also to the amount of time spent on work-related activities (Weiner and Gechman, 1977). Work orientation was significantly related to productivity in a study by Kazanas (1978), who found that those with intrinsic orientations had higher productivity than extrinsically-oriented workers. The relationship between values and managerial success has been demonstrated by England (1975), and Watson and Williams (1977). More specifically, work ethic values have also been associated with performance. Those who endorsed work ethic values spent more time on repetitive tasks (Merrens and Garrett, 1975), and had higher performance than those with low work ethic values (Greenberg, 1977).

These results suggest that work meanings do indeed function to influence behavior in organizations. It is the purpose of this chapter to attempt to explain the nature of this influence. The impact of work meanings on behavior is analyzed from a motivational perspective. Theories of motivation attempt to specify the variables and processes involved that determine the choices among alternate actions made by individuals, the effort, and persistence of behavior (Campbell and Pritchard, 1976; Vroom, 1964). A motivational perspective assumes that work meanings will influence behavior through these variables and processes. A general model of the motivation process has been developed through summarizing the concepts involved in major theories of work motivation. This model is shown in figure 4–1.

Basically, this model posits that motivation and behavior take place in the context of a specific environmental situation. Behavioristic models of motivation have traditionally focused solely on environmental variables to explain work behavior. However, most theories also include the individual as a determinant of action, for individuals must perceive and interpret the environment in order to act upon it. Thus, cognitive appraisals of the situation

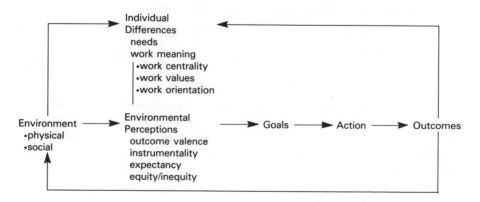

Figure 4–1. Model of Motivation

precede action. Several theories focus on this aspect of the motivation process. Expectancy-value models (Vroom, 1964; Naylor, Pritchard, and Ilgen, 1980; Heckhausen and Kuhl, 1984) state that people decide on the action to take by forming expectancies of success for various actions, and by evaluating the desirability or valence of the outcomes of actions. Equity theory (Adams, 1965) proposes that individuals evaluate the situation in terms of its perceived fairness, by comparing their own contributions to the situation and outcomes received from it to those of others. If the contribution suggests they are being treated unfairly, they change their behavior to reduce the inequity.

According to the model, several factors influence these perceptions. One is the objective work environment. Factors such as the reward structure, physical environment, and task characteristics inform individuals of the likely outcomes of behaviors, their probability of attainment, and their usefulness for obtaining other rewards. A second important influence is the social environment. The work of Salancik and Pfeffer (1977; 1978), Weiss (1978), and others has called attention to the impact that an individual's managers and co-workers can have on perceptions of the environment. The objective task setting contains many stimuli which can be overwhelming and ambiguous. Therefore, individuals depend on others to understand and interpret this information. Managers and co-workers define the relevant attributes of the environment, make certain stimuli more salient, and also suggest how these stimuli should be evaluated. Thus, the perceived environment is at least partly a function of social factors. People construct meaning through the expressions of others (O'Reilly and Caldwell, 1985)

The third influence on perceptions noted in the model are individual differences. These typically refer to relatively stable, long-term characteristics or attributes of the individual (Naylor et al., 1980) that are brought to the job setting. One type of individual difference important in theories of work motivation are needs, hypothesized to affect the perceived value of job outcomes (Alderfer, 1969; Herzberg, 1966; Maslow, 1943). Expectancy-value theorists have proposed other personality variables which influence not only outcome value, but also expectancies and instrumentalities (Naylor et al., 1980). Work meaning dimensions are included in the model as another individual difference variable. Like needs, work values, centrality, and orientation are believed to be relatively stable, formed through early socialization and work experiences.

Even though these individual differences are believed to be enduring traits, it has been argued that the immediate work environment, particularly the social environment, can influence these attributes (Salancik and Pfeffer, 1978). In interactions with others, individuals learn not only how to perceive and interpret specific environmental stimuli, but also what needs one ought to possess and what values are appropriate and rewarded (Buchanan, 1974; Pfeffer, 1980). Thus, work meanings can change as a result of social interactions in the workplace. Although meaning is brought to the workplace, its stability/invariance in the face of new information cannot be assumed.

Thus, the physical and social environment and individual differences lead to perceptions about the relative value and likelihoods of attaining various outcomes in the job setting. In the next step of the model, these perceptions result in a specific goal or intention to act. The theories of Locke (1968) and Ryan (1970) propose that goals are the most immediate result of initial environmental perceptions, and are also the most important precursors of action. In the last box of the model, outcomes resulting from behavior modify the environment, influence subsequent cognitions and action. Models of feedback (e.g., Taylor, Fisher, and Ilgen, 1984) and cognitive evaluation theory (Deci, 1975) have focused on this phase of the motivation process, and suggest that different kinds of outcomes, such as extrinsic versus intrinsic rewards, or positive and negative feedback, will have different effects on behavior. Experienced outcomes in turn also modify work meanings. The work meaning dimensions involve beliefs about the sources and value of outcomes available through work. The types of outcomes actually experienced by the individual may modify or enhance these beliefs. Thus, motivation and behavior are not only influenced by work meanings: work meanings themselves are in turn affected by behavior and its consequences.

Work Meanings and Job Outcome Value

As is clear from the model, work meaning dimensions are generally believed to influence motivation and behavior through their impact on environmental perceptions. By far, the most commonly hypothesized function of the meaning of work is that it determines the valence of job outcomes. This view was especially apparent in popular writings of the 1970s. During that decade many believed that cultural changes in work meaning had resulted in workers' no longer valuing traditional work rewards such as money, praise, and pride in hard work (Taylor and Thompson, 1976). The widespread endorsement of job enrichment was based on this assumption. Job enrichment was believed to provide rewards of more value to workers, such as variety, interesting work, and responsibility. For the younger worker with a new meaning of work, these outcomes would effectively function as motivators (Rose, 1985). Thus, the meaning of work was believed to influence the desirability of available rewards.

Much of the research conducted on work meaning dimensions has been directed toward testing this hypothesis. A number of studies examine the relationship between centrality indices and outcome value or importance. Significant relationships between job involvement and growth need strength have been reported in several studies (Rabinowitz and Hall, 1981; Rabinowitz,

Hall, and Goodale, 1977). These studies suggest that centrality is related to preferences for jobs having challenge, freedom, participation, and personal growth over jobs characterized by friendly relationships with co-workers and management, high salary, and job security. Dubin, Hedley, and Taveggia (1976) reported associations between outcome value and "central life interest." Subjects were asked to indicate their most important outcomes from a list of 124 choices. Substantial differences in the outcomes endorsed were found between job- and nonjob-oriented groups. Job-oriented employees valued positive outcomes that reflected high investment in the job such as challenge and job responsibility. In contrast, the nonjob-oriented valued outcomes concerned with withdrawal from the workplace (Dubin et al., 1976). Good hours, holidays and vacations, and being left alone to work, were among the outcomes most frequently chosen as important.

Other studies have found no relationships between centrality and outcome value. Gorn and Kanungo (1980) classified managers into intrinsic and extrinsic preference groups based on their rankings of the importance of fifteen job outcomes. The job involvement scores of these groups did not differ significantly. Similarly, Taveggia and Ziemba (1978) reported no relationship between central life interest and the importance ratings of twenty-two outcomes in a sample of 1,112 employees, and concluded that centrality and outcome value were totally independent constructs.

While this pattern of results may appear contradictory, differences in methodology may partially explain the mixed results. Recall that centrality refers to the value of job rewards relative to those available outside the work setting. Thus, job- and nonjob-oriented groups should differ most when the relative values of work and nonwork outcomes are compared. When comparisons are made only among work-related rewards, significant relationships between centrality and outcome value seem more likely to occur when absolute ratings rather than relative rankings of value are compared. Work outcomes may be ranked similarly in both groups, but the absolute value of work outcomes should be lower for the nonjob-oriented. Some support for this hypothesis is found in a study by Dubin, Champoux, and Porter (1975), who compared job- and nonjob-oriented employees. The relative attractiveness ratings of twelve organizational features did not differ by group; however, the absolute attractiveness ratings did. The job-oriented group rated virtually all of the features as more attractive than did the nonjob-oriented.

Hypotheses concerning the relationships between work values and outcome valence are prominent in theoretical discussions. Values are reference points, the standards by which evaluations of the goodness or worth of experiences and objects are made (Rokeach, 1973). Events or experiences are appealing or desirable to the extent that they are instrumental for attaining one's values. Ronen (1978) provides evidence for a relationship between values and the importance of job outcomes. Employees with self-realization values placed more importance on intrinsic job outcomes than extrinsic ones, while those holding aggrandizement values valued extrinsic outcomes more than intrinsic. Other studies relating values to outcome desirability focus exclusively on the work ethic. There is a substantial amount of evidence that this value system is related to preferences for job outcomes such as challenge and opportunities for personal growth—that is, the attributes included on measures of growth need strength. Wanous (1974), Wollack et al. (1971), and Aldag and Brief (1975; 1979) report correlations of around .40 between work ethic scores and growth need strength scales. In addition, work ethic scores have been found to moderate relationships between job scope and job satisfaction (Wanous, 1974; Morrow, 1983). Higher relationships between job scope and satisfaction are reported for those employees who endorse the work ethic. These results also suggest that the work ethic is related to preferences for challenge, autonomy, and personal growth.

Although these studies provide consistent and convincing evidence of a relationship between values and the valence of job outcomes, they fail to provide much information concerning the nature of that relationship. For example, are the outcomes considered on growth need strength scales the only ones for which preference differences exist between work ethic endorsement groups? Studies have failed to consider other outcomes on which valence differences might be found, and have limited their focus instead to job outcomes inherent in the job characteristics model (e.g., Hackman and Oldham, 1976). In addition, while statements can be made about the preferences of work ethic endorsers, detailed information is lacking about the outcome preferences of other employees who do not adhere to the work ethic. Employees without work ethic values, typically lumped together for research purposes, are not a homogeneous group. Buchholz (1978) identified four other coherent work value systems, which together were endorsed more frequently than the work ethic. How do the outcome preferences of such various groups differ from each other? Answers to such questions are unknown, for the research in this area has focused on only one value system and one domain of job outcomes.

The existing literature provides no information on the relationship of work orientation to outcome valence, for orientation has not been assessed independent of the valence or importance of job outcomes. Yet, given a content free measure of work orientation, should such a relationship exist? One might expect that the extrinsically oriented, whatever the content of their values, would place less importance than intrinsic individuals on job outcomes concerned solely with work content or process. An extrinsic orientation is specifically defined in terms of the absence of value for work content. However, beyond this general speculation, it is difficult to make any specific hypotheses. The valence of job outcomes is likely to depend more on the content of one's value systems than on its orientation.

Studies of demographic group differences in outcome preferences have also been used to provide evidence for a work meaning-outcome value linkage. This approach is believed to yield indirect evidence of a relationship, based on the following rationale: work meanings, values, and beliefs are the result of early upbringing and socialization. If one can assume different socialization experiences among the demographic groups that differ on outcome preferences, one can also infer that the groups differ in the meaning they give to work. This kind of reasoning can be seen in the early work of Turner and Lawrence (1965) on the job scope–job satisfaction relationship. These authors explained urban-rural differences in the importance of job characteristics through positing concomitant differences in work values between the two groups. Thus, the relationship between a demographic variable and outcome preferences was interpreted as a relationship between work values and preferences.

Later studies within the job scope framework went on to directly test the relationship between work values and job characteristics importance. However, most research using group differences has stayed at the inferential level, and assumes that the relationship hypothesized between the demographic variable and work meaning in fact exists. For example, sex differences in outcome preferences have long been cited as evidence of a relationship between work meaning and outcome importance. Research often indicated that women placed less importance on intrinsic factors than did men. This was explained as a result of girls' early socialization, which taught them to value family roles over an occupation (Kaufman and Fetters, 1980). Hence, such differences in preference should be expected. Similar arguments have been made to explain age and racial group differences in work outcome importance (Buchholz, 1978; Cherrington, Condie, and England, 1979).

There are obvious problems with this approach. Preference differences among various subgroups can be attributed to many factors other than work beliefs and meanings. As Andrisani and Miljus (1977) have argued, opportunities for rewards or levels of financial security may also cause differences in preferences. More recent studies on group differences have held economic and job factors constant when attempting to determine if socialization could in fact be responsible for preference differences. The results of these studies are mixed. While sex and race differences in outcome preferences tend to disappear when other factors are controlled (Brief, Rose, and Aldag, 1977; Lacy, Bokemeier, and Shepard, 1983; Mossholder et al., 1985), relationships between age and preferences are still found (Cherrington et al., 1979). However, these relationships can still not be unequivocally attributed to socialization and work meaning differences (Rhodes, 1983). All things considered, this kind of research provides little information on the relationship between work meaning and the valence of job outcomes.

Work Meanings and Other Environmental Perceptions

Although the relationship between outcome valence and the meaning of work has received the most attention in research and theory, work meanings may also influence other perceptions of the environment. In figure 4–1, expectancy, instrumentality, and perceptions of fairness are included as additional motivational concepts.

Expectancy-value theorists have long hypothesized that individual difference variables contribute to the formation of expectancies and instrumentalities. For example, Lawler (1973) suggested that successful experiences with the task and high self-esteem would increase expectancies of task success. Naylor et al. (1980) proposed that other personality factors may be operating as well, and specifically pointed to locus of control as a determinant of both expectancy and instrumentality. People with a high internal locus of control, who believe that events are under their control, may in general have high expectancies of success and also perceive strong relationships between performance and the attainment of outcomes. Those with an external locus of control may perceive lower relationships, and feel that performance and outcome attainment are more dependent on luck or chance than on their own efforts. Work meanings should also influence the perceptions of contingency relationships, for they reflect the individual's experiences in obtaining outcomes and beliefs about relationships between effort, performance, and outcomes. For example, work values include beliefs not only about desired end states, but the means by which these ends should be attained. Consider two of the items from the Mirels and Garrett (1971) Protestant ethic scale: "People who fail at a job have usually not tried hard enough," and "Most people who don't succeed in life are just plain lazy." These items imply a strong relationship between effort and success; and their endorsement should be related to general task expectancies.

Another dimension of work meanings—work centrality—has particular relevance to the instrumentality of job performance. Those who hold the job to be a "central life interest" perceive work to be a source of many valued rewards. They are likely to see more and stronger associations between performance and outcomes than those who find few valued outcomes in the job setting. While someone who is not job-oriented may see strong relationships between performance and pay, the job-oriented individual may not only perceive the performance-pay relationship, but also see strong links between performance and self-worth, growth, and personal satisfaction. Thus, for job-oriented individuals, performance should be instrumental for obtaining many more valued outcomes.

Work orientation may not influence instrumentality levels, but rather influence decisions about outcomes for which work performance is seen as instrumental. The extrinsically-oriented, for example, are likely to perceive work as leading to money, security, leisure, or social change, while the intrinsically-oriented may perceive linkages between work and spiritual or psychological growth. However, there are virtually no data to address such hypotheses. Only one study (Lied and Pritchard, 1976) examined Protestant ethic values and expectancy-instrumentality perceptions. As expected, Protestant ethic endorsement was positively related to effort-performance expectancies and the instrumentality of performance. No other studies were found that tested the relationship of work meaning dimensions to these expectancy-value components.

Recent research has begun to examine individual differences not in the formation, but in the utilization of the expectancy-value model components. Vroom (1964) had proposed earlier that individuals made decisions about effort by combining their valence, expectancy, and instrumentality estimates in a multiplicative manner. This method of decision making assumes that choices are rational, and intended to maximize expected gain. However, recent evidence suggests that not all individuals combine information in such an optimal way. Information processing theorists (Slovik, Fischoff, and Lichtenstein, 1977) have proposed that most decisions are not optimal, and that multiplicative models are too complex for most individuals to handle. Some support for this hypothesis was found in a study by Stahl and Harrell (1981). Sixty-three percent of their sample used a simple additive model to combine valence and expectancies. Since use of the additive model was negatively related to age and education, the authors proposed that ability factors may determine one's decision-making process. Other authors have suggested additional factors that may influence decision making. For instance, circumstances may determine the way that decisions are made. According to Heckhausen and Kuhl (1984), commitment to a course of action does not always follow from a rational expectancy analysis. Deadlines and sudden opportunities can also precipitate a decision to act. Staw (1984) suggested that the magnitude of the consequences of the decision will influence the process of decision making used. If the consequences of the decision are large, people may carefully screen and combine expectancies and valences in the multiplicative fashion suggested by the model. But when the decision involves few consequences of small magnitude, individuals may be more likely to rely on a *noncognitive* process.

These theories suggest that work meaning dimensions may play a role in determining the processing of environmental information. For example, individuals with low work centrality may not perceive large consequences for performance (or any work) goals, and hence may be less likely to use multiplicative processing of expectancy-value information in making work-related decisions. Such individuals may instead become committed to work-related goals on the basis of pressure or other situational variables. In contrast, those with high job centrality who perceive that their performance decisions have many important consequences may be more likely to make work-related decisions in accordance with expectancy-value theory. Values should influence the decision process in a similar way. Those decisions critical for value attainment may be processed more carefully.

Another model to emphasize the role of perceptions on behavior is equity theory (Adams, 1965). This model assumes that individuals have beliefs about what is a fair or equitable return for their contributions to an exchange relationship (such as a job), and seek to maintain equity in that relationship. To determine equity, individuals consider their contributions, or inputs that they bring to the job, and also their outcomes, or benefits received from the job setting. Equity is not determined solely on the level of inputs and outcomes perceived. Rather, the model posits that a social comparison process is crucial to the determination of equity. If the individual perceives that his or her ratio of outcomes to inputs equals that of a comparison other, the situation is deemed fair, and the individual is content. However, any perceived inequality between the individual's and other's ratios will be perceived as an inequitable situation. This results in a tension that increases motivation to reduce the inequality. Restoration of equity may be accomplished in several ways, depending on the nature of the situation. If individuals feel underrewarded relative to the other, they will attempt to increase outcomes and decrease inputs. Conversely, individuals feeling overrewarded will attempt to decrease their outcomes and increase their inputs. Thus, equity theory predicts behavior through knowing the individual's perceptions of his or her own inputs and outcomes, and those of the comparison other.

Several authors have recently suggested that work meanings will influence equity processes. First, values may determine the individual's definition of *fairness*. Currently, equity theory operates on the assumption that fairness means a correspondence between inputs and outcomes (Mowday, 1987). This definition implies a correlation between the two, where those who contribute more to the job should also receive more benefit. This assumption is incorporated into the common formulas for determining equity. According to the theory, fairness exists if the other who receives more is also perceived as having greater input.

This definition of fairness, however, is not universal (Birnbaum, 1983). To some, fairness may mean strict equality of outcomes for all concerned, or outcome distribution based not on input but on need (Mowday, 1987). Adams (1965) speculated that values determined one's definition of fairness, and thus the conditions under which inequity would be experienced. Several studies support this hypothesis. Greenberg (1979) reported that subjects who endorsed Protestant work ethic values preferred to maintain a correspondence between inputs and outcomes in allocating rewards, while low scorers on the work ethic scale preferred to distribute outcomes equally. Vecchio (1981) found that moral values influenced preferences for input-outcome correspondence. Subjects high in moral maturity responded as predicted to an overpayment condition, by lowering their own outcomes. However, subjects low in moral maturity failed to respond to this form of inequity. These studies indicate that values reflect different conceptions of fairness and hence, different responses to job conditions. The results suggest that work ethic endorsers are more likely to behave as hypothesized by equity theory, because their definition of fairness seems to correspond to that of the model. However, individuals endorsing other value systems may not be as predictable from the theory. They may respond only to outcome inequality, and ignore relative inputs.

Work meaning dimensions may influence equity processes in terms other than definitions of fairness. Centrality, values, and orientation reflect beliefs about valued job inputs and the job attributes that represent valued outcomes. Thus they may affect the factors that are used to compute an equity ratio and the salience of different components of the ratio (Weick, Bougon, and Maruyama, 1976). Although there is little research in this area, work ethic values have been associated with recognition of different types of inputs. Those with low work ethic values were less likely to base rewards on inputs under the workers own control, while high work ethic scorers rewarded internal inputs (Greenberg, 1979). Thus, work meanings may also influence equity processes and responses to the job through their effects on the nature and value of the inputs and outcomes considered.

Work Meanings and Goals

In the next step of figure 4–1, perceptions of the environment are translated into a goal or specific intention to act. Goal theories (see, e.g., Locke et al., 1981; Ryan, 1970) stress the importance of goals or intentions as the primary determinants of action. In these theories valences, expectancies, or instrumentalities are not directly related to action. Rather, they contribute to the development of intentions (Ryan, 1970). Individual difference variables, such as work meanings, are believed to impact goals through their influence on environmental perceptions (Ryan, 1970; Pinder, 1984). This process is illustrated in figure 4–1.

There is support for this conceptualization of the motivation process. Expectancy-value variables correlate with stated performance goals and goal commitment (Dachler and Mobley, 1973; Klinger, Barta, and Maxeiner, 1980; Roberson, 1986). In addition, Mento, Cartledge, and Locke (1980) found goal valence to be a determinant of goal acceptance.

In the previous sections, evidence was found suggesting that work meaning facets influence valences, expectancies, instrumentalities, and even the processing of this information. Through this impact on perceptions, work meanings should also influence goal choice and goal acceptance. Let us first consider work centrality. If, as has been suggested, the job involved perceive more plentiful and more valued work outcomes, these individuals may set a greater number of work-related goals in the job setting than would the nonjob involved. Commitment to task performance goals may also be related to job involvement, for individuals with high centrality should perceive more valued outcomes as being contingent upon task accomplishment.

One would also expect substantial relationships between work value dimensions and goals. Goals are the mechanisms through which values are translated into action (Locke and Henne, 1986). Goal objects thus directly reflect an individual's values. Given a situation where individuals are free to choose their own goals, there should be a substantial correspondence between the content of values and goals that are decided on. Even when free goal choice is not permitted (such as when goals are assigned), commitment to a given goal should reflect one's values. For example, work ethic values are associated with high expectancies of goal attainment and also with high value for effort (Lied and Pritchard, 1976). Those who endorse this belief system should set more difficult goals than those who endorse other values. Indirect support for this hypothesis was found by Yukl and Latham (1978). In this study, need for achievement—a correlate of the work ethic belief system (Furnham, 1984)—was positively related to goal difficulty.

Unfortunately, there has been no other research testing these hypothesized links. Although there have been numerous studies of goal setting and its impact on behavior, the role of individual differences in determining goal choice and goal acceptance has not been systematically examined. Our ignorance of individual differences in this area is in large part due to the predominant design used in goal setting studies (see Weiss and Adler, 1984). Experimental interest has been in goal setting as an intervention. Goals are usually assigned to subjects, with little attention paid to self-set goals (Rakestraw and Weiss, 1981). These conditions have drastically diminished the impact of individual differences on goal setting behavior (Locke et al., 1981). Self-set goals cannot be studied with goal assignment, and the variance in goal acceptance is reduced. To begin to investigate relationships among work meanings and goals, changes in research design and strategy are sorely needed.

Recently, researchers have attempted to understand the process by which goals influence performance. A control theory perspective has been suggested to explain why goal setting works (Campion and Lord, 1982). Within this framework, behavior is a result of continual comparison between the individual's goal and environmental feedback concerning goal attainment. The goal serves as a standard or desired end state of affairs to which the feedback is compared. Any discrepancy between the feedback and the standard creates a motivation to remove the difference. Depending on the individual and situation, the difference may be removed in any of a number of ways: increasing effort, changing strategies, or modifying the goal (Campion and Lord, 1982).

It is important to note that in this theory, the goal in part determines the kind of environmental feedback that will be monitored by the individual (Ashford and Cummings, 1983; Taylor et al., 1984). For example, given a goal of pleasing one's co-workers, the individual will seek feedback information relevant to this goal. Co-workers' smiles, frowns, and opinions may be attended to closely, while information not seen as relevant to the goal will be ignored. Klinger (1977) has hypothesized that this screening of the environment occurs on a preconscious level. That is, goal irrelevant information is not ignored, but is just not consciously perceived or attended to. Several studies have demonstrated that greater attention is paid to cues related to goals, and that goal irrelevant information is less well attended to or remembered (Klinger, 1978; Hoelscher, Klinger, and Barta, 1981).

This perspective suggests additional hypotheses about the impact of work meanings on motivation and behavior. As work meanings influence goals, they will also influence the environmental information that individuals attend to. Different goals result in a differential sensitivity to types of information. Through their influence on goals, work meanings may also affect the utility of feedback sources used by the organization to maintain performance. Ashford and Cummings (1983) propose that sources or types of feedback seen as irrelevant to the individual's goals will be less effective for maintaining performance. Studies by Baron and associates (Baron and Ganz, 1972; Baron et al. 1974) reported that children with an external locus of control outperformed those with internal control when the experimenter provided verbal feedback on task performance. However, internals outperformed externals when performance feedback intrinsic to the task was used. The authors interpreted their results in terms of value differences between internals and externals. Because externals place a higher value on social approval than on achievement, social feedback was more effective than task information in maintaining their performance. Internals, however, who value achievement more than affiliation, were more responsive to task information. Greenberg (1977) also found that values influenced responses to feedback. Negative feedback improved the task performance of those with high scores on a Protestant ethic scale, but lowered the performance of low scorers. The interpretation was consistent with Ashford and Cummings' proposal about the effects of feedback. As high work ethic scorers value success and the expenditure of effort, the discrepant information provided by the negative feedback spurred them on to higher performance in an effort to meet their standards. However, low work ethic scorers were less interested in working hard or succeeding. These goals, of less value to them, were easily abandoned in light of negative information, which resulted in decreased performance.

In conclusion, theories of goals and their impact on performance suggest a number of possible avenues through which work meanings may influence behavior. Through their influence on goal content and value, work meanings not only affect the direction of behavior, but also the individual's attention and responsiveness to the environment. Work meanings may enhance the salience of certain sorts of stimuli and information, and also *decrease* the salience of irrelevant information.

Work Meanings and the Effect of Rewards

In the last section of the model depicted in figure 4–1, the outcomes or consequences of behavior are received. As indicated by the feedback loop, these outcomes serve as environmental stimuli that influence levels of need arousal and perceptions such as expectancies, instrumentalities, and equity. In this way, outcomes of behavior impact subsequent motivation and behavior.

Most theories of motivation have assumed that the effects of consequences on behavior are additive. Thus, when two or more valued outcomes are received for a particular action, subsequent motivation to perform the act should be greater than when only one outcome is provided.

However, there is some evidence that rewards may not always be additive. Several researchers (Deci, 1971; Calder and Staw, 1975; Lepper and Greene, 1975) have demonstrated that the addition to extrinsic contingent pay to a task that provides intrinsic rewards will reduce, not enhance, subsequent intrinsic motivation to perform the task. These results have led to the conclusion that intrinsic and extrinsic outcomes combine in a nonadditive fashion to influence task motivation (Staw, 1977). It is hypothesized that when both intrinsic and extrinsic rewards are received, individuals experience oversufficient justification for their actions, and respond by devaluing the intrinsic reward (Staw, 1976; Deci, 1975).

Although the overjustification effect was originally hypothesized to occur only when intrinsic and extrinsic rewards were combined, recent evidence suggests that nonadditivity may be applicable to all outcomes, regardless of their content. Porac and Salancik (1981) demonstrated nonadditivity using only extrinsic rewards. The value of one extrinsic reward (money) was devalued by another extrinsic outcome (credit) provided contingently to college students for the same activity. The authors suggested that the salience of rewards, rather than their content, determines when nonadditivity will occur. If multiple outcomes are differentially salient, the more salient outcomes will control behavior and the other will be devalued.

This interpretation was supported in a study by Phillips and Freedman (1985). Although using the extrinsic-intrinsic dichotomy, they hypothesized that differential reward salience was the crucial factor determining the nonadditivity effect. Thus, contingent pay should undermine intrinsic motivation only when pay is more salient than the intrinsic rewards. In addition, they suggested that work values would determine the salience of outcomes. Pay should be a more salient reward for those with extrinsic values. Therefore, nonadditivity of extrinsic and intrinsic rewards should be more likely to occur for those with high extrinsic values. Their results supported the hypotheses. For subjects with extrinsic work values, nonadditivity of intrinsic and extrinsic rewards was reported. These subjects, for whom pay was most salient, devalued intrinsic rewards after receiving extrinsic pay. However, for subjects with intrinsic values, additivity of rewards was found. Intrinsics reported greatest task motivation when both intrinsic and extrinsic rewards were present. The value of intrinsic rewards remained high regardless of the presence of contingent pay.

If reward salience is the crucial factor determining nonadditivity of rewards, the intrinsic-extrinsic dichotomy is no longer useful for predicting the effect of multiple rewards (Pearce, 1987). Instead, the effect of rewards must be predicted through knowledge of their relative salience to the individual. The literature reviewed in this chapter indicates that work meaning dimensions may be a major determinant of reward salience. The results of Phillips and Freedman (1985) suggest that greater knowledge of work meanings and their impact will also facilitate our understanding of the effects of multiple reward contingencies.

Summary and Conclusions

How do work meanings influence motivation and behavior? This chapter suggested that work meaning dimensions may influence a number of motivational concepts. It was hypothesized that outcome valences, expectancies, equity, goals, and responses to feedback are all at least partly a function of the meaning one gives to work. The chapter has also revealed that there is little empirical evidence supporting such hypotheses. The available data allow only the conclusion that work ethic values are associated with preferences for the intrinsic outcomes prominent in the Herzberg two-factor and job characteristics models. Although this finding does indeed support a more general statement that work meaning dimensions influence the valence of job outcomes, it demonstrates only one of what should be numerous and complex linkages between the two domains. The research in this area, which studies only one value system, does not address the question of how networks of values and work meanings influence outcome valence.

Evidence concerning the relationships between other environmental perceptions (such as expectancies, instrumentalities, and equity perceptions) and work meanings is virtually nonexistent. However, additional research on these motivational concepts may do little to illuminate our understanding of the role work meanings play in determining organizational behavior. Reviews of the motivation literature suggest that those theories involving concepts closest to action are the most valid in predicting performance and behavior. Goal theories, in particular, have demonstrated more validity than other approaches to work motivation (Locke and Henne, 1986; Pinder, 1984). In this light, it may be most fruitful to concentrate research efforts on investigating relationships between work meanings and goals. How do work meanings influence goal content, goal choice, and goal commitment? Do work meanings affect responses to feedback and the salience of different types of environmental information? This review suggests that through their impact on goals, work meanings have far-reaching effects on organizational behavior and performance. Research on such issues, previously neglected, is likely to yield the most understanding.

This chapter has focused on the affect of work meanings on motivation and behavior. But, as is clear from the model, behavior and its outcomes in turn affect work meaning dimensions. There has been little research on this topic. Studies have shown that organizational and job tenure are related to values or needs (Buchanan, 1974; Pfeffer, 1980). However, the ways in which work participation modify work meanings have not been addressed. Similarly, social influences on work meanings also need to be investigated. Weiss (1978) found greater similarity between the values of a manager and subordinate when managers were perceived as having high status and competence. This suggests that social influences on work meanings will be strong only under certain conditions. Such issues concerning the development and change of work meanings are also important to address. If work meanings are indeed related to behavior and performance, then it is important to know how they can be modified in ways consistent with organizational goals.

It is also clear that attention to methodology is necessary for substantial gains in knowledge. This review has noted serious limitations in measures of some work meaning dimensions. Especially in the cases of work values and orientation, large discrepancies exist between conceptual and operational definitions of the dimensions. In order to remedy this, researchers must begin to consider a greater diversity of types of work meanings. Work values other than the work ethic need to be identified. For example, Nord et al. (1988) suggested attention be directed to nonsecular work values and the value systems of other cultures. In an attempt to extend the types of work values considered, Cornelius et al. (1985) utilized critical incident technology to identify values apparent in employee actions. Researchers should also attempt to measure and define work orientation in a content free manner, without reference to a specific set of outcomes.

Another way to expand definitions of work meaning would be to pay more attention to the negative functions of work. Early researchers tended to emphasize the positive meaning of work (e.g., Friedman and Havighurst, 1954), and subsequent investigations have followed this lead. Overwhelmingly, we consider only positively valued work outcomes, although, historically, cultures have often defined work solely in terms of its negative functions. Our preoccupation with positive work meanings may be giving a very one-sided view of the concept (Friedman and Havighurst, 1954). Another interesting aspect of work meaning may well be the positive/negative orientation of the individual toward work. Is work defined primarily in terms of the positive things it brings, or in terms of its negative results? A negative orientation to work may also mean that work is perceived not as bringing positive outcomes, but as averting negative consequences. Such a dimension of work meaning may also have important consequences for work motivation.

A final point must be mentioned. So far, this chapter has looked at dimensions of work meaning singularly, taking each one and considering its implications for motivation and behavior. This approach reflects the nature of research in this area, but it is an oversimplification of the work meaning concept. The meaning of work is a multidimensional construct. This chapter focused on three dimensions, and has suggested a fourth. Other researchers have proposed additional work meaning dimensions that may be important (MOW International Research Team, 1981). The multidimensional nature of the construct means that an individual's work meaning can not be characterized solely by any one of the dimensions alone. Rather, the individual's work meaning, in a larger sense, refers to the pattern defined by all of the dimensions. This is something that research and theory has not considered, yet it may be crucial. For example, it is useful to know how centrality alone is related to behavior. However, values and orientation may interact with centrality for different behavioral consequences. In order to accurately predict the effects of centrality, we may also need to know the individual's standing on the other two dimensions. This means that the behavioral implications resulting from different patterns of work meaning dimensions also need to be explored. We must begin to study the meaning of work as a multidimensional construct.

References

Adams, J.S. (1965). Inequity in social exchange. In L. Berkowitz (ed.), *Advances in experimental social psychology*. New York: Academic Press, pp. 267–300.

Aldag, R.J., and Brief, A.P. (1975). Some correlates of work values. *Journal of Applied Psychology, 60*, pp. 757–60.

———. (1979). Examination of a measure of higher-order need strength. *Human Relations, 32*, pp. 705–18.

Alderfer, C.P. (1969). An empirical test of a new theory of human needs. *Organizational Behavior and Human Performance, 4*, pp. 142–75.

Andrisani, P.J., and Miljus, R.C. (1977). Individual differences in preferences for intrinsic vs. extrinsic aspects of work. *Journal of Vocational Behavior, 11*, pp. 14–30.

Ashford, S.J., and Cummings, L.L. (1983). Feedback as an individual resource: Personal strategies of creating information. *Organizational Behavior and Human Performance, 32*, pp. 370–98.

Baron, R.M., and Ganz, R.I. (1972). Effects of locus of control and type of feedback on the task performance of lower-class black children. *Journal of Personality and Social Psychology, 21*, pp. 124–30.

Baron, R.M., Cowan, G., Ganz, R.I., and McDonald, M. (1974). Interaction of locus of control and type of performance feedback: Considerations of external validity. *Journal of Personality and Social Psychology, 30*, pp. 285–92.

Birnbaum, M.H. (1983). Perceived equity of salary policies. *Journal of Applied Psychology, 68*, pp. 49–59.

Blood, M.R. (1969). Work values and job satisfaction. *Journal of Applied Psychology, 53*, pp. 456–9.

Brief, A.P., Rose, G.L., and Aldag, R.J. (1977). Sex differences in preferences for job attributes revisited. *Journal of Applied Psychology, 62*, pp. 645–6.

Buchanan, B. (1974). Building organizational commitment: The socialization of managers in work organizations. *Administrative Science Quarterly, 19*, pp. 533–46.

Buchholz, R.A. (1977). The belief structure of managers relative to work concepts measured by a factor-analytic model. *Personnel Psychology, 30*, pp. 567–87.

———. (1978). An empirical study of contemporary beliefs about work in American society. *Journal of Applied Psychology, 63*, pp. 219–27.

Calder, B.J., and Staw, B.M. (1975). Self-perception of intrinsic and extrinsic motivation. *Journal of Personality and Social Psychology, 31*, pp. 599–605.

Campbell, J.P., and Pritchard, R.D. (1976). Motivation theory in industrial and organizational psychology. In M.D. Dunnette (ed.), *Handbook of industrial and organizational psychology.* Chicago: Rand McNally, pp. 63–130.

Campion, M.A., and Lord, R.G. (1982). A control systems conceptualization of the goal-setting and changing process. *Organizational Behavior and Human Performance, 30*, pp. 265–87.

Cherrington, D.J. (1980). *The work ethic: Working values and values that work.* New York: Amacom.

Cherrington, D.J., Condie, S.J., and England, J.L. (1979). Age and work values. *Academy of Management Journal, 22*, pp. 617–23.

Cornelius, E.T., Ullman, J.C., Meglino, B.M., Czajka, J., and McNeely, B. (1985). A new approach to the study of worker values and some preliminary results. Paper presented at the Southern Management Association, Orlando, FL.

Cummings, T.G., and Manring, S.L. (1977). The relationship between worker alienation and work-related behavior. *Journal of Vocational Behavior, 10*, pp. 167–79.

Dachler, H.P., and Mobley, W. (1973). Construct validation of an instrumentality-expectancy-task-goal model of work motivation: Some theoretical boundary conditions. *Journal of Applied Psychology, 58*, pp. 397–418.

Deci, E.L. (1971). Effects of externally mediated rewards on extrinsic motivation. *Journal of Personality and Social Psychology, 18*, pp. 105–115.

———. (1975). *Intrinsic motivation.* New York: Plenum Publishing.

Dubin, R. (1956). Industrial workers' worlds: A study of the *Central Life Interests of industrial workers. Social Problems, 3,* pp. 131–42.

Dubin, R., Champoux, J.E., and Porter, L.W. (1975). Central life interests and organizational commitment of blue-collar and clerical workers. *Administrative Science Quarterly, 20,* pp. 411–21.

Dubin, R., Hedley, R.A., and Taveggia, T.C. (1976). Attachment to work. In R. Dubin (ed.), *Handbook of work, organization, and society.* Chicago: Rand McNally, pp. 281–341.

England, G.W. (1975). *The manager and his values: An international perspective from the United States, Japan, Korea, India, and Australia.* Cambridge, MA: Ballinger.

Fox, A. (1980). The meaning of work. In G. Esland, and G. Salaman (eds.), *The politics of work and occupations.* Toronto: University of Toronto Press, pp. 139–91.

Friedlander, F., and Greenberg, S. (1971). Effect of job attitudes, training, and organization climate on performance of the hard-core unemployed. *Journal of Applied Psychology, 55,* pp. 287–95.

Friedman, E.A., and Havighurst, R.J. (1954). *The meaning of work and retirement.* Chicago: University of Chicago Press.

Furnham, A. (1984). The Protestant work ethic: A review of the psychological literature. *European Journal of Social Psychology, 14,* pp. 87–104.

Gorn, G.J., and Kanungo, R.N. (1980). Job involvement and motivation: Are intrinsically motivated managers more job involved? *Organizational Behavior and Human Performance, 26,* pp. 265–77.

Greenberg, J. (1977). The Protestant work ethic and reactions to negative performance evaluations on a laboratory task. *Journal of Applied Psychology, 62,* pp. 682–90.

———. (1979). Protestant work ethic endorsement and the fairness of equity inputs. *Journal of Research in Personality, 13,* pp. 81–90.

Hackman, J.R., and Oldham, G.R. (1976). Motivation through the design of work: Test of a theory. *Organizational Behavior and Human Performance, 16,* pp. 250–79.

Harpaz, I. (1985). Meaning of working profiles of various occupational groups. *Journal of Vocational Behavior, 26,* 25–40.

Heckhausen, H., and Kuhl, J. (1984). From wishes to action: The dead ends and short-cuts on the long way to action. In M. Frese, and J. Sabini (eds.), *Goal directed behavior: Psychological theory and research on action.* Hillsdale, N.J.: Erlbaum, pp. 134–60.

Herzberg, F. (1966). *Work and the nature of man.* Cleveland, OH: World Publishing.

Herzberg, F., Mausner, B., and Snyderman, B.B. (1959). *The motivation to work.* New York: Wiley.

Hoelscher, T.J., Klinger, E., and Barta, S.G. (1981). Incorporation of concern- and nonconcern-related verbal stimuli into dream content. *Journal of Abnormal Psychology, 90,* pp. 88–91.

Kanungo, R.N. (1982). *Work alienation: An integrative approach.* New York: Praeger.

Kaufman, D., and Fetters, M.L. (1980). Work motivation and job values among professional men and women: A new accounting. *Journal of Vocational Behavior, 17,* pp. 251–62.

Kazanas, H.C. (1978). Relationship of job satisfaction and productivity to work values of vocational education graduates. *Journal of Vocational Behavior, 12,* pp. 155–64.

Klinger, E. (1977). *Meaning and void: Inner experience and the incentives in people's lives.* Minneapolis, MN: University of Minnesota Press.

———. (1978). Modes of normal conscious flow. In K.S. Pope and J.L. Singer, (eds.), *The stream of consciousness: Scientific investigations into the flow of human experience.* New York: Plenum Press, pp. 225–54.

Klinger, E., Barta, S.G. and Maxeiner, M.E. (1980). Motivational correlates of thought content frequency and commitment. *Journal of Personality and Social Psychology, 39,* pp. 1222–37.

Korman, A.K., Greenhaus, J.H., and Badin, I.J. (1977). Personnel attitudes and motivation. *Annual Review of Psychology, 28,* pp. 175–96.

Lacy, W.B., Bokemeier, J.L., and Shepard, J.M. (1983). Job attribute preferences and work commitment of men and women in the United States. *Personnel Psychology, 36,* pp. 315–29.

Lawler, E.E. (1973). *Motivation in work organizations.* Monterey, CA: Brooks/Cole.

Lawler, E.E., and Hall, D.T. (1970). Relationships of job characteristics to job involvement, satisfaction, and intrinsic motivation. *Journal of Applied Psychology, 54,* pp. 305–12.

Lepper, M.R., and Greene, D. (1975). Turning play into work: Effects of adult surveillance and extrinsic rewards on children's intrinsic motivation. *Journal of Personality and Social Psychology, 31,* pp. 479–86.

Lied, T.R., and Pritchard, R.D. (1976). Relationships between personality variables and components of the expectancy-valence model. *Journal of Applied Psychology, 61,* pp. 463–7.

Locke, E.A. (1968). Toward a theory of task motivation and incentives. *Organizational Behavior and Human Performance, 3,* pp. 157–89.

Locke, E.A., and Henne, D. (1986). Work motivation theories. In C.L. Cooper and I. Robertson (eds.), *International review of industrial and organizational psychology.* New York: Wiley, pp. 1–35.

Locke, E.A., Shaw, K.N., Saari, L.M., and Latham, G.P. (1981). Goal setting and task performance: 1969–1980. *Psychological Bulletin, 90,* pp. 125–52.

Lodahl, T.M., and Kejner, M. (1965). The definition and measurement of job involvement. *Journal of Applied Psychology, 49,* pp. 24–33.

Maslow, A.H. (1943). A theory of motivation. *Psychological Review, 50,* pp. 370–96.

McGregor, D.M. (1973). The human side of enterprise. In V.H. Vroom and E.L. Deci (eds.), *Management and Motivation.* Baltimore, MD: Penguin Books, pp. 302–19.

Mento, A.J., Cartledge, N.D., and Locke, E.A. (1980). Maryland vs. Michigan vs. Minnesota: Another look at the relationship of expectancy and goal difficulty to task performance. *Organizational Behavior and Human Performance, 25,* pp. 419–40.

Merrens, M., and Garrett, J. (1975). The Protestant ethic scale as a predictor of repetitive work performance. *Journal of Applied Psychology, 60,* pp. 125–27.

Mills, C.W. (1973). The meanings of work throughout history. In F. Best (ed.), *The future of work.* Englewood Cliffs, N.J. Prentice Hall, pp. 6–14.

Mirels, H.L., and Garrett, J.B. (1971). The Protestant ethic as a personality variable. *Journal of Consulting and Clinical Psychology, 36,* pp. 40–4.

Morrow, P.C. (1983). Concept redundancy in organizational research: The case of work commitment. *Academy of Management Review, 8,* pp. 486–500.

Morse, N.C., and Weiss, R.S. (1955). The function and meaning of work and the job. *American Sociological Review, 20,* pp. 191–8.

Mossholder, K.W., Bedeian, A.G., Touliatos, J., and Barkman, A.I. (1985). An examination of intraoccupational differences: Personality, perceived work climate, and outcome preferences. *Journal of Vocational Behavior, 26,* pp. 164–76.

MOW International Research Team (1981). The meaning of working. In G. Dlugos, and K. Weiermair (eds.), *Management under differing value systems: Political, social, and economical perspectives in a changing world.* Berlin and New York: deGruyter, pp. 565–92.

Mowday, R.T. (1987). Equity theory predictions of behavior in organizations. In R.M. Steers, and L.W. Porter (eds.), *Motivation and Work Behavior.* 4th ed. New York: McGraw-Hill, pp. 89–110.

Naylor, J.C., Pritchard, R.D., and Ilgen, D.R. (1980). *A theory of behavior in organizations.* New York: Academic Press.

Nord, W.R., Brief, A.P., Atieh, J.M., and Doherty, E.M. (1985). Work values and the conduct of organizational behavior. In B.M. Staw, and L.L. Cummings (eds.), *Research in organizational behavior, 10,* pp. 1–42.

O'Reilly, C.A., and Caldwell, D.F. (1985). The impact of normative social influence and cohesiveness on task perceptions and attitudes: A social information processing approach. *Journal of Occupational Psychology, 58,* pp. 193–206.

Pearce, J.L. (1987). Making sense of volunteer motivation: The sufficiency of justification hypothesis. In R.M. Steers, and L.W. Porter (eds.), *Motivation and work behavior.* 4th ed. New York: McGraw-Hill, pp. 545–53.

Pfeffer, J. (1980). A partial test of the social information processing model of job attitudes. *Human Relations, 33,* pp. 457–76.

Phillips, J.S., and Freedman, S.M.. (1985). Contingent pay and intrinsic task interest: Moderating effects of work values. *Journal of Applied Psychology, 70,* pp. 306–13.

Pinder, C.C. (1984). *Work motivation: Theory, issues, and applications.* Glenview, IL: Scott, Foresman.

Porac, J.F., and Salancik, G.R. (1981). Generic overjustification: The interaction of extrinsic rewards. *Organizational Behavior and Human Performance, 27,* pp. 197–212.

Pryor, R. (1982). Values, preferences, needs, work ethics, and orientations to work: Toward a conceptual and empirical integration. *Journal of Vocational Behavior, 20,* pp. 40–52.

Rabinowitz, S., and Hall, D.T. (1977). Organizational research on job involvement. *Psychological Bulletin, 84,* pp. 265–88.

Rabinowitz, S., Hall, D.T., and Goodale, J.G. (1977). Job scope and individual differences as predictors of job involvement: Independent or interactive? *Academy of Management Journal, 20,* pp. 273–81.

Rabinowitz, S., and Hall, D.T. (1981). Changing correlates of job involvement in three career stages. *Journal of Vocational Behavior, 18,* pp. 138–44.

Rakestraw, T.L., and Weiss, H.M. (1981). The interaction of social influences and task experience on goals, performance, and performance satisfaction. *Organizational Behavior and Human Performance, 27,* pp. 326–44.

Rhodes, S.R. (1983). Age-related differences in work attitudes and behavior: A review and conceptual analysis. *Psychological Bulletin, 93,* pp. 328–67.

Roberson, L. (1989). Assessing personal work goals in the organizational setting: Development and evaluation of the Work Concerns Inventory. *Organizational Behavior and Human Decision Processes, 44,* pp. 345–67.

Rokeach, M. (1973). *The nature of human values.* New York: Free Press.

Ronen, S. (1978). Personal values: A basis for work motivational set and work attitude. *Organizational Behavior and Human Performance, 21,* pp. 80–107.

Rose, M. (1985). *Re-working the work ethic: Economic values and socio-cultural politics.* New York: Schocken Books.

Ryan, T.A. (1970). *Intentional behavior: An approach to human motivation.* New York: Ronald Press.

Salancik, G.R., and Pfeffer, J. (1977). An examination of need-satisfaction models of job attitudes. *Administrative Science Quarterly, 22,* pp. 427–56.

———. (1978). A social information processing approach to job attitudes and task design. *Administrative Science Quarterly, 23,* pp. 224–53.

Saleh, S.D., and Hosek, J. (1976). Job involvement: Concepts and measures. *Academy of Management Journal, 19,* pp. 213–24.

Slovik, P., Fischoff, B., and Lichtenstein, S. (1977). Behavioral decision theory. *Annual Review of Psychology, 28,* pp. 1–39.

Stahl, M.J., and Harrell, A.M. (1981). Modeling effort decisions with behavioral decision theory: Toward an individual differences model of expectancy theory. *Organizational Behavior and Human Performance, 27,* pp. 303–15.

Staw, B.M. (1976). *Intrinsic and extrinsic motivation.* Morristown, NJ: General Learning Press.

———. (1977). Motivation in organizations: Toward synthesis and redirection. In B.M. Staw, and G. Salancık (eds.), *New directions in organizational behavior,* vol. 1. Chicago: St. Clair Press, pp. 54–95.

———. (1984). Organizational behavior: A review and reformulation of the field's outcome variables. *Annual Review of Psychology, 35,* pp. 627–66.

Taveggia, T.C., and Ziemba, T. (1978). Linkages to work: A study of the *Central Life Interests* and *Work Attachments* of male and female workers. *Journal of Vocational Behavior, 12,* pp. 305–20.

Taylor, M.S., Fisher, C.D., and Ilgen, D.R. (1984). Individual's reactions to performance feedback in organizations: A control theory perspective. *Research in Personnel and Human Resources Management, 2,* pp. 81–124.

Taylor, R.N., and Thompson, M. (1976). Work value systems of younger workers. *Academy of Management Journal, 19,* pp. 522–36.

Turner, A.N., and Lawrence, P.R. (1965). *Industrial jobs and the worker.* Cambridge: Harvard University Press.

Vecchio, R.P. (1981). An individual differences interpretation of the conflicting predictions generated by equity theory and expectancy theory. *Journal of Applied Psychology, 66,* pp. 470–81.

Vroom, V.H. (1964). *Work and motivation.* New York: Wiley.

Wanous, J. (1974). Individual differences and reactions to job characteristics. *Journal of Applied Psychology, 59,* pp. 616–22.

Watson, J., and Williams, J. (1977). Relationship between managerial values and managerial success of black and white managers. *Journal of Applied Psychology, 62,* pp. 205–7.

Weick, K.E., Bougon, M.G., and Maruyama, G. (1976). The equity context. *Organizational Behavior and Human Performance, 15,* pp. 32–65.

Weiss, H.M. (1978). Social learning of work values in organizations. *Journal of Applied Psychology, 63,* pp. 711–8.

Weiss, H.M., and Adler, S. (1984). Personality and organizational behavior. In B.M. Staw, and L.L. Cummings (eds.), *Research in organizational behavior,* vol. 6. Greenwich, CT: JAI Press, pp. 1–50.

Wiener, Y., and Gechman, A.S. (1977). Commitment: A behavioral approach to job involvement. *Journal of Vocational Behavior, 10,* pp. 47–52.

Wiener, Y., and Vardi, Y. (1980). Relationships between job, organizational, and career commitments and work outcomes—An integrative approach. *Organizational Behavior and Human Performance, 26,* pp. 81–96.

Wollack, S., Goodale, J.G., Witjing, J.P., and Smith, P.C. (1971). Development of the survey of work values. *Journal of Applied Psychology, 55,* pp. 331–8.

Yukl, G.A., and Latham, G.P. (1978). Interrelationships among employee participation, individual differences, goal difficulty, goal acceptance, goal instrumentality, and performance. *Personnel Psychology, 31,* pp. 305–23.

5

Stress, Coping, and
the Meaning of Work

Edwin A. Locke
M. Susan Taylor

No I'm not disturbed any more. If I was just starting on this job, I probably would. But the older I get, I realize its a farce. You just get used to it. It's a job. I get my paycheck—that's it. It's all political anyway.

—Terkel (1972, p. 155)

And working is my life. If you took that away from me, it would be worse than killing me. I've inherited the Yorkshire value of work from my father. Being idle wasn't what my father believed in.

—Henry Moore (in Chandler, 1982, p. 183)

As these two quotations indicate, the meaning of work varies widely among individuals in our society. While each of us can observe this variation from personal experience, the research literature provides even stronger evidence of such differences. In one of the earliest studies on the meaning of work, Morse and Weiss (1955) examined a sample of 401 American males, and found that individuals in middle-class and farming occupations tended to emphasize the intrinsic interest and significance of their work, whereas those in lower-class occupations viewed work simply as an activity that kept them busy. Similarly, Near, Rice, and Hunt (1980) reviewed the literature on work and nonwork domains and concluded that the importance of work varied by occupation; people in higher skilled jobs saw their work as more important than those in lower skilled jobs. Finally, Buchholz (1978) examined the work beliefs of over one thousand individuals including employees, union leaders, and managers and found individual differences according to age, education, and occupation. Young people displayed a stronger pro-work ethic than did older people, and those with graduate education expected more intrinsic outcomes (for instance, interest or challenge) from their work than those with less education.

These findings reflect considerable inter-individual variance in the meaning of work. By the *meaning of work* we mean the totality of values including their importance that individuals seek and expect to derive from work. Values themselves are what individuals desire or consider to be good or beneficial. They have been defined as "that which one acts to gain and/or keep" (Rand,

1964), and they serve to govern individuals' emotional responses as well as to guide their choices and actions (Locke, 1976). Values have been described as the motivational link between inborn needs and action (Locke and Henne, 1986).

Although individuals generally begin work with a set of work values, we believe these values both affect and are affected by the experiences encountered in the workplace. These experiences are due partly to factors within the individuals' control (for instance, effort, or new learning) and partly to factors outside their control (such as, economic conditions). Therefore people may succeed in getting what they want from work or they may fail and experience conflict between what they desire and expect and what is experienced. This conflict may yield disappointment, frustration, and/or stress, causing individuals periodically to appraise and draw conclusions about their work experiences. As a result they may change their actions, expectations, values—or all of these. Depending on how individuals respond or cope after appraisal, work may come to hold either more or less personal meaning.

In this chapter we shall explore the process described above, by: identifying the values that individuals seek to derive from work; showing how conflicts between these values and work experiences may produce stress; identifying the methods used to cope with stress; and discussing the implications of different coping methods for the meaning of work. We begin with a discussion of work values.

Work Values and the Meaning of Work

Our review of the literature suggests that there are at least five different categories of values that people may seek to fulfill at work. These are similar but not identical to the categories developed by Rokeach (1960; 1973) for values in general and include: 1) material values (such as Rokeach's comfortable life, money, family security); 2) achievement-related values (Rokeach's sense of accomplishment, freedom, and wisdom; 3) a sense of purpose (Rokeach's inner harmony); 4) social relationships (Rokeach's true friendship and social recognition); and 5) enhancement or maintenance of the self-concept (Rokeach's self-respect).

For a relatively large segment of the population, work seems to be of value primarily because of its association with material outcomes, especially money. This meaning has been termed the *economic function by Morse and Weiss (1955) and the instrumental* function by Locke, Sirota, and Wolfson (1976). In an explanation of clerical workers' indifferent reactions to job enrichment, Locke et al. (1976) offered the following observations about the relative importance of material and achievement-related values:

The workers' greatest concern was to get good ratings so that they could get promoted and get more pay. Many had given up more interesting jobs in order to take their present ones. They were quite willing, if not anxious, to have more interesting tasks but only on the condition that some practical benefit would result. (p. 710)

Those who work primarily to fulfill material values are not limited to lower status occupational groups. Mortimer and Lorence (1979) surveyed a male sample of 513 college students at graduation and followed them up ten years later. The researchers found that the students who placed a high value on extrinsic (material) rewards later chose the highest paying jobs. However, to say that material outcomes are important to people is not to say that these are the only values people derive from work. For example, Yankelovich and Immerwahr (1983) found that only 31 percent of a national sample agreed with the statement that work was "purely a business transaction."

A second meaning of work concerns achievement-related values such as autonomy, success, challenge, growth, interest, and variety. This meaning was emphasized by the *Work in American Report* (1973) which proclaimed that all was not well with work in the United States because significant numbers of employed workers were locked into "dull, repetitive, [and] seemingly meaningless tasks, offering little challenge or autonomy" (pp. xv). Indeed the assumed desirability of job characteristics such as autonomy, significance, and variety, forms the conceptual basis for much of the job enrichment literature (Aldag and Brief, 1979; Griffin, 1982; Hackman and Oldham, 1976, 1980). Furthermore, like material values, the achievement-related values also seem to affect subsequent job choice. In the study described earlier by Mortimer and Lorence (1979), those college students who valued achievement-related outcomes most highly in their senior year were found in jobs providing the highest levels of autonomy when resurveyed ten years later.

Research findings suggest that the achievement-related aspects of work are primary for only a small segment of society. For example, Morse and Weiss (1955) reported that only 5 percent of their sample listed "feelings of interest" and only 12 percent listed "the kind of work performed" as reasons for continuing to work. Furthermore, the work of Dalton and Thompson (1986) on the career stages of professionals seems to restrict the primacy of an achievement-focused work meaning to an even smaller subgroup—professionals working on individual tasks. The researchers noted:

Why do most of the instances that we heard about concerning a deep interest in work involve unusual circumstances? Perhaps it is because in our society, a certain level of interest in one's work is expected among professionally trained individuals. But even if a certain level of interest is considered normal, we did not find that a deep and absorbing interest in one's work was a universal condition among professionals. . . . Interestingly, both White's examples of "deeply interested" individuals, and our own examples tended to be individuals performing individual tasks. (p. 226)

Work may also provide individuals with a sense of purpose. It may help them to keep active, to organize their activities and their lives on a daily basis, and to feel that they are doing something significant. For example, Super (1986) noted that in our society being without a job symbolizes a loss of role, purpose, and meaning, and proposed that one major function of work was to provide a way of structuring time. Similarly, Sofer (1970) stated that work provides individuals with ways to structure the passage of time and to demonstrate their productive ability. Finally, 47 percent of Morse and Weiss's (1955) sample reported that they would continue to work even if economically secure because of positive reasons related to the purposeful aspect of work (e.g., keeps one occupied—32 percent; justifies one's existence—5 percent; keeps one healthy—10 percent). Another 37 percent listed negative reasons relevant to the structuring meaning (e.g., feel lost—14 percent; feel useless—2 percent; feel bored—4 percent; not know what to do with one's time—10 percent; habit—6 percent; "keep out of trouble"—1 percent).

A fourth meaning of work is based on social relationships that provide opportunities to interact with others, share information, attain visibility, and receive feedback and recognition for one's accomplishments. Super (1986) has identified social support and the prestige of others as primary meanings of work, while Sofer (1970) noted that having a work role provides opportunities simply to interact with others. Furthermore, a full 31 percent of the Morse and Weiss (1955) sample listed "the people known through or at work" as one of the things that would be missed if they stopped working. The importance of the social relationship meaning is further emphasized by the fact that a primary method of job analysis classifies jobs according to the level of interactions required with people (Fine and Wiley, 1971).

A final meaning of work concerns its significance for the self-concept. In an extensive study of adult developmental stages conducted on a cross section of American males, Levinson and his colleagues (1978) found that one of the primary tasks of early adulthood is forming the "Dream"—individuals' sense of self-in-the-adult-world that generally involve vocational accomplishments. Levinson et al. (1978) found that individuals' timely progression toward achievement of the Dream during early adulthood was highly related to their self-concept and life purpose. In their words:

If the Dream remains unconnected to his life, it may simply die and with it his sense of aliveness and purpose. Those who betray the Dream in their twenties will have to deal later with the consequences. Those who build a life structure around the Dream in early adulthood have a better chance for personal fulfillment, though years of struggle may be required to maintain the commitment and work towards its realization. (p. 92)

Similarly, Markus (1986) has introduced the concept of possible selves which represents individuals' ideas of what they might become, would like to become, and are afraid of becoming. The possible self is believed to be a conceptual link between cognition and motivation that may provide means-ends patterns for new behavior, as well as additional meaning for current behavior. Markus has included occupational fields, or work, as one of the six proposed domains of the possible self.

The relationship of work to individuals' self-concept is also supported by other research. Morse and Weiss (1955) found that 9 percent of their sample indicated that "feelings of doing something important or worthwhile," and "feelings of self-respect" would be the things missed if they did not work. Bailyn (1977) classified a sample of MIT graduates into two categories—those who said that family needs were primary and those who said career success was most important. Ten to twenty years later, individuals who displayed a marked subordination of career to family interests tended to demonstrate low self-confidence, low interest in the nature of their work, and a lower probability of holding managerial positions. Finally, Evans and Bartolome (1980) interviewed a sample of 532 business managers and their wives from several different countries. Managers who had not yet reached their mid-forties reported that what happened at work had powerful effects on life at home, but there were few reports of spillover in the opposite direction. However, the researchers noted that after forty, managers' family lives seemed to have a greater impact on their self-concepts. Thus, there is considerable evidence that individuals' work experiences may be central to their self-concepts, at least in the case of males prior to age forty.

In summary, we have provided evidence that the value or meaning of work varies across individuals; and we have proposed that individuals may expect and desire to fulfill five different categories of values from their work—material values, achievement-related values, a sense of purpose, social relationships, and the enhancement or maintenance of the self-concept. The extent to which work is personally meaningful to people may change over time as individuals have successful or unsuccessful experiences and make changes in their actions, expectations, and/or values. Furthermore, previous research suggests that there is a cyclical process whereby work values influence individuals' occupational choices, and that the experiences encountered in the chosen occupations may reinforce their original values (Brousseau, 1978; Brousseau and Prince, 1981; Kohn and Schooler, 1978, 1982; Mortimer and Lorence, 1979). However, for most people the attainment of work-related values, even when earnestly sought after, is virtually never automatic.

Attainment entails overcoming obstacles, setbacks, and challenges. Insofar as such situations are perceived as a threat, the individual will experience stress. How the individual copes with such stress may have profound implications for subsequent health and well-being. Let us therefore consider the nature of stress in some detail.

The Nature of Stress

Although the topic of stress has been the subject of tens of thousands of articles over the past decades, it has rarely been defined intelligibly. Selye's (1976) well-known conceptualization: "the nonspecific response of the body to any demand," is frequently cited; however, this definition is useless from a psychological perspective because it describes only the body's reaction to physical stress. Psychologically-based definitions, even when given, are often excessively vague. Thus we believe it important to clearly identify the nature of stress. We shall begin by identifying the key elements of the stress situation and then provide a working definition. We conceptualize stress as involving four elements (see Locke and Latham, 1984).

1. Threat. We agree with Lazarus and Folkman (1984) and Arnold (1960) that stress is experienced when the individual appraises a state or condition as threatening to his safety or well-being. More specifically, there is a perceived object, event, idea, or situation which the individual is aware of directly or peripherially and which he judges subconsciously to be a threat to his values (see Lazarus and Folkman (1984) who use the term *commitments*). The more fundamental values typically used as implicit standards for appraisal are: (a) the value of one's own person qua physical entity. This threat involves something appraised as physically dangerous, harmful, or painful, such as, electric shock, radiation, germs, a robber or rapist, a swerving car, or an enemy soldier; or (b) the value of one's own person qua psychological entity or qua total person. The threats in this case are to individuals' self-esteem, their estimates of their worth, and sense of adequacy as persons. Thus, for example, individuals who base their self-esteem almost totally upon the approval of others and are then criticized by a "significant other" will feel deeply inadequate or feel fundamental doubt about their adequacy.

2. Felt Need for Action. Implicit in the stress situation is the assumption that action must be taken to deal with the threat, whether physical or psychological, such as the need to regain self-control in the face of anxiety. This feature of the stress situation is so taken for granted that people are typically not aware of it, but its significance can be seen by observing the reaction of people who conclude—at the deepest level—that no action of any significance can be taken. For example, in cases of fatal illnesses, when individuals have totally accepted the fact that nothing can be done and that there is no hope whatever, they then become calm, withdrawn, and disinterested in life (Kübler-Ross, 1969). There is passive resignation but no stress. Similarly, concentration camp inmates who give up all hope no longer experience stress. They become living corpses—and then dead ones (Dimsdale, 1974).

3. Uncertainty. If there is certainty—again, at the deepest level—that nothing can be done and that the situation is clear and will not change, then there is, as noted above, no stress but instead passive resignation. On the other side of the same coin, if the individual is totally certain that he can cope with the situation, then, again, there is no stress. We make no specific assumptions here regarding the effects of different degrees of uncertainty. Lazarus and Folkman (1984), however, suggest that the greater the uncertainty the greater the stress.

There are many different types of uncertainties involved in stress situations (see Folkman, Schaefer, and Lazarus, 1979). These include uncertainties about: (a) what the exact nature of the threat is (e.g., Will the plant close, or will there just be layoffs or a shortened work week?); (b) whether the situation will change sooner or later (e.g., Will the economy slump?); (c) what action is the appropriate one to take (e.g., Should I look for a new job or wait things out?); (d) whether or not one can take the requisite cognitive and overt actions (e.g., Can I find another job? Can I learn another skill? Can I make myself act when I am so afraid?); (e) what the outcome(s) will be and whether or not one can deal with them (e.g., If I lose my job will I then lose my house? My spouse? Will I start drinking again?).

The core uncertainty, in terms of its implications for stress, may be the individual's perceived ability to take the requisite overt action: the higher the confidence that one can take the needed action, the lower the degree of stress that will be experienced (Anderson, Hellriegel, and Slocum, 1977). Bandura (1982) calls the conviction that one can carry out a specific course of action *self-efficacy*. Self-efficacy refers to task specific self-confidence. Research has shown that the higher the degree of self-efficacy in a given situation, the lower the degree of stress or fear that will be experienced by individuals in that situation (Bandura, 1988, p. 443). One reason for this is that self-efficacy is based to a considerable extent on mastery experiences (demonstrated skill); thus individuals with high self-efficacy are less threatened because they know they have dealt with such situations successfully in the past and can do so again.

Without high self-efficacy, the freedom to make choices as such in a stress situation does not necessarily lead to reduced stress (Averill, 1973). Similarly, predictability as such does not always reduce stress. What seems to be more essential is the conviction not that one can choose or predict but that one can exert *control* over the situation, even if the belief about having control is false

(Bandura, 1986; Geer, Davison, and Gatchel, 1970; Gilmore, 1978; Glass, Singer, and Friedman, 1969; Glass, Reim, and Singer, 1971). Choice and predictability actually can increase experienced stress, if there are doubts about whether the situation can be controlled (Bandura, 1986).

Information as such can reduce stress by reducing uncertainty (Hamburg and Adams, 1967; Miller, 1979). Relevant information might include (a) information about the meaning of sensory experiences (see, e.g., Holmes and Houston, 1974); or (b) information about how to cope or respond, behaviorally or cognitively (Averill, 1979). Such information can diminish the threat of a situation (Doering and Entwisle, 1975) and/or heighten self-efficacy—and therefore result in better coping (Egbert et al., 1964). People who feel confident about being in control experience less stress and are more likely to perform well under pressure. Subsequently, they feel more in control. The opposite is true of those who lack confidence and then perform poorly (Anderson, 1977). Thus the relation between self-efficacy and successful coping is reciprocal.

Self-efficacy, however, is not based solely on past performance. It also reveals the implicit conclusions individuals have reached about themselves from past performance. If they conclude, for example, that, although they did well, they were very nervous and might go to pieces next time, their self-efficacy will be lower than that of people who performed equally well in the past but who concluded that they were in total control. Individuals who have high self-efficacy estimates for many situations presumably would develop high generalized self-efficacy and would be likely to respond (with equanimity) even to totally new stress situations. In contrast people who habitually "freak out" when anything goes wrong would be likely to react with high anxiety to new threat situations. One means of increasing self-efficacy is through acquiring self-control (self-regulation) skills that enable one to decrease anxiety caused by new situations and thereby increase the chances of performing effectively (Rosenbaum and Merbaum, 1984).

Finally, it should be noted that we are not in full agreement with Lazarus and Folkman (1984) concerning when feelings of self-efficacy come into play during stress situations. These authors distinguish between primary appraisal (response to the threat itself) and secondary appraisal (response to the threat in view of one's perceived ability to cope). While agreeing that there can be multiple appraisals (reappraisals) of any situation as events develop and new knowledge is discovered, we believe that *every* appraisal includes current estimates about one's current coping ability in relation to the situation. Thus there are not two separate appraisals of each situation but only one. We believe that people with high self-efficacy actually appraise situations more benignly than do low self-efficacy individuals. To contrast the difference between Lazarus and Folkman's (1984) position and ours, we disagree with their implied view that high self-efficacy people first experience threat, then realize that they can cope, and then experience less threat; while low self-efficacy people experience threat, then realize they cannot cope, and then experience more threat. Rather, we believe that individuals high in self-efficacy experience less threat from the very beginning. Thus, we propose that *all appraisals automatically include one's evaluation of the total situation* as it is implicitly perceived, including potential threats in relation to one's ability to deal with them.

4. Emotions and Other Symptoms. As a result of appraising a situation as threatening, believing that action is needed, and feeling that the outcome is uncertain, individuals experience an emotional reaction. The type of emotion experienced differs depending on the nature of the threat. In the case of a direct physical threat, the emotion is fear. When self-esteem is threatened the person experiences self-doubt and anxiety (Packer, 1985/1986). When something of value is lost, people experience sadness. Upon concluding that something of great importance is irreparably lost, including their own self-worth, people experience depression. If they believe others are in some way responsible for their plight, anger will be experienced. However, fear and especially anxiety are usually the core emotions in stress situations, whether acute or chronic.

The intensity of the emotional reaction will depend on such factors as the perceived degree, chronicity, and duration of the threat, the importance of the value, the perceived ability to cope, and probably one's personal physiology, since some people seem to be temperamentally more reactive than others. In addition, individuals under stress may experience various physical symptoms or physiological reactions (e.g., asthma, faintness, headaches, etc.) which, because they are painful, unpleasant, and even dangerous, become an added source of stress.

Another aspect of the stress situation is that of conflict (Space Science Board, 1972). On the one hand, there is an implicit or explicit desire to escape from the situation in order to eliminate the fear or anxiety; and on the other hand, there is a desire to deal with or remove the threat in order to preserve or protect the value. For example, to avoid failure on the job, one might be tempted to resign; but then one might lose both self-respect and practical benefits such as pay, so there is also a desire to stay and succeed. Similarly, a person who gives up his or her job or career and yet still longs for satisfaction from it would continue to experience some conflict and therefore some stress.

In summary, we have integrated the previous points about stress and now provide a comprehensive definition of it:

Stress is the emotional response, typically consisting of fear and/or anxiety and associated physical symptoms, resulting from: (a) the appraisal of an object, situation, outcome, or idea, as threatening to one's physical or psycho-

logical well-being or self-esteem; (b) the implicit belief that action needs to be taken to deal with the threat thus producing conflict; and (c) felt uncertainty regarding one's ability to successfully identify and carry out the requisite action.

The experience of stress generally stimulates individuals' attempts to cope with the situation. Let us now consider the nature of coping.

Coping with Stress

Our definition of stress and the model on which it is based imply the existence of alternative ways of coping. One basic categorization of coping techniques, which has been suggested many times in the literature (see e.g., Lazarus and Folkman, 1984), is the dichotomy of emotion-focused or symptomatic versus problem-focused or causal coping. In the former case, individuals attempt merely to alleviate the bad feelings stemming from the stress; and in the latter, they try to remove the factors that brought about the feelings.

The cause-symptom dichotomy is related to Roth and Cohen's (1986) recently offered approach-avoidance dichotomy in coping, whereby one displays activity that is oriented toward or away from the threat. However, there are problems with their dichotomy. Sometimes coping can entail both approach and avoidance (e.g., confronting a poor employee, then firing him). Also it fails to distinguish between cognitive and behavioral coping mechanisms. Latack (1984) added cognitive reappraisal (a type of causal focus) to the previous two categories to make a trichotomy. To complete the categorization, we propose a 2 × 2 breakdown with: symptom focus versus causal focus on the one hand, and intra-psychic focus (cognitive reappraisal) versus action focus on the other. This model is shown in figure 5–1. The cognitive (intra-psychic) behavior distinction is admittedly hard to make because thought and action typically go together and because thoughts can focus on both symptoms and planned actions. Nevertheless we believe it to be a useful conceptual distinction because the effectiveness of cognitive and behavioral coping mechanisms seems likely to vary with the circumstances. Therefore, individuals who are able to use the most suitable approach are likely to deal more effectively with stress than those who use the same approach to every situation.

Observe that in the model in figure 5–1, social support is placed in the middle of the figure, rather than in any one cell because social support can pertain to many different coping procedures depending on the specific actions that other people take. Thus it will be discussed last.

Symptom/Cognitive Focus. The classic method of coping in this category is the use of defense mechanisms. *Defense mechanisms* are subconscious mental

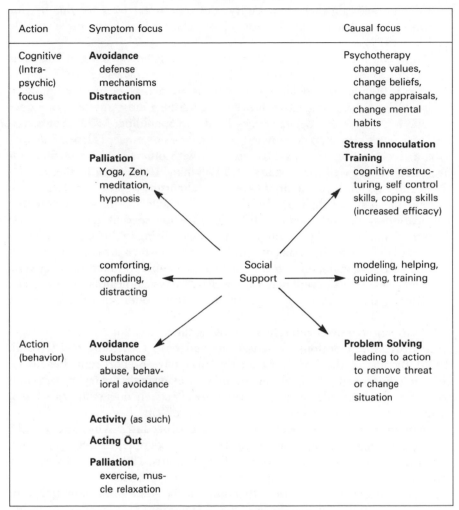

Action	Symptom focus		Causal focus
Cognitive (Intra-psychic) focus	**Avoidance** defense mechanisms **Distraction**		Psychotherapy change values, change beliefs, change appraisals, change mental habits
	Palliation Yoga, Zen, meditation, hypnosis		**Stress Innoculation Training** cognitive restruc- turing, self control skills, coping skills (increased efficacy)
	comforting, confiding, distracting	Social Support	modeling, helping, guiding, training
Action (behavior)	**Avoidance** substance abuse, behav- ioral avoidance		**Problem Solving** leading to action to remove threat or change situation
	Activity (as such) **Acting Out** **Palliation** exercise, mus- cle relaxation		

Figure 5–1. Coping Model

habits which act to protect the individual in the short term from painful feel-ings and threats to self-esteem. Psychodynamic therapists would argue that the core defense mechanism is repression, in which painful emotions or the appraisals leading to such emotions are blocked from entering awareness.

There is no denying that defense mechanisms "work" in the short run in the sense of protecting people from painful feelings. In extreme situations such as concentration camps, defense mechanisms may even be necessary (even if not sufficient) for survival (Benner, Roskies, and Lazarus, 1980; Dimsdale, 1974). Similarly children who come from very disturbed homes may need to defend, such as by repression and distancing themselves from their parents, in order to maintain their own sanity. But they suffer later for this by, for example, being unable to develop close relationships with other people (Lublin, 1979).

Some confusion exists in the literature regarding how defense mechanisms contribute to psychological functioning. A continuing legacy of Freudian thought is the idea that defense mechanisms are necessary for psychological health. Advocates of this view, however, describe almost anything one does to cope with stress as a defense (e.g., Ford and Spaulding, 1973). For example, a patient's refusal to acknowledge a diagnosis of cancer is labeled *denial,* as is a second patient's refusal to discuss it with others or the assertion that he surely will get well (see Lazarus and Folkman, 1984, for a further discussion of this issue). If one defines defense mechanisms as mental habits which prevent the acknowledgment of reality, when reality has actual or potential implications for action, then it is difficult to see how (except in extreme cases) such mechanisms could promote health and well-being in the long run. Thus, we regard defense mechanisms as unhealthy habits which distort or deny reality and therefore make one, in the long run, less able to function effectively. Such mechanisms can even increase the risk to physical health—for example, by denying the existence of a treatable medical condition (Benner et al., 1980).

Distraction or diversion refers to moving the focus of one's attention away from distressing emotions or sensations and onto something else (Averill, 1979; Bloom, et al., 1977). Again this may have a short-term benefit by reducing the tendency to dwell on and thereby exaggerate the feeling or symptom. It may also enable one to perform more effectively on a temporary basis, although it does not resolve the underlying problem.

Cognitive palliation refers to cognitive procedures which help make negative feelings or symptoms less intense. For example, in Zen, yoga, and meditation (Goleman and Schwartz, 1976; Shapiro, 1985) the individual attempts to relax while removing thoughts about the external world from his mind and focusing inward on either nothing or some innocuous image or sound. By becoming passive, he lets stressful emotions fade away, so to speak.

A more active cognitive method is biofeedback which helps the individual develop physical self-regulation skills. It has been used with some success to treat headaches (Adams, Feuerstein, and Fowler, 1980; Blanchard, Ahles, and Shaw, 1979; Feuerstein and Gainer, 1982). However, the mechanisms underlying its success are not clear. Andrasik and Holroyd (1980) found that subjects under biofeedback treatment employed multiple headache control strategies including new behaviors; thus more than palliation was involved. Like defense mechanisms and distraction, palliation does not remove the underlying problem.

Symptom/Action Focus. Actions in this category function essentially in the same way as mental operations such as defense mechanisms in the symptom/cognitive category. One can avoid situations just as one avoids thoughts—and with the same result. For example, consider the agoraphobic who avoids leaving the house. He feels better in the short term but this does not solve the underlying problem and may make it worse. A claustrophobic who begins avoiding small rooms may soon feel he has to avoid elevators, closets, offices, buses, cars, and planes. The end result is an extremely restricted life style in which every moment is governed not by desire but by fear.

Similarly, *substance abuse* (drinking, narcotics) does not cure the problem causing the bad feelings, but only makes one temporarily unaware of those feelings—and may bring about long-term physical harm as well.

Activity for the sake of activity functions much like cognitive distraction (Chodoff, Friedman, and Hamburg, 1984). It takes one's mind temporarily off the negative thoughts and feelings, as in, for example, a housewife worried about her husband's infidelity frantically doing housework.

Acting out might be considered a method of *noncoping* since it refers simply to expressing the bad feelings one has, as when an angry boss screams at a subordinate for spending too much time at a work task. According to the Freudian steam-kettle model of mental health (the other side of the Freudian coin which says that mental health requires repression), such actions are useful in that they release tension (let off steam). However, it seems more likely that they simply develop bad habits (e.g., acting on one's every emotion) and lead ultimately to more, rather than fewer, explosions while the underlying cause remains unresolved (Tavris, 1982).

Behavioral palliation in this category would include such activities as exercise (Ledwidge, 1980; Mihevic, 1982) and muscle relaxation. Lavey and Taylor (1985) claim that the main elements of relaxation are: a quiet setting; muscle relaxation; deep breathing; internal focusing on something innocuous; and a passive attitude. Thus cognitive elements are involved.

Typically behavioral palliation tecniques are used to moderate the physical symptoms of stress rather than the emotions themselves. They are most frequently used to treat: migraine headaches, hypertension, insomnia, postsurgical pain, and asthma (Lavey and Taylor, 1985; Patel, 1977). There is evidence that they are of some help with the first four (Blanchard, Ahles and Shaw, 1979; Blanchard and Miller, 1977; Egbert et al., 1964), but the evidence with respect to asthma is less consistent (Alexander, Cropp, and Chai, 1979; Kinsman et al., 1980; Knapp and Wells, 1978).

In considering the effectiveness of methods in the symptom-focused categories (both cognitive and behavioral) with respect to reducing the incidence of stress, the least helpful of the group is likely to be the acting out method since it is virtually equivalent to noncoping (Kuhlmann, 1986). Avoidance techniques, both cognitive and behavioral, would be slightly more effective because they yield some relief in the short term. Palliation techniques would be the most effective of all because they allow short-term relief at probably less cost than avoidance.

However, none of the coping techniques in the symptom categories deal with underlying causes; thus they generally must be presumed to be less effective in the long term than methods which attack stress at its source. One study (Schwartz, Davidson, and Goleman, 1978), for example, showed that exercise reduced bodily tension but not cognitive anxiety. Attacking the causes of stress, if successful, would ultimately serve to *prevent* further stress, thus obviating the need to reduce the stress that it habitually experienced (LaGreca, 1985).

Cognitive/Causal Focus. The paradigm procedure in this category is *psychotherapy/counseling.* There is no doubt that, on the average, psychotherapy works in that it helps people feel and function better as compared to others who do not undergo therapy (Stiles, Shapiro, and Elliott, 1986). However, it is not clear exactly why therapy works; for example, many studies have shown relatively few differences between formal "brands" of therapy with respect to effectiveness (Stiles et al., 1986).

If one observes what therapists (including behavior therapists—see Locke, 1971) actually do, the procedures fall into only a limited number of categories: namely, show warmth and empathy; help to change (self-defeating) values; help to change erroneous beliefs; help to interpret and modify emotions by changing beliefs and values and modifying habitual methods of appraising situations (Packer, 1985/1986); help to improve self-esteem; uncover repressed feelings, beliefs, and conflicts; give practical suggestions for coping with life's stresses; and support and encourage new behaviors. Thus, therapy, unlike the symptom-focused methods, attempts to help the client modify the causes of stress.

Especially significant in the therapy category is the uncovering of the bases for a client's self-esteem. If the client's self-esteem is based on something which is inherently self-destructive (e.g., how much one can drink, how subservient one can be), or something not in one's control (how rich one's family is, the important people one's parents know, etc.), or something nonfundamental (how much money one makes, how big one's muscles are), then one is highly vulnerable to being threatened by everyday events. One is then compelled to develop defenses against the threats. When the defenses themselves are threatened, the individual becomes even more vulnerable. If the basis of one's self-esteem is something which contradicts reality, then sooner or later the individual will experience the following conflict: either deal with reality or protect self-esteem.

Individuals are likely to be more in control of their lives and less vulnerable to stress from threats to self-esteem if it is based upon their ability to use rational thought. Rand (1961) has argued that the need for self-esteem is based specifically on the implicit belief that one will use one's mind (reason) to identify and understand reality in order to guide one's choices and actions. To quote Rand (1961):

Every form of causeless self-doubt, every feeling of inferiority and secret unworthiness is, in fact, man's hidden dread of his inability to deal with existence. . . . *Self-esteem* is reliance on one's power to think. (pp. 176–77)

Figure 5–2 concretizes this theory further by indicating a number of specific choices and actions that would be involved in using one's mind properly and which, when made habitual, would raise self-esteem and foster effective coping.

Stress inoculation training or cognitive restructuring is a cognitive coping procedure narrower in scope than psychotherapy (Goldfried, Linehan, and Smith, 1978; Meichenbaum, 1972, 1975, 1977; Forman, 1980). This procedure does not attempt to discover the historical roots of psychological problems but rather to directly inculcate new mental habits aimed at helping the individual deal with a particular, troublesome situation (Hussian and Lawrence, 1978). A complete stress inoculation treatment would include three stages: cognitive preparation, skill acquisition and rehearsal, and application/practice. For example, students with test anxiety are trained to focus on the test itself rather than on their bad feelings about it or about themselves (Dweck and Wortman, 1982; Arnkoff, 1986). People quick to anger are shown how to talk themselves into a calmer reaction to situations which habitually set them off (Feindler and Fremouw, 1983; Novaco, 1977). Modified expectations and attributions regarding oneself and others are used to reduce headaches (Holroyd, Andrasik, and Westbrook, 1977; Holroyd and Andrasik, 1978). Similar procedures have been used to increase pain tolerance (Horan et al., 1977; Scott and Barber, 1977), to reduce stressful postoperative responses to surgery (Johnson et al., 1978; Langer, Janis, and Wolfer, 1975), to decrease fear of dating (Jaremko, 1983) and of public speaking (Jaremko, Hadfield and Walker, 1980), and to cope with the trauma of being raped (Forman, 1980). Overall the studies have shown very positive results for this method (Meichenbaum, 1977). Even relaxation can be taught as an active coping skill (Goldfried and Trier, 1974; Houston, 1982).

Spontaneous cognitive coping was used by prisoners in the Pueblo incident. The more effective copers focused on the real meaning of the North Korean actions and used more coping mechanisms in general than the less effective copers (Ford and Spaulding, 1973). Similarly, headache sufferers who after training used many coping techniques achieved more relief than those who used few (Mitchell and White, 1977).

Causal/Action Focus. The essence of this category is the taking of action which removes or negates the threat(s) to one's values. For example, if one was confronted by a rabid dog, one would take action to protect oneself by going inside, shooting the dog, or calling the animal shelter. Or, confronted by the failure of a new product, a marketing manager would develop a new

1. Take facts seriously: don't evade. (If you make $20,000 a year, do not pretend that you can get away with spending $40,000.) Learn to distinguish between man-made facts (wrong government policies) which can be changed and metaphysical facts (you need food to live) which cannot.

2. Exert mental effort. Do not give up thinking or trying to understand things just because they are difficult. Grow in your knowledge; do not stagnate.

3. Use your own independent judgment. Do not follow others blindly even if they expect you to.

4. Do not substitute emotions for thoughts. The fact that you feel something is good or right does not make it so. Emotions are not tools of knowledge.

5. Think long-range. Don't claim you want to be a doctor and then not study in school. Don't smoke without being prepared to pay the price later.

6. File firm conclusions when you make decisions, e.g., I'll do this; I'll do that; or I'll wait and get more information. Filing "maybe's," ("Maybe I should have spoken up") is a way of filing self-doubt.

7. Make firm, contextual decisions. Do not expect to have perfect certainty for a decision. Use the information available or get more and then choose.

8. Do not give others the benefit of your self-doubt. Do not give in to others without good reason just because they appear to be more certain than you.

9. Introspect. Be aware of your own subconscious values and beliefs. Identify any defenses that you use. Change faulty thinking.

10. Choose rational standards to judge yourself by based on your personal context, needs, and goals. Do not use arbitrary standards of perfection. Do not have pretentious aspirations.

11. Take yourself as a value. Assume in principle that you are worthy of pleasure and happiness and have the right to pursue your own values. Take your values seriously.

12. Take action based on your judgment (e.g., including nos. 1–11 above). If you make a judgment and fail to act on it when appropriate, your subconscious will file "You don't mean it and you can't do it, therefore you can't cope and are no good."

Figure 5–2. Types of Choices that Bolster Self-Esteem

plan (e.g., by modifying the product or taking action to minimize the loss caused by the failure).

Anderson, Hellriegel, and Slocum (1977) found that small business owners who were flood victims were most likely to recover if they used task-centered (problem-solving) coping techniques rather than emotion-centered, palliative techniques. Nezu et al., (1986) found that effective problem solvers were not adversely affected by negative life events whereas ineffective problem solvers were adversely affected by such events. Innes and Clarke (1985) obtained a parallel finding for those high versus low in job involvement: high involvement may indicate a pro-active approach toward work and life whereas low involvement may indicate passivity and a lack of problem-solving attempts. Andreasen and Norris (1972) reported that effort toward rehabilitation helped the recovery of burn victims. Overburdened managers mentioned that actions such as using new strategies helped them cope (Burke and Belcourt, 1974). Job changers coped by working longer hours (Feldman and Brett, 1983). Depressed patients who successfully controlled their depression were far more likely to have taken steps to change their social environments than those who were unsuccessful (Doerfler and Richards, 1981). Among the elderly, the most aggressive and demanding coped best with radical life changes (Lieberman, 1975). Gal and Lazarus (1975) have summarized the beneficial effects of action as a method of coping. Even in concentration camps, taking small actions contributed to survival (Benner et al., 1980; Dimsdale, 1974).

However, it cannot be assumed that taking action is necessarily more appropriate than intrapsychic mechanisms such as changing one's values, beliefs, or appraisals. Consider, for example, obsessive-compulsive, Type A, perfectionists (Friedman and Rosenman, 1974). These individuals do not fail to deal with obstacles or solve problems; rather, their constant striving for perfection creates too many problems to solve or unrealistic standards by which to judge a solution appropriate. Practical success will not remove the stress because they would condemn themselves for not having succeeded faster or better and would set five new goals to replace each one that they achieved. The proper solution in this case is to change their standards (values).

Similarly, it is not necessarily inappropriate to take action which involves leaving a stress-producing situation—a method which we previously called *avoidance*. For example, take the insecure man who is in a bar with his date and is threatened by a huge, drunken lout. He might feel that a "real man" would stand up and punch the man out, whereas more rational solutions would be to call the manager, leave, or call the police—that is, avoid fighting. If individuals hate their job or some aspect of it (for instance, the boss), the most rational solution may not be to adapt themselves to the job but to find another job (or even another career).

The appropriate solution or solutions in each case must be based on the total situation: namely, the environment, the individual, and the relationship between them (Folkman et al., 1979). However, in cases where sources of stress are at least partly under the individual's control, dealing with stress from the causal side is generally preferable (in terms of preventing future reoccurrence of the stress) to dealing with it from the symptomatic side. Latack (1986), for example, found that people who use pro-active control strategies for dealing with potential job stressors experience less stress and more satisfaction than those who use escape or symptom-focused strategies. Nevertheless, the most effective method of dealing with the causes (i.e., action versus cognition) ultimately depends on the context. Since stress is caused by *the environment in relation to oneself* (one's appraisal of it), one can, in principle, deal with it by focusing either inwardly or outwardly, or both.

Social Support. As noted earlier social support cannot be placed in any one cell of our 2 × 2 model because it can involve any or all of them depending upon the type of support given (Barrera, 1981; Beehr, 1985; Cohen and Wills, 1985; DiMatteo and Hays, 1981; Lazarus and Folkman, 1984). For example, friends could suggest that the stressed persons not think about the problem (distraction), encourage them to blame (incorrectly) someone else (defense mechanism), tell them to relax (palliation), give them some drug (substance abuse), or just talk. Similarly, friends could instruct them how to cope (tell yourself that you can do it—restructuring), or give suggestions as to how to solve the problem (problem solving). Support can also involve direct, tangible help such as providing food, shelter, or money (action). Sometimes support simply involves understanding what the other person is going through. Gottlieb (1981) referred to this as a *confiding relationship*. Hirsch (1980) found that cognitive guidance (counseling, cognitive restructuring) was the most beneficial aspect of support whereas having dense social networks (suggesting extreme dependency) was associated with higher stress levels (Gottlieb, 1981a and b; Hirsch, 1981). Generally high support is associated with lower stress (Cohen and Wills, 1985).

Some research work has indicated that social support entails an indirect benefit called *buffering* in which others emotionally moderate the effects of stress (Cohen and Wills, 1985; Gore, 1978). LaRocco and Jones (1978) found this "buffering" did not occur with respect to job stress. Kaufman and Beehr (1986) actually found a reverse buffering effect: the relationship between situational stressors and experienced stress was higher under conditions of high rather than low social support. The authors suggest that support seeking may follow rather than precede or prevent the experience of stress.

In summary, we have argued that coping responses can be classified as symptom- or cause-focused and as cognitive or behavioral. Social support may be involved in any or all of these categories. We have further suggested that in the long run cause-focused coping will be more successful than symptom-focused coping, but that there is no inherent superiority of cognitive to behavioral coping or vice versa, especially since they may often be used in combination.

We may now define successful, long-term coping as *the identification of the causal elements in the precipitating situation (both external and internal) followed by cognitive and/or physical actions aimed at modifying one or more of these causal elements so as to reduce or eliminate associated negative emotions and physical symptoms.* Successful coping leaves the individual free to enjoy positive emotions and to deal with situations objectively, unencumbered by cognitive distortions or fears which restrict action and the achievement of values.

Let us now apply this model to the categories of values (discussed earlier) which people seek on the job.

Coping and Job Values

The major types of threats to each of the five categories of job values discussed earlier are shown in figure 5–3. We shall use many examples, some taken from the first author's clinical practice and some taken from other sources, to illustrate various coping techniques.

Work Values and Meanings	Threats (Potential Stress Initiators)
1. Material values	1. No raise. No promotion Loss of job Loss of other values Loss of identity Poverty

2. Achievement-related values	2. Failure
	Job or career change
	Loss of control
	    Boundary spanning role
	    Role conflict
	    Role overload
	    Time pressure
	Loss of interesting work

3. Sense of purpose	Loss of job Career failure Career success
4. Social relationships	Conflict, criticism Isolation alienation Rejection
5. Self-concept	All of the above Failure to pursue values Irrational standards Self-concept—work environment discrepancy

Figure 5–3. Major Threats to Job Values

1. Material Values. There are several ways in which material values can be associated with stress. One is that individuals may base their self-concept almost entirely on material outcomes, in particular on the amount of money they earn. As a result, they attempt to relieve any self-doubt by compulsive attempts to make more and more money. Individuals' heavy reliance on money and material goods as a basis for their self-esteem can result in stress in two ways. First, they are easily devastated by the loss of material outcomes such as the failure to get an expected raise or promotion or loss of a job. Such losses have negative consequences far beyond any practical threat, such that individuals feel they are worthless failures, regardless of whether they in any way caused the event to occur (e.g., they may have been laid off due to a merger or to poor economic conditions). The threat to their self-esteem may be so great that they take refuge in defense mechanisms (repression, withdrawal), and substance abuse. They may be unwilling to accept other employment, or to remain in the same position (after being passed over for promotion) because their self-esteem will not permit any compromises in the area of material outcomes. Loss of job, of course, can have serious practical consequences, such as poverty—which can entail various physical threats.

A second way in which stress can result from individuals' overreliance on material outcomes for their self-esteem is that other important values such as those pertaining to interest in one's job or to the meaning of one's family relationships become de-emphasized and even lost permanently. Thus, individuals may be shocked to find that the attainment of large quantities of material outcomes do not prove nearly as satisfying as expected because they were achieved at the expense of other important values. Consider the case of Professor A.

> Professor A moaned and groaned for years that Eastern University did not pay its professors enough and that he was losing potential earnings by staying there. Finally, he accepted an offer at Atlantic University at a substantial raise. However two years later he tried (unsuccessfully) to get his old job back. Atlantic University did not have the same caliber of faculty research focus as Eastern University and he felt intellectually and professionally frustrated.

Korman (1980) and Maccoby (1976) have provided other examples of how individuals' overemphasis on material outcomes (such as career success) may cause them to ignore another important value, that of social relationships. As Maccoby (1976) has explained:

> Careerism demands detachments. To succeed in school the child needs to detach himself from a crippling fear of failure. To sell himself, he detaches himself from feelings of shame and humiliation. To compete and win, he detaches himself from compassion for the losers. To devote himself to success at work, he detaches himself from family. (p. 104)

Korman (1980) has proposed that the sacrifice of social relationships (termed *affiliative satisfactions*) in order to achieve material outcomes is one of the greatest sources of personal and social alienation among today's managers. Unfortunately, individuals may erect strong defenses against the recognition of conflicts between the attainment of material outcomes and other values, such as interesting work or social relationships, so that the negative implications of these trade offs go unrecognized for many years. By the time these conflicts are recognized, it may be much more difficult to attain them.

The value of material outcomes may also result in stress because individuals have failed to choose appropriate standards by which to judge themselves. They may strive solely to impress others with highly visible material outcomes. This case is exemplified by the response of Mr. B, when asked to describe a fantasy that would reflect what he really wanted in life.

> I see a big house with white columns sitting on a hill. I drive up to it in a Cadillac. My beautiful wife meets me at the door trailed by two large dogs and the kids. It is the most expensive house around. Everyone else is envious of me.

Individuals like Mr. B rely on others for their standards because they lack a set of personal values that would enable them to make their own choices. They are often threatened because they can never acquire enough. There is always someone with a bigger house, a more expensive car, or a more attractive spouse in relation to whom they feel inadequate. Further, these individuals often have difficulty establishing relationships with others because they have nothing unique to contribute to the relationship. Underneath the facade of confidence, there is no self—only a mirror of others' desires.

In each of the previous examples, effective coping with stress requires cognitive changes. These individuals must learn to disengage their self-esteem from the material outcomes they have acquired, develop their own unique set of values, and/or become more aware of other values that are just as important as material outcomes. Frequently, a significant setback, such as the failure to obtain an important promotion, loss of a job, or the loss of a meaningful personal relationship, is required before these individuals are willing to change. Furthermore, they may be quite defensive and require assistance in identifying the causes of the setback. Once the causes are identified, the individuals have to learn to act differently in similar situations, to acquire new skills, to develop better relationships with organizational superiors, and to put more time into important personal relationships.

We do not wish to imply from the foregoing discussion that trying to make money and increase one's earning power is bad. It is not. Improving one's skills and abilities and progressing through a series of higher and more demanding jobs, tasks, and responsibilities which produce increasingly higher salaries is an important and legitimate source of pride and self-esteem. Such progress indicates the increasingly effective and productive use of one's mind. We strongly approve of people being proud of their earning power, but this is not the same as being obsessed with it and using it to relieve profound self-doubt.

Furthermore, being poor is itself a source of stress, not just because (for some) it is associated with failure (lack of skill, lack of motivation to work hard), but because it can pose many practical difficulties in living (e.g., problems in housing, transportation, nutrition, medical care, freedom to take vacations, and so forth). Thus one way to eliminate some sources of stress is to make *more* money, not less. This requires a great deal of proactive behavior: for example, getting a good education, doing well in school, acquiring marketable skills, learning new things, working hard at one's job, looking for a better job, and being willing to move and take risks. Some people remain in poverty because of their failure to take such actions either out of laziness or fear of failure. Increasing one's earning power can be an indication of growth and the failure to increase it an indication of intellectual and career stagnation (though there are exceptions to this association).

Thus one can feel stressed in the realm of material values for two broadly different reasons: because one (due to self-doubt) makes money too important and thus feels constantly threatened because it is never enough, or because one earns too little and is beset by practical difficulties and the recognition that one failed to grow.

2. Achievement-Related Values. The key threats to achievement-related values are the loss of feelings of competence (failure), of work that is interesting or challenging, or of personal control over one's work. In the case of threats due to failure, it is important for individuals to examine the standards they are using to judge their effectiveness, since these may be inappropriate. Individuals who strive to achieve such standards often experience extreme, albeit partially subconscious, conflict because they feel hopelessly tied to standards that they suspect may be impossible to achieve. In actuality, the standards may be totally arbitrary. Consider the case of Ms. C.

> Ms. C was contemplating suicide. When asked what the problem was, she said that she was a failure because she was unable to make any progress on the book she was writing. When asked how long she had studied the topic she was writing about, she responded that she had studied it for about two months and had read a couple of books on it. Ms. C was shocked to learn that the reason she could not write about the topic was that she knew hardly anything about it.

The standard that Ms C. was using to judge her performance was that of omniscience—a standard divorced from reality. She expected herself to master any new topic with a minimum amount of effort. When she could not meet this arbitrary and impossible standard, she judged herself a failure. Thus, effective coping in cases such as Ms. C's involves the development of more rational standards by which to judge success and failure. Such standards must reflect a realistic assessment of task difficulties vis-à-vis the individual's ability level.

On the other hand if individuals' failures are judged on the basis of a rational standard—namely, if the failures are real—then effective coping would lie in the realm of action. Such individuals must identify the causes of their failures and proceed to develop the needed skills or work habits. Sometimes this will require switching jobs or even careers to better match skills and interests with job requirements. At other times, they may need to discuss conflicting role requirements with superiors in order to increase the likelihood of success.

Threats to individuals' achievement values may also occur when there is a loss of personal control over their work and/or a loss of interest in what they are doing. For example, boundary spanning roles that place individuals in an interface position between two conflicting groups may offer them little personal control with respect to the scheduling of job tasks or the results of those tasks. Job changes may bring about significant time pressures or work overload that cause similar decreases in personal control. Furthermore, as noted in the material outcomes section, individuals may trade away work that is inherently interesting in order to attain material outcomes such as the status of a managerial position or a higher salary.

Individuals who feel their choice of work activities is externally controlled may subsequently lose interest in performing the activities for their own sake (Deci, 1975). Consider a Nobel laureate's description of what happened upon assuming his first faculty position as a physicist:

> At Cornell I'd work on preparing my courses, and I'd go over to the library a lot and read through the *Arabian Nights* and ogle the girls that would go by. But when it came time to do some research, I couldn't get to work. I was a little tired; I was not interested; I couldn't do research. . . . Then I had another thought: Physics disgusts me a little bit now, but I used to *enjoy* doing physics. Why did I enjoy it? I used to *play* with it. I used to do whatever I felt like doing—it didn't have to do with whether it was important for the development of nuclear physics, but whether it was interesting and amusing for me to play with. (Feynman, 1985, pp. 155, 157)

In cases where individuals' values for achievement-related outcomes are threatened by a lack of personal control over, or interest in, their work, effective coping generally involves both cognitive and behavioral methods. Such individuals often must consciously decide, as did Feynman, that they will not allow others to exert an unreasonable amount of control over their work and they then must respond behaviorally to reduce this control (e.g., negotiate with the organization to decrease time pressures, or reduce workloads by delegating and utilizing time management techniques). Similarly, individuals often must also decide that the performance of interesting work is an important value that is worth the loss of some material outcomes. If their diminished interest in work is not caused by a loss of personal control but rather by the nature of the work itself, objective changes in job tasks may be required to restore this interest. Recall that Dalton and Thompson (1986) found individual, rather than group, work was more likely to be intrinsically interesting. Further, Katz (1980) has argued that no matter how stimulating individuals' work is, periodic changes in job tasks are required in order for it to remain interesting and challenging.

3. Sense of Purpose. As noted earlier, work may have meaning for individuals because it gives them a sense of purpose, thus adding structure to their lives and providing the feeling of doing something meaningful. This sense of purpose can be threatened in a number of different ways. Much has been written on the demoralizing effect of job loss on the structure and sense of purpose that work provides (Cobb and Kasl, 1977; Cohn, 1978; Feather and Davenport, 1981). However, it is not necessary for individuals to lose their jobs in order to feel such a threat. They may experience failure when changes in the goals or technology of the organization undermine the nature of their contribution. Consider the case of Professor D.

> Professor D says that she feels "like dirt" upon going home from work. She was tenured at the associate level in 1953 when Southern University was mainly a teaching-oriented university. She is a good teacher but has neither the interest nor skill to be a good researcher. Over the years Southern University has gradually become a publish-or-perish institution. Professor D has found herself cut off intellectually from the younger faculty who talk mainly about their research. She feels penalized by the reward system since pay raises and promotions are based increasingly on publications. She has begun to see her contribution to the university—being a good teacher—as invalid and thus meaningless and has lost interest in her teaching as well as the day-to-day life of the university.

Professor D has several coping alternatives at this point. She probably will need to deal both cognitively and behaviorally with the threat. She might, for example, cognitively reappraise the situation, telling herself that different people have different values and that, while what she values is not extrinsically rewarded, it is still something that she thinks is important, loves, and finds pleasurable. The cognitive reappraisal might be bolstered by behaviors that emphasize teaching, such as putting in more time and effort, or trying to attain some outside recognition by striving for teaching awards. These might also include finding consulting activities to replace the income she will forfeit under the current university reward structure.

However, Professor D's reappraisal of her teaching contribution may not be convincing enough to keep her satisfied in the face of few extrinsic rewards. If not, she may cope behaviorally by moving to a work environment that values her teaching contribution more highly or by acquiring the research skills that would allow her to be rewarded in her current environment. The latter behavior would also require some additional cognitive change in her beliefs about the relative values of teaching and research. Finally, Professor D might attempt to cope with the threat by shifting the high value she places on her work to another arena (e.g., volunteer activities). If she is successful, Professor D would then need to make behavioral changes that focus on this arena.

People also may experience *self-induced* threats to the sense of purpose derived from their work. As noted earlier, when individuals become so obsessed with "career success' that they sacrifice the attainment of other valued outcomes such as family relationships or interesting work, work may come to hold little meaning (Korman, 1980). At this point, effective coping often involves the decision to pursue these other values—for example, building new personal relationships or changing careers.

People may also lose their sense of purpose at work after *attaining* highly valued, long-term goals. The realization that one has achieved the "epitome" of success in their chosen occupational area (e.g., an olympic gold medal in swimming, going to the moon, etc.) may result in the feeling that further work is no longer meaningful because nothing can match what one has already achieved. In this situation, individuals may decrease the threat by assessing whether the goal itself was really the factor that gave their work meaning, or whether it was simply a surrogate for other attributes of the work, such as high quality performance, or creativity. If the sense of purpose derived from work was based upon achievement of the particular goal, effective coping may consist of problem-solving activities undertaken to identify other occupational fields where individuals feel they can make a contribution. Conversely, if a sense of purpose was derived from other attributes of work that subsequently were overlooked, cognitive reappraisal may be effective in diminishing the threat to one's sense of purpose.

People may also still feel conflict after achieving a long-range goal because they never wanted it in the first place. Consider Mr. E:

> Mr. E got out of the Army and decided that what he really wanted was to be a lawyer. But various family members pointed out that this would be a high-risk choice, and that it would be a long time paying off. These comments plus his own self-doubts led him to take a secure job with the federal government instead. By most standards he has "succeeded" in this job. He

has received several promotions, makes good money, and has job security. But the job means nothing at all to him; he experiences his work as unbearable drudgery. It is not what he really wanted to do, and never was.

Even at middle age, however, Mr. E could change if he had the courage to do so.

4. Social Relationships. Social relationships serve both an expressive and an instrumental function at work (Locke, 1976). That is, individuals' interactions with their co-workers and customers often provide enjoyment in their own right as well as a mechanism for accomplishing cooperative aspects of their work.

People's value for social relationships at work may be threatened in several different ways. First, people may value the expressive aspect of these relationships so highly that job requirements involving even minor conflicts with others prove very threatening. Consider the case of Ms. F.

Ms. F managed a small number of employees as part of her administrative duties. One of them was chronically late for work, rude to customers, and unproductive. It was F's job to confront this employee but she was too terrified to do so. "If she gets mad at me, I think I'll go to pieces," she confessed. Her self-esteem was quite low because she would not deal with situations involving confrontation in any sphere of her life.

Effective coping in Ms. F's case involved cognitive and behavioral methods. Through therapy she was able to change her beliefs about the importance of receiving constant approval from others and to rely more on her internal standards for correct and incorrect behavior. In addition, through the use of role play techniques she learned how to depersonalize disciplinary episodes and conflict situations at work so that she was more effective and comfortable when engaged in the less pleasant interpersonal demands of her job.

A second threat to individuals' interpersonal relationships at work occurs when they respond by totally ignoring other people. As Korman (1980) has noted, individuals may become so obsessed with career success that they experience personal alienation from others in the work environment. Korman (1980) proposed that the competitive, compulsive behavior believed to contribute to career success destroys the expressive aspect of work relationships and results in the loss of an important value for many individuals.

Effective coping in the case of personal alienation might involve getting individuals to reappraise the threat situation and explicitly acknowledge the trade off in values that may result (preferably prior to accepting such jobs). Then, if such a trade off is undesirable, they may also have to move to work environments that do not require such behaviors in order to be effective.

Another threat to people's value for social relationships at work may be caused by their poor social skills and pessimistic expectations of others. Consider the case of Mr. G.

> From the time he was two years old (his earliest memories), Mr. G., concluded that people, including his parents, did not like him. Gradually he withdrew from people and as a result developed few social skills. Talking to him is an uncomfortable experience. He does not smile. He looks scared and nervous and yet on guard, ready to attack if he is attacked. At work, people either ignore him or talk about him disparagingly behind his back. Being "supervigilant," he often can hear them do this and feels strong anger towards them and a desire for revenge. He does not get along with the neighbors where he lives. He expects people not to like him, and they usually don't.

The behavior and attitudes of individuals such as Mr. G frequently eliminate both the expressive and instrumental aspects of work relationships. Others do not even wish to be around him, much less to assist him in accomplishing job tasks. If Mr. G is unfortunate enough to become a manager, he will undoubtedly fail.

Effective coping in Mr. G's case might involve the examination of his beliefs about why others respond to him as they do and some changes in his value for others' feelings. The strengthening of major social skills (e.g., conversational skills, learning to smile and laugh, showing greater restraint in his personal attacks on others, etc.), would also be helpful. Finally, the use of problem-solving techniques to identify work environments where he would be more effective and feel less threatened would be important.

5. Self-Concept. Individuals' self-concept is esssentially their view of themselves with respect to abilities, interests, knowledge, skills, and values as well as their overall evaluation of themselves—that is, their self-esteem. Of these, values are the most critical. Packer (1984) writes: "The key to personal identity is values. The more developed, integrated, and intensely held are a person's values, the stronger is his sense of identity" (p. 2). Thus, all of the threats mentioned in previous sections also constitute threats to the self-concept.

Work is an important arena for threats to the self-concept because the job offers a means to sustain life and provides key opportunities for individuals to develop and achieve the values that constitute the self-concept. The threat to the self-concept is especially acute among individuals who have a poorly developed set of work values. As noted previously, individuals who fail to develop their work values may rely solely on material values as a basis of self-evaluation (e.g., Mr. B). Thus they are threatened by situations involving the loss of, or failure to attain, material outcomes. Furthermore, they tend to overemphasize material outcomes so that they neglect to pursue other important, but initially unrecognized, values. The opposite may also be true. Individuals may undervalue material outcomes and the values that make them possible (e.g., the desire to better themselves) and thus suffer material as well as psychological impoverishment.

The failure to pursue values at work may have long-term negative implications for their mental health. As Kornhauser (1965) expressed it:

> The unsatisfactory mental health of working people consists in no small measure of their dwarfed desires and deadened initiative, reduction of their goals, and restriction of their efforts to a point where life is relatively empty and only half meaningful. (p. 270) [Kornhauser arbitrarily attributes all such problems to the nature of the job and never to the workers themselves.]

Coping with such threats requires both thinking and acting; individuals need to identify and pursue important work-related values.

A second threat to the self-concept results from failures in the work arena. As noted earlier, these failures may occur because the standards individuals use to evaluate themselves (the basis of their self-esteem) are irrational; that is, the standards are impossibly difficult or based on attributes not under their control (e.g., Ms. C). In such cases effective coping involves changing the individuals' ways of thinking; specifically, they must realize that the standards are irrational and change them. In other cases, however, the self-concept is threatened by failures determined by rational standards. In order to cope effectively with these threats, individuals generally must make behavioral changes that increase the probability of future success; they must, for example, develop new skills or work harder.

A third source of threat results from a lack of congruence between individuals' self-concepts and the requirements of their work environment. Thus individuals who view themselves as slow, methodical thinkers will feel threatened by work environments that require fast, intuitive decisions. Persons who view themselves as very family oriented will be threatened by work environments that usurp family activities by requiring frequent overtime, relocations, and travel. Effective coping with such threats may sometimes be accomplished by preventive, cognitive methods whereby individuals predict the likelihood of such threats and choose environments where requirements are consistent with their self-concepts. However, as Professor D discovered, job requirements may change over time; thus, no one choice can guarantee permanent success. In instances of incongruence, effective coping will involve behavioral and cognitive methods that either bring the work environment into congruence with the self-concept (e.g., leave the organization to act or change organizational requirements) or the self-concept into congruence with the environment (e.g., change abilities, values, etc.).

Summary and Conclusion

A job or career allows the pursuit of many important values. It allows one to make money so as to earn a living. It can give one a sense of achievement and accomplishment as well as the pleasure of doing something one considers interesting. It gives one's life a sense of purpose. It allows one to develop meaningful social relationships. And it helps to define one's self-concept.

However, the actual achievement of these values is neither easy nor automatic. Inevitably there will be obstacles in the way of value attainment. These obstacles may be self-imposed in that the value standards which one uses to judge oneself are irrational and arbitrary. Or they may be externally imposed by other people or nature. When one perceives these obstacles as a threat to one's physical well-being or self-esteem, stress is experienced. Stress is experienced emotionally as fear or anxiety.

When faced with stress, one has a choice between several alternatives. One can attempt to identify the actual causes of stress (inappropriate values and/or external blocks) and take mental and/or physical actions to remove them. One can ignore the causes and deal only with symptoms through defense mechanisms, palliation, or substance abuse. Worse yet, one can repress one's desires and stop pursuing meaningful values in the realm of work. The result is that work loses meaning because important values can no longer be attained from it. If work loses meaning, life too can lose meaning, since a considerable part of one's life is spent at work. When this happens, one can feel burned out—and old. Whatever "dream" or vision of the future one started with is gone. The feelings of youthful vigor, purpose, and meaning are lost.

Meaning in work and in life can only be achieved by the pursuit and attainment of important values. To quote Ayn Rand (1957), "To hold an unchanged youth is to reach, at the end, the vision with which one started."

References

Adams, H.E., Feuerstein, M., and Fowler, J.L. (1980). Migraine headache: Review of parameters, etiology, and intervention. *Psychological Bulletin, 87,* pp. 217–37.

Aldag, R.J., and Brief, A.P. (1979). *Task design and employee motivation.* Glenview, IL: Scott, Foresman.

Alexander, A.B., Cropp, G.J.A., and Chai, H. (1979). Effects of relaxation training on pulmonary mechanics in children with asthma. *Journal of Applied Behavior Analysis, 12,* pp. 27–35.

Anderson, C.R. (1977). Locus of control, coping behaviors, and performance in a stress setting: A longitudinal study. *Journal of Applied Psychology, 62,* pp. 446–51.

Anderson, C.R., Hellriegel, D., and Slocum, J.W. (1977). Managerial response to environmentally induced stress. *Academy of Management Journal, 20,* pp. 260–72.

Andrasik, F., and Holroyd, K.A. (1980). A test of specific and nonspecific effects in the biofeedback treatment of tension headache. *Journal of Consulting and Clinical Psychology, 48,* pp. 575–86.

Andreasen, N.J.C., and Norris, A.S. (1972). Long-term adjustment and adaptation mechanisms in severely burned adults. *Journal of Nervous and Mental Disease, 154* (5), pp. 352–62.

Arnkoff, D.B. (1986). A comparison of the coping and restructuring components of cognitive restructuring. *Cognitive Research and Therapy, 10,* pp. 147–58.

Arnold, M.B. (1960). *Emotion and personality: Psychological aspects,* vol. 1. New York: Columbia University Press.

Averill, J.R. (1973). Personal control over aversive stimuli and its relationship to stress. *Psychological Bulletin, 80,* pp. 286–303.

———. (1979). A selective review of cognitive and behavioral factors involved in the regulation of stress. In R.A. Depue (ed.), *The psychobiology of the depressive disorders.* New York: Academic Press, pp. 365–87.

Bailyn, L. (1977). Involvement and accommodation in technical careers: An inquiry into the relation to work at mid-career. In J. Van Maanen (ed.), *Organizational careers: Some new perspectives.* New York: Wiley, pp. 120–8.

Bandura, A. (1982). Self-efficacy mechanism in human agency. *Americal Psychologist, 37,* pp. 122–47.

———. (1988). Self-efficacy mechanism in physiological activation and health-promoting behavior. In J. Madden, S. Matthysse, and J. Barchas (eds.), *Adaptation, learning, and affect.* New York: Raven Press.

Barrera, M. (1981). Social support in the adjustment of pregnant adolescents. In B.H. Gottlieb (ed.), *Social networks and social support.* Beverly Hills, CA: Sage, pp. 69–96.

Beehr, T.A. (1985). The role of social support in coping with organizational stress. In T.A. Beehr and R.S. Bhagat (eds.), *Human stress and cognition in organizations.* New York: Wiley, pp. 375–98.

Benner, P., Roskies, E., and Lazarus, R.S. (1980). Stress and coping under extreme conditions. In J.E. Dimsdale (eds.), *Survivors, victims, and perpetrators.* Washington, DC: Hemisphere, pp. 219–58.

Blanchard, E.B., Ahles, T.A., and Shaw, E.R. (1979). Behavioral treatment of headaches. In M. Hersen, R.M. Eisler, and P.M. Miller (eds.), *Progress in behavior modification,* vol. 8. New York: Academic Press, pp. 207–47.

Blanchard, E.B., and Miller, S.T. (1977). Psychological treatment of cardiovascular disease. *Archives of General Psychiatry, 34,* pp. 1402–13.

Bloom, L.J., Houston, B.K., Holmes, D.S., and Burish, T.G. (1977). The effectiveness of attentional diversion and situation redefinition for reducing stress due to a nonambiguous threat. *Journal of Research in Personality, 11,* pp. 83–94.

Brousseau, K.R. (1978). Personality and job experience. *Organizational Behavior and Human Performance, 22,* pp. 235–52.

Brousseau, K.R., and Prince, J.B. (1981). Job—person dynamics: An extension of longitudinal research. *Journal of Applied Psychology, 66,* pp. 59–62.

Buchholz, R.A. (1978). An empirical study of contemporary beliefs about work in American society. *Journal of Applied Psychology, 63,* pp. 219–27.

Burke, R.J., and Belcourt, M.L. (1974). Managerial role stress and coping responses. *Journal of Business Administration, 5* (2), pp. 55–68.

Chandler, C. (1982). *The ultimate seduction.* Garden City, NY: Doubleday.

Chodoff, P., Friedman, S.B., and Hamburg, D.A. (1984). Stress, defenses, and coping behavior: Observations in parents of children with malignant disease. *American Journal of Psychiatry, 120,* pp. 743–9.

Cobb, S., and Kasl, S.V. (1977). *Termination: The consequences of job loss.* Cincinatti, OH: U.S. Department of Health, Education and Welfare.

Cohen, S., and Wills, T.A. (1985). Stress, social support, and the buffering hypothesis. *Psychological Bulletin, 98,* pp. 310–57.

Cohn, R.M. (1978). The effect of employment status change on self-attitudes. *Social Psychology, 41,* pp. 81–93.

Dalton, G.W., and Thompson, P.H. (1986). *Novations, strategies for career management.* Glenview, IL: Scott, Foresman.

Deci, E. (1975). *Intrinsic motivation.* New York: Plenum.

DiMatteo, M.R., and Hays, R. (1981). Social support and serious illness. In B.H. Gottlieb (ed.), *Social networks and social support.* Beverly Hills, CA: Sage, pp. 117–48.

Dimsdale, J.E. (1974). The coping behavior of Nazi concentration camp survivors. *American Journal of Psychiatry, 131,* pp. 792–7.

Doerfler, L.A., and Richards, C.S. (1981). Self-initiated attempts to cope with depression. *Cognitive Therapy and Research, 5,* pp. 367–71.

Doering, S.G., and Entwisle, D.R. (1975). Preparation during pregnancy and ability to cope with labor and delivery. *American Journal of Orthopsychiatry, 45,* pp. 825–37.

Dweck, C.A., and Wortman, C.B. (1982). Learned helplessness, anxiety, and achievement motivation. In H.W. Krohne and L. Laux (eds.), *Achievement, stress, and anxiety.* Washington, DC: Hemisphere, pp. 93–105.

Egbert, L.D., Battit, G.E., Welch, C.E., and Bartlett, M.K. (1964). Reduction of postoperative pain by encouragement and instruction of patients. *New England Journal of Medicine, 270,* pp. 825–7.

Evans, P.A., and Bartolome, F. (1980). The relationship between professional life and private life. In C.B. Derr (ed.), *Work, family, and the career.* New York: Praeger, pp. 281–317.

Feather, N.T., and Davenport, P.R. (1981). Unemployment and depressive affect: A motivational and attributional analysis. *Journal of Personality and Social Psychology, 41,* pp. 422–36.

Feindler, E.L., and Fremouw, W.J. (1983). Stress inoculation training for adolescent anger problems. In D. Meichenbaum and M.E. Jaremko (eds.), *Stress reduction and prevention.* New York: Plenum, pp. 451–85.

Feldman, D.C., and Brett, J.M. (1983). Coping with new jobs: A comparative study of new hires and job changers. *Academy of Management Journal, 26,* pp. 258–72.

Feuerstein, M., and Gainer, J. (1982). Chronic headache: Etiology and management. In D.M. Doley, R.L. Meredith, and A.R. Ciminero (eds.), *Behavioral medicine: Assessment and treatment strategies.* New York: Plenum, pp. 199–249.

Feynman, R.P. (1985). *Surely you're joking, Mr. Feynman.* Toronto: Doubleday.

Fine, S.A., and Wiley, W.A. (1971). *An introduction to functional job analysis: A scaling of selected tasks from the social welfare field.* Kalamazoo, MI: W.E. Upjohn Institute of Employment Research.

Folkman, S., Schaefer, C., and Lazarus, R.S. (1979). Cognitive processes as mediators of stress and coping. In V. Hamilton and D.M. Warburton (eds.), *Human stress and cognition.* New York: Wiley, pp. 265–98.

Ford, C.V., and Spaulding, R.C. (1973). The Pueblo incident. *Archives of General Psychiatry, 29,* pp. 340–43.

Forman, B.D. (1980). Cognitive modification of obsessive thinking in a rape victim: A preliminary study. *Psychological Reports, 47,* pp. 819–22.

Friedman, M., and Rosenman, R.H. (1974). *Type A behavior and your heart.* New York: Knopf.

Gal, R., and Lazarus, R.S. (1975). The role of activity in anticipating and confronting stressful situations. *Journal of Human Stress, 1* (4), pp. 4–20.

Geer, J.H., Davison, G.C., and Gatchel, R.I. (1970). Reduction of stress in humans through nonveridical perceived control of aversive stimulation. *Journal of Personality and Social Psychology, 4,* pp. 731–38.

Gilmore, T.M. (1978). Locus of control as a mediator of adaptive behavior in children and adolescents. *Canadian Psychological Review, 19,* pp. 1–26.

Glass, D.C., Singer, J.E., and Friedman, L.N. (1969). Psychic cost of adaptation to an environmental stressor. *Journal of Personality and Social Psychology, 12,* pp. 200–10.

Glass, D.C., Reim, B., and Singer, J.E. (1971). Behavioral consequences of adaptation to controllable and uncontrollable noise. *Journal of Experimental Social Psychology, 7,* pp. 244–57.

Goldfreid, M.R., and Trier, C.S. (1974). Effectiveness of relaxation as an active coping skill. *Journal of Abnormal Psychology, 83,* pp. 348–55.

Goldfried, M.R., Linehan, M.M., and Smith, J.L. (1978). Reduction of test anxiety through cognitive restructuring. *Journal of Consulting and Clinical Psychology, 46,* pp. 32–39.

Goleman, D.J., and Schwartz, G.E. (1976). Mediation as an intervention in stress reactivity. *Journal of Consulting and Clinical Psychology, 44,* pp. 456–66.

Gore, S. (1978). The effects of social support in moderating the health consequences of unemployment. *Journal of Health and Social Behavior, 19,* pp. 157–65.

Gottlieb, B.H. (1981a). Social networks and social support in community mental health. In B.H. Gottlieb (ed.), *Social networks and social support.* Beverly Hills, CA: Sage.

———. (1981b). Preventive interventions involving social networks and social support. In B.H. Gottlieb (ed.), *Social networks and social support.* Beverly Hills, CA: Sage.

Griffin, R.W. (1982). *Task design: An integrative approach.* Glenview, IL: Scott, Foresman.

Hackman, J.R., and Oldham, G.R. (1976). Motivation through the design of work: Test of a theory. *Organizational Behavior and Human Performance, 16,* pp. 250–79.

———. (1980). *Work redesign.* Reading, MA: Addison-Wesley.

Hamburg, D.A., and Adams, J.E. (1967). A perspective on coping behavior. *Archives of General Psychiatry, 17,* pp. 277–84.

Hirsch, B.J. (1980). Natural support systems and coping with major life changes. *American Journal of Community Psychology, 8,* pp. 159–72.

———. (1981). Social networks and the coping process. In B.H. Gottlieb (ed.), *Social networks and social support.* Beverly Hills, CA: Sage, pp. 149–70.

Holmes, D.S., and Houston, B.K. (1974). Effectiveness of situation redefinition and affective isolation in coping with stress. *Journal of Personality and Social Psychology, 29,* pp. 212–18.

Holroyd, K.A., Andrasik, F., and Westbrook, T. (1977). Cognitive control of tension headache. *Cognitive Therapy and Research, 1,* pp. 121–33.

Holroyd, K.A., and Andrasik, F. (1978). Coping and the self-control of chronic tension headache. *Journal of Consulting and Clinical Psychology, 46,* pp. 1036–45.

Horan, J.J., Hackett, G., Buchanan, J.D., Stone, C.I., and Demchik-Stone, D. (1977). Coping with pain: A component analysis of stress inoculation. *Cognitive Therapy and Research, 1,* pp. 211–21.

Houston, B.K. (1982). Trait anxiety and cognitive coping behavior. In H.W. Krohne and L. Laux (eds.), *Achievement, stress, and anxiety.* Washington, DC: Hampshire, pp. 195–206.

Hussian, R.A., and Lawrence, P.S. (1978). The reduction of test, state, and trait anxiety by test-specific and generalized stress innoculation training. *Cognitive Therapy and Research, 2,* pp. 25–37.

Innes, J.M., and Clarke, A. (1985). Job involvement as a moderator variable in the life events stress-illness relationship. *Journal of Occupational Behavior, 6,* pp. 299–303.

Jaremko, M.E. (1983). Stress-innoculation training for social anxiety, with emphasis on dating anxiety. In D. Meichenbaum and M.E. Jaremko (eds.), *Stress reduction and prevention.* New York: Plenum, pp. 419–50.

Jaremko, M.E., Hadfield, R., and Walker, W.E. (1980). Contribution of an educational phase to stress innoculation of speech anxiety. *Perceptual and Motor Skills, 50,* pp. 495–501.

Johnson, J.E., Rice, V.H., Fuller, S.S., and Endress, M.P. (1978). Sensory information, instruction in a coping strategy, and recovery from surgery. *Research in Nursing and Health, 1,* pp. 4–17.

Katz, R. (1980). Time and work: Toward an integrative perspective. In B. Staw and L. Cummings (eds.), *Research in organizational behavior,* vol. 2. Greenwich, CO: JAI Press, pp. 81–127.

Kaufman, G.M., and Beehr, T.A. (1986). Interactions between job stressors and social support: Some counterintuitive findings. *Journal of Applied Psychology, 71,* pp. 522–6.

Kinsman, R.A., Dirks, J.F., Jones, N.F., and Dahlem, N.W. (1980). Anxieity reduction in asthma: Four catches to general application. *Psychosomatic Medicine, 42,* 397–405.

Kohn, M.L., and Schooler, C. (1978). The reciprocal effects of substantive complexity of work and intellectual flexibility: A longitudinal assessment. *American Journal of Sociology, 84,* pp. 24–52.

———. (1982). Job conditions and personality: A longitudinal assessment of their reciprocal effects. *American Journal of Sociology, 87,* pp. 1257–86.

Knapp, T.J., and Wells, L.A. (1978). Behavior therapy for asthma: A review. *Behavior Research and Therapy, 16,* pp. 110–15.

Korman, A.K. (1980). *Career success and personal failure.* Englewood Cliffs, N.J.: Prentice Hall.

Kornhauser, A. (1965). *Mental health and the industrial worker.* New York: Wiley.

Kübler-Ross, E. (1969). *On death and dying.* New York: McMillan.

Kuhlmann, T.M. (1986). Coping with occupational stress among urban bus and tram drivers. Nurnberg, W. Germany; Sozialwissenschaftlichen Institut.

La Greca, G. (1985). The stress you make. *Personnel Journal* (September), pp. 42–7.

Langer, E.J., Janis, I.L., and Wolfer, J.A. (1975). Reduction of psychological stress in surgical patients. *Journal of Experimental Social Psychology, 11,* pp. 155–65.

LaRocco, J.M., and Jones, A.P. (1978). Co-worker and leader support as moderators of stress-strain relationships in work situations. *Journal of Applied Psychology, 63,* pp. 629–34.

Latack, J.C. (1984). Career transitions within organizations: An exploratory study of work, nonwork, and coping strategies. *Organizational Behavior and Human Performance, 34,* pp. 296–322.

Latack, J. (1986). Coping with job stress: Measures and future directions for scale development. *Journal of Applied Psychology, 71,* pp. 377–85.

Lavey, R.S., and Taylor, C.B. (1985). The nature of relaxation therapy. In S.R. Burchfield (ed.), *Stress, psychological, and physiological interactions.* Washington, DC: Hemisphere, pp. 329–58.

Lazarus, R.S., and Folkman, S. (1984). *Stress, appraisal and coping.* New York: Springer.

Ledwidge, B. (1980). Run for your mind: Aerobic exercise as a means of alleviating anxiety and depression. *Canadian Journal of Behavioral Science, 12,* pp. 126–40.

Levinson, D.J., Darrow, C.N., Klein, E.B., Levinson, M.H., and McKee, B. (1978). *The seasons of a man's life.* New York: Ballantine.

Lieberman, M.A. (1975). Adaptive processes late in life. In N. Daten and L.H. Ginsberg (eds.), *Life-span developmental psychology: Normative life crises.* New York: Academic Press, pp. 135–59.

Locke, E.A. (1971). Is "behavior therapy" behavioristic? (An analysis of Wolpe's psychotherapeutic methods). *Psychological Bulletin, 76,* pp. 318–27.

———. (1976). The nature and causes of job satisfaction. In M. Dunette (ed.), *Handbook of industrial and organizational psychology.* New York: Rand McNally, pp. 1297–349.

Locke, E.A., and Henne, D. (1986). Work motivation theories. In C. Cooper and L. Robertson (eds.), *International review of industrial and organizational psychology.* Chichester, England: Wiley, pp. 1–35.

Locke, E.A., and Latham, G.P. (1984). *Goal setting: A motivational technique that works.* Englewood Cliffs, NJ: Prentice Hall.

Locke, E.A., Sirota, D., and Wolfson, A.D. (1976). An experimental case study of the successes and failures of job enrichment in a government agency. *Journal of Applied Psychology, 61,* pp. 701–11.

Lublin, J.S. Stress research seeks clues to why children can't cope with life. *Wall Street Journal,* 10 April 1979.

Maccoby, M. (1976). *The gamesman.* New York: Simon and Schuster.

Markus, H. (1986). Possible selves. *American Psychologist, 14,* pp. 954–69.

Meichenbaum, D.H. (1972). Cognitive modification of test anxious college students. *Journal of Consulting and Clinical Psychology, 39,* pp. 370–80.

———. (1975). A self-instructional approach to stress management: A proposal for stress inoculation training. In C. Spielberger and I. Sarason (eds.), *Stress and anxiety,* vol. 1. New York: Wiley, pp. 237–58.

———.(1977). *Cognitive behavior-modification: An integrative approach.* New York: Plenum.

Mihevic, P.M. (1982). Anxiety, depression, and exercise. *Quest, 33,* 140–53.

Miller, S.M. (1979). Controllability and human stress: Method, evidence, and theory. *Behavior Research and Therapy, 17,* 287–304.

Mitchell, K.R., and White, R.G. (1977). Behavioral self-management: An application to the problem of migraine headaches. *Behavior Therapy, 8,* pp. 213–21.

Morse, N.C., and Weiss, R.S. (1955). The function and meaning of work and the job. *The American Sociological Review,* (April), pp. 191–8.

Mortimer, J.T., and Lorence, J. (1979). Work experience and occupational value socialization: A longitudinal study. *American Journal of Sociology, 84,* pp. 1361–85.

Near, J.P., Rice, R.W., and Hunt, R.J. (1980). The relationship between and nonwork domains: A review of empirical research. *Academy of Management Review, 5,* pp. 415–29.

Nezu, A.M., Nezu, C.M., Saraydarian, L., Kalmar, K., and Rona, G.F. (1986). Social problem solving as a moderating variable between negative life stress and depressive symptoms. *Cognitive Therapy and Research, 10,* pp. 489–98.

Novaco, R.W. (1977). Stress inoculation: A cognitive therapy for anger and its application to a case of depression. *Journal of Consulting and Clinical Psychology, 45,* pp. 600–08.

Packer, E. (1984). The psychological requirements of a free society. *The Objectivist Forum, 5*(1), 1–11.

———. (1985/1986). The art of introspection. *The Objectivist Forum, 6*(6), pp. 1–10; 7(1), pp. 1–8.

Patel, C.H. (1977). Biofeedback-aided relaxation and meditation in the management of hypertension. *Biofeedback and Self-Regulation, 2,* pp. 1–41.

Rand, A. (1957). *Atlas shrugged.* New York: New American Library.

———. (1961). *For the new intellectual.* New York: Signet.

———. (1964). The objectivist ethics. In A. Rand (ed.), *The virtue of selfishness.* New York: Signet, pp. 13–35.

Rokeach, M. (1960). *The open and closed mind.* New York: Basic Books.

———. (1973). *The nature of human values.* New York: Free Press.

Rosenbaum, M., and Merbaum, M. (1984). Self-control of anxiety and depression: An evaluative review of treatments. In C.M. Franks (ed.), *New developments in behavior therapy: From research to clinical application.* New York: Haworth Press, pp. 105–54.

Roth, S., and Cohen, L.T. (1986). Approach, avoidance, and coping with stress. *American Psychologist, 41,* 813–19.

Schwartz, G.E., Davidson, R.J., and Goleman, D.J. (1978). Patterning of cognitive and somatic processes in the self-regulation of anxiety: Effects of meditation versus exercise. *Psychosomatic Medicine, 40,* pp. 321–8.

Scott, D.S., and Barber, T.X. (1977). Cognitive control of pain: Effects of multiple cognitive strategies. *Psychological Record, 2,* pp. 373–83.

Selye, H. (1976). *The stress of life.* New York: Van Nostrand Reinhold.

Shapiro, D.H. (1985). Meditation and behavioral medicine. In S.R. Burchfield (ed.), *Stress: psychological and physiological interactions.* Washington, DC: Hemisphere.

Sofer, C. (1970). *Men in mid-career.* London: Cambridge University Press.

Space Science Board. (1972). *Human factors in long-duration space flight.* Washington, DC: National Academy of Sciences.

Stiles, W.B., Shapiro, D.A., and Elliot, R. (1986). Are all psychotherapies equivalent? *American Psychologist, 41,* 165–80.

Super, D.E. (1986). Life career roles: Self-realization in work and leisure. In D.T. Hall (ed.), *Career development in organization.* San Francisco: Dorsey Press, pp. 95–119.

Tavris, C. (1982). Anger defused. *Psychology Today* (November), pp. 25–35.

Terkel, S. (1972). *Working people talk about what they do all day and how they feel about what they do.* New York: Avon Books.

Work in America (1973). Report of a special task force sponsored by the U.S. Secretary of Health, Education, and Welfare. Prepared under the auspices of the W.E. Upjohn Institute for Employment Research. Cambridge, Mass.: MIT Press.

Yankelovich, D., and Immerwahr, J. (1983). *Putting the work ethic to work: A Public agenda report on restoring America's competitive vitality.* New York: The Public Agenda Foundation.

6

Work and Nonwork Connections

Arthur P. Brief
Walter R. Nord

T he raw materials from which individuals construct the meaning of work are the experiences they associate with work. There are two general sets of these experiences. One set consists of events on the job, such as the nature of one's task and the workplace itself. Modern applied psychologists have given most of their attention to this source of meaning.

The experiences in the second set are generated by what social scientists call *role* relationships. These experiences arise from the patterns of relationships within and among the various social positions (or roles) that a given person occupies in the social system. Each social position is associated with certain role expectations. Role expectations, as defined by Sarbin and Allen (1968), consist of the "rights and privileges, [and] the duties and obligations, of any occupant of a social position in relation to persons occupying other positions in the social structure" (p. 497).

It is commonly accepted that any given role occupant is subject to two classes of expectations. One class—*intrarole*—consists of expectations people may have about how the person should behave in that particular role. Intrarole conflicts in the work context may arise when the expectations of some co-workers require different actions than the expectations of some other co-workers. For example, the conflicting expectations of management and those of workers are known to have dramatic effects on the way first line supervisors experience their jobs.

A second class of expectations arises from the multiple roles most individuals occupy. For example, an employee may also occupy roles such as father, mother, or shop steward. Often some of the various expectations may contradict each other, such as when meeting the expectations of one's boss is in tension with meeting those of one's spouse. This latter conflict—*interrole* conflict—is the focus of the current chapter.

For several decades, social scientists have shown a growing interest in interrole conflict. In the study of work, interrole relationships are often treated under the broad headings of *work* and *nonwork*. A large literature has developed and a major purpose of this chapter is to review that literature, in abbreviated fashion. As will be seen, the literature suggests that relatively little is understood about the nature of the relationship between work and non-work. Thus, a second purpose of this chapter is to introduce an alternative way of viewing the connection.

We begin our treatment of the work-nonwork literature by addressing why the matter of connectedness emerged. The review itself follows and leads to our alternative perspective.

The Origins of the Issues

Concern with life domains is a thoroughly modern phenomenon; intellectual treatment of work's connectedness with other aspects of life stems from changes in the structure of society. The earliest discussions of work in Western intellectual history are found in the writings of the ancient Greeks (Tilgher, 1931). While the Greeks, and later the Romans, interpreted work in religious and political terms, they did not explicitly treat the connections between work and other purposeful activities in life. In fact, throughout much of human history, work was not distinguished from nonwork. As Zuboff (1983) observed: "The concept of 'work' as a generic description of meaningful, productive activity typically emerges only after the introduction of cash crops and wage labor" (p. 153). In traditional societies the activities that produced human subsistence were not seen as unique from other aspects of human intercourse.

Earlier societies were (and some of today's simpler societies are still) characterized by a focal or dominant institution such that a person's participation and position in the focal institution dictated behaviors in subordinate institutions (Dubin, 1973). A contemporary U.S. example of such a society is the Amish community of Lancaster County, Pennsylvania, in which the church, as the dominant institution, prescribes and enforces school, work, and family role behaviors. Other examples abound in the anthropological literature (e.g., Wallman, 1979). In such societies, since most significant social behaviors are determined by the focal institution, coherence and unity are readily achieved. Perhaps unfortunately, this is not so for modern, urban, industrialized societies (e.g., Champoux, 1981; Dubin, 1973; Wilensky, 1960).

As societies industrialize, typically the number of social institutions to which the individual is attached increases (e.g., Simmel, 1955); and, the nature of the relationships among these institutions changes.[1] More specifically, Dubin (1973) and others (e.g., Berger, 1964; Cooley, 1962; Durkheim, 1933; Weber, 1968; Wilensky and Lebeaux, 1958) have argued that industrial and postindustrial societies (in contrast to hunting/gathering and horticultural societies) have institutions that are physically, temporally, and functionally segregated. For instance, in modern societies economic, religious, and educational needs are largely met by highly specialized institutions: each institution occupies its own physical setting and requires relatively significant amounts of time from its participants.

Under these conditions, individuals play multiple roles and are not likely to be bound together by a set of prescriptions emanating from any single source. Whether this means, as James (1891) noted some time ago, that a person has multiple selves, or instead that the same "self" plays different parts, is debatable. Most modern writers seem to hold the latter view, seeing the individual as being pulled in several directions. As Champoux (1981) noted, it is this image of the self being segmented across institutional roles that gave rise to questions about how individuals connect work to the other domains of their lives, if in fact they do. Below we examine the pertinent social science literature to ascertain what may be known about such work-nonwork linkages. First, we review alternative theoretical approaches and then sample from the available empirical results.

Propositions about Work and Nonwork Connections[2]

Many of the propositions about work-nonwork connections address the relation between work and leisure. Our review, accordingly, reflects this emphasis. Generally speaking, there are two sorts of work-nonwork propositions, universalistic and particularistic. The universalistic propositions assert that the relationship between work and nonwork is constant—for instance, across people and situations. Alternatively, particularistic propositions are more complex in that work-nonwork relationships are postulated to vary as a function of some other variable(s). The sorts of other variables that have been proposed to modify the nature of the work-nonwork relationship include various individual differences (e.g., age and education) and a number of contextual factors (e.g., job level and task complexity). Often the universalistic versus particularistic distinction is not made explicitly, but is easily inferred from what a given writer appears to assume and/or take as problematic.

Universalistic Propositions. Essentially, there are three competing universalistic propositions. The most common labels for the three are *spillover, compensatory,* and *segmentation* hypotheses.

The *spillover* hypothesis states that a person's work experiences carry over to other domains of life and affect attitudes and behaviors in these other domains. It appears that Adam Smith (1937), in observing eighteenth-century factory life, was one of the first to assert that the negative effects of work produce dysfunctions outside of work. Karl Marx, of course, held a similar view as do many critics of modern work (Argyris 1957; Kohn and Schooler, 1982;

Sennett and Cobb, 1973). Argyris' treatment of the hypothesis is one of the clearest examples and we use it as representative.

Argyris argued that members of many formal work organizations are unable to satisfy important psychological needs and that the dissatisfaction at work is associated with passive participation in leisure activities which the worker finds, like his/her work, to be meaningless and uninvolving. The converse of Argyris' argument is equally plausible under the spillover hypothesis. That is, the hypothesis also implies that those workers who find satisfaction in their work will generalize these positive attitudes to their nonwork domains. While, of course, any correlation coefficient indexing the work-nonwork relationship speaks empirically to the potential of both positive and negative spillover effects, it seems, in some quarters at least, that when support is found for the spillover hypothesis, emphasis in interpretation is placed on the negative effects of work on life in general. This can be seen in the job stress literature (e.g., Brief, Schuler, and Van Sell, 1981) where the adverse effects of work invariably are discussed and its possible therapeutic effects largely ignored.

It is also important to note that the spillover proposition asserts that both the "good" (e.g., being calm and relaxed) and the "bad" (e.g., feeling distressed and fearful) about work generalize to the nonwork domains of life. Evidence for the positive effects can be found, for example, in Kohn (1980). Correspondingly, the proposition can be seen as holding that both the good and the bad about the nonwork domains of life generalize to work—it is not only work that can spill over. In short, the spillover hypothesis implies that spillover can be both positive and negative and can have two-way flows. Most users of the hypothesis, however, have focused mainly on the negative impact of work on nonwork.

The second, and perhaps the most frequently advanced universalistic proposition, is the *compensatory* one. Here, it is asserted that in their nonwork activities, workers seek satisfaction of those needs they are unable to fulfill at work, and that they do not look to the nonwork domains of their life to satisfy needs fulfilled at work. The compensatory hypothesis appears in many forms and is rationalized by an even greater variety of arguments (e.g., Anderson, 1964; Friedmann, 1960; Green, 1968; Gross, 1901; Pangburn, 1922; Robinson, 1920; Sapora and Mitchell, 1961; Slavson, 1946).

The compensatory hypothesis is often associated with the assumption that prior to the industrial revolution, work provided considerable intrinsic satisfaction which modern work does not. Following Bottomore's (1964) interpretation of Karl Marx, Marx appears to have held a compensatory view: specifically, workers had to seek fulfillment in their leisure because fulfillment could not be found in work. Marx attributed the dissatisfactoriness of work to its organization within capitalist societies where workers are exploited to the benefit of owners. [See Fromm, 1966; Israel, 1971; and Meszaros, 1970. Wilensky (1960) noted that Engels (1892) advanced essentially the same reasoning.] The validity of this historical scenario as support for the compensatory view, although widely shared, has been seriously challenged (Anthony, 1977; Clayre, 1974). Clayre, for example, tested the assumption by study of the oral history of workers prior to the industrial revolution and found no evidence that there was any great pleasure derived from the intrinsic nature of work. Moreover, people found a great deal missing from their work and wanted to fuse work with play which they did by putting their work aside from time to time and singing and dancing. This is not to question the validity of the compensation hypothesis. People may indeed lead segmented lives, achieving different satisfactions in different arenas. However, it does appear that the common version of the hypothesis that sees the quest for compensation as stemming from industrialization is problematic.

Also, those who share the compensatory hypothesis typically take a directional stance analogous to what we observed of the spillover hypothesis. Generally, work is taken as the starting point and the analysis centers on nonwork activities as sources of self-esteem, intrinsic satisfaction, and so forth that compensate for deficiencies in work. As Parker (1983) observed, however, it is also possible to start with leisure and inquire how work may compensate for deficiencies in leisure. In fact, it is not at all unreasonable to suppose that some people derive more benefits from intrinsic interest and esteem from their work than from their nonwork activities. Indeed, some inquiries into "workaholism" (Machlowitz, 1977) suggest this fact. In short, tests of the compensatory hypothesis should attend to two sources of compensation—those from work and those from nonwork.

In addition, it is one thing to say that nonwork activities *can* compensate for "deficiencies" of work and quite another to say they actually do. Undoubtedly, if people are deprived of certain valued rewards in one aspect of their lives, they are likely to seek them elsewhere. However, motivation by itself does not mean that compensation will be achieved: other factors are also important. Suppose, for example, that the resources needed to compensate are not available elsewhere or that people lack the wealth to gain the resources they need. Moreover, people may lack sufficient knowledge of how to consume resources (even if they have them) in a way to satisfy their needs. Following the noted welfare economist Tibor Scitovsky (1976), it simply cannot be assumed that people know how to consume effectively. In the absence of skill in consuming and/or the absence of appropriate wares, compensation will be frustrated. Finally, the quest for compensation can be denied in another way. It is possible that demands from aspects of life other than work (e.g., family) are so great that people simply do not have time to obtain and enjoy the rewards that might be compensatory.

Putting these ideas together we see that the compensatory hypothesis demands a thorough understanding of the nature of the conditions of nonwork; simply assuming the motivation to compensate and finding evidence that some compensation takes place is only a start. To date, inquiry guided by this hypothesis has been limited mainly to describing the compensation process or proposing ways to change work so as to provide for some of the desired rewards. However, in order to realize the potential of the hypothesis for discovering ways to enhance the overall quality of life, more careful study of nonwork activities (both existing and possible ones) and of ways to help people "consume" what is available seems to be indicated.

Segmentation, the third universalistic proposition, essentially represents a null hypothesis: There is no relationship between work and the other spheres of life. As a universalistic idea, few have advanced this hypothesis. A notable exception, however, is Dubin (1956; 1958), who viewed social experience in industrial society as being highly segmented with each social segment of a person's life generally lived out independently of the rest. Counter to many proponents of the compensatory proposition, Dubin found positive value in work characteristics such as repetitiveness and specialization. Building on Durkheim (1933), Dubin suggested that these characteristics might signal to the individual that while work institutions, like the rest of society, are segmented by the divisions of labor, their seemingly disparate parts are bound together in meaningful interdependencies. Alternatively stated, through observing their work environments, workers learn that essential dependencies exist among attitudinally and behaviorally insular social segments of their lives. Dubin, at least in his earlier writings, limited his segmentalist reasoning to only those workers who found their central life interests outside of work. His ideas, however, are labeled as universalistic here because in his view the lives of most urban-industrial workers are not centered in their work or, for that matter, in any single institution.

Particularistic Propositions. The particularistic propositions of work/nonwork connections are more complex and difficult to categorize further. Most of these propositions do, however, contain a spillover, compensatory, and/or segmentation hypothesis and combine it with varying other factors used to specify when a given relationship is expected to hold. A frequently cited example of this sort of particularistic model is the one proposed by Wilensky (1960; 1961).[3]

In part, Wilensky argued that the relationship between labor and leisure is contingent upon the technical and social organization of work that an individual experiences. More specifically, he asserted that occupational status can facilitate the integration of the work and nonwork domains of life. He wrote, "Does the job yield no readily-visible status claim? Then it is as neighbor and family man that he will find his chief identity. . . . The work role, if it is status-invisible, will be checked at the workplace door" (Wilensky, 1960, p. 559). Overall, the lower the status of the worker's occupation, the more likely the segmentation hypothesis will hold for the worker. Conversely, as occupational status increases, work will be more likely integrated with (i.e., spill over to) the nonwork spheres of life. Wilensky made analogous claims for the role of job complexity—as it increased, so would the likelihood of integration.

An intuitively appealing alternative to Wilensky's notions, advanced by Parker and Smith (1976), serves as another example of the particularistic approach. They argued that the extremeness of one's affective reactions to work specifies the work-nonwork connection. The spillover hypothesis, for instance, will hold only for those workers highly satisfied or highly dissatisfied with their work. For workers without such extreme work-related experiences, it would appear as if the workers' lives were segmented.

A final example of the use of particularistic proposition can be found in the literature dealing with *occupational community*. Salaman (1974) proposed: "Members of occupational communities build their lives on their work; their work-friends are their friends outside work and their leisure interests and activities are work-based" (p. 19). In other words, the spillover proposition holds among members of such communities but not necessarily among individuals whose occupations cannot be so identified. After Gusfield (1975), van Maanen and Barley (1984) suggested that *consciousness in kind* or an agreement on the occupation's boundaries among the members themselves is the fundamental identifying property of an occupational community. Van Maanan and Barley also provided insights into the ways that the occupational community can condition work-nonwork connections. They asserted that the distinction between work and leisure is blurred to the extent that (a) members of the occupational community are geographically or organizationally clustered; (b) the occupation restricts social relations outside the community through shift work, night work, isolated posting, and the like; (c) entry to the occupational community is kin-based (e.g., sons follow fathers into the occupation); and (d) after Goffman (1961), the occupational community is a "total work institution" as it is for fighter pilots, submariners, intelligence workers, and other such groups. Consequently, the relations between work and nonwork cannot be universal—they depend on the nature of the occupational community and other "participants."

Again, the above examples and other particularistic propositions (e.g., Allport, 1933; Faunce and Dubin, 1975; Kelly, 1972; Neulinger, 1974; Shepard, 1974) specify that the particular relation between work and nonwork depends on some additional variables. As we noted previously, the specific moderator (or mediator) candidates in these propositions vary widely. Interestingly, the advocates of particularistic propositions, in most instances, have looked only to the world of work to isolate contingency variables. Few particularistic model builders have examined the nonwork domains of life for conditions which might influence the nature of work-nonwork connections. As will be shown in the next section, when the relevant empirical literature is reviewed, such conceptual omissions have left us with only a very limited number of studies which examine potential nonwork modifiers of the relation between work and nonwork. The seriousness of these omissions will become apparent later.

Some Empirical Evidence

There are several well-developed streams of research bearing on work-nonwork connections. The flavor of this research and the conclusions which might or might not be drawn from it can be derived from a cursory sampling of the literature. Many investigators have pitted one universalistic proposition against another rather than design their research to assess the more complex, particularistic type of model.[4] These universalistic types of studies are reviewed first, beginning with the evidence bearing on work-leisure connections and evidence on job-life satisfaction relationships. We then review evidence of the particularistic view.

Work-Leisure. There is considerable controversy surrounding the definition of *leisure* (Wilson, 1980) that can not be resolved here. For simplicity, we adopt Kabanoff's (1980) broad-scoped definition. Kabanoff defined *leisure* as a "set of activities that individuals perform outside of their work context and [which] excludes essential maintenance functions" (p. 69). [For alternative definitions, see, for example, DeGrazia (1964), Kelly (1972), Neulinger (1974), and Rapaport and Rapaport (1974).] Most of the empirical research on leisure can be subsumed under this definition.

The results of a number of work-leisure investigations are consistent with the spillover hypothesis. Some examples follow. Kornhauser (1965), in a study principally concerned with the mental health of four hundred Detroit factory workers, found routine work activities to be associated positively with routine leisure activities. These routine leisure activities were reported as affording limited opportunities for self-expression or self-development. Meissner (1971), based on an intensive study of various dimensions of work and leisure, concluded "the job has a long arm indeed" (p. 260), with limited opportunities for the exercise of discretion or social interaction at work being associated positively with limited participation in nonwork-related, voluntary social organizations. Among a sample of workers in an occupation classified as high-risk (namely, air traffic controllers), Musolini and Hershenon (1977) found a greater preference for challenging leisure activities than was expressed among a sample of low-risk, civil service workers. Kohn and Schooler (1973), using a representative sample of civilian, employed men in the United States, observed a significant positive association between doing mentally demanding work and engaging in similar nonwork activities. Finally, Rousseau (1978), in a sample of workers drawn from two organizations, found that those who described their work as having task characteristics such as high degrees of variety and autonomy described their leisure activities in a similar manner.

Why Rousseau and the other researchers cited here found the work-leisure connection that they did is unclear because research addressing the "why" question is sparse. There are a number of possible explanations. For instance, it may be that the income one obtains defines the set of leisure activities one can choose from. This is a point we will raise again later. For now, the examples provided, which are representative of other work-leisure studies supportive of the spillover hypothesis, could lead one to conclude that, in general, there is a correspondence between the nature of one's work and one's choice of leisure activities. But such a conclusion is premature; one must examine the evidence that supports the spillover model in context with competing results. Moreover, the work-leisure evidence that seems to support the spillover proposition may be of the spurious sort (that is, some unmeasured variable may be a cause of the reported correlation between work and leisure, which would lead us to conclude erroneously that work and leisure themselves are causally connected). Although little empirical evidence is available to support the idea that observed work-leisure relationships may be spurious, one study (Kabanoff and O'Brien did research in 1986 on the relationship between stress and leisure needs) suggests that occupation may be such a factor. Other variables that might play important roles include educational level and social class.

The compensatory proposition, like the spillover one, has received some support in the work-leisure literature. Social isolation at work has been found to be compensated for through involvement in community associations (Hagedorn and Labovitz, 1968). In addition, Spreitzer and Snyder (1974) found that workers who derived little satisfaction from their work reported their leisure to be their principal area of self-identification. Champoux (1978), found that persons occupying jobs in high variety, creativity, and challenge compensate with nonwork activities characterized by less of these task attributes. Numerically, however, relatively few studies can be found which substantiate the often advocated, universalistic proposition of compensation.

Support for the segmentation proposition is also sparse. The clearest support comes from two studies by Bacon (1975; 1978). In his first investigation, apparently following the reasoning of Seemen (1971), Bacon sought to ascertain whether the alienating work of the English male manual workers he studied carried over to their nonwork spheres of life, such that they (a) generated false consumption obsessions, (b) participated in passive, uninvolving leisure pursuits, and/or (c) engaged in violent, compensatory leisure behavior. Instead, Bacon (1975) observed no relationship between work and leisure; in his words, "Men who found their work totally involving and interesting were just as likely to be home centered and physically passive in their leisure time as men who found their work a totally alienating experience" (p. 187). In his later study of the carpentry classes, he also found the segmentation hypothesis to hold.

In sum, evidence on the work-leisure relationship presents an unclear picture regarding the three competing universalistic models: at least some data support each alternative. The more ample job-life satisfaction literature, to which we now turn, improves our understanding only marginally.

Job-Life Satisfaction. There is a substantial body of research on the contribution of satisfaction with work to one's avowed happiness in life. Much of it is structured around the spillover, compensatory, and segmentation propositions.

The strategy of job-life satisfaction researchers has generally been to survey a sample of workers to measure their (a) overall job satisfaction or satisfaction with specific facets of their jobs (e.g., promotional opportunities, coworker relations, supervision, pay, and the content of the work itself); and (b) overall life satisfaction or, more rarely, satisfaction with specific nonwork domains of life, and then compute some index of association between the measures of job and life satisfaction. Positive associations are usually interpreted as supporting the spillover hypothesis, negative ones as supporting the compensatory hypothesis, and no observed association as supporting the segmentation hypothesis. The samples employed in these studies have been quite diverse, including, for example, life insurance agents, auto workers, first level supervisors, as well as national probability samples of noninstitutionalized adults.

To make a potentially long story short, in very, very few studies has any support been found for the compensatory proposition (e.g., Mansfield and Evans, 1975); that is, it does not seem that job and life satisfaction are associated negatively. Moreover, while it is often claimed that support for the spillover proposition has been found (e.g., Kavanaugh and Halpern, 1977; Near, Rice, and Hunt, 1978; Orpen, 1978), the observed positive associations between job and life satisfaction are quite modest: the contribution of satisfaction with work to the variance in avowed happiness is less than 10 percent (Rice, Near, and Hunt, 1980). To make matters worse, for methodological reasons even these small relationships are suspect. At least conceptually, since job satisfaction is part of life satisfaction, any index of association between the two may quite likely be inflated (Quinn, Staines, and McCullough, 1974). Inflation is also expected because of the tendency of respondents to answer similarly phrased questions, asked at the same point in time, about their job and life satisfactions, in a like manner (Rice et al., 1980). Given these problems, much of the modest relationship between job and life satisfaction is probably as much methodological as substantive.

Overall, then, as was the case with the research on work-leisure, the job-life satisfaction evidence supplies very weak support for the spillover proposition *or,* alternatively interpreted, for the segmentation proposition. Taking together the work-leisure and job-life satisfaction research on competing universalistic models, it seems plausible to argue that no simple, general work-nonwork connection exists. This conclusion suggests that one look to tests of the various particularistic propositions.

Evidence on the Particularistic Propositions. Probably the most comprehensive particularistic study conducted was reported by London, Crandall, and Seals (1977). The study was comprehensive in the sense that it examined a number of variables which might modify the work-nonwork connection. Based on a probability sample of noninstitutionalized U.S. adults, London et al. (1977) found the job-life satisfaction relationship to be more positive (indicating more of a spillover effect) for (a) white-collar versus blue-collar occupational members, (b) those high versus low in socioeconomic status, (c) college versus noncollege educated, (d) Caucasian versus minority group members, and (e) older versus younger persons. But other studies have contradicted these findings. For example, Kelly (1976) found that as age increased so did the chances of seeing leisure as compensatory. In addition, Brief and Hollenbeck (1985), who also used a probability sample of U.S. adults, found that occupation played no meaningful role in explaining the nature of the relationship between job and life satisfaction.[5] Beyond the dimensions on which London et al. (1977) reported significant findings, gender is the only other potential modifier of the work-nonwork connection that has received more than passing attention. Here, most evidence suggests the connection is stronger among males; but, regrettably again, the results are somewhat mixed (cf. Rice et al., 1980).

Overview. The streams of research reviewed above have led us to no firm conclusions. This pessimistic statement implies that none of the universalistic or particularistic propositions of the work-nonwork connection which have been advanced appear to be uniformly consistent with real world observations. Admittedly, the above review of the literature is not complete. A notable omission is the exclusion of research that is not traditionally construed as focusing on work-nonwork connections.[6]

Nevertheless, the evidence surveyed does indicate that at least some dimensions of work and nonwork sometimes are connected meaningfully. When this connection occurs and why, however, remain unknown. But there are clues available to aid in seeking answers to these questions. In the following section, these clues are presented and built upon to frame an alternative way of viewing when and how the work-nonwork domains of life are linked.

A Suggested Alternative

Clearly, our interests lie in the study of work; but, as others have suggested (e.g., Andrews and Withey, 1974; Seashore, 1975), to understand the connections among work and other life domains, we must adopt an orientation to the whole of life—that is, to the total collection of roles a person plays. At the extreme, this orientation implies that there exists some underlying structure which ties all of life together. Our position is more moderate, and postulates only that parts of experience are stored in some form within the individual and that these residues interact with each other. These residues include cognitive components (e.g., expectations) as well as affective and behavioral predispositions. Experiences of work are related to experiences of leisure in the same way as experiences related to leisure are linked to those concerning the family. It is not assumed, however, that the resulting linkages between any two pairs of life domains are of the same character; rather, the assumed *consistency is at a process level*—concerning *the ways* by which the linkages come about. Congruent with this idea is the suggestion that people are consistent in the reasons why they choose their work and their diversions; and not necessarily that their work has an effect on their choice of leisure activities (e.g., Mansfield, 1972).[7]

Also, congruent with the idea that consistencies exist in the way linkages among life domains come about, is the far from startling observation that there is some tendency for individuals to be consistent in the way they respond to a variety of diverse stimuli or situations. By this we mean that while people may exhibit attitudes and behaviors that are specific to particular roles and situations, they also carry somewhat enduring attributes—knowledge, skills, abilities, needs, wants, desires, and so forth, across life domains. In the propositions and research we reviewed earlier, it seems that all too often James's (1891) description of multiple social selves was carried too far; in effect, by using it, an individual in different role-situations somehow comes to be seen as a differentiable social being rather than as a physically and psychologically whole person. However, the view we adopt here is that while the roles a person performs (e.g., father and worker) may be distinguishable, the person him/herself cannot be thought of as neatly divisible across those roles. In particular, we examine the processes contributing to people's exhibiting role invariant value structures. To the degree such a structure exists, it ties much of life together, at least in terms of the way linkages among life domains come about. The construct of values describes such a structure.

Values: The Integrating Structure. The construct of *values* so central to our reasoning here is influenced strongly by Rokeach (e.g., 1973). Therefore, we begin by summarizing the key aspects of his perspective. Rokeach (1973) wrote:

A *value* is an enduring belief that a specific mode of conduct or end-state of existence is personally or socially preferable to an opposite or converse mode of conduct or end-state of existence. A *value system* is an enduring organization of beliefs concerning preferable modes of conduct or end-states of existence along a continuum of relative importance. (p. 5)

Rokeach's elaborations of these definitions are noteworthy. By *enduring,* Rokeach did not mean that values do not change. Rather he asserted explicitly that there is a "relative quality of values" (p. 6). Values receive their enduring quality from the fact that they are taught in isolation as absolute or always desirable. On the other hand, as people face reality, values come into conflict. Over time, however, people integrate the values into a hierarchically structured system. Behavior can be a product of only one value being activated or, if more than one value is activated, of the relative importance of values that are activated.

In defining a value as a belief, Rokeach limited the scope to a particular class of beliefs—prescriptive or proscriptive beliefs that judge some means or end as desirable or undesirable. Like all beliefs, Rokeach asserted, values have cognitive, affective, and behavioral components. The cognitive component refers to the desirable—to what a peron knows as the correct way to behave or the end-state to pursue. The affective component treats the emotional dimension—to feel for or against some stimulus, such as a type of behavior or those who exhibit it. A value is behavioral in that, when activated, it leads to action.

In asserting that a value refers to a mode of conduct or end-state of existence, Rokeach was proposing two kinds of values. Values referring to modes of conduct are *means* values or *instrumental* values. Alternatively, values referring to end-states of existence can be thought of as *terminal.* While terminal values may be self-centered (e.g., peace of mind) or society-centered (e.g., world peace), instrumental values concern either morality (e.g., being honest) or competence (e.g., being imaginative). In noting that a value is something that is personally or socially preferable, he acknowledged that beliefs can apply to a number of different people or groups.

In addition, Rokeach maintained that a value is part of a system of values. A preferable mode of behavior is ordered among other instrumental values in terms of its relative importance. Correspondingly, a preferable end-state is ordered among other terminal values in terms of its relative importance. All systems, like the values comprising them, are enduring. Finally, the two systems are separate yet functionally interconnected.

Rokeach's systems of terminal and instrumental values refer to the processes that work to interrelate the various domains of a person's life. Thus, we turn to Rokeach's (1973) assertion that values function as standards that guide ongoing activities, such as general plans employed to resolve conflicts and make decisions, and give expression to human needs. Such functionality, in fact, has often been demonstrated, at least in regards to *domain or role specific* thoughts, feelings, or actions. Among students, for instance, values have been shown to be predictive of educational choices and adjustments. The impressive research program of Norman T. Feather (1975) supports this claim.

Feather found that university students matched their values to those attributed to the programs of study they entered (e.g., Feather, 1970; 1971; Feather and Collins, 1974).[8] For example, business administration students reported a median rank of two for a comfortable life as a terminal value. This value was ranked considerably lower by students choosing other majors (e.g., humanities majors ranked it seventeen and social sciences majors fourteen). Moreover, Feather (1972a; 1972b) found students more satisfied with school the more congruent their values were with those they saw their school promoting. Our confidence in the general validity of Feather's findings is enhanced by their consistency with theories of vocational choice (e.g., Holland, 1966, 1973; Rosenberg, 1957) and the empirical results of others (Dukes, 1955).

More relevant to the current thesis are students addressing the functionality of values across domains; however, such research is relatively rare (e.g., Atieh, Brief, and Vollrath, 1987; Furnham, 1985a, 1985b). Once again, the exemplary research has been provided by Feather (1984).

Feather (1984) studied the impact of values on work beliefs conceptualized in terms of Weber's (1930) notion of the Protestant ethic *and* on conservative attitudes such as enforcement of the death penalty, white superiority, and chastity. He found rankings of the terminal values of salvation and of the instrumental values of obedience and self-control to be positively associated both with orientations toward the Protestant ethic and conservatism. Also, Feather found rankings of the instrumental values of broad-mindedness and imaginativeness to be negatively associated with the Protestant ethic and conservatism. These results take on special importance for the study of work and nonwork when they are linked to other research that has shown measures of Protestant ethic endorsement to be related to factors such as internal work motivation; performance levels on boring, repetitive tasks; and commitment to one's employer (cf. Furnham, 1984). In addition, the conservative social attitudes studied by Feather have been shown in other studies (cf. Wilson, 1973) to be related to various religious, political, and superstitious behaviors. These findings, coupled with the results of Feather, suggest the utility of a *process* perspective for understanding how the relationship between work and nonwork are experienced. Specifically, one's values (at least values as treated by Rokeach) may produce consistency across domains of life in terms of what may appear to be disparate, domain-specific thoughts, feelings, and actions.

Additional support for the process view to understanding across-domain consistency can be derived from the quality-of-life literature. Most of this literature begins with the question, "How much does job satisfaction contribute to life satisfaction?" (Life satisfaction is viewed as an index of quality of life or subjective well-being.) This perspective is a "bottom-up" one; that is, a person's avowed happiness in life is seen as a function of the aggregations of his or her satisfaction with each of the domains comprising his or her life. Diener (1984) notes that this bottom-up perspective of a happy life is often contrasted with a "top-down" perspective, which suggests that causation proceeds from higher order elements down through more elemental levels. [As an aside, it should be noted that recent efforts in personality (e.g., Watson and Clark, 1984) and organizational (e.g., Brief et al., 1988; Staw, Bell, and Clawsen, 1986) psychology also emphasize a top-down approach.] Here, we view the process through which one comes to judge his or her quality of life as lying somewhere between the bottom-up and top-down views. In particular, causation is seen as proceeding from a person's value structure down to the relationships among the role or situation that person occupies; however, these relationships also are seen as molded by the social realities that the individual finds in the role or situation he or she occupies. Below, we address the top-down element of our argument; later, we turn to the effects of social context.

Recall that the elements within each value system (terminal or instrumental) are seen as organized by their importance as guiding principles in life (e.g., Williams, 1968). Now we introduce a second dimension along which a value may vary relative to others within its systems. That dimension is called applicability. A given value—say a world at peace, which was ranked as most important in a 1968 probability sample of American men and women—may be seen by an individual as a highly desirable end-state or mode of conduct. Nevertheless, it might not exert much functional influence over the person's life, because the value is not viewed by the individual as applicable across a range of life domains.

The term *applicable* means that, within a life domain, the value is salient and actionable; indeed, progress toward its attainment is deemed as feasible. As a citizen, one may vote for a presidential candidate that he or she believes will contribute to world peace; but, what acts can a person take to obtain world peace in another life domain role (e.g., as a husband or a wife)? A world at peace is simply not as applicable in some domains as it is in others.

The notion of applicability is related to other concepts used to describe human psychological processes. It is close to the concept of *expectancy* contained in various theories of human motivation (Mitchell and Biglan, 1971). Generally, expectancy refers to the perception that one's efforts will produce an outcome. If the outcome is desired and it is perceived that one's efforts will lead to the outcome, then the person is said to be motivated to exert that effort. The notion of applicability also has parallels in structural versions of symbolic interactions (e.g., Stryker, 1968; 1980). There, the term *relative salience* is used to denote the specific probability of enacting an identity in a given role situation. Thus, extending Rokeach's conceptualization to capture the idea of applicability appears to be consistent with both psychological theorizing about motivation (e.g., Fishbein, 1967; Vroom, 1964) and sociological models of how one's self-identity becomes socially enacted (e.g., Rosenberg, 1979; Turner, 1978).

If a value is important *and* applicable in two domains, then because of the functionality of this value, one will observe a person's thoughts, feelings, and/or actions in the two domains to be linked. The greater the number of important values the person applies to both domains, the stronger the observed bond between the two. For instance, if a sense of accomplishment is an important guiding principle in a person's life and she applies that value to her work and leisure domains, then one might see a degree of consistency in the achievement-related characteristics of her work and leisure activities. Alternatively, if a sense of accomplishment is not applied to the work domain because of low expectations, then no such consistency would be seen. Thus, to ascertain the connection between work and another domain, one must know what a person values *and* where those values are sought. In addition, one must know the psychological processes an individual uses to make sense of his/her environment. These processes differ widely across individuals (see McCaulley, 1985).

The universalistic spillover, compensation, and segmentation propositions simply are not developed sufficiently to give adequate guidance for comprehending this process. In our view, the nature of the relationship between work and nonwork is particularistic—varying as a function of the person's value and information processing structures. The failure of students using these general perspectives to incorporate these mediating processes in their research may explain at least some of the conflicting empirical evidence on work-nonwork connections we reviewed earlier. But we do not know this for sure, because these processes and their applicability to work and nonwork domains remain to be investigated by those concerned with how work is bound up in the rest of life.

Rokeach's model provides one final set of ideas for refining our understanding of the processes affecting work-nonwork connections—namely, the distinction between terminal and instrumental values. It is anticipated that instrumental values will have wider applicability than terminal ones. Therefore, greater connections between work and nonwork can be expected in the mode of conduct across domains than in the desired end-states these behavioral means are aimed at. This is so because instrumental values, (e.g., being helpful, honest, and responsible) probably are seen as more obtainable, and thus more applicable, across a broader range of role situations than such terminal values as wisdom and mature love. If we are right, then the current search for connections between work and nonwork needs to broaden its focus from satisfaction and task linkages, to encompass modes of conduct across domains. For instance, people who value being helpful are unlikely to limit their helpfulness to the confines of a single domain; thus, it is expected that if a person is found to be helpful at work, it is likely he/she also will be found to behave helpfully toward others at home, at play, and elsewhere. The point is, we must not only broaden our horizons to consider the ways in which value structures may affect how work and nonwork are bound together; we also need to consider what it is about work and nonwork that may be connected. While we have noted numerous studies of how job satisfaction may be bound to life satisfaction, we are virtually unaware of any study of how a particular mode of conduct at work (e.g., helpfulness) may be bound to that mode as evidenced in other life domains. Dependent on a person's value structure, it would not surprise us to find a wide array of thoughts, feelings, and actions to be connected across domains. Again, however, we do not know, given the narrow focus of past research.

Thus far, our sketch of an alternative perspective has dealt primarily with the person's value structure in terms of value importance and applicability. However, the processes linking work and nonwork are vitally affected by the social context in which the person is embedded. Now we turn to the roles social context might play in molding work-nonwork connections. This exploration will demonstrate that our current intraindividual orientation toward explaining work-nonwork connections is incomplete.

The Social Context. Here, the term *social context* refers to the institutional and cultural surroundings of a people. This broad use of the term encompasses social relationships and organizations as well as the customs (behavioral and otherwise), which transcend the institutional boundaries within a society. As noted by Rokeach (1973), these features of the social environment shape one's values. While this influence of social context on values is pervasive, our attention here is limited to work-nonwork connections.

Our treatment of social context is also a limited one. Social context is a very broad construct. It could easily encompass almost everything. In order to set some boundaries and maintain a focus on work-nonwork matters that have been studied systematically, we opted for one attribute of the work role-situation, namely, occupation. As will become clear, occupation is an important construct about which much can be inferred as to its effects on work-nonwork connections.

From a macrosociological perspective, at least in industrial societies, the concept of occupation is very helpful in analyzing social structure. Social structures or the stratification of them are attributable to two processes—social differentiation and social ranking (cf. Sheppard, 1974). Social differentiation is the assigning of specialized duties to specific social positions; it is the division of labor. Social ranking is the evaluation and location of social positions in a hierarchy. Social positions which have a sufficiently similar hierarchical location are termed a *social class*. In fact, in Western societies, the most general index of social status (or ranking) is social class (Miller and Form, 1980).

Class, and thus, status, are fundamentally determined, though not exclusively, by one's occupation (e.g., Warner, Meeker, and Eels, 1949; Friedman et al., 1954). Class and status, along with power (or using Weber's term, *party*) have long been recognized as the key criteria for stratifying a social structure (Gerth and Mills, 1946). The occupational structure of a society, therefore, can be seen as that society's infrastructure or at least a key defining property of it. This macro-organizing function of occupations has broad implications for individuals. As addressed below, an individual's occupation as a facet of the social context of his/her work sphere of life has substantial influence on the nonwork domains of that person. Again, these influences are tied to the role of occupational membership as a key determinant of a society's social structure.

Occupational work supplies material rewards in the form of income (Dubin, 1958; Caplow, 1964; Moore, 1969). The impact of this income is probably the most obvious of occupational influences across life domains (Andrews and Withey, 1974, Brief and Aldag, in press; Dubin, Hedley, and Taveggia, 1976). Members of higher earning occupational groups (or classes) are afforded greater *life chances*, to use Weber's term, than members of low earning groups. These life chances are the likelihood of securing various desired goods and services that are consumed, more often than not, outside the work domain. In the case of leisure, for example, as one's income level rises so does the absolute amount of money spent on leisure (Meisell, 1978). In this way, occupational earnings shape the leisure domain by placing limits on the activities that can be afforded (Cheek and Burch, 1976; Owen, 1969). While measuring the cognitive and emotional aspects of one's values may indicate a propensity for certain sorts of leisure activities, the person's financial resources earned through occupational work may constrain enactment of those values. Thus, an individual's occupation can be seen as moderating the effects of value structure on work-nonwork connections. Demonstrating the potentially pervasive influence of occupation income is the often reported finding that as income increases so does overall life satisfaction (cf. Diener, 1984). That is, it appears money *may* buy one happiness. This might occur because money is a vehicle for satisfying certain values (e.g., a comfortable life and family security). While evoking the construct of needs rather than values, this, is precisely the argument advanced by Brief and Aldag (in press) who further reason that money's potential to satisfy goes beyond the material realm to impact on social relations and even personal growth and development.

Alternatively, the observed income-life satisfaction relationship may be confounded by other factors, such as access to psychologically rewarding work. To our knowledge, however, analyses addressing the plausibility of such confounding remain to be conducted.

In less material ways, as suggested above, occupational membership exerts a number of other influences. For example, occupational prestige [which is associated closely with, yet distinct from, income (Salz, 1944)] has been found to be related to numerous nonwork activities (Nosow, 1962). Warner (1953), for instance, in his classic Yankee City study found (a) while 70 percent of the upper strata belonged to community associations, only 40 percent and 25 percent, respectively, of the middle and lower stratum did so; and (b) the types of associations participated in also varied by strata with upper strata members belonging to garden clubs, historical societies, civic groups, country clubs, and the like; and members of lower stratum more often joining such associations as fraternal orders, patriotic groups, and religion-based clubs. Warner's results dealing with associational participation rates have been replicated often for urban workers (e.g., Axelrod, 1956; Bell and Boat, 1957). More generally, occupational prestige has been tied to choice of friends, style of dress, language, religious affiliation, political activities, as well as to community association membership (e.g., Anderson, 1961; Champoux, 1981; Lynd and Lynd, 1929; Sorokin, 1928).

In our view, these observed differences, at least in part, are attributable to how others react socially to another's occupational prestige, and these reactions serve to affect a person's ability to enact his/her values. Support for this assertion can be found in the group dynamics literature, where it is known that others act more positively toward those occupying more rather than less prestigious positions (Shaw, 1981). Doors appear to open to all sorts of activities for members of prestigius occupations which are closed to members of less occupationally prestigious groups. These opportunities bring members of prestigious occupations into interactions with others in settings from which lower status persons are excluded.[9] In these social settings, norms governing thoughts, feelings, and actions evolve which further differentiate the classes. These norms suggest to people the "right" ways to dress, talk, and possibly even what one's religious affiliation should be. Thus, occupational prestige may cause people to find themselves behaving with others in social settings in ways over which they have relatively limited conscious control. That is to say, the social forces attached to occupational prestige are not only strong, but they, to a degree, are hidden. The lawyer, for instance, who values equality and freedom, may find him/herself, upon entering a corporate practice, acting inconsistently with these desired end-states. It not only is the lawyer's work environment which creates this inconsistency; the other, nonwork social contexts to which his/her occupational prestige has led him/her contributes meaningfully to producing the effect. Of course, cognitive dissonance theories (e.g., Festinger, 1957) tell us that, over time, location in these contexts will leave the lawyer with a different set of values, thereby reducing value-behavior conflicts. Indeed, this is what adult socialization is.

Membership in some occupations dictates time and space relationships which specify certain work-nonwork connections that reduce the effects of values on behavior. For example, at times, occupations like firefighters (Smith, 1972) and railroaders (Salaman, 1974) require their members to work physically isolated from typical nonwork activities. Perhaps to a lesser degree, the same can be said about occupations involving shift work or "deviant" work schedules. Other occupations [e.g., soldiering (Janowitz, 1960) and carnival work (Bryant, 1972)] create *total work institutions* (Van Maanen and Barley, 1984) which, through their physical isolation, force occupational members to eat, sleep, and play together rather than with "outsiders." Simply, some forms of occupational work require physical isolation, in varying degrees, from certain nonwork activities; and those who perform such work may face special constraints in acting on their values. Again, however, values are dynamic. It is expected, for example, that the soldier serving an extended period in an isolated station will begin to modify his value structure consistent with the dictates of his isolated work.

In sum, occupational membership has been used as an exemplary facet of social context; and, through it, we have suggested the ways in which social context may moderate the effects of value structure on work-nonwork connections. Moreover, it was indicated that, over time, context may serve to shape values. Thus, to understand the ways in which a person connects the work-nonwork domains of life, the individual's value structure, the nature of the social contexts in which the person is embedded, the positions he/she occupies in those contexts, and the process that link these together—perhaps in a somewhat unique way for each individual—must be examined. Recalling that occupational membership is a mere example of how one might construe social context, the difficulty in trying to understand work-nonwork connections becomes readily apparent.

Conclusions

Conventional theoretical and empirical analyses of work-nonwork connections have been reviewed; and from this review, it has been concluded that the ways in which people connect the work and nonwork domains of their lives is not well understood. As an alternative to conventional approaches, it has been suggested that a person's value structure guides the processes that bind work-nonwork domains. If those values important to an individual are seen as applicable by him/her to two or more domains, then, it was argued, covariation in the individual's thoughts, feelings, and/or actions across these domains is to be expected. These expectations, it was argued further, must be tempered, however, by the realities of the social context in which the individual is embedded. That is, facets of the individual's social environment were construed as moderating the effects of value structure on work non-work connections. It has also been noted briefly that social context may serve, over time, to shape one's values.

The alternative model introduced is an extremely crude heuristic for understanding how people connect the work-nonwork domains of their lives. Its crudeness is attributable to the vagueness with which remarkably complex relationships are dealt. This vagueness is reflective of gaps in knowledge. It is not known how people come to prioritize their values, or how they come to see these values as applicable or not to particular life domains; and, it is not known how social contexts function in either of these two processes. Moreover, we seem to be ill-equipped to conceptualize and investigate the complex, longitudinal processes through which individuals cope with their changing life situations. Without this knowledge, we are left with making poorly grounded inferences about the interplay among values, social contexts, and work/nonwork connections. We do know that conventional thinking in the area has not been particularly productive; thus, our alternative is offered as a starting point for beginning to rethink the ways the components of a person's life become intertwined such as they are. Its crudeness aside, the alternative perspective does show some promise. Previous universalistic and particularistic thinking about work/nonwork connections has generally ignored the psychological *process* by which the domains of a person's life become connected. One consequence of this lacuna was that the social context might affect this process, also was not attended to. Thus, the currently proposed heuristic is conceptually richer than its alternatives. We offer it as a framework for guiding thinking and empirical inquiry to encompass the complex and perhaps idiographic processes that characterize work/nonwork connections.

Notes

1. The term *social institutions* refers to clusters of norms, values, beliefs, roles, statuses, and groups that guide social action toward the fulfillment of one or more of the basic needs of society (Sheppard, 1984). Examples of the sorts on institutions being referred to include economic, educational, family, political, and religious ones.

2. The propositions discussed, in large part, were identified in reviews of the literature by Champoux (1981), Kabanoff (1980), Parker and Smith (1976), and Wilson (1980).

3. While Wilensky's (1960; 1961) work is cited widely, it is almost invariably misrepresented (cf. Brief and Hollenbeck, 1985). More often than not he is treated as advancing the three previously introduced universalistic propositions. Our discussion of his ideas, however, clearly shows they are of the particularistic sort.

4. Indeed, later in the chapter, we note that the typical universalistic study yields results salient to all three of the present universalistic predictions.

5. Brief and Hollenbeck (1985), to be precise, did detect that occupation moderated the job-life satisfaction relationship, at least in a statistical sense. But, since the incremental variance explained in life satisfaction by the interaction between job satisfaction and their occupational variable was less than 1 percent, they concluded that the effect was of limited practical significance. Others, however, have interpreted similar results quite differently. For example, Bamundo and Kopelman (1980) found the incremental variance explained by the interaction to be just 1 percent; yet, they perceived this to mean that occupation is an important moderator variable.

6. For example, there is a facet of stress research concerned with the interplay between work and family roles. It is clear from reading summaries of this research (Brief, Schuler, and Van Sell, 1981; Burke and Bradshaw, 1981; Greenhaus and Beutell, 1985) that work and family somehow are intertwined. But, here too, ambiguity abounds. For instance, while Jones and Butler (1980) found the extent of stress producing conflict between work and family roles was negatively related to work perceived as challenging and interesting, Burke, Weir, and Duwors (1980) found no support for such a relationship. For more on the research not traditionally construed as focusing on work-nonwork connections, see Brief and Aldag (in press) and Brief and Atieh (1987).

7. We use the words *choose* and *choice* rather loosely. By doing so, we in no way assert that people are free to define the various role-situations in which they find themselves embedded. That is, the alternatives available (or perceived to be so) to an individual are limited. They are limited not only by the now well-known cognitive constraints on rationality of judgment and choice (e.g., Kahneman and Tversky, 1982; Simon, 1957; Tversky and Kahneman, 1974; 1981). More important to us, one's choices in life are limited by a host of economic, political, and social factors which generally can be construed as being beyond the control of the individual. Simply, for instance, the life chances afforded a baby born to a black, unwed, high school dropout in the South Bronx are not comparable to those of the baby born to white, educated parents residing in an affluent suburb. Indeed, as the baby from the South Bronx matures, she may feel her life's course is predetermined.

8. Feather measured values by using the Rokeach Value Survey which requires respondents first to rank eighteen terminal values in order of their importance as guiding principles in life and then to rank eighteen instrumental values in order of their importance. Rather elaborate conceptual and empirical procedures used to identify the particular values gauged are described by Rokeach (1973). Considerable evidence bearing on the widely used survey's reliability and validity has been accumulated (e.g., Braithwaite and Law, 1985; Gorsuch, 1970; Jones, Sensenig, and Ashmore, 1978). The values contained in the survey are listed in Appendix 6a.

9. Also, higher status people may be excluded from full participation in lower status groups, but these exclusions do not seem to be recognized as being as important to most people.

References

Allport, F.H. (1933). *Institutional behavior.* Chapel Hill, NC: University of North Carolina Press.

Anderson, N . (1961). *Work and leisure.* London: Routledge and Kegan Paul.

————. (1964). *Dimensions of work: The sociology of a work culture.* New York: David McKay.

Andrews, F.M., and Withey, S.B. (1974). Developing measures of perceived life quality: Results from several national surveys. *Social Indicators Research, 1,* pp. 1–26.

Argyris, C. (1957). *Personality and organizations: The conflict between systems and individual.* New York: Harper and Row.

————. (1964). *Integrating the individual and the organizations.* New York: Wiley.

Atieh, J.M., Brief, A.P., and Vollrath, D.A. (1987). The Protestant work ethic-conservatism paradox: Beliefs and values in work and life. *Personality and Individual Differences, 8,* pp. 577–80.

Axelrod, M. (1956). Urban structures and social participation. *American Sociological Review, 21,* pp. 13–18.

Bacon, W. (1975). Leisure and the alienated worker: A critical ressessment. *Journal and Leisure Research, 7.* pp. 179–90.

————. (1978). Leisure and the craft-workers. In M. Smith (ed.), *Leisure in urban society.* Salford, England: Salford University Research Center of Leisure Studies.

Bamundo, P.J., and Kopelman, R.E. (1980). The moderating effects of occupation, age, and urbanization on the relationship between job satisfaction and life satisfaction. *Journal of Vocational Behavior, 17,* pp. 106–23.

Bell, W., and Boat, M.D. (1957). Urban neighborhoods and informal social relations. *American Journal of Sociology, 52,* pp. 391–8.

Berger, P.L. (1964). Some general observations on the problem of work. In P.L. Berger (ed.), *The human shape of work.* New York: Macmillan, pp. 211–41.

Bottomore, T.B. (1964). *Karl Marx: Early writings.* New York: McGraw-Hill.

Braithwaite, V.A., and Law, H.G. (1985). Structure of human values: Testing adequacy of the Rokeach Value Survey. *Journal of Personality and Social Psychology, 49,* pp. 250–63.

Brief, A.P., Schuler, R., and Van Sell, M. (1981). *Managing job stress.* Boston: Little, Brown.

Brief, A.P., and Hollenbeck, J.R. (1985). Work and the quality of life. *International Journal of Psychology, 20,* pp. 199–206.

Brief, A.P., and Atieh, J.M. (1987). Studying job stress: Are we making mountains out of molehills? *Journal of Occupational Behavior, 8.* 115–26.

Brief, A.P., and Aldag, R.J. (In press). The economic functions of work. In K.M. Rowland and G.R. Ferris (eds.), *Research in Personnel and Human Resources Management.* Greenwich, CT.: JAI Press.

Brief, A.P., Burke, M.J., George, J., Robinson, B., and Webster, J. (1988). Should negative affectivity remain an unmeasured variable in the study of job stress? *Journal of Applied Psychology, 73,* pp. 193–8.

Bryant, C.D. (1972). Sawdust in their shoes: The carnival as a neglected complex organization and work culture. In C.D. Bryant (ed.), *The social dimensions of work.* Englewood Cliffs, NJ: Prentice Hall, pp. 180–203.

Burke, R.J., Weir, T., and DuWors, R.E. (1980). Work demands on administrators and spouse well-being. *Human Relations, 33,* 253–78.

Burke, R.J., and Bradshaw, P. (1981). Occupational and life stress and the family. *Small Group Behavior, 2,* pp. 329–75.

Caplow, T. (1964). *The sociology of work.* New York: McGraw-Hill.

Champoux, J.E. (1978). Perceptions of work and nonwork: A reexamination of the compensatory and spillover models. *Sociology of Work and Occupations, 5*, pp. 402–22.

———. (1981). A sociological perspective on work involvement. *International Review of Applied Psychology, 30*, pp. 65–86.

Cheek, N., and Burch, W. (1976). *The social organization of leisure in human society.* New York: Harper and Row.

Clayre, A. (1974). *Work and play: Ideas and experiences of work and leisure.* New York: Harper and Row.

Cooley, C.H. (1962). *Social organization: A study of the larger mind.* New York: Schocken.

DeGrazia, S. (1964). *Of time, work, and leisure.* Garden City, NY: Doubleday.

Diener, E. (1984). Subjective well-being. *Psychology Bulletin, 95*, 542–75.

Dubin, R. (1956). Industrial worker's worlds: A study of the *central life interest* of industrial workers. *Social Problems, 3*, pp. 131–42.

———. (1958). *The world of work.* Englewood Cliffs, NJ.: Prentice Hall.

———. (1973). Work and nonwork: Institutional perspectives. In M.D. Dunnette (ed.), *Work and nonwork in the year 2001.* Belmont, CA: Wadsworth, pp. 53–89.

Dubin, R., Healey, A., and Taveggia, T.C. (1975). Attachment to work. In R. Dubin (ed.), *Handbook of work, organization, and society.* Chicago: Rand McNally.

Dukes, W.F. (1955). Psychological studies of values. *Psychological Bulletin, 52*, pp. 24–50.

Durkheim, E. (1933). *On the division of labor in society.* New York: MacMillan.

Engels, F. (1892). *The condition of the working class in England in 1844.* London: Allen and Unwin.

Faunce, W.A., and Dubin, R. (1975). Individual investment in work and living. In L.E. Davis, and A. Cherns (eds.), *The quality of working life.* New York: Free Press, pp. 299–316.

Feather, N.T. (1970). Educational choice and student attitudes in relation to terminal and instrumental values. *Australian Journal of Psychology, 22*, pp. 127–44.

———. (1971). Similarity of value systems as a determinant of educational choice at the university level. *Australian Psychologist, 6*, pp. 181–8.

———. (1972a). Value similarity and school adjustment. *Australian Journal of Psychology, 24*, pp. 305–15.

———. (1972b). Value similarity and value systems in state and independent secondary schools. *Australian Journal of Psychology, 24*, pp. 305–15.

———. (1975). *Values in education and society.* New York: Free Press.

———. (1984). Protestant ethic, conservatism, and values. *Journal of Personality and Social Psychology, 46*, pp. 1132–41.

Feather, N.T., and Collins, J.M. (1974). Differences in attitudes and values of students in relation to program of study at a college of advanced education. *Australian Journal of Educations, 18*, 16–29.

Festinger, L. (1957). *A theory of cognitive dissonance.* Stanford, CA.: Stanford University Press.

Fishbein, M. (1967). Attitude and the prediction of behavior. In M. Fishbein (ed.), *Readings in attitude theory and measurement.* New York: Wiley, pp. 477–92.

Friedman, E.A., Havighurst, R.J., Hartan, W.H., Bowers, J., Gruen, D.C., Ireland, R.A., and Jhanas, E. (1954). *The meaning of work and retirement.* Chicago: University of Chicago Press.

Friedmann, G. (1960). Leisure and technological civilization. *International Social Science Journal, 12,* pp. 509–21.

Fromm, E. (1966). *Marx's concept of man.* New York: Ungar.

Furnham, A. (1984). The Protestant work ethic: A review of psychological literature. *European Journal of Social Psychology, 14,* 87–104.

———. (1985a). Why do people save? Attitudes to, and habits of, saving money in Britain. *Journal of Applied Social Psychology, 15,* pp. 354–73.

———. (1985b). Determinants of attitudes toward social security recipients. *British Journal of Social Psychology, 24,* 19–27.

Gerth, H.H., and Mills, C.W. (1946). *From Max Weber, Essays in sociology.* New York: Oxford University Press.

Goffman, E. (1961). *Encounters.* Indianapolis: Bobbs-Merrill.

Gorsuch, R.L. (1970). Rokeach's approach to value systems and social comparisons. *Review of Religious Research, 11,* pp. 139–43.

Green, T.F. (1968). *Work, leisure, and the American schools.* New York: Random House.

Greenhaus, J.H., and Beutell, N.J. (1985). Sources of conflict between work and family roles. *Academy of Management Review, 10,* pp. 76–88.

Gross, K. (1901). *The play of man.* New York: Appleton.

Gusfield, J.R. (1975). *Community: A critical response.* New York: Harper and Row.

Hagedorn, R., and Labovitz, S. (1968). Participation in community associations by occupation: A test of three theories. *American Sociological Review, 33,* pp. 272–83.

Hauser, R.M., and Featherman, D.L. (1977). *The process of stratification: Trends and analyses.* New York: Academic Press.

Holland, J.L. (1966). *The psychology of vocational choice: A theory of personality types and model environments.* Waltham, MA: Blaisdell.

———. (1973). *Making vocational choices: A theory of careers.* Englewood Cliffs, NJ: Prentice Hall.

Israel, J. (1971). *Alienation: From Marx to modern sociology.* Boston: Allyn and Bacon.

James, W. (1891). *The principle of psychology.* London: MacMillan.

Janowitz, M. (1960). *The professional soldier.* Glencoe, IL: Free Press.

Jones, A.P., and Butler, M.C. (1980). A role transition approach to the stress of organizationally-induced family role disruptions. *Journal of Marriage and the Family, 42,* pp. 367–76.

Jones, R.A., Sensenig, J., and Ashmore, R.D. (1978). Systems of values and their multidimensional representations. *Multivariate Behavioral Research, 13,* pp. 255–70.

Kabanoff, B. (1980). Work and nonwork. A review of models, methods and findings. *Psychological Bulletin, 88,* pp. 60–77.

Kahneman, D., and Tversky, A. (1982). Psychology of preferences. *Scientific American, 246* (January), pp. 161–73.

Kavanaugh, M.G., and Halpern, M. (1977). The impact of job level and sex on the relationship between life and job satisfaction. *Academy of Management Journal, 20,* pp. 66–73.

Kelly, J.R. (1972). Work and leisure: A simplified paradigm. *Journal of Leisure Research, 4,* pp. 50–62.

———. (1976). A critique of *Leisure and the alienated worker: A critical reassessment of three radical theories,* by Bacon. *Journal of Leisure Research, 8,* pp. 129–31.

Kluckhohn, C. (1951). Values and value orientations in the theory of action. In T. Parsons, and E.A. Shils (eds.), *Toward a general theory of action.* Cambridge: Harvard University Press.

Kohn, M.L. (1980). Job complexity and adult personality. In N.J. Smelser and E.H. Erikson (eds.), *Themes of work and love in adulthood.* Cambridge, MA: Harvard University Press, pp. 193–210.

Kohn, M.L., and Schooler, C. (1973). On occupational experience and psychological functioning. *American Sociological Review, 38,* pp. 97–118.

———. (1982). Job conditions and personality: A longitudinal assessment of their reciprocal effects. *American Journal of Sociology, 87,* pp. 1257–86.

Kornhauser, A.W. (1965). *Mental health of the industrial worker.* New York: Wiley.

London, M., Crandall, R., and Seals, G.W. (1977). The contribution of job and leisure satisfaction to quality of life. *Journal of Applied Psychology, 62,* pp. 328–34.

Lynd, R.S., and Lynd, H.M. (1929). *Middletown: A study in contemporary American culture.* New York: Harcourt and Brace.

Machlowitz, M. (1977). Workaholics. *Across the Board, 14* (10), pp. 30–7.

Mansfield, R. (1972). Need satisfaction and need importance in and out of work. *Studies in Personnel Psychology, 14,* pp. 21–7.

Mansfield, R., and Evans, M.G. (1975). Work and nonwork in two occupational groups. *Industrial Relations, 6,* pp. 48–54.

McCaulley, M.H. (1985). *A guide to the development and use of the Myers-Briggs Type Indicator.* Palo Alto, CA: Consulting Psychologists Press.

Meisell, J. (1978). Leisure, politics, and political science: A preliminary exploration. *Social Science Information, 17,* pp. 185–229.

Meissner, M. (1971). The long arm of the job: A study of work and leisure. *Industrial Relations, 10,* pp. 239–60.

Meszaros, I. (1970). *Marx's theory of alienation.* New York: Harper and Row.

Miller, D.C., and Form, W.H. (1980). *Industrial sociology.* New York: Harper and Row.

Mitchell, T.R., and Biglan, A. (1971). Instrumentality theories: Current uses in psychology. *Psychological Bulletin, 76,* pp. 432–54.

Moore, W.E. (1969). Changes in occupational structures. In W.A. Faunce and W.H. Form (eds.), *Comparative perspectives on industrial society.* Boston: Little, Brown, pp. 107–25.

Musolino, R.F., and Hershenon, D.B. (1977). Advocational sensation seeking in high and low risk-taking occupations. *Journal of Vocational Behavior, 10,* pp. 358–65.

Near, J.P., Rice, R.W., and Hunt, R.G. (1978). Work and extra-work correlates of life and job satisfaction. *Academy of Management Journal, 21,* pp. 248–64.

Neulinger, J. (1974). *The psychology of leisure.* Springfield, IL: Charles C. Thomas.

Nosow, S. (1962). Social correlates of occupational membership. In S. Nosow, and W.H. Form (eds.), *Man, work, and society.* New York: Basic Books, pp. 517–36.

Orpen, C. (1978). Work and nonwork satisfaction: A causal correlation analysis. *Journal of Applied Psychology, 63,* pp. 530–2.

Owen, J.D. (1969). *The price of leisure.* Rotterdam: Rotterdam University Press, 1969.

Panghurn, W. (1922). The worker's leisure and his individuality. *American Journal of Sociology, 27,* pp. 433–41.

Parker, S. (1983). *Leisure and work.* London: George Allen & Unwin.

Parker, S.R., and Smith, M.A. (1976). In R. Dubin (ed.), *Handbook of work, organization, and society.* Chicago: Rand McNally, pp. 37–62.

Quinn, R.P., Staines, G.L., and McCollough, M.R. (1974). *Job satisfaction: Is there a trend?* Manpower Research Monograph No. 30. Washington, DC: U.S. Department of Labor.

Rapaport, R., and Rapaport, R.N. (1974). Four themes in the sociology of leisure. *British Journal of Sociology, 25,* pp. 215–29.

Rice, R.W., Near, J.P., and Hunt, R.G. (1980). The job satisfaction/life satisfaction relationship: A review of research. *Basic and Applied Social Psychology, 1,* pp. 37–64.

Riesman, D., and Bloomberg, W. (1957). Work and leisure: Fusion or polarity? In C.M. Arensberg, S. Barkin, W.E. Chalmers, H.L. Wilensky, J.C. Worthy, and B.D. Dennis (eds.), *Research in industrial and human relations.* New York: Harper and Brothers, pp. 68–85.

Robinson, E.S. (1920). The compensatory function of make-believe play. *Psychological Review, 27,* pp. 429–39.

Rokeach, M. (1973). *The nature of human values.* New York: Free Press.

Rosenberg, M. (1957). *Occupations and values.* Glencoe, IL: Free Press.

———. (1978). *Occupations and values.* Glencoe, IL: Free Press.

———. (1979). *Conceiving the self.* New York: Basic Books.

Rousseau, D.M. (1978). Relationship of work to nonwork. *Journal of Applied Psychology, 63,* pp. 513–7.

Salaman, G. (1974). *Community and occupation.* Cambridge: Cambridge University Press.

Salz, A. (1944). Occupations in their historical perspective. *Encyclopedia of the Social Sciences, 11–12,* pp. 424–8.

Sapora, A.V., and Mitchell, E.D. (1961). *The theory of play and recreation.* New York: Ronal Press.

Sarbin, T.R., and Allen, V.L. (1968). Role theory. In G. Lindzey and E. Aronson (eds.), *The handbook of social psychology, vol. I.* Reading, MA: Addison Wesley.

Scitovsky, T. (1976). *The joyless economy.* New York: Oxford.

Seashore, S.E. (1975). Defining and measuring the quality of life. In L.E. Davis and A.B. Cherns (eds.), *The quality of working life.* New York: Free Press.

Seeman, M. (1971). The urban alienations: Some dubious theses from Marx to Marcuse. *Journal of Personality and Social Psychology, 19,* pp. 135–43.

Sennett, R., and Cobb, S. (1973). *The hidden injuries of class.* New York: Vintage.

Shaw, M.E. (1981). *Group dynamics.* New York: McGraw-Hill.

Sheppard, J. (1974). A status recognition model of work-leisure relationships. *Journal of Leisure Research, 6,* pp. 58–63.

Sheppard, J.M. (1984). *Basic sociology.* New York: Harper and Row.

Simmel, G. (1955). *Conflict and the web of group affiliations.* New York: Free Press.

Simon, H.A. (1957). *Models of man.* New York: Wiley.

Slavson, S.R. (1946). *Recreation and the total personality.* New York: Association Press.

Smith, A. (1937). *An inquiry into the nature and causes of the wealth of nations.* New York: Modern Library.

Smith, D. (1972). *Report from engine company eight-two.* New York: Dutton.

Sorokin, P.A. (1928). *Contemporary sociological theories.* New York: Harper and Row.

Spreitzer, E., and Snyder, E. (1974). Work orientation, meaning of leisure, and mental health. *Journal of Leisure Research, 6,* pp. 207–19.

Staw, B.M., Bell, N.F., and Clawsen, J.A. (1986). The dispositional approach to job attitudes: A longitudinal test. *Administrative Science Quarterly, 31,* pp. 56–77.

Stryker, S. (1968). Identity salience and role performance. *Journal of Marriage and the Family, 30,* pp. 558–64.

———. (1980). *Symbolic interactionism: A social structural version.* Menlo Park, CA: Benjamin/Cummings.

Swell, W.H., and Hauser, R.M. (1975). *Education, occupations, and earnings: Achievement in the early career.* New York: Academic Press.

Tilgher, A. (1931). *Work: What is has meant through the ages.* London: George C. Harrap.

Turner, R.H. (1978). The role and the person. *American Journal of Sociology, 84,* pp. 1–23.

Tversky, A., and Kahneman, D. (1974). Judgment under uncertainty: Heuristics and biases. *Science, 185,* pp. 1124–31.

———. (1981). The framing of decisions and the psychology of choice. *Science, 211,* pp. 454–63.

Van Maanen, J., and Barley, S.R. (1984). Occupational communities: Culture and control in organizations. *Research in Organizational Behavior, 6,* pp. 287–365.

Vroom, V.H. (1964). *Work and motivation.* New York: Wiley.

Wallman, S. (1979). *Social anthropology of work.* London: Academic Press.

Warner, W.L. (1953). *American life: Dream and reality.* Chicago: University of Chicago Press.

Warner, W.L., Meeker, M., and Eels, D. (1949). *Social class in America.* Chicago: Science Research Associates.

Watson, D., and Clark, L.A. (1984). Negative affectivity: The disposition to experience aversive emotional states. *Psychological Bulletin, 96,* pp. 465–90.

Weber, M. (1968). *Economy and society.* Berkeley, CA: University of California Press.

Wilensky, H.L. (1961). Orderly careers and social participation: The impact of work history on social integration in the middle mass. *American Sociological Review, 26,* pp. 521–39.

Wilensky, H.L., and Lebeaux, C.N. (1958). *Industrial society and social welfare.* New York: Russell Sage Foundation.

Wilensky, H.L. (1960). Work, careers, and social integration. *International Social Science Journal, 12,* pp. 543–60.

Williams, R.R. (1968). Values. In D.L. Sills (ed.), *International Encyclopedia of the Social Sciences.* New York: Cromwell Collier and MacMillan, pp. 283–87.

Wilson, G.D. (1973). *The psychology of conservatism.* New York: Academic Press.

Wilson, J. (1980). Sociology of leisure. *Annual Review of Sociology, 6,* pp. 21–40.

Zuboff, S. (1983). The work ethic and work organization. In J. Barbash, R.J. Lampman, S.A. Levitan, and G. Tyler (eds.), *The work ethic—a critical analysis.* Madison, WI: Industrial Relations Research Association, pp. 153–81.

Appendix
Rokeach's Terminal and Industrial Values

Terminal Values	Instrumental Values
A comfortable life	Ambitious
An exciting life	Broadminded
A sense of accomplishment	Capable
A world at peace	Cheerful
A world of beauty	Clean
Equality	Courageous
Family security	Forgiving
Freedom	Helpful
Happiness	Honest
Inner harmony	Imaginative
Mature love	Independent
National security	Intellectual
Pleasure	Logical
Salvation	Loving
Self-respect	Obedient
Social recognition	Polite
True friendship	Responsibility
Wisdom	Self-controlled

7
Work and the Family

Arthur P. Brief
Walter R. Nord

A t the time of the industrial revolution, the spatial connection
between the institutions of work and family, in large part, was
severed (Smelser, 1959). Subsequently, each institution has tended to
be viewed as a separate field of study (Mortimer, Lorence, and Kumka 1986;
Zedeck, 1987). The spatial separation appears to have led students of
organizational psychology and behavior to give little attention to the many
ways that the family affects the meaning of work and vice versa. To a considerable degree, work and family seem to be studied as if they were separate
social systems.

To some extent, this discreteness is justified because of the separation
experienced by people who participate in both systems concurrently. As Renshaw (1976) found, individuals often behave as if the particular system they
are in at the moment is the only system they live in. Bartolome and Evans
(1979) reported that nearly all of the 453 managers they surveyed viewed the
ideal life style as "one in which professional and private life are both separate
and independent" (p. 6). Some (e.g., Kanter, 1977) have argued that the
separation is fostered by the interests of the large corporation.

Of course, long after the industrial revolution, work and family are tied
together in several ways. In fact, even today, there are many family businesses. More importantly, however, even for people whose employment is
totally separate from any members of their family, work and family are interdependent in important ways. For instance, Parsons and Smelser (1956) noted
that work provides income or wages for the family household, thereby setting
limits on the consumer goods and services it can acquire. The family, in
return, provides a present and future source of willing labor as well as demand
for the economy's products. Also, since both one's work and one's family
make claims on a person's time and both can utilize and replenish an individual's energy, emotions, and other personal resources, the daily experience at work is almost certainly influenced by the family and vice versa.

Moreover, the reciprocal effects extend well beyond to more sociological
matters than the daily experiences of those currently working. Families play

an important role in socializing each new generation for the world of work, and in doing so are affected by the current and anticipated nature of what work requires. These sociological effects of the family are not central to this chapter, rather, attention is limited to the social psychological processes of working at the present time.

As we noted, for the most part organizational behaviorists have concentrated their attention inside the workplace. Recently, however, they have begun to expand their horizons from the effects of various conditions of work on work-related attitudes and behaviors of the workers (e.g., job satisfaction and job performance) to consideration of components of life outside of the workplace. Growth of interest in the family has been an early result of this shift, as evidenced in the work of Burke (1986), Burke and Greenglass (1987), Evans and Bartolome (1986), and Greenhaus and Beutell (1985).

Undoubtedly, this broadened scope is linked to social changes that have made it clear that separating the study of family and work has had mixed effects. On the one hand, by ignoring the mutual effects of work and other systems such as the family, organizational behaviorists have been more able to focus on ways to improve work and organizations in the work setting; "externalities" could be ignored. On the other hand, the lack of attention to potentially negative externalities associated with an exclusive emphasis on productivity and other outcomes thought to be desired by managers, makes such inquiry vulnerable to the charge of being managerially biased (Baritz, 1960). However, matters may be less contentious than they seem because employees and their families can benefit from the same outcomes as managers do (such as improvements in the financial performance of the organization). In any case, when only some of the outcomes of work are taken as problematic, the risk of suboptimization is great.

Our intent here is to introduce the literature on the interaction of work and the family to those students of work who have given little attention to the dynamic relationship between work and family. We have two more specific purposes. First, we want to encourage organizational behaviorists and other managerially-oriented scholars to expand the set of dependent variables they consider, and especially to recognize that work has meaning to the family. Second, we want to show that the meanings of work to individuals cannot be assessed without consideration of other roles they play concurrently, perhaps the most important of which are centered in the family.

Family Defined

Although it is probably easier to define the word *family* than to define *work*, the definitional problems surrounding family cannot be ignored. Typically, a family refers to a group of people who are related to each other by blood or marriage. In addition, various criteria (e.g., degree of common ancestry and living patterns) are used to denote special types of family relationships (such as, nuclear and extended families). In Western culture, discussions of work and the family usually seem to be most concerned with the family unit of a father, mother, and their children. This will be the unit we refer to by the word *family*. However, before going further, it is instructive to note some of the trappings of this definition that limit the value of the term as a scientific construct.

The most obvious problem is that many variations between and within such social units make it impossible to assume that individuals from two different families are responding to anything approaching a common stimulus. Moreover, due to such processes as aging, the nature of any given family and people's relationships to it change over time; therefore, research that uses the family as a unit of analysis must be interpreted in ways that recognize that the family is not a uniform stimulus even to the same individual. To serve as an adequate construct for building theory, a great deal of refinement in our understanding of family is needed.

In addition, what psychological processes can be assumed to be properties of the family? Presumably simply being related by blood or marraige without being influenced by certain social overlays (e.g., norms, dependency, and physical proximity) has few direct consequences. Therefore, the family is in some sense a unit within which fundamental social and psychological processes take place. Many of these processes stem from physical proximity and emotional bonding which can be part of relationships with people who are not part of one's family. For instance, one's relationship with a spouse may be far more distant than another person's relationship with a roommate.

In addition, just as the nature of work changes over time, so does the family. Young and Willmott's (1973) description of the evolution of the family during the last two centuries in London illustrates this point. Young and Willmott suggested that the nature of the family and its relationship to work passed through three forms during this period. During the preindustrial period (lasting well into the nineteenth century) the family was usually the unit of production. In contrast, during stage two, family members became wage earners. The family was no longer a business partnership. As work moved away from the home, the family changed dramatically. Husbands and wives could no longer observe the activities and earnings of each other. Moreover, childhood changed dramatically. Children could no longer learn by observing their fathers work. To a considerable degree, despite the existence of considerable child labor, children became "breadeaters." Over time, childhood became institutionalized as compulsory education and other laws came into existence. During this stage, husbands had enormous power. They had control of the purse. Moreover, their physically taxing labor gave them a legitimate claim on the most and best food to sustain themselves. Stage three, starting early in the twentieth century, saw an increase in symmetry. Many changes in technology, social norms, and increased earnings of women were responsible for these changes. In this stage, Young and Willmott assert that the unity of the family was restored, but around consumption rather than production. Whereas earlier expenditures on entertainment centered on alcohol and tobacco, much of which men consumed away from home, inventions including water in the home, gas and electric light, and the gramophone, radio, and television, made the house more attractive and helped make the home a locus of entertainment. Young and Willmott suggest that a partnership in leisure succeeded the partnership in work.

Moreover, even at the same point in time, there are wide variations within a given society concerning what impact the family has on the behavior expected of its members. Although intrasocietal contrasts in parental behavior in socializing children are well-known (see, for example, Zigler and Child, 1969), far less attention has been given to intersocietal patterns. In a society with a melting-pot history such as the United States, it seems reasonable to expect substantial intrasocietal variation; the relationships between parents and their children (as well as those between parents and among children) would seem likely to vary among families whose ancestors came from different cultures. Moreover, Zigler and Child report considerable evidence of variations in child-rearing practices among societal classes within the United States. Perhaps regional and other intrasocietal variations exist as well. The existence of these differences suggests yet another problem with using the family as a construct and searching for consistent relations between it and some other social process (e.g., work). If changes in technology, norms, and work roles spread unevenly across families (say between rural and urban setttings or upper and lower classes), then variations in the nature of the family itself are being introduced constantly. Other problems with using the family as a construct could be noted. As with work, the use of social categories in attempting to understand human experiences is fraught with a number of problems. Unfortunately, we have little else to go on at present. Therefore, we organize our review of the existing knowledge about the relationship of work and important life events outside work using the word *family* as a general category under which a number of variables are operating.

The concept of family entails much complexity; and yet, existing research on work and the family has for the most part viewed the concept as if it were a uniform construct. It is likely, therefore, that the research to date has yielded only partially valid conclusions. As Zedeck (1987) noted, ultimately to understand the relationship *between* family and work requires that we understand the *person's* relationship *to each*. The need for idiographic studies that clarify these relationships is clear. In the interim, however, existing research reveals some interesting patterns. We review it by considering income and the family, social processes, and qualities of particular family configurations.

Income and the Family

We have defined work as what one does to earn a living in ways that are separated from other roles [see chapter 1]. In the current social context, *earning a living,* of course, often means providing a living for others as well—especially one's family. One's income has a major impact on the quality—material and social—of how the worker and his/her family live.

Even the earliest observers of modern industrial societies recognized that a person's work-related income affected both his/her own status as well as that of the individual's family. Veblen (1934), for example, in his *The Theory of the Leisure Class* (first published in 1899), noted the role of "conspicuous consumption." He observed that the "gentleman" of the leisure class "not only consumes of the staff of life beyond the minimum required for subsistence and physical efficiency, but his consumption undergoes a specialization as regards the quality of the good consumed. He consumes freely and of the best" (p. 73). Veblen added that "since the consumption of these more excellent goods is an evidence of wealth, it becomes honorific; and, conversely, the failure to consume of due quantity and quality becomes a mark of inferiority and demerit" (p. 74). Since "the members of each stratum accept as their ideal of decency the scheme of life in vogue in the next higher stratum" (p. 84), the members of the middle and lower classes also seek to consume conspicuously. Veblen further reasoned, however, that the household heads of these classes, by the economic necessity of earning the family unit's livelihood, vicariously consume through other members of the unit.

Contemporary evidence in line with Veblen's reasoning can be extrapolated from Andrews and Withey's (1974) research on interconnections among the satisfactions of individuals with specific domains of their lives and how these satisfactions combine to yield overall life satisfaction. For instance, the researchers found satisfaction with housing to be a primary contributor to overall life satisfaction—considerably more important than satisfaction with work. Moreover, they found that satisfaction with income was linked strongly to satisfaction with housing. It would seem, therefore, that work-related income does indeed act on the family unit through consumption, in this case through the housing purchased.

Perhaps a less obvious effect of work-related income is evident in the literature pertaining to child-rearing practices. In that literature, the work variable is often captured by social class. This is justified on the basis that occupational position is a principle component of social class (Kohn, 1979). [See Hoffman (1984a) for a further discussion of social class as a proxy for income in child-rearing research.[1]]

At the most general level, it has been observed that middle- versus working-class parent-child relationships are more acceptant and egalitarian and place less emphasis on the maintenance of order and obedience than those found in working-class families (Bronfenbrenner, 1958). This conclusion is well-documented by the program of research conducted by Kohn and his associates (Kohn, 1959, 1963, 1977; Kohn and Carroll, 1960; Kohn and Schooler, 1969). This research included an early study of two hundred white-collar and two hundred blue-collar Caucasian families in Washington, DC; 861 parents in Turin, Italy; and a national survey of 3,101 American men. He found parents in the middle and upper classes to stress the traits of happiness, curiosity, responsibility, dependability, and self-control; while, in contrast, working- and lower-class parents emphasized such characteristics as obedience, neatness, cleanliness, ability to defend oneself, good manners, and honesty. Many other findings from Kohn's research have been replicated both in the United States and in other nations (e.g., Gecas, 1979; Gecas and Nye 1974; Inkeles, 1955, 1960; Pearlin, 1970). Similarly, Minton, Kagan, and Levine (1971) observed middle- and lower-class children and their mothers over a five- to six-hour period. They found lower-class mothers on average issue a prohibition (e.g., "Don't do that") once every five minutes, and middle-class mothers do so only every ten minutes.

The consequences of these class differences in child-rearing practices are both subtle and important. According to Kagan (1978), who has summarized much of the research, the typical ten-year-old, lower-class child questions his/her ability to possess the talents and instrumental competencies that the middle-class child commands; in addition, the middle-class child's expectations of success in intellectual situations is greater, and he/she is more reflective and less likely to take extreme risks when given alternatives. Moreover, associations have been found between parents' work and the values they instill in their children. The work and child-rearing relationships we have described are a primary mechanism for establishing this association. As recognized by Mortimer (1975; 1976), such transmitted values help shape the meanings children attach to work. This meaning, in turn, influences vocational preferences and, ultimately, occupational choices (Mortimer and Kunka, 1982; Spenner, 1981).

Again, the effects of income on child-rearing practices may not be particularly obvious; but, as noted by Hoffman (1986), certain of the consequences of income on the family are quite apparent. For example, she noted its effects on nutrition, security, resources available for coping and stressors, and opportunities for education. While these and other obvious effects suggest that high income is associated with positive family outcomes and, correspondingly, low income is not, some evidence indicates otherwise. For example, Kemper and Reichler (1976) found that very low income may foster shared life orientations of a husband and wife, such as when a stronger bond results from a shared feeling of being treated unfairly.

In short, the economic consequences of work for the family are pervasive.

Rather than dwell on them further, we focus on some of the seemingly less obvious ways work influences the social functioning of family unit. However, even when we attempt to focus on social processes, the influence of income is so strong that it will appear again and again.

Work and Social Processes of the Family

The following overview of the literature is organized initially by type of family unit (i.e., "traditional," dual-provider, and single-parent-provider). This approach was taken in order to accommodate the structure of much of the contemporary research on the family. It highlights, in addition, the fact that the issues of concern tend to vary by type of family unit.

The "Traditional" Family: Husband as Sole Breadwinner

In hunting and gathering societies and in early agricultural villages, the efforts of females provided about 80 percent of human subsistence (Boulding, 1976). It was not until the appearance of large trading towns that males began to provide at a level equal to the contributions of females; and, with the beginning of true cities, the female role as provider tended to become invisible (Bernard, 1981). Thus, the conception of males as "good providers" or as the family "breadwinner" is a thoroughly modern occurrence.

Despite its recency, in our society the breadwinner role has become a defining characteristic of contemporary notions of masculinity. That is, by performing it, males confirm their manliness and are able to demonstrate their strength, cunning, inventiveness, endurance, and a host of other traits stereotypically labeled as *masculine* (e.g., Brenton, 1966; Demos, 1974; Gould, 1974; Pleck, 1983; Rubin, 1976). The breadwinner role undoubtedly has helped males gain power within the family unit.

Without doubt, the position of sole breadwinner for the family unit enhanced the male's power at home through his wife's and children's dependency on him for every purchase (Kormarowsky, 1940; Lopata, 1971; Young and Willmott, 1973). For example, not only did the man control the purse strings, but, as noted earlier, the importance of his health and energy for sustaining the family's income gave him first claim on the most and the best food (Young and Willmott, 1973). Dependency, however, had dual effects. It led to power and real responsibilities and fears associated with failing to meet them. Consequently, when males fail to adequately perform their breadwinner role, their psychological well-being is adversely affected, often with depression being a resultant condition (see Kessler, 1982). Other evidence of the burdens placed on males is the fact that married males work more hours than bachelors (Moore and Hedges, 1971) and, among fathers, working hours increase with the number of children (Bosserman, 1975). Consistent with this evidence is Gould and Werbel's (1983) finding that psychological involvement in one's job is lower among married men whose wives share the breadwinner role than among those whose wives do not engage in paid work.[2]

The breadwinner role has other social psychological effects. Many observers of the modern male breadwinner role, ranging from de Tocqueville to Freud (Bernard, 1981), have recognized the implicit conflict men confront between devotion to their work and meeting the other demands of family life. The impact of this conflict on wives is shown clearly in a study by Burke, Weir, and DuWors (1980a) of eighty-five male senior administrators and their spouses. Burke et al., in part found that wives whose husbands experienced greater occupational demands were, in comparison with wives of husbands who experienced fewer such demands, more likely to cope with daily stresses of life in less constructive ways—such as by reliance on alcohol and drugs, explosive outbursts, and withdrawal and escapism. In addition, these women were likely to smoke more cigarettes and to drink more cups of coffee per day. These results imply that, in the long run, wives of husbands with greater occupational demands may be running real risks to their health.[3] Barling and Rosenbaum (1986) reported evidence of more immediate effects: Husbands who physically abused their wives were found to report significantly more stressful events and a greater impact of stressful events at work than nonabusive husbands.

Studies of the relationships between the *Type A* behavior of husbands and their wives' satisfaction and well-being by Burke et al. (1979; 1980b) revealed other consequences of job demands for the family. Type A behavior is a significant predictor of coronary heart disease. It encompasses working long and hard hours, being constantly under deadline pressures and conditions of overload, carrying work home on evenings and weekends, showing an inability to relax, cutting vacations short to get back to work, and other behaviors indicative of a work addict with an exaggerated sense of the success ethic (Friedman and Rosenman, 1974; Jenkins, 1975). Burke et al. found that high levels of husbands' Type A behavior were associated with wives' reporting less marital satisfaction, fewer friends, fewer social contacts with friends, and a weaker sense of belonging to a social network from which they might draw needed psychological support. In addition to Burke et al., other researchers have demonstrated that Type A males, in fact, invest highly in their jobs (e.g., Howard, Cunningham, and Rechnitzer, 1975) and that such investment[4] can result in alienation of the male from his spouse and the placing of great pressures on the family unit (e.g., Kanter, 1977; Maccoby, 1976). Explicitly, by *investment* we mean the duration and amount of physical and mental energy expended. This includes expenditures at work as well as expenditures preparing for work (e.g., training).

High levels of investment by the breadwinner in his work do more than impact negatively on his wife; they also may have adverse effects on the bread-winner's children. These effects are illustrated in an interesting study by Sostel and Sherman (1977) of executives' children whose thoughts, feelings, and actions were surveyed over an eight-year period. The executives' children often expressed bitter resentment, and saw their parents as making rigid, non-negotiable demands and showing no interest in understanding their points of view. Moreover, the children expressed fears of failure and low aspirations, indicating a lack of self-confidence and a low achievement orientation.

If a high level of investment by the male breadwinner in his work can have such deleterious effects, why then does the family unit tolerate or, possibly, condone his work behaviors? According to Grieff and Munter (1980), the answer, at least for wives, is that they accommodate their husband's work in exchange for the promise of increased income and economic security. The wives' accommodations for these economic benefits often go beyond coping with increased family responsibilities (e.g., Bailyn, 1971; Pahl and Pahl, 1971; Young and Willmont, 1973). Social obligations, travel requirements, and geographic relocations exemplify other male breadwinner role activities that may require the wife's active support (e.g., Culbert and Renshaw, 1972; Levinson, 1964; Renshaw, 1976). Moreover, a wife's active support may entail participation in her husband's work (e.g., Handy, 1978; Helfrich, 1965; Whyte, 1956). This participation often has been documented for the wives of husbands employed as managers in large-scale business organizations (cf. Mortimer and London, 1984) as well as for the wives of husbands engaged in academe (Hochschild, 1975), diplomacy (Hochschild, 1969), medicine (Fowles, 1980), the military (Finlayson, 1976), the ministry (Taylor and Hartley, 1975), and politics (MacPherson, 1975). A variety of activities including: making appointments, editing, attending meetings, and serving as a "sounding board" (Kanter, 1977; Machlowitz, 1980; Mortimer and London, 1984), have been found to be undertaken by wives participating in their husband's work. Papanek (1973) labeled the types of husband-wife work activities we have been describing as a *two-person single career;* Kanter (1977) referred to the *career progression* of corporate wives and described the costs many of the women reported, including losses of privacy and friendships.

Not all effects of work investment are negative for the family. In fact, Kemper and Reichler (1976) found that wives' satisfaction with the marriage may increase with husbands' job involvement because it lowers the demands husbands make on their wives. In Kemper and Reichler's words:

> If husband likes his work and is eager to get back to it after time away, this
> means he is less dependent on wife to gratify his psychic whims and needs;
> and while this appears to enhance his own satisfaction with the marriage,
> since he probably does not demand so much from it, his intrinsic satisfac-

tions with work enhance even further wife's satisfaction with the marriage, since demands on her are also less. (p. 939)

Our use of the term *investment* in the last few paragraphs implies that the family unit exercises voluntary choice about the level at which the breadwinner invests in his work. Often, the "choice" is so constrained, however, that for many families, such choices are hardly experienced as voluntary. Even where the opportunity to participate in a husband's career exists, it often is not experienced as a real choice (Kanter, 1977).

Absence of choice may be most apparent for wives in lower classes. Piotrkowski (1978) has observed that lower-class families often strain to meet the demands of the breadwinner's merely maintaining his income, even when doing so causes deterioration in family relationships. Many breadwinners are locked into work that does not even supply much in the way of economic security; they live in fear of a reduction in overtime pay, a cutback in their hours, or, even worse, being laid off (Mortimer and London, 1984). Essentially, these workers can be thought of as struggling to maintain their family's financial position. Considerable research documents the harmful consequences of such marginal employment on the family (e.g., Elder, 1974; Sennett and Cobb, 1972). Again, these families bear such costs because essentially they have no choice. The breadwinner sees no alternative work that would allow him to lower his investment yet maintain whatever level of income and security his current work supplies.

The negative consequences for lower-class wives may be particularly intense for other reasons. For one, the opportunities to participate in her husband's career (the two-person single career) does not exist for many wives—most blue-collar jobs simply do not have such corollary roles for wives. Moreover, the wife is not apt to see her husband's time away from home as leading to career advancement as in the middle and upper classes (Halle, 1984).

Qualities of Particular Families. Our treatment of the traditionally structured family (with the male as the sole breadwinner) has centered on the negative effects of work on the family. Indeed, much of the research has a similar bent. However, as we have noted, not all the effects are negative. In fact, as Zedeck's (1987) directive toward a more idiographic approach implied, the impact of work characteristics on the experiences of family members is moderated by many qualities of particular individuals and families. Specifically, the impact of a breadwinner's investment in work can be a function of a number of factors.

First, not all people invest heavily in their jobs for the same reasons. Personality characteristics and person/job fit must be taken into account. For some people, work involvement is more akin to play than anything else; for others, work is an addiction (Schaef and Fassel, 1988); for still others, involvement in work may be an escape from an uncomfortable family situation. Even though the time "taken away" from the family for work may be the same in all three cases, the quality of any spillover into the family may be quite different.

Second, not all facets of work that demand the breadwinner's involvement have the same effects on the family. Some might include frequent or extended travel and long or off-cycle working hours. Other facets may demand strong involvement, but not physical separation. Job investment is too gross a variable to capture such differences.

Third, and perhaps most important, the dynamics of a family itself moderate the effects. Brett's (1980) research on the effects of job transfers on the family illustrates such dynamics. She proposed that the effect of a transfer on a family is a function of its sources of identity, social class support, and numerous other factors that contribute to the attributions family members make and the actions that they take. Extending Brett's ideas, we believe it is reasonable to suggest that other contingencies that work imposes on a family will have quite different consequences across families. In this vein, Bartolome and Evans' (1979) and Renshaw's (1976) research provide clear evidence that it is not job events themselves but how they are conceived of by the family which determines their consequences.

In short, efforts to uncover the effects of investment of the breadwinner in work (as well as other features of work) on the family cannot assume that some apparently objective event or state of being impacts directly on the psychological well-being of people. Rather, intervening social and psychological processes of all the actors involved may influence the nature of the responses of individual family members and the family unit. These must be taken into account.

Breadwinner Role and the Family: Next Steps. Although this brief review of the effect of the work of the male breadwinner on the family is far from complete, the factors identified are reflective of current knowledge. (For more comprehensive reviews see Burke, 1986; Burke and Greenglass, 1987; Hoffman, 1986.) Much needs to be done; and, students of work could make major contributions. Given their knowledge of, for instance, job security issues, fringe benefit programs, and compensation schemes, organizational psychologists are especially well-equipped to study how these "extrinsic" features of modern employment affect the quality of family life. We note these extrinsic aspects of the workplace because, to date, work-family research has appeared to have been preoccupied with the work itself (i.e., the content or "intrinsic" features of work). In addition, students of work can make important contributions by exploring the various *processes* that mediate and moderate the relationships between these events at work and individual and family responses.

Processes has been italicized to emphasize a very important point. To study the effects of work, simple assumptions about either the nature of work and social units (e.g., the dynamics of particular families) in which the effects are assumed to occur will not be adequate. To study the effects of work, the dynamic nature of these systems must be comprehended. A focus on processes is more apt to aid such comprehension than is analysis focused on entities. (The latter is much more prone to errors stemming from assumptions that units are fixed and general rather than evolving and idiosyncratic.)

From a process view, we see the need to reevaluate our understanding of the family. Much of what we have said about the influence of work on the traditional family is germane to the well-being of any family unit, regardless of its form. But, as was implied earlier, the traditional family is far less prevalent than it was even a few decades ago. Still, its social residues cannot be ignored. Despite dramatic movement away from the traditional form, recent research indicates that many husbands may not be ready yet to abandon, at least psychologically, the traditional role of being sufficiently resourceful as a provider so that one's wife does not have to enter the labor force (e.g., Ross, Mirowsky, and Huber, 1983; Slocum and Nye, 1976; Staines, Pottick, and Fudge, 1986). Although matters are changing, these residues are still operative and deserve study, especially as a new set of relationships—those of the dual-provider family—take hold. It is this form we turn to now.

The Dual-Provider Family

As noted above, the traditional family faces considerable financial difficulties if the income generated by the husband, as sole breadwinner, is inadequate. At least two strategies for the family to cope with these difficulties can be identified (Mortimer and London, 1984). First, the husband can increase the hours he works by working overtime or taking a second job. Second, the wife (or some other family member) can enter the labor market. When husband and wife both are engaged in paid work, a dual-provider family is constituted. The impact of work on this type of family is the concern of the current section.

The great trek of married women into the labor force, through its impact on work roles of men and women and on the family, constitutes a subtle revolution (Bernard, 1981; Smith, 1979). In 1890, only 18 percent of women in the United States participated in the labor force; over the next fifty years, the participation rate increased by about 11 percent (Sheppard, 1984). Understandably, World War II dramatically increased the female participation rate; it was not until 1961 that the female rate once again achieved the peak obtained during the war years (Blau, 1978). The rate has increased continually since 1961 with 38 percent of the civilian labor force being comprised of women in 1970 and 43 percent in 1981 (U.S. Department of Commerce,

1982a). The trend appears to be unaffected by the presence of children; that is, the traditional housewife-mother position will likely be occupied by less than half of the married mothers in the United States during the decade of the 1990s.

Explaining the increased participation of women in the labor market requires attention to factors affecting both supply and demand. Felt economic need has undoubtedly played a major role on the supply side. Indeed, it is clear that the lower the husband's income the more likely it is that the wife will enter the labor market (e.g., Cain, 1966; Kreps, 1971; Sweet, 1973). At least in an economic sense, the wife's movement into the market is an effective response to economic need—married women who are employed full-time contribute about 40 percent of the family income (Hayghe, 1979). But, it is unlikely that economics alone explains the female labor force participation trend described.

A number of other mutually causal changes may be involved, including: (a) rising educational levels of women; (b) marital instability increasing the need for women to attain occupational competence (Hoffman, 1986); (c) the presence of labor-saving devices for housework; (d) the fact that since American women are having fewer children, they are still in their mid-twenties when their last child is born and, thus, have more time to work; and (e) the increased freedom women have to choose how they will fulfill their gender roles (Sheppard, 1984). This increased freedom probably is attributable to a number of changes in social norms regarding the role of women as well as to governmental efforts to reduce sex discrimination in the marketplace (Frieze et al., 1978). Of course, laws are seldom changed unless the status quo is problematic in some way and norms seldom change unless behavior is changed. We envision a positive feedback relationship in which substantial social change is produced as economic, legal, social, and technological factors build on each other.

On the demand side, technological and economic developments have undoubtedly played a role. Young and Willmott (1973) noted that inventions such as the typewriter and telephone generated a number of semiskilled jobs. Moreover, a long period of economic prosperity (e.g., post-World War II) keeps the employment rate high, encouraging employers to hire qualified applicants regardless of gender and reducing opposition from other employees protecting their jobs. Perhaps, also, the gradual shortening of the typical work day and the increase in the use of part-time and temporary employees have played a role.

Given the increasing prevalence of dual-provider families, the question becomes "What effects do the work roles of dual-providers have on the family?" Sheppard (1984) described five relationships between the increasing size of the female labor force and the family. First, as we have already noted, the net income of dual-provider families is higher than in families with only one adult member employed. For example, the median family income comparison figures for 1981 were $26,860 and $17,630, respectively (U.S. Department of Commerce, 1982b). Second, in households with the wife-mother working, men increasingly share housework and child-care. Third, a growing portion of children are being cared for by persons other than their parents (Levitan and Belous, 1981). Fourth, because of their greater economic independence, women can be expected to marry later, have fewer children, and be more willing to end unsatisfying marriages. Finally, given the role model working women provide, new generations of female children can be expected to engage in paid work. Rather than analyze each of Sheppard's conclusions, we will focus primarily on those which directly concern the impact of the wife-mother's work role on her husband and her children. As will be seen, our posture will not always be congruent with that of Sheppard.

Satisfaction with Marriage. To begin, Sheppard's summary did not consider feelings about marriage itself. Evidence suggests that the husbands of working wives are less satisfied with their marriages than those whose wives are not employed (Burke and Weir, 1976; Kessler and McRae, 1982). This pattern has been attributed to a decrease in the active support of occupational endeavors husbands of working women receive from their wives and having imposed on them family tasks previously performed by their wives (e.g., Gupta and Jenkins, 1985).

Second, with respect to imposed household tasks, Sheppard's conclusion regarding men sharing housework and child-care duties with their wives must be tempered by the fact that employed wives now spend 50 percent more time doing family chores than their husbands. That is, a wife's employment does not necessarily result in equality at home. To be sure, ample data indicate that wives engaged in paid work spend less time performing family tasks than those not so employed (Meissner et al., 1975; Robinson, Juster, and Stafford, 1976; Walker, 1969) and that the husbands of these working women do pick up some of the hours of housework and child-care dropped by their wives (Blood and Wolfe, 1960; Lein et al., 1974; Oakley, 1972). But, data also show that time devoted to family chores by husbands is far from equal to the time their employed wives spend on such chores. According to a study by Walker and Woods (1976) of 1296 upper New York State families, men's family work occupied about 1.6 hours of their day; and the comparable figure for employed wives was 4.8 hours—over twenty-two hours more per week. Similar findings were reported by Robinson (1977). Moreover, employed men, after their contributions to the family, still have 50 percent more leisure time than employed women (Szalai, 1973). [For more on the division of family work, see, for example, Barnett and Baruch (1987), and Yogev and Brett (1985)]. Thus, husbands of working women may be less satisfied than other men; but, their relative dissatisfaction probably is not due to the burdensome number of family work time hours they are required to spend.

Job Involvement. In addition, we reported earlier that the husbands of working wives are less psychologically involved in their jobs than husbands who are sole providers. Thus, it would be expected that because they are less involved in their jobs, the husbands of working women might also be less sensitive to their wives' reduced role in their occupational endeavors. If, in fact, the relative dissatisfaction of the husbands of working women is not generally attributable either to the increase in the time they spend on family chores or to the reduction in occupational support they receive from their wives, then what is the root cause of the presumed difficulty?

Threats to Male Dominance. It has often been speculated that one cause of the male's discomfort may be that some husbands see their wife's paycheck as a threat to their dominance in the household (Bahr, 1974). Recalling our discussion of the entwining of the masculine and breadwinner role, it becomes apparent why some men may value dominating their households (Komarousky, 1940) and why threats to such authority would be associated with a decline in satisfaction. This reasoning is substantiated in a series of studies by McClelland and his associates (e.g., McClelland et al., 1976; Winter, McClelland, and Steward, 1977). In essence, they found men with a high need for power (presumably a reasonably stable personality characteristic) to be less likely to tolerate the sharing of power implied in their wives engaging in paid work (cf. Burke and Broadshaw, 1981). Other research findings support the picture of men with this high need for power as distrusting and exploitative of women (e.g., Stewart and Rubin, 1976).

Clearly, however, not all men exhibit such a maladjusted posture toward women. One would expect, therefore, that the effects on husbands of having wives who are employed outside the home are not uniformly negative. Data are available to indicate that a wife's work can have no effect (e.g., Locksley, 1980) or even a positive effect (e.g., Newberry, Weissman, and Myers, 1979) on marital satisfaction. Recently, Yogev (1982) and Chassin, (1985) have reasoned that the marital satisfaction of dual-provider couples, in part, is a function of the congruence between each partner's self-concept and the requirements of his/her family and work multiple roles. Their reasoning is consistent with what has been said about the husband's need for power and the variable impact of the wife's work on marital satisfaction.

In sum, then, it seems that here is no simple answer to the question of what effects a wife's work has on her husband. Analyses of the partner's values and the extent to which those values are realized is required. In conducting such analyses, it is important not to neglect the economic motives behind the decision of a wife to enter the labor force and the impact of her labor force participation on her family's financial well-being.

Child-Rearing Practices. Another important way the dual provider family might differ from the traditional one is with respect to child-rearing practices.

While investigators often have studied the effects of maternal employment on children (Hoffman, 1986) research which specifically focuses on the parenting of dual-provider as contrasted with that of the "traditional" father and mother is rare (Gupta and Jenkins, 1985). Viewing the available data broadly, however, some tentative conclusions can be drawn.

Although some have argued the dual-provider family promotes improper child-care (Rossi, 1977; Sawhill, 1977), most research results indicate otherwise. For instance, the husbands of working women are capable of performing their increased parenting role (Lynn, 1974) and willing to do so (Levine, 1976). In addition, employed mothers appear to be more attentive to their children than are nonemployed mothers (Hoffman, 1984b). [This is particularly the case in regards to their daughters (Stuckey, McGhee, and Bell, 1982).] In addition, it seems employed mothers are more likely to encourage independence in their children than are nonemployed mothers (Hoffman, 1974). Moreover, Blood (1965) has asserted that the presence of a working mother may result in daughters being more masculine and sons more feminine; and, Madani and Cooper (1977) reasoned that such a trend is desirable in that it may promote greater gender role conversion and equality across the sexes. [Also see Hoffmann (1974; 1980).] Finally, St. John-Parsons (1978) found, based upon an indepth study of twenty dual-provider families, that their children were independent, resourceful, and self-confident with no indication of the children's having fared poorly because of their mothers' engagement in paid work.

Institutional Changes and Constants in the Family. One of the major changes stemming from the increase in dual-career families may be on the institution of the family itself. What appears to have happened is a fundamental change in the role of the wife. As Hoffman (1986) observed, several decades ago women who worked outside the home felt guilty; in contrast, now, women who do not do so are apt to feel guilty. Hoffman (1986) wrote:

> Whereas employed mothers of the past responded with guilt and over-mothering, as one study in the 1950s showed, guilt is less likely to be the response now that maternal employment is so prevalent. In fact, more recent data suggests that unemployed mothers may be on the defensive today, and to justify their nonemployment, they may be overmothering. (pp. 193–4)

Again we see the dynamic interaction of the social institutions of work and the family and therefore the difficulty of viewing the impact of one on the other without recognizing this dynamism. Adequate conceptual understanding of the constantly changing relationship between work and family may depend on analysis of the underlying social psychological processes.

Of course, there is one aspect of the traditional family which will not change: Women bear the children. The work-related issues that this fact generates in the modern work context received a great deal of attention in the popular press following an article by Felice Schwartz (1989) in the *Harvard Business Review*. Whether or not a woman is or would like to be the major breadwinner, the requirements of maternity place her at a competitive disadvantage in the career derby as it is run in modern organizations. Schwartz argued that this "immutable, enduring difference between men and women" (p.66) is associated with differences in how men and women are socialized and in how they are perceived in organizations. Clearly such differences affect how women are treated at work, including what roles they are permitted to play—and also including how they are perceived as candidates for top-level positions. Obviously, in this context, the requirements of motherhood affect the meaning work will have for women.

Summary. We have been able to isolate no uniformly negative effects of work by dual-provider couples on their family units. Even the tendency for husbands in these families to experience somewhat lower levels of satisfaction is far from universal. In addition, it seems likely that the relatively greater income of these families generally is beneficial to the family, since a wife's income is likely to reduce the economic pressures the family unit experiences and to enhance the material standard of living (e.g., food, clothing, and housing) each family member is able to enjoy. While the income effects seem reasonably clear, learning about other consequences is more difficult in part because the process involved is dynamic. For example, as behaviors change, so do roles (i.e., expected behavior) and therefore, so do feelings about any particular behaviors. (To illustrate feelings about being part of a traditional family may well be different today even though behaviorally such families might be exactly the same.) Assessing the effects of dual careers by comparing today's dual-career families with today's traditional families cannot detect such changes.

The Single Parent-Provider Family

The number of one-parent families doubled between 1970 and 1981 with 12.6 million children in the United States living with only one parent (Sheppard, 1984). A substantial portion of this dramatic rise was due to the growing numbers of children born out of marriage and of divorces. For instance, the divorce ratio (i.e., the number of divorced persons per 1,000 persons who are married and living with their spouses) rose from forty-seven in 1970 to 109 in 1981 (U.S. Department of Commerce, 1982a). Other factors also played a role. For one, good economic conditions appear to fuel the divorce rate—divorce rates increase during times of prosperity and decrease during recessions and depressions. In addition, as we have noted, increased labor force participation by women means greater economic independence for them and, probably, a greater willingness to dissolve unhappy marriages (Sells, 1979).

Even though general economic gains seem to increase the number of single-parent families, economic well-being is often the central problem that particular single-parent families face (Kamerman, 1980). About 90 percent of single-parent families are headed by women and about a third of these families are poor (Rudd, 1981). Only 60 percent of divorced mothers receive child support and only half of these receive the full amount due them (Mortimer and London, 1984). The children of divorced mothers, along with those who are widowed or deserted, are about six times more likely to grow up in poverty than are children living in households headed by men (Bane, 1976).

The above picture suggests that the meaning of the economic aspect of work has special salience in single-parent families, simply because the economic aspect of life is more problematic for the single parent. Economic demands undoubtedly contribute to the fact that almost 60 percent of females who do head households participate in the labor force (Adams, Milner, and Schrepf, 1984). Perhaps children of a working mother pay a price for her work (Poznanski, Maxey, and Mersden, 1970); but at least some data simply do not bear out this argument (Taveggia and Thomas, 1974). Whatever the costs, however, when the alternative is poverty, which brings with it to the child feelings of inadequacy and inferiority (Coleman and Cressey, 1984), it is hard to see the net results as negative.

An Interpretation

In abstracting from what has been said about the influence of work on the family, three general themes emerge. The first concerns the economic role of work and the second its effects on child-rearing. The third deals with the tradeoffs between work and the family and raises the matter of achieving some optimal level—a good "rate of return."

First, and probably foremost, a provider's work has obvious and direct effects on the financial well-being of his/her family. The size of these effects probably depends on the proportion of income the provider's work supplies to the pool of monies the family expends. The more the family is dependent on a provider's earned income to maintain or enhance its standard of living, the greater the effect that income will have on the family. As we have noted, these effects will be felt by the family in several different ways. In many cases, the provider's work means nothing less than survival. Many families depend on a sole provider whose work supplies the income the family requires to exist on in terms of what society defines as minimal levels of food, clothing, and shelter. At the other extreme is the provider's work which contributes at most a very small percentage of the money a family spends. (For example, a family may have inherited wealth or have two income earners, with the primary earner supplying more than enough income to maintain the family's life style and the secondary earner accounting for only a small fraction of the family's income.) Clearly, a family's place on this continuum can be expected to influence what a person's work means to him/her and to the family.

Second, work is seen as having a developmental influence on the family in that parental work gives shape to the values of the child. By a *developmental influence,* we simply mean that parents' work affects many dimensions of child-rearing. Of special relevance here, is what children come to expect from work. Specifically, we hypothesize that the meaning of work experienced by a family perpetuates itself through the family's children. The beliefs and values that are communicated impact on occupational choice, attitudes toward authority, commitment to work, and so forth. The effects of this transfer of values cannot be underestimated, for one's values may constitute the linking pins between the work and nonwork domains of life, and in particular between work and the family.

Third, work appears to influence the family through the tradeoffs it involves. Simply, the economic gains derived from work are not cost free to the family—work demands an investment of time and energy on the part of the provider, and, as in the case of the corporate wife, of other family members. This investment implies that the family does not have available the full physical, mental, and emotional resources of the provider to be expended on a host of family tasks, such as, for example, cooking, cleaning, and loving. Thus, investment in work, at least at high levels, can be a source of family strain. Hoffman (1986) put this well: "Work steals time, energy, and involvement" (p. 169). Much of the meaning work has for an individual family is indicated through the way the family members handle the necessary tradeoffs.

Implicit in the idea of tradeoffs and in much of the literature we have reviewed is some notion of *rate of return*—the ratio of the gains (economic and other) a family unit derives from a provider's work to the costs of work to the family. Costs of work include, but are not limited to, investment in work. Earlier in this chapter, *investment in work* was defined in terms of the duration and amount of physical and mental energy the *individual* expended. From the family's perspective the time, energy, and involvement the family loses due to its members' engagement in and preparation for paid work can be defined as costs. In addition to investment there are other costs of work to the family. For example, some conditions of work may promote stresses and strains (Brief and Atieh, 1987) which spill over at home (e.g., Burke and Weir, 1981; Buss and Redburn, 1983); and, as was noted in our discussion of the "traditional" family, one family member may need to actively support another member's occupational role (such as by meeting various social obligations).

The sum of all such "costs" to the family can be viewed as an investment by the family. This investment is experienced subjectively by each family member as negative consequences stemming from any family member's engagement in work. The experiences are also idiographic. For example, the time work takes away from the family may be experienced as far less negative (perhaps even positive) by some families than by others.

Gains are construed broadly to include not only the work-related income the provider currently supplies to the family but also other factors such as the long-term financial security the family acquires through the provider's efforts of work, and the stimulation that excitement and achievement at work may transfer into the family. The gains are also experienced subjectively. For instance, financial security cannot be indexed through a mere count of dollars; rather, one is required to think of the family's standard of living, current and future, as appraised by the family itself.[5]

The ratio of these gains from work to the costs of work represents the subjective rate of return of work to the family. We suggest that a broad framework of this sort, that deals with the idiographic and subjective aspects of experience, is essential for understanding the effects of work on families. As we noted earlier in this chapter, the meaning of *family* is constantly changing. Recall, for example, our brief discussion of the subjective effects of the passage of time. What we are studying are families existing at different points in time, under different social and economic conditions. The notions of tradeoffs and rates of return help call attention to the nature of the particular experiences that researchers attempt to aggregate as the "impact of work on the family." The effort to aggregate in this sphere without having an appreciation of the dynamics of the individual cases may be counterproductive.

Our ideas about rate of return are speculative and other noneconomic frameworks may serve the same orienting function. The important point is to suggest a productive avenue for investigation. Aggregation may be our ultimate aim, but the materials we aggregate must map the underlying processes—the dynamics of the individual family.

Effects of Family on Work

It was not the intent of this chapter to explore the effects of the family on work. Since, however, the work-family relationship is a reciprocal one, before closing, a few comments on the effects of the family on the worker are needed.

Support from the Family. The family's role in work-related distress is often discussed (e.g., Burke and Bradshaw, 1981) but has not been particularly well-researched. It does appear, however, that the family can be a source of strain at work. For instance, Nieva (1979) has shown that as family demands for time, energy, and involvement increase, the worker experiences more negative reactions to his/her job. On the other hand, more data speak to the positive effects of the family as a support system. The family, for example, can aid the worker in solving problems at work, be a haven for rest and recuperation, and contribute to the worker's mastering his/her emotions (Caplan, 1976). Moreover, Kahn and Antonucci (1980) suggested that the family can support the worker by expressing admiration, respect, and love; by affirming what he/she said and did was right; and by giving assistance such as money, time, labor, or information. To the worker, such family support may serve to prevent job-related distress or to act in a therapeutic or buffering manner; but, our previous discussion of the family's investment in work suggests that the support family members provide is not necessarily a free good. For example, the energy expended on supporting a worker in the family unit may detract from that available for child-rearing.

Family as Socializing Unit. In terms of family effects on work, the most germane to the current endeavor is how it influences the meaning of work. We have already shown how work affects parenting and, thus, children's work values. A more likely immediate effect is how the family shapes the worker's view of his/her job. Our previous analyses suggest that economics is a key factor involved in the meaning a worker attaches to his/her job. In support of this view, George and Brief (1988) have found that financial requirements, indexed by the worker's family size and economic role in it, condition the effect job outcomes have on a worker's psychological well-being. In particular, the greater the family-related financial requirements the worker has, the more his or her well-being in life is associated with the economic outcomes of work. That is, family responsibilities appear to promote an economic interpretation of work. [Also, see Brief and Atieh (1987) and Brief and Aldag (in press).]

Effects of Particular Families. Of course, as we have just emphasized in discussing the effects of work on families, treatment of the effects of families on work must also recognize the dynamics of particular families. Moreover, workplaces are obviously not uniform. For example, the effects a worker's family has when her children are ages two, four, and eight are probably quite different than when they are twenty-three, twenty-five, and twenty-nine. Therefore, it is important that dynamics of individual workplaces be mapped appropriately before general statements about the effects of families on work can be comprehended adequately.

Conclusion

We have only scratched the surface of the interrelationships between work and the family. We have indicated, however, by recognizing early on the dangers of treating the family as constant across time and space, that research must become more grounded. The family as an institution evolves historically. Similarly, as an individual worker's family unit evolves over time, so do the effects of that unit on his/her work and vice versa.

As we have noted throughout the book, the institution of work and the individual's experience of work also are evolving. The reciprocal relationship between work and the family needs to be viewed from a developmental or evolutionary perspective—a perspective that encompasses the evolution of *both* phenomena at the institutional and individual level. To date, there is little evidence of research based on such a perspective.

Notes

1. Unless otherwise noted, the word *income* will be used throughout the text for the longer phase *work-related income*.
2. We interpret this as evidence for the burdens of the breadwinner role, but it is possible that the low involvement contributed to rather than resulted from the entrance of wives into the work force.
3. Again, causality could run in other directions.
4. The term *investment* is used in place of the often used alternative *involvement*. This is done to avoid confusion with the psychological construct of "job involvement" (Rabinowitz and Hall, 1977), to which positive connotations invariably have been attached.
5. Consistent with our subjective view of economic gains is Veblen's (1934) observation that: "The desire for added comfort and security from want is present as a motive at every stage of the process of accumulation in a modern industrial community; although, the standard of sufficiency in these respects is in turn greatly affected by the habit of pecuniary emulation. To a great extent this emulation shapes the methods and selects the objects of expenditure for personal comfort and decent livelihood" (p. 32). In addition, Rainwater (1974) has asserted that "mainstream American" families compare what they have to the "standard packages" people like themselves have; and these standard packages represent a conception of the going standard of living the majority of Americans can and do enjoy. Living levels below this going standard is making do and getting by; levels above is having extras. Thus, the promotion and pay increase earned by a provider may be considered by one family as allowing the unit to make do and by another as affording the family some extras.

References

Adams, P.L. Milner, J.R., and Schrepf, N.A. (1984). *Fatherless children*. New York: John Wiley and Sons.

Andrews, F.M., and Withey, S.B. (1974). Developing measures of perceived life quality: Results from several national surveys. *Social Indicators Research, 1,* pp. 1–26.

Bahr, S. (1974). Effects on power and division of labor in the family. In L.W. Hoffman and F.I. Nye (eds.), *Working mothers.* San Francisco: Jossey-Bass, pp. 167–85.

Bailyn, L. (1971). Career and family orientation of husbands and wives in relation to marital happiness. In A. Theodore (ed.), *The professional woman.* Cambridge, MA: Schenckman, pp. 545–67.

Bane, M.J. (1976). *Here to stay: American families in the twentieth century.* New York: Basic Books.

Baritz, L. (1960). *The servants of power.* New York: Wiley.

Barling, J., and Rosenbaum, A. (1986). Work stressors and wife abuse. *Journal of Applied Psychology, 71,* pp. 346–8.

Barnett, R., and Baruch, G.K. (1987). Determinants of father's participation in family work. *Journal of Marriage and the Family, 49,* pp. 29–40.

Bartolome, F., and Evans, P.A.L. (1979). *Organizational Dynamics, 7,* no. 4 (Spring), pp. 2–30.

Bernard, J. (1986). Marital stability and patterns of status variables. *Journal of Marriage and the Family, 28,* pp. 421–39.

———. (1981). The good-provider role: Its rise and fall. *American Psychologist, 36,* pp. 1–12.

Blau, F.D. (1978). The data on women workers: Past, present, and future. In A.H. Stromberg, and S. Harkess (eds.), *Women working.* Palo Alto, CA: Mayfield, pp. 29–62.

Blood, R.O. (1965). Long-range causes and consequences of the employment of married women. *Journal of Marriage and the Family, 27,* pp. 43–7.

Blood, R.O., and Wolfe, P. (1960). *Husbands and wives.* New York: Free Press.

Bosserman, P. (1975). Some interpretations of the dynamics of time in industrial society. *Sociology of Leisure, 7.* pp. 155–64.

Boulding, E. (1976). Familial constraints on women's work roles. *Signs, 1,* pp. 95–118.

Brenton, M. (1966). *The American male.* New York: Coward-McCann.

Brett, J.M. (1980). The effect of job transfer on employees and their families. In C.L. Cooper and R. Payne (eds.), *Current concerns in occupational stress.* New York: Wiley, pp. 99–136.

Brief, A.P., and Atieh, J.M. (1987). Studying job stress: Are we making mountains out of molehills? *Journal of Occupational Behavior, 8,* pp. 115–26.

Brief, A.P. and Aldag, R.J. (In press). The economic functions of work. In K.M. Rowland and G.R. Ferris (eds.), *Research in personnel and human resources management.* Greeenwich, CT: JAI Press.

Bronfenbrenner, U. (1958). Socialization and social class through time and space. In E.E. Maccoby, T.M. Newcomb, and E.L. Hartley (eds)., *Readings in social psychology.* New York: Holt, Rinehart and Winston, pp. 400–25.

Burke, R.J. (1986). Occupational and life stress and the family: Conceptual frameworks and research findings. *International Review of Applied Psychology, 35,* pp. 347–69.

Burke, R.J., and Weir, T. (1981). The impact of occupational demands on nonwork experiences. *Group and Organization Studies, 6,* pp. 472–85.

Burke, R.J., and Greenglass, E.R. (1987). Work and family. In C.L. Cooper and I.T. Robertson (eds.), *International review of industrial and organizational psychology.* New York: Wiley, pp. 273–320.

Burke, R.J., and Bradshaw, P. (1981). Occupational and life stress and the family. *Small Group Behavior, 12,* pp. 329–75.

Burke, R.J., and Weir, T. (1976). Relationship of wives' employment status to husband, wife, and pair satisfaction and performance. *Journal of Marriage and the Family, 39,* pp. 279–87.

Burke, R.J., Weir, T., and DuWors, R.E., Jr. (1979). Type A behavior of husbands' and wives' satisfaction and well-being. *Journal of Applied Psychology, 64,* pp. 57–65.

———. (1980a). Work demands on administrators and spouse well-being. *Human Relations, 33,* pp. 253–78.

———. (1980b). Perceived type A behavior of husbands' and wives' satisfactions and well-being. *Journal of Occupational Behavior, 1,* pp. 139–50.

Buss, T., and Redburn, F.S. (1983). *Mass unemployment: Plant closings and community mental health.* Beverly Hills, CA: Sage.

Cain, G.G. (1966). *Married women in the labor force: An economic analysis.* Chicago: University of Chicago Press.

Caplan, G. (1976). The family as a support system. In G. Caplan and M. Killilea (eds.), *Support systems and mutual help.* New York: Grune and Stratton, pp. 19–36.

Chassin, L., Ziess, A., Cooper, K., and Reaven, J. (1985). Role perceptions, self-role congruence, and marital satisfaction in dual-workers couples with preschool children. *Social Psychology Quarterly, 48,* pp. 301–11.

Coleman, J., and Cressey, D. (1984). *Social problems.* New York: Harper and Row.

Culbert, S.A., and Renshaw, J.R. (1972). Coping with the stresses of travel as an opportunity for improving the quality of work and family life. *Family Process, 11,* pp.321–37.

Demos, J. (1974). The American family in past time. *American Scholar, 43,* pp. 422–46.

Dubin, R. (1976). Theory building in applied areas. In M.D. Dunnette, (ed.), *Handbook of industrial and organizational psychology.* Chicago: Rand McNally, pp. 17–39.

Elder, G.H., Jr. (1974). *Children of the Great Depression: Social change in life experience.* Chicago: University of Chicago Press.

Evans, P., and Barolome, F. (1986). The dynamics of work-family relationships in managerial lives. *International Review of Applied Psychology, 35,* 371–95.

Finlayson, E.M. (1976). A study of the wife of the Army officer: Her academic and career preparations, her current employment, and volunteer services. In H.I. McCubbin, B.B. Dahl, and E.J. Hunter (eds.), *Families in the military system.* Beverly Hills, CA: Sage.

Fowles, M.R. (1980). *Behind every successful man: Wives of medicine and academe.* New York: Columbia University Press.

Friedman, M., and Rosenman, R.H. (1974). *Type A behavior and your heart.* New York: Knopf.

Frieze, I.H., Parsons, J.E., Johnson, P.B., Rable, D.N., and Zellman, G.L. (1978). *Women and sex roles*. New York: Norton.

Gecas, V. (1979). The influence of social class on socialization. In W.R. Burr, R. Hill, F.I. Nye, and I..L. Reiss (eds.), *Contemporary theories about the family, vol. 1*. New York: Free Press, pp. 365–404.

Gecas, V., and Nye, F.I. (1974). (1974). Sex and class differences in parent child interactions: A test of Kohn's hypothesis. *Journal of Marriage and the Family*, 36, pp. 724–49.

George, J., and Brief, A.P. (1988). *The economic instrumentality of work: An examination of the moderating effects of financial requirements and sex on the pay-life satisfaction relationship*. Unpublished manuscript submitted to New York University for review.

Gould, R.E. (1974). Measuring masculinity by the size of the paycheck. In J.E. Pleck J. Sawyer (eds.), *Mean and masculinity*. Englewood Cliffs, NJ: Prentice Hall.

Gould, S., and Werbel, J.D. (1983). Work involvement: A comparison of dual wage earner and single wage earner families. *Journal of Applied Psychology*, 68, pp. 313–19.

Greenhaus, J.H., and Beutell, N.J. (1985). Sources of conflict between work and family roles. *Academy of Management Review*, 10, 76–88.

Grieff, B.S., and Munter, P.K. (1980). *Tradeoffs: Executives, family, and organizational life*. New York: Mentor.

Gupta, N., and Jenkins, G.D., Jr. (1985). Dual career couples: Stress, stressors, strains, and strategies. In T. Beehr and R.S. Bhagat (eds.), *Human stress and cognition in organizations*. New York: Wiley and Sons, pp. 141–75.

Halle, D. (1984). *America's working man*. Chicago: University of Chicago Press.

Handy, C. (1978). The family: Help or hindrance? In C.L. Cooper and R. Payne (eds.), *Stress at work*. New York: Wiley and Sons, pp. 107–23.

Hayghe, H. (1979). Working wives' contributions to family income in 1977. *Monthly Labor Review*, 102, pp. 62–4.

Helfrich, M.L. (1965). *The social role of the executive's wife*. Columbus, OH: Ohio State University, Bureau of Business Research.

Hicks, M.W., and Platt, M. (1970). Marital happiness and stability: A review of the research of the sixties. *Journal of Marriage and the Family*, 32, pp. 553–75.

Hochschild, A.R. (1975). Inside the clockwork of the male career. In F. Howe (ed.), *Women and the power to change*. New York: McGraw Hill, pp. 47–80.

Hoffman, L.W. (1974). Effects on child. In L.W. Hoffman and F. I. Nye (eds.), *Working mothers*. San Francisco: Jossey-Bass, pp. 126–66.

———. (1980). Effects of maternal employment on children. In C.D. Hayes, (ed.), *Work, family, and community: Summary proceedings of an ad hoc meeting*. Washington, DC: Proceedings of the National Academy of Science's Committee on Child Development and Public Policy, Appendix C, 21–22 February, pp. 47–54.

———. (1984a). Work, family, and the socialization of the child. In R.D. Parke (ed.) *The family: Review of child development research*. Chicago: University of Chicago Press.

———. (1984b). Maternal employment and the young child. In M. Perlmutter (ed.), *Parent-child interaction and parent-child relations in child development. The Minnesota symposia on child psychology*. Hillsdale, NJ: Erlbuam, pp. 101–27.

———. (1986). Work, family, and the child. In M.S. Pallak and R.O. Perloff (eds.), *Psychology and work: Productivity, change, and employment.* Washington, DC: American Psychological Association, pp. 173–220.

Holland, J.L. (1976). Vocational preferences. In M.D. Dunnette (ed.), *Handbook of industrial and organizational psychology.* Chicago: Rand McNally, pp. 521–70.

Howard, J.H., Cunningham, D.A., and Rechnitzer, P.A. (1975). Work patterns associated with Type A behavior: A managerial population. *Journal of Human Stress, 2,* pp. 24–31.

Inkeles, A. (1955). Social change and social character: The role of parental mediation. *Journal of Social Issues, 11,* pp. 12–23.

———. (1960). Industrial man: The relation of status to experience, perception, and values. *The American Journal of Sociology, 66,* pp. 1–31.

Jenkins, C.D. (1975). The coronary-prone personality. In W.D. Gentry and R.B. Williams, Jr. (eds.), *Psychological aspects of myocardial infarction and coronary care.* St. Louis: Mosby, pp. 5–23.

Kagan, J. (1978). The child in the family. In A.S. Rossi, J. Kagan, and T.K. Hareven (eds.), *The Family.* New York: Norton, pp. 33–56.

Kahn, R.L., and Antonucci, T. (1980). Convoys over the life course: Attachment roles and social support. In P.B. Baltes and O. Brim (eds.), *Life-span development and behavior.* Orlando, FL: Academic Press.

Kamerman, S.B. (1980). *Parenting in an unresponsive society: Managing work and family life.* New York: Free Press.

Kanter, R.M. (1977). *Work and family in the United States: A critical review and agenda for research and policy.* New York: Russell Sage.

Kemper, T.D., and Reichler, M.L. (1976). Work integration, marital satisfaction, and conjugal power. *Human Relations, 29,* pp. 929–44.

Kessler, R.C. (1982). A disaggregation of the relationships between socioeconomic status and psychological distress. *American Sociological Review, 47,* pp. 752–64.

Kessler, R.C., and McRae, D. (1982). The effect of wives' employment on the mental health of married men and women. *American Sociological Review, 47,* pp. 216–27.

Kohn, M.L. (1959). Social class and parent-child relationships: An interpretation. *American Sociological Review, 68,* pp. 471–80.

———. (1963). Social class and parental values. *American Journal of Sociology, 64,* pp. 337–51.

———. (1977). *Class and conformity.* Chicago: University of Chicago Press.

———. (1979). The effects of social class on parental values and practices. In D. Reiss and H.H. Hoffman (eds.), *The American Family: Dying or developing.* New York: Plenum Press.

Kohn, M.L., and Carroll, E.E. (1960). Social class and the allocation of parental responsibilities. *Sociometry, 23,* pp. 372–92.

Kohn, M.L., and Schooler, C. (1969). Class, occupation, and orientation. *American Sociological Review, 34,* pp. 659–78.

———. (1978). The reciprocal effects of the substantive complexity of work and intellectual flexibility: A longitudinal assessment. *American Journal of Sociology, 84,* pp. 24–52.

Komarovsky, M. (1940). *The unemployed man and his family: The effect of unemployment upon the status of the man in fifty-nine families.* New York: Dryden Press.

Kreps, J. (1971). *Sex in the marketplace: American women at work*. Baltimore, MD: Johns Hopkins Press.

Lein, L., Durham, M., Schudson, M., Thomas, R., and Weiss, H. (1974). *Final report: Work and family life*. National Institute of Education, project no. 3–33094. Cambridge, MA: Center for the Study of Public Policy.

Levine, J.A. (1976). *Who will raise the children? New options for fathers (and mothers)*. Philadelphia, PA: Lippincott.

Levinson, H. (1964). *Emotional problems in the world of work*. New York: Harper and Row.

Leviton, S., and Belous, R.S. (1981). *What's happening to the American Family?* Baltimore, MD: Johns Hopkins University Press.

Locksley, A. (1980). On the effects of wives' employment on marital adjustment and companionship. *Journal of Marriage and the Family, 42*, pp. 337–46.

Lopata, H. (1971). *Occupation housewife*. New York: Oxford University Press.

Lynn, D.B. (1974). *The father: His role in child development*. Monterey, CA: Brooks/Cole.

Maccoby, M. (1976). *The gamesman*. New York: Simon and Schuster.

Machlowitz, M. (1980). *"Workaholics": Living with them, working with them*. New York: Mentor.

MacPherson, M. (1975). *The power lovers: An intimate look at politicians and their marriages*. New York: Putman.

Madani, H., and Cooper, C.L. (1977). The impact of dual career family development on organizational life. *Management Decision, 15*, pp. 487–93.

McClelland, D.C., Coleman, C., Finn, K., and Winter, D.G. (1976). *Motivation and maturity patterns in marital success*. Cambridge: Harvard University, Laboratory for Social Relations.

McCormick, E.J. (1976). Job and task analysis. In M. Dunnette (ed.), *Handbook of industrial and organizational psychology*. Chicago: Rand McNally, pp. 651–83.

Meissner, M., Humphreys, E., Meis, S., and Scheu, W. (1975). No exit for wives: Equal division of labor and the cumulation of household demands. *Canadian Review of Sociology and Anthropology, 12*, pp. 424–39.

Minton, C., Kagan, J., and Levine, J.A. (1971). Maternal control and obedience in the two-year-old child. *Child Development, 42*, pp. 1873–4.

Moore, G., and Hedges, J. (1971). Trends in labor and leisure. *Monthly Labor Review, 9*, pp. 3–11.

Mortimer, J.T. (1975). Occupational value socialization in business and professional families. *Sociology of Work and Occupations, 2*, pp. 29–53.

———. (1976). Social class, work, and the family: Some implications of the father's occupation for familial relations and sons' career decisions. *Journal of Marriage and the Family, 38*, pp. 241–56.

Mortimer, J.T., and Kumka, D.S. (1982). A further examination of the "occupational linkage hypothesis." *Sociological Quarterly, 23* (1), pp. 3–16.

Mortimer, J.T., and London, T. (1984). The varying linkages of work and family. In P. Voydanoff (ed.), *Work and family*. Palo Alto, CA: Mayfield, pp. 20–42.

Mortimer, J.T., Lorence, J., and Kumka, D.S. (1986). *Work, family, and personality: Transition to adulthood*. Norwood, NJ: Ablex.

Newberry, P., Weissman, M.M., and Myers, J.K. (1979). Working wives and housewives: Do they differ in mental status and social adjustment? *American Journal of Orthopsychiatry, 49*, pp. 282–91.

Nieva, U.F. (August 1979). *The family's impact on job-related attitudes of men and women: Report of work in progress.* Paper presented at the American Psychological Association annual meeting, New York.

Oakley, A. (19972). Are husbands good housewives? *New Society, 112,* pp. 377–9.

Pahl, J.M., and Pahl, R.E. (1971). *Managers and their wives.* London: Allen Lane.

Papanek, H. (1973). Men, women, and work: Reflections on the two-person career. *American Journal of Sociology, 78,* pp. 852–72.

Parsons, T., and Smelser, N.J. (1956). *Economy and society.* Glencoe, IL: Free Press.

Pearlin, L.I. (1970). *Class context and family relations: A cross-national study.* Boston: Little, Brown.

Piotrkowski, C.S. (1978). *Work and the family system.* New York: Free Press.

Pleck, J. (1983). Husbands' paid work and family roles: Current research issues. In H. Lopata and J. Pleck (eds.), *Research in the interweave of social roles: Families and jobs.* Greenwich, CT: JAI Press, pp. 251–333.

Poznanski, E., Maxey, A., and Marsden, G. (1970). Clinical implications of maternal employment: A review of research. *Journal of the American Academy of Child Psychiatry, 9,* pp. 741–61.

Rabinowitz, S., and Hall, D.T. (1977). Organizational research on job involvement. *Psychological Bulletin, 84,* pp. 265–88.

Rainwater, L. (1974). *What money buys: Inequality and social meaning of income.* New York: Basic Books.

Renne, K.S. (1970). Correlates of dissatisfaction in marriage. *Journal of Marriage and the Family, 32,* pp. 54–67.

Renshaw, J. (1976). An exploration of the dynamics of the overlapping worlds of work and family. *Family Process, 15,* pp. 143–65.

Robinson, J.P. (1977). *How Americans use time: A social psychological analysis of everyday behavior.* New York: Praeger.

Robinson, J., Juster, T., and Stafford, F. (1976). *Americans' use of time.* Ann Arbor, MI: Institute for Social Research.

Ross, C.E., Mirowsky, J., and Huber, J. (1983). Dividing work, sharing work, and in-between: Marriage patterns and depression. *American Sociological Review, 48,* pp. 809–29.

Rossi, A.S. (1977). A biosocial perspective on parenting. *Daedalus, 106,* pp. 1–31.

Rubin, L.B. (1976). *Worlds of pain: Life in the working-class family.* New York: Basic Books.

Rudd, N. (1981). *Dual-earner families: Issues and implications.* Paper presented at Dual Earner Family Symposium, Purdue University, West Lafayette, Indiana.

St. John-Parsons, D. (1978). Continuous dual-career families: A case study. In J.B. Bryson and R. Bryson (eds,), *Dual-career couples.* New York: Human Sciences, pp. 30–42.

Sawhill, I.V. (1977). Economic perspective on the family. *Daedalus, 106,* pp. 115–25.

Schaef, A.W., and Fassel, D. (1988). *The addictive organization.* San Francisco: Harper and Row.

Schwartz, F.N. (1989). Management women and the new facts of life. *Harvard Business Review, 67* (January–February), pp. 65–76.

Sello, K.D. (1979). Divorce law reform and increasing divorce rates. In J.G. Wells (ed.), *Current issues in marriage and the family.* New York: MacMillan, pp. 290–308.

Sennett, R., and Cobb, J. (1972). *The hidden injuries of class.* New York: Vintage Books.

Sheppard, J.M. (1984). *Sociology.* St. Paul, MN: West.

Slocum, W.L., and Nye, F.I. (1976). Provider and housekeeper roles. In F. Nye (ed.), *Role structure and analysis of the family.* Beverly Hills, CA: Sage, pp. 81–99.

Smelser, N.J. (1959). *Social change in the industrial revolution.* Chicago: University of Chicago Press.

Smith, R.E. (1979). *The subtle revolution.* Washington, DC: Urban Institute.

Sostel, A., and Sherman, S. (1977). Report on children of executives. *Behavioral Science.*

Spenner, K.I. (1981). Occupational role characteristics and intergenerational transmission. *Sociology of Work and Occupations, 8,* pp. 89–112.

Staines, G.L., Pottick, K.J., and Fudge, D.A. (1986). Wives' employment and husbands' attitudes toward work and life. *Journal of Applied Psychology, 71.* pp. 118–28.

Stewart, A.J., and Rubin, Z. (1976). Power motivation in the dating couple. *Journal of Personality and Social Psychology, 34,* pp. 305–9.

Strong, E.K. (1955). *Vocational interests eighteen years after college.* Minneapolis: University of Minnesota Press.

Stuckey, M.R., McGhee, P.E., and Bell, N.J. (1982). Parent-child interaction: The influence of maternal employment. *Developmental Psychology, 18,* pp. 635–44.

Super, D.E., Starishevsky, R., Matlin, N., and Jordan, J.P. (1963). *Career development: Self-concept theory.* Princeton, NJ: College Entrance Examination Board.

Sweet, J.A. (1973). *Women in the labor force.* New York: Seminar.

Szalai, A. (1973). The quality of family life—traditional and modern: A review of sociological findings on contemporary family organization and role differentiation in the family. Paper presented at the United Nations Interregional Seminar on the Family in the Changing Society: Problems and Responsibilities of its members, London.

Taveggia, T.C., and Thomas, E.M. (1974). Latchkey children. *Pacific Sociological Review, 17,* pp. 27–34.

Taylor, M.G., and Hartley, S.F. (1975). The two-person career: A classic example. *Sociology of Work and Occupations, 2,* pp. 354–72.

U.S. Department of Commerce. (1982a). *Population profile of the United States.* Current population reports, ser. P–20, no. 374. Washington, DC: GPO.

———. (1982b). *Money income and poverty status of families and persons in the United States: 1981 (Advance data from the March 1982 Current population survey).* Current population reports. ser. P–60, no. 134. Washington, DC: GPO.

Veblen, T. (1934). *The theory of the leisure class.* New York: Modern Library.

Walker, K.E. (1969). Time spent in household work by homemakers. *Family Economics Review, 3,* pp. 5–6.

Walker, K., and Woods, M.E. (1976). *Time use: A measure of household production* of family goods and services. Washington, DC: American Home Economics Association.

Watson, D., and Clark, L.A. (1984). Negative affectivity: The disposition to experience oversize emotional states. *Psychological Bulletin, 96,* pp. 465–90.

Whyte, W.H. (1956). *The organizational man.* New York: Doubleday.

Winter, D.G., McClelland, D.C., and Stewart, A.J. (1977). Husband's motives and wife's career level. *Journal of Personality and Social Psychology, 35,* pp. 159–66.

Yogev, S. (1982). Happiness in dual-career couples: Changing research, changing values. *Sex Roles, 8,* pp. 593–605.

Yogev, S., and Brett, J. (1985). Perceptions of the division of housework and childcare and marital satisfaction. *Journal of Marriage and the Family, 47,* pp. 609–18.

Young, M., and Willmott, P. (1973). *The symmetrical family.* New York: Pantheon.

Zedeck, S. (1987). *Work, family, and organization: An untapped research triangle.* Presidential address to the Society of Industrial and Organizational Psychology presented at the American Psychological Association's convention, New York, NY.

Zigler, E., and Child, I.L. (1969). Socialization. In G. Lindzey and E. Aronson (eds.) *The handbook of social psychology.* 2nd ed., vol. 3. Reading, MA: Addison-Wesley, pp. 450–589.

8
The Absence of Work

Arthur P. Brief
Walker R. Nord

I n the behavioral sciences, gaining an understanding of a phenomenon is often aided by considering its absence. This is obvious, for instance, in experimental psychology when researchers compare treatment and control groups with the control group *not* having been exposed to the phenomenon of interest. Additionally, in experimental psychology, designs are employed in which subjects serve as their own controls; that is, they are observed exposed and *not* exposed to the phenomenon of interest. Somewhat analogously, the intent of this chapter is to seek a better understanding of the meaning of work through examining the literature concerned with the effects of the absence of work on those previously employed.

The literature on two groups in particular will be reviewed briefly. First, attention will be focused on those willing and able to engage in paid work but who cannot find a job—in other words, those conventionally labeled as *unemployed*. Second, attention will shift to those retired from paid work. Again, our intent in looking at how unemployed and retired persons (as well as their families) react to the absence of work is to gain additional insights into what work might mean in the lives of people.

The Unemployed

According to the U.S. Department of Labor (1976), the unemployed are defined as those not now employed but looking for work in the last four weeks and those waiting for recall from layoff or due to report to work in the next thirty days. The major cause of being counted among the officially unemployed, at least for adult males, is job loss (Tiffany, Cowan, and Tiffany, 1970). It is these job losers that are the primary though not exclusive focus of the literature to be reviewed below.

Perceptions of the Unemployed

Some time ago, Bell (1958) argued (and we believe his point still holds) that the unemployed—those seeking work—are largely invisible. This is so because, at least proportionally, they represent a small segment of society and because the daily lives of many of us are so structured that if we ever encounter an unemployed person, that contact is a brief one.

Even though our direct experience with unemployed people is limited, we still have images of the unemployed and an explanation for their circumstances (e.g., Feagin, 1972; Feather, 1974; Furnham, 1982a). Some of these images feature negative, individualistic explanations for unemployment. As Jacoby (1985) pointed out, historically in the United States, the unemployed have been viewed as responsible for their own condition. In fact, it was not until the depression of 1893 that "for the first time it was widely acknowledged that the unemployed might not be entirely to blame for their situation" (p. 105). Other accounts blame the "system" for people being out of work (e.g., Furnham, 1982b). The assumed causes are associated with more general sets of beliefs and values. People who are less tolerant of and less sympathetic to those out of work also tend to endorse Weber's (1905) notion of the Protestant work ethic which he argued provided a moral justification for the accumulation of wealth (cf. Furnham, 1984). The other side of the coin, of course, is that the failure to gain wealth (in the extreme—poverty) stems from not working.

In American culture at least, certain attributions are frequently made about those who do not work. Typically, these attributions place personal responsibility on the unemployed for economic failure and are consistent with an *ideology of individualism* (Feagin, 1975). The tenets of this ideology include: (1) individuals should work hard and strive to succeed in competition with others; (2) those who work hard should be rewarded with success (e.g., wealth, power, and prestige); (3) because of widespread and equal opportunity, those who work hard, in fact, will be rewarded with success; and, (4) economic failure is an individual's own fault and reveals lack of effort and other character defects. Feagin, based upon the results of a nationwide survey, argued that the ideology of individualism remains a potent force in American life and, correspondingly, most Americans hold individuals responsible for economic failures such as losing their jobs.

While such findings regarding "lay" reactions to the unemployed may be provocative, our primary concern is with the reactions of the unemployed themselves to being without paid work. By examining these reactions, one might not only better understand what work means to the unemployed; one might also be better able to attribute responsibility for the unemployed's circumstance. That is, if it is found that the effects of unemployment are devastating personally, then assuming that the unemployed in some way choose their condition becomes less plausible.

Effects of Unemployment on Individuals

Studies of the effects of unemployment on individuals and their families began to appear in substantial numbers in response to the depression period (e.g., Bakke, 1940a, 1940b; Hall, 1934; Israeli, 1935; Komarovsky, 1940; Lazarsfeld, 1932; Rudquist and Sletto, 1936; Williams, 1933). First and foremost, these studies demonstrated that the unemployed of the 1930s experienced their condition as restrictive poverty. Because the phrase *restrictive poverty* and its equivalents are evoked not only in this early literature but also throughout later writings on the unemployment experience, the following two more recent examples are used to convey what is meant by use of the phrase.

Sinfield and Sinfield (1968) studied ninety-two unemployed men and their families living in North Shields which is located in northeast England and another group of sixty unemployed men and their families living in Syracuse, New York. They reported:

> The women spoke of the struggle to keep the children's clothes in good shape longer and the ways in which they managed to ensure that they could still put a good meal on the table at weekends for Sunday dinner. The narrowed economic aspirations were often brought home vividly. "What have you cut down on, now that your husband's out of work?"—"Well, we've never had any luxuries lately."—"What are luxuries?"—"Oh, fresh or tinned fruit, cream, biscuits, and cheese." Or, "Is there anything you bought while your husband was out of work that you felt you really shouldn't have because you couldn't afford it?"—"Well, yes. On a Friday night when Jack collected his money on the dole [Employment Exchange], he would stop at the shop on the corner and buy us some pastry and bacon and eggs. I know it was extravagant, but we had to have something to cheer us up." (pp. 359–60)

The second vehicle for illustrating *restrictive poverty* is Lebeaux's (1968) study of ninety-three needy families in Detroit. His findings included the following:

1. Only about half of the children's clothing was purchased. For the other half, the children depended upon gifts from relatives, neighbors, and schoolteachers.

2. About 80 percent of the boys and about 50 percent of the girls had but one pair of shoes; and, about 50 percent of the children had no rubbers or boots of any kind and about 75 percent had no raincoats of any description.

3. Hardly any mothers had as much as a half gallon of milk on hand and very little meat; the meat they often listed was an inexpensive cut like neck bones or a canned variety.

4.   Nearly universally the mothers reported "No fruit" and frequently it was volunteered "No vegetables either."

Simply, it can be seen through the two examples provided that phrases like *restrictive poverty* mean *getting by* or *surviving,* at least in regards to the standard of living enjoyed by mainstream Americans (Rainwater, 1974).

Beyond the obvious economic consequences of unemployment, Jahoda (1982) reports other consistent results, more psychological in nature, in the depression literature: (1) the loss of a habitual (albeit, culturally imposed) time structure; (2) feeling that one's life is without purpose; (3) a shrunken social experience given the absence of regular contact with a collectivity and its purposes; and, (4) a loss of status and identity. Moreover, some data document how these effects unfold. The initial response is fear and distress; this is followed by numbness and apathy which gradually are replaced by some adaptation and efforts to obtain employment; as the futility of these adaptive efforts become obvious, hope weakens; and finally, complete loss of hope occurs which gradually changes to apathy or sober acquiescence (Zawadski and Lazarsfeld, 1935). Also, a limited amount of depression era data suggest what the effects of unemployment are on children. According to Eisenberg and Lazarsfeld (1938), studies conducted in Germany before Hitler's rise to power showed that the academic performance of children dropped with the onset of parental unemployment; and, further deterioration occurred when parental unemployment lasted three or more years. These findings were attributed to inadequate nutrition; but, the very rapid onset of the school performance decline suggests that the effects of unemployment on family atmosphere may have been a contributing factor (Jahoda, 1982).

Based on the limited results reviewed above, as well as those from a number of other studies (e.g., Bakke, 1933; Dunn, 1934; Kardiner, 1936), it is obvious that unemployment during the 1930s was a traumatic, often devastating experience for the job loser as well as for his/her family. Some additional research helps us understand why those who lost their jobs reacted so negatively to the loss of their work and hence gives us more insight into the meaning of work.

After a critical review of the research evidence on the effects of unemployment during the depression period, O'Brien (1986) concluded that when extreme despair and hopelessness did occur following job loss, they were often the result of progressive economic deterioration and concomitant poor physical health. He adds, "It is a distortion to say that the loss of job activities were essential for the maintenance of psychological health. Few of the unemployed regretted the loss of unsatisfying work. They did regret the loss of income, or regular time structure and social status" (p. 196). O'Brien viewed the loss of income as especially salient and argued that the failure of psychologists to give appropriate emphasis to economic factors has interfered with their understanding of the meaning of work. "Psychologists have tended to understate the importance of economic factors by focusing on the loss of activity, time structure, and job prestige. Certainly, these factors were salient and were mentioned, at times, by the unemployed as contributing to their mood of discouragement. Yet, on balance, the researchers attributed the main cause to poverty" (p. 206).

Thus, O'Brien's conclusions point out that the manifest function or meaning of work in the lives of the unemployed during the depression period was the provision of income, a position echoed in other quarters (e.g., Carnegie Trust, 1943; Kardiner, 1936; Jahoda, Lazarsfeld, and Zeisel, 1933; Zawadski and Lazarsfeld, 1935).

How general are O'Brien's conclusions? It is possible that concerns over income are intensified during an economic depression and, therefore, O'Brien's findings are limited to certain economic conditions. Moreover, many things about work and its surroundings have changed during the five decades since the depression. In other words, we must ask under what conditions (e.g., economic, political, and/or social) can the results on which such conclusions are based be generalized over time? This question is explored below.

Effects of Unemployment. Many studies of the effects of unemployment on the unemployed have appeared in recent years. Several macro- or aggregate-level studies indicate that negative changes in general economic conditions (e.g., an increase in the unemployment rate) are positively associated with various indicators of poorer mental health (e.g., Catalano and Dooley, 1977; Dooley and Catalano, 1977, 1979, 1980; Pearlin, et al., 1981). For instance, Brenner (1976) has demonstrated that for society as a whole the negative consequences of unemployment are substantial. He has related increases in unemployment to proportional increases in social pathology (e.g., crime); and, importantly, this result holds across racial, sexual, and age groups and across nations. Brenner has also shown that the rate of admissions to mental health hospitals in New York State from 1910 to 1960 was associated positively with the state's unemployment rate; and, in a later study Brenner (1979) showed that the unemployment rate was also associated positively with deterioration of physical health (i.e., with an increase in cardiovascular disease, mortality, and cirrhosis of the liver).

Two points regarding Brenner's latter results are worthy of emphasis. First, the relationships he observed are not weak. For example, his findings suggest that a 1.0 percent increase in the unemployment rate is associated with almost a 2.0 percent increase in cirrhosis of the liver mortality. Second, the social pathologies he observed did not appear immediately after a change in the unemployment rate. Again taking the case of cirrhosis as an example, the chronic reaction increased about three years after a change in the unemployment rate. Thus, it seems that changes in the unemployment rate are tied to subsequent and substantial changes in aggregated indicators of both psychological and physical well-being. But, what do such macro-results mean for the affected individual and his/her family?

Over the past decade or so, considerable effort has focused on identifying the effects of job loss—particularly job loss driven by plant closings or some other form of organizational cutback (e.g., Brief and Atieh, 1987; Jick, 1985; Kaufman, 1982; Powell and Driscoll, 1973; Scholzman and Verba, 1978; Slote, 1969). Overall, these writers indicate that while in the last forty or fifty years social legislation has given workers greater protection against the negative effects of unemployment, being voluntarily without paid work remains a significantly harmful life event for those experiencing it. For instance, unemployment has been tied to anomia (e.g., Aiken, Ferman, and Sheppard, 1968), guilt and hostility (e.g., Stokes and Cochrane, 1984), depression (e.g., Feather and Barber, 1983), poorer physical health in general (e.g., O'Brien and Kabanoff, 1979) and, in particular, myocardial infarction (e.g., Burr and Sweetnan, 1980). The following examples provide some detail on the methods used and results obtained in the recent literature on unemployment.

For two years, Kasl and Cobb (1979) studied the blood pressure changes in married, stably employed men who lost their jobs because of a permanent plant shutdown. They found blood pressure levels during anticipation of job loss and unemployment (or probationary reemployment) were clearly higher than after subsequent stabilization on new jobs; and, men whose blood pressure levels remained higher longer had more severe unemployment, reported longer-lasting subjective stress, and failed to show much improvement in reported well-being. Warr (1983) found, in an extensive program of research on the unemployment problem in Britain, that psychological health of the unemployed (as indexed by levels of anxiety, depression, insomnia, irritability, self-confidence, listlessness, and concentration) was poorer than that of employed individuals; *and* that this poor health was the result of unemployment since a return to paid employment commonly was followed by an improvement in psychological health.

Consistent with these findings, Kahn (1981) concluded that: "Studies of plant closings have documented the ramifying effects of job loss: the distress and pessimism, the psychological depression, the sharply reduced standard of living, the occasional suicide" (p. 83). Moreover, Kahn noted that job insecurity has been shown to have an adverse impact on physical health—"the threat of unemployment triggers some physiological changes long before actual job loss occurs" (p. 100).

Interestingly, some recent evidence on gender differences in psychological distress also confirms that the male's attachment to the traditional role of breadwinner is alive and well. McLanahan and Glass (1985) argued that for men, in general, the employment role remains a major source of identity and self-esteem, their achievement and status being measured in terms of occupational status and career mobility; thus, unemployment and intermittent employment for males indicates role failure which nearly always leads to a loss of face. Ross and Huber (1985) reported that a husband's personal earnings directly decreased his level of depression while a wife's personal earnings did not affect her depression. These findings support McLanahan and Glass's position. Despite changes in sex roles that have occurred in recent decades, there remains, in many families, an attachment of the husband to the breadwinner role that impacts the meaning of work—or, in this case, the absence of work.

In sum, from a review of the effects of job loss on individuals, it is clear that job losers, almost universally, express dissatisfaction with becoming unemployed (e.g., Hartley, 1980; Swinburne, 1981; Warr, 1978); and, as the time one remains unemployed increases, psychological and physical health deteriorate (e.g., Cobb and Kasl, 1977; Hepworth, 1980; Warr and Jackson, 1984). Time unemployed may also be associated with a deteriorating financial position and such increasing economic hardship itself may have a direct, adverse effect on the individual. Indeed, some data suggest that it is the economic loss attached to unemployment which produces many of the adverse effects observed following job loss (Aiken et al., 1968; Cohn, 1978; Estes and Wilensky, 1978; Little, 1976; Oliver and Pomicter, 1981). These findings, coupled with the previously mentioned reasoning advanced by McLanahan and Glass (1985) regarding the effects of failure to perform as a breadwinner, indicate a reasonable degree of consistency between the research results of the 1930s and more current findings. That is, recent findings on the effects of unemployment add credence to the assertion that the manifest function of work is income. Over time, at least, what it seems the unemployed miss most from working is the income they earned; and the available data have little, if anything, to say about the loss of activity, time structure, or job prestige.

Effects on the Family. Contemporary evidence also documents the effects of unemployment on the family. These effects go beyond the psychological spill-over of the unemployed person's strains and concerns to affect other family members (Root, 1977). Unemployment of the breadwinner is associated with increased conflicts between spouses (e.g., Fagin, 1981; Liem and Liem, 1979; Moen, 1976). Moreover, while the available data do not speak to the specific reactions of husbands to their wives' unemployment, evidence does show that the wives of unemployed men experience, for example, depression, anxiety, fearfulness, and helplessness. The major impact of such reactions appears to emerge several months after husbands become unemployed (e.g., Liem and Rayman, 1982) and seems to be greater among the wives of blue-collar than white-collar workers (e.g., Buss and Redburn, 1983). Since the duration of time unemployed and lower occupational status are apt to be associated with the financial hardship attached to unemployment, these results extend at least indirectly the *manifest function of work is income* notion beyond the unemployed worker to the family.

Unemployment of a major family provider is also associated with a shift in the pattern of labor force participation and earnings among family members (Ferman and Gardner, 1979). Spouses may obtain employment outside the home or increase their level of labor force participation from part-time to full-time (Voydanoff, 1983). Moreover, with the unemployed family member spending substantially more time at home, family routines may be disrupted and tensions increased (LeMasters, 1975). Disruption additionally may be manifest through the loss of power in the family of the unemployed breadwinner. This is especially so if the breadwinner's respect and authority were contingent on his or her earnings (e.g., Kanter, 1977).

The disruptions in family life from unemployment can be particularly devastating when they adversely affect the well-being of the family's children. The children of the unemployed are exposed to higher risks of being physically ill (Margolis and Farron, 1981). As will be discussed shortly, this exposure may be attributable to the lower standard of living experienced by the families of the unemployed. Socially and psychologically, children of the unemployed have been found: (a) to experience strained relationships with their peers and to avoid interacting with them; (b) to be more moody at home; (c) to have increased problems in school; and, (d) to feel distrustful, immobilized, helpless, and victimized (Leim and Rayman, 1982; Buss and Redburn, 1983). Moreover, some evidence suggests that unemployment is associated with child abuse (Justice and Justice, 1976; Steinberg, Catalano, and Dooley, 1981).

In summarizing the effects of unemployment on the family, Moen (1983) painted a picture of lasting gloom. She asserted that unemployment and the economic losses attached to it force families to reappraise their current situation *and* prospects for the future which, in turn, results in the reduction of both short- and long-term family goals. For example, in the short run, preventive health care may be delayed. Similarly, due to an uncertain financial future, aspirations for the higher education of the family's children may be curtailed or even eliminated. Thus, the family, in reacting to a current economic crisis and in planning for a seemingly dim financial future, lowers its aims in ways which may have multiple negative consequences for generations to come (Price, 1984).

Implications. Most of the evidence we have cited paints a gloomy picture of the unemployed and their families. It is important to recognize, however, that the magnitude of the effects of unemployment do vary. Few writers, unfortunately, have attempted to articulate those factors which may moderate or mediate the effects of unemployment. What is known suggests that financial resources (e.g., spouse's income, savings, homeownership, and lack of debt) are major factors in constraining the negative effects of unemployment (cf., Brief and Atieh, 1987). Another important constraining factor appears to be a relatively low level of financial need—low need being reflected by few dependents, a comparatively austere life style, and being at a stage in life when demands on economic resources are minimal, such as when one's children have completed their formal education. Other family-oriented constraints on the negative effects might include a family life prior to unemployment characterized by (1) cohesiveness, adaptability, and an authority pattern based on love and respect rather than earnings (Voydanoff, 1983), and (2) high levels of social supportiveness (Gore, 1978).

Beyond the family, other factors may reduce the negative effects of unemployment. These include an employer who supplies extensive services and generous severance pay to discharged employees, and a government that has sought to regulate the job loss process humanely and that ensures adequate amounts of unemployment compensation.

Finally, personal attributes of the unemployed person that can limit the magnitude of the negative effects should not be overlooked. Here, we refer principally to the person's performance capabilities in terms of his or her motivation to work and his or her work-relevant skills and abilities. Also, the employment opportunities derived from the economic demand for his or her talents and from members of the occupational group to which he or she belongs must be recognized. [For more on potential moderators see, for example, Brief and Atieh (1987) and Leana and Ivancevich (1987).]

In sum, a rather clear picture emerges of the effects of unemployment on the unemployed. Work serves an array of functions in life including, for example, a source of purpose (Morse and Weiss, 1955) and self-image (Wilensky, 1966) and even a tie to reality (Freud, 1930). As Kahn (1981) observed in discussing unemployment and the meaning of work, "For most men and for increasing numbers of women there is no viable alternative to work, no other activity that uses the energy, demands the attention, [and] provides regular social interaction around some visible outcome on which the larger society confers some dollar value" (p. 69). However, from this array, the economic outcomes seem to be particularly salient. Friedmann and Havighurst (1954), based on the results of their research on the meaning of work among members of several different occupations, concluded that while work does serve a number of functions in life, only one was identified by all of the men they interviewed. The one universal function was that work is a means of earning a living. Consistent with our analysis, unemployment has many consequences, most of which appeared to be tied to the economic functions of work. [For more on this point, see Brief and Aldag (in press).]

The unemployed, as we suggested earlier, are part of a stigmatized class of persons. That is, their economic failure is often seen by others as a product of some defect in character. Being labeled as *unemployed,* therefore, is a socially illegitimate condition. However, not all forms of being without paid work are labeled as unemployed. When being without paid work is labeled differently, it can be a more legitimate state of being. For example, retirement is a seemingly more acceptable state.

The Retired

The experiences concerning retirement of three groups of people can help us understand the meaning of work by considering special forms of its absence. One group consists of a growing number of people who retire early. The second group includes those who retire at the conventional time. The final group embodies those who work beyond the age at which most others retire.

Early Retirement. While some individuals are forced into retirement because they are not physically or mentally capable of continuing in their paid work roles, others who have the option of continuing to work and are capable of doing so, elect to retire. By examining the reasons of this latter group for voluntarily selecting so-called "early retirement," one can gain an understanding of the psychology of the retirement decision. Several studies indicated that financial considerations are the single most important criterion in making a retirement decision (e.g., Boskin, 1977; Parnes et al., 1974; Quinn, 1977).

These findings should not be interpreted to suggest that economic factors are the only ones people consider. Indeed, research has developed a rather long list of reasons for the decision to retire early. Job satisfaction, occupational level and status, and activities planned for in retirement (cf. McGoldrick and Cooper, 1985) appear to be some of the most important reasons. However, health appears to be even more important. In early retirement studies relying on samples in which those who might retire for health reasons are not necessarily excluded, poor health emerged as the primary reason for early retirement (e.g., Parker, 1980; Reno, 1971). [Even in so-called normal retirement studies (Parker, 1982), poor health was also an often identified reason (e.g., Anderson and Cowan, 1956; Palmore 1971).]

Normal Retirement. Many investigators who have examined the experience of "normal" retirement, have reported finding considerable dissatisfaction with retirement. These investigators generally agree that this dissatisfaction is largely attributable to poor health and/or inadequate finances (see McGoldrick and Cooper, 1985). Importantly, however, the evidence also suggests that poor health is *not* a function of retirement (e.g., Kasl and Cobb, 1980). For example, while many may assume retirement adversely affects a person's mental health, evidence indicates that this is not the case (e.g., Bell, 1974; Campbell, Converse, and Rogers, 1976; Streib, 1956; Streib and

Schneider, 1971). Indeed, it appears that sufficient positive values are obtainable in retirement to maintain people's psychological well-being (e.g., Atchley, 1971). Thus, it seems that those attributes of work which people find meaningful—other than income—can be found or substituted for in retirement.

Such a conclusion is supported by Parker's (1982) qualitative study of the meanings pre-retirees attach to retirement. The two meanings most frequently reported were: (a) "A feeling of freedom and being able to please yourself," and (b) "Looking forward to more leisure, time for hobbies" (p. 105). Analogously, Jones (1974) listed several gains seen in retirement, including freedom from the clock, freedom from taking orders, not having to get up in the morning, and not having to put up with bad traveling conditions. Thus, many of the elements often assumed to be causes of dissatisfaction in retirement could be, but often are not, the major complaint.

The most consistently reported complaints center on finances. Considerable research points in this direction. Draper, Lundgren, and Strother (1967) found that white-collar, supervisory, and skilled workers were more satisfied with retirement than service, semiskilled, and unskilled workers. Likewise, Smith, Kendall, and Hulin (1969) found retirees from blue-collar occupations to be less satisfied with their lives than retirees from white-collar occupations. In addition, Smith et al. also found the blue-collar retirees to be less satisfied with their finances. These results suggest that the economic outcomes attached to one's preretirement occupation are associated with adjusting well to retirement. Indeed, Friedman and Orbach (1974) found satisfaction with retirement to be correlated substantially with financial resources. Most recently, McGoldrick and Cooper (1985) found that the *chief* concern among retirees was finances—not the loss of an habitual time structure, feeling that their life is without purpose, experiencing a shrunken social existence, or a loss of status and identity.

Working Past Normal Retirement. In opening our consideration of the retired, we addressed the question "Why do people retire?" In closing, we very briefly consider why people continue to work past normal retirement age. The pattern that emerges suggests that, on one hand, when finances are problematic, people who continue to work report doing so primarily for the money. In a study of retired recipients of social security benefits (prior to the indexing of those benefits to the Consumer Price Index), Stecker (1951) found interest in continuing to work tied to obtaining the income required to maintain something like one's previous standard of living rather than to being busy or feeling useful. In a more recent study in Britain, Parker (1980) found 42 percent of the men and 40 percent of the women he studied reported the "Need for money" to be a main reason for continuing work after normal retirement age. For men, the next most frequent response was "Would be bored otherwise" (21 percent); and, for women, it was "Like to work" (21 percent).

On the other hand, when one's finances are secure, those who continue to work report doing so for other reasons. The available research suggests that among those members of occupational groups who are relatively secure financially, work-related income does not appear to be a factor in the decision to continue working. For example, Kratcoski, Huber, and Gaulak (1974), in a study of retired professors, found that the factor most frequently reported as aiding in adjustment to retirement was continued work activities. Also, wanting to continue professional contacts was frequently reported as a reason for stying on. Acuff and Allen (1970), in their study of retired professors, likewise found that those who continued to work seemed to do so to maintain a sense of purpose in life.

Implications. It appears that, among those approaching or in retirement, the decision to disengage from paid work is influenced to a large degree by health and financial considerations; and, these same two factors also appear to play major roles in determining how well people adjust to their retirements. From these conclusions and the limited direct evidence available, it seems what many, if not most, retirees miss significantly about working are the economic outcomes that were attached to their work. Moreover, it seems that while other features of working also are missed, they surface as difficulties primarily among thoses retirees who feel financially comfortable.

It is also worth noting that poor adjustment to retirement, financial concerns aside, appears to be a problem for only a minority of retirees. Slightly less than one-third of retirees have difficulty adjusting to retirement; and among those who do, only 7 percent attribute it to missing their jobs while the rest assign blame to financial limitations, health problems, or death of a spouse (see Atchley, 1976).

It is also important to recognize that significant new patterns of retirement may be emerging. In the past decade, numerous companies have encouraged some of their employees to retire long before the traditional age sixty-five. Some of these plans call for people to work part time or as consultants rather than abruptly to sever their ties to the organization. In addition, it seems that the number of workers seeking early retirement is on the increase. In this regard, Johnson and Williamson (1987, p. 13) observed, "Although researchers continue to look for problems retirees faced because of the removal of work as a source of meaning in their lives, more and more workers in the 1960s and 1970s appeared to believe that a retirement earlier than was required by mandatory retirement regulations or than was necessary for the receipt of full social security benefits, was personally and financially preferable to continued employment: in 1957, 83 percent of men aged sixty to sixty-four were in the labor force; in 1982, 57 percent were participants (Schulz,

1985)." In addition, changes in federal laws and improved health of workers in their sixties are likely to mean that more people will work beyond age sixty-five.

These trends, taken together, mean that increasingly greater choice about the decision to retire or not will reside in the individual. Moreover, a larger number of people may have second careers that they begin quite late in life— late at least by past norms. In the context of our discussion in chapter 1 concerning the interrelationships between components of the social context and the meaning of work, these new patterns may well prove to be very important changes not only in the meaning of work but in society more generally. At the very least, they suggest the need for students of work and nonwork to recognize that the labels used in previous research may need to be revised to adequately capture the experiences of today's people. As the nature of social experience changes, so must the categories used to map it.

Conclusions

Our analyses of the unemployed and the retired lead to similar conclusions. That is, while the effects of unemployment are devastating and those of retirement are not necessarily so, the feature of work most sorely missed by both groups appears to be income. Other features of work have their meaning too; but when one is without work and, therefore, in economic need, it is the income which is attached to working that repeatedly surfaces as the outcome of work both unemployed and retired persons value most. This should be an obvious conclusion given that we are addressing the meaning of *paid* work. However, there is a tendency in the research literature to overintellectualize what work means to people. Our analysis of those out of work might serve as a clear warning against the tendency to glorify certain psychological functions of work, while paying too little attention to the basics.

Finally, we have seen how changes in the social system have operated to alter the experience of unemployment and, perhaps to an even greater degree, the experience of retirement. Again, the study of work demands the student to be aware that the concepts he or she uses are in need of constant updating if they are to map the human experience with sufficient fidelity.

References

Acuff, G., and Allen, D. (1970). Hiatus in meaning: Disengagement for retired professors. *Journal of Gerontology, 25,* pp. 126–28.

Aiken, M., Ferman, L.A., and Sheppard, H.L. (1968). *Economic failure, alienation, and extremism.* Ann Arbor, MI: University of Michigan Press.

Anderson, W.F., and Cowan, N.R. (1956). Work and retirement: Influences on the health of older men. *Lancet, 271,* pp. 1344–47.

Atchley, R.C. (1971). Retirement and leisure participation: Continuity or crisis. *The Gerontologist, 11,* pp. 13–7.

———. (1976). *The sociology of retirement.* Cambridge, MA: Schenkman.

Bakke, E.W. (1933). *The unemployed man.* London: Nisbet.

———. (1940a). *Citizens without work.* New Haven: Yale University Press.

———. (1940b). *The unemployed worker.* New Haven: Yale University Press.

Bell, D. (1958). The "invisible" unemployed. *Fortune, 15* (July), pp. 105–11, 198, 200, 202, 204.

Bell, B.D. (1974). Cognitive dissonance and the life satisfaction of older adults. *Journal of Gerontology, 29,* pp. 564–71.

Borrero, I.M. (1980). Psychological and emotional impact of unemployment. *Journal of Sociology and Social Welfare, 7,* pp. 916–34.

Boskin, M. (1977). Social security and the retirement decision. *Economic Enquiry,* pp. 1–25.

Brenner, H.M. (1967). Economic change and mental hospitalization: New York, 1910–1960. *Social Psychiatry, 2,* pp. 180–8.

———. (1974). *Mental illness and the economy.* Cambridge: Harvard University Press.

———. (1976). *Estimating the social costs of national economic policy.* Washington, DC: U.S. Government Printing Office.

———. (1979). Influence of the social environment on psychopathology: The historic perspective. In J.E. Barrett, R.M. Rose, and G.L. Kerman (eds.), *Stress and mental disorder.* New York: Raven Press, pp. 161–77.

Brief, A.P., and Aldag, R.G. (N.d.). The economic functions of work. In K.M. Rowland and G.R. Ferris (eds.), *Research in personnel and human resources management.* Greenwich, CT: JAI Press. In press.

Brief, A.P., and Atieh, J.M. (1987). Studying job stress: Are we making mountains out of molehills? *Journal of Occupational Behavior, 8,* pp. 115–26.

Burr, M.L., and Sweetnan, P.M. (1980). Family size and paternal unemployment in relation to myocardial infarction. *Journal of Epidemiology and Community Health, 34,* pp. 43–95.

Buss, T.F., and Redburn, F.S. (1983). *Mass unemployment: Plant closings and community mental health.* Beverly Hills, CA: Sage.

Campbell, A., Converse, P.E., and Rogers, W.L. (1976). *The quality of American life.* New York: Russell Sage.

Carnegie Trust. (1943). *Disinherited youth.* Ediburgh: T. and A. Constable.

Catalano, R.A., and Dooley, D. (1977). Economic predictors of depressed mood and stressful life events in a metropolitan community. *Journal of Health and Social Behavior, 18,* pp. 292–307.

Clague, E., Couper, W.J., and Bakke, E.W. (1934). *After the shutdown.* New Haven: Yale University Press.

Cobb, S., and Kasl, S.V. (1977). *Termination: The consequences of job loss.* Cincinnati, OH: U.S. Department of Health, Education and Welfare.

Cohn, R.M. (1978). The effects of employment status change on self-attitudes. *Social Psychology Quarterly, 41,* pp. 81–93.

Dooley, D., and Catalano, R. (1977). Money and mental disorder: Toward behavioral cost accounting for primary prevention. *American Journal of Community Psychology, 5,* pp. 217–27.

———. (1979). Economic life, and disorder changes: Time series analyses. *American Journal of Community Psychology, 7,* pp. 381–96.

———. (1980). Economic change as a cause of behavioral disorder. *Psychological Bulletin, 87,* pp. 450–68.

Draper, J.E., Lundgren, E.F., and Strother, G.B. (1967). *Work attitudes and retirement adjustment.* Madison, WI: University of Wisconsin, Bureau of Business Research and Service.

Dunn, M. (1934). Psychiatric treatment of the effects of depression: Its possibilities and limitations. *Mental Hygiene, 18,* pp. 279–86.

Eisenberg, P., and Lazarsfeld, P.F. (1938). The psychological effects of unemployment. *Psychological Bulletin, 87,* pp. 450–68.

Estes, R.J., and Wilensky, H.L. (1978). Life cycle squeeze and morale curve. *Social Problems, 25,* pp. 277–92.

Fagin, L. (1981). *Unemployment and health in families.* Washington, DC: U.S. Government Printing Office.

Feagin, J. (1972). Poverty: We still believe that God helps them who help themselves. *Psychology Today, 6,* pp. 101–29.

Feagin, J.R. (1975). *Subordinating the poor.* Englewood Cliffs, NJ: Prentice Hall.

Feather, M. (1974). Explanations of poverty in Australian and American samples: The person, society, and fate? *Australian Journal of Psychology, 26,* pp. 109–26.

Feather, M.T., and Barber, J.G. (1983). Depressive reactions and unemployment. *Journal of Abnormal Psychology, 92,* pp. 185–95.

Ferman, L.A., and Gardner, J. (1979). Economic deprivation, social mobility, and mental health. In L.A. Ferman and J.P. Gordus (eds.), *Mental health and the economy.* Kalamazoo, MI: W.E. Upjohn Institute.

Freud, S. (1930). *Civilization and its discontents.* London: Hogarth.

Friedman, E.A., and Havighurst, R.J. (1954). *The meaning of work and retirement.* Chicago: University of Chicago Press.

Friedman, E.A., and Orbach, H.L. (1974). Adjustment to work and retirement. In S. Arieti (ed.), *American handbook of psychiatry,* vol. 1. New York: Basic Books.

Furnham, A. (1982a). Explanation for unemployment in Britain. *European Journal of Social Psychology, 12,* pp. 335–52.

———. (1982b). The Protestant work ethic and attitudes towards unemployment. *Journal of Occupational Psychology, 55,* pp. 277–86.

———. (1984). The Protestant work ethic: A review of the psychological literature. *European Journal of Social Psychology, 14,* pp. 87–104.

Gore, S. (1978). The effect of social support in moderating the health consequences of unemployment. *Journal of Health and Social Behavior, 19,* pp. 157–65.

Hall, O.M. (1934). Attitudes and unemployment: A comparison of the opinions and attitudes of employed and unemployed men. *Archives of Psychology, 25* (165).

Hartley, J. (1980). The personality of unemployed managers: Myth and measurement. *Personnel Review, 9,* pp. 12–18.

Hartley, J., and Freyer, D. (1984). The psychology of unemployment: A critical appraisal. In G. Stephenson and J. Davis (eds.), *Progress in Applied Social Psychology,* vol. 2. Chichester, England: Wiley, pp. 3–30.

Hepworth, S.J. (1980). Moderating factors of the psychological impact of unemployment. *Journal of Occupational Psychology, 53,* pp. 139–46.

Israeli, N. (1935). Distress in the outlook of Lancashire and Scottish unemployed. *Journal of Applied Psychology, 19,* pp. 67–9.

Jacoby, S.M. (1985). *Employing bureaucracy: Managers, unions, and the transformation of work in American industry 1900–1945.* New York: Columbia University Press.

Jahoda, M. (1982). *Employment and unemployment.* Cambridge: Cambridge University Press.

Jahoda, M., Lazarsfeld, P.F., and Zeisel, H. (1933). *Marienthal: The sociography of an unemployed community.* London: Tavistock.

Jick, T.D. (1985). As the ax falls: Budget cuts and the experience of stress in organizations. In T.A. Beehr and R.S. Bhagat (eds.), *Human stress and cognition in organizations.* New York: Wiley, pp. 83–114.

Johnson, E.S., and Williamson, J.B. (1987). Retirement in the United States. In K.S. Markides and C.L. Cooper (eds.), *Retirement in industrialized societies.* Chichester, England: Wiley.

Jones, A. (1974). Work and leisure. In M. Pilch (ed.), *The retirement book.* London: Hamish Hamilton.

Justice, B., and Justice, R. (1976). *The abusing family.* New York: Human Services Press.

Kahn, R.L. (1981). *Work and health.* New York: John Wiley & Sons.

Kanter, R.M. (1977). *Work and family in the United States: A critical review and agenda for research and policy.* New York: Russell Sage.

Kardiner, E. (1936). The role of economic security in the adaptation of the individual. *The Family, 17,* pp. 187–97.

Kasl, S.V. (1979). Changes in mental health status associated with job loss and retirement. In M.E. Barrett, R.M. Rose, and G.L. Klerman (eds.), *Stress and mental disorder.* New York: Raven Press.

Kasl, S.V., and Cobb, S. (1979). Some mental health consequences of plant closing and job loss. In L.A. Ferman and J.P. Gordus (eds.), *Mental health and the economy.* Kalamazoo, MI: W.E. Upjohn Institute for Employment Research.

———. (1980). The experience of losing a job: Some effects on cardiovascular functioning. *Psychotherapy and Psychosomatics, 34,* pp. 88–109.

Kaufman, H. (1982). *Professionals in search of work: Coping with the stress of job loss and underemployment.* New York: Wiley-Interscience.

Komarovsky, M. (1940). *The unemployed man and his family: The effect of unemployment upon the status of the man in fifty-nine families.* New York: Dryden Press.

Kratcoski, P.C., Huber, J.H., and Gaulak, R. (1974). Retirement satisfaction among emeritus professors. *Industrial Gerontology, 1,* pp. 78–81.

Lazarsfeld, P. (1932). An unemployed village. *Character and Personality, 1*, pp. 147–51.

Leana, C.R., and Ivancevich, J.M. (1987). Involuntary job loss: Institutional interventions and a research agenda. *Academy of Management Review, 12*, pp. 301–12.

Lebeaux, C. (1968). Life on A.D.C.: Budget of despair. In L.A. Ferman, J.L. Kornbluh, and A. Haber (eds.), *Poverty in America*. Ann Arbor, MI: University of Michigan Press, pp. 519–28.

LeMasters, E.E. (1975). *Blue-collar aristocrats: Life-styles at a working class tavern*. Madison, WI: University of Wisconsin Press.

Liem, G.R., and Liem, J.H. (1979). Social support and stress: Some general issues and their application to the problem of unemployment. In L.A. Ferman and J.P. Gordis (eds.), *Mental health and the economy*. Kalamazoo, MI: W.E. Upjohn Institute for Employment Research.

Liem, R., and Rayman, P. (1982). Health and social costs of unemployment: Research and policy considerations. *American Psychologist, 37*, pp. 1116–23.

Little, C.B. (1976). Technical-professional unemployment: Middle-class adaptability to personal crisis. *Sociological Quarterly, 17*, pp. 262–71.

Margolis, L.H., and Farran, D.C. (1981). Unemployment: The health consequences in children. *North Carolina Medical Journal, 42*, pp. 849–50.

McGoldrick, A.E., and Cooper, C.L. (1985). Stress at the decline of one's career. In T.A. Beehr and R.S. Bhagat (eds.), *Human stress and cognition in organizations*. New York: Wiley-Interscience, pp. 177–201.

McLanahan, S.S., and Glass, J.L. (1985). A note on the trend in sex differences in psychological distress. *Journal of Health and Social Behavior, 26*, 328–35.

Moen, P. (1976). Family impact of the 1975 depression: Duration of unemployment. *Journal of Marriage and the Family, 41*, pp. 561–72.

Moen, P. (1983). Unemployment, public policy, and families: Forecasts for the 1980s. *Journal of Marriage and the Family, 48*, pp. 751–60.

Morse, W.C., and Weiss, R.S. (1955). The function and meaning of work and the job. *American Sociological Review*, pp. 191–8.

O'Brien, G.E. (1986). *Psychology of work and unemployment*. Chichester, England, Wiley and Sons.

O'Brien, G.E., and Kabanoff, B. (1979). Comparison of unemployed and employed workers on work values, locus of control, and health variables. *Australian Psychologist, 14*, pp. 143–54.

Oliver, J.M., and Pomicter, (1981). Depression in automotive assembly-line workers as a function of unemployment variables. *American Journal of Community Psychology, 89*, pp. 507–72.

Palmore, E.B. (1971). Why do people retire? *Aging and Human Development, 2*, pp. 269–83.

Parker, S. (1980). *Older workers and retirement*. London: HMSO.

———. (1982). *Work and retirement*. London: George Allen and Unwin.

Parnes, H.S., Arvil, V.A., Andrisani, P.J., Kohen, A.I., and Gilbert, N. (1974). *The pre-retirement years: Five years in the work lives of middle-aged men*, vol. 4. Washington, DC: U.S. Department of Commerce.

Pearlin, L.I., Lieberman, M.A., Menaghan, E.G., and Mullan, J.T. (1981). The stress process. *Journal of Health and Social Behavior, 22,* pp. 337–56.

Powell, D.H., and Driscoll, P.F. (1973). Middle-class professionals face unemployment. *Society, 10,* pp. 18–26.

Price, R.H. (1984). The effects of long-term unemployment on children, youth, and families: Policy options. Testimony submitted to the Select Committee on Children, Youth, and Families, U.S. House of Representatives.

Quinn, J. (1977). Microeconomic determinants of early retirement: A cross-sectional view of white married men. *Journal of Human Resources, 12,* pp. 329–46.

Rainwater, L. (1974). *What money buys.* New York: Basic Books.

Reno, V. (1971). Why men stop working at or before age sixty-five. *Social Security Bulletin, 34,* pp. 3–17.

Root, K. (1977). Workers and their families in a plant shutdown. Paper presented at the annual meeting of the American Sociological Association, Chicago, IL.

Ross, C.E., and Huber, J. (1985). Hardship and depression. *Journal of Health and Social Behavior, 26,* pp. 312–27.

Rundquist, E.A., and Sletto, R.F. (1936). *Personality in the depression: A study in measurement of attitudes.* Minneapolis, MN: University of Minnesota Press.

Scholzman, K.L., and Verba, S. (1978). The new unemployment: Does it hurt? *Public Policy, 26,* pp. 333–58.

Schulz, J.H. (1985). *The economics of aging.* Belmont, CA: Wadsworth.

Sinfield, D., and Sinfield, A. (1968). (1968). Out of work in Syracuse and Shields. In I. Deutscher and E.J. Thompson (eds.), *Among the people: Encounters with the poor.* New York: Basic Books, pp. 353–71.

Slote, A. (1969). *Termination.* New York: Bobbs-Merrill.

Smith, P., Kendall, L., and Hulin, C. (1969). *The measurement of satisfaction in work and retirement.* Chicago: Rand McNally.

Stecker, M.L. (1951). Beneficiaries prefer to work. *Social Security Bulletin, 14,* pp. 15–17.

Steinberg, L., Catalano, R., and Dooley, D. (1981). Economic antecedents of child abuse and neglect. *Child Development, 51,* pp. 975–85.

Stokes, G., and Cochrane, R. (1984). A study of the psychological effects of the redundance of unemployment. *Journal of Occupational Psychology, 57,* pp. 309–22.

Streib, G.F. (1956). Morale of the retired. *Social Problems, 3,* pp. 270–6.

Streib, G.F., and Schneider, C.J. (1971). *Retirement in American society: Impact and process.* Ithaca, NY: Cornell University Press.

Swinburne, P. (1981). The psychological impact of unemployment on managers and professional staff. *Journal of Occupational Psychology, 54,* pp. 47–64.

Tiffany, D.W., Cowan, J.R., and Tiffany, P.M. (1970). *The unemployed.* Englewood Cliffs, NJ: Prentice Hall.

U.S. Department of Labor. (1976). *BLS Handbook of Methods.* Bulletin 1910. Washington, DC: GPO.

Voydanoff, P. (1983). Unemployment: Strategies for family adaptation. In C.R. Figley and H.I. McCubbin (eds.), *Stress and the family. Catastrophic stressors,* vol. 2. Brunner Mazel.

Warr, P.B. (1978). A study of psychological well-being. *British Journal of Psychology, 69,* pp. 111–21.

———. (1983). Work, jobs, and unemployment. *Bulletin of the British Psychological Association, 36,* pp. 305–11.

Warr, P.B., and Jackson, P. (1984). Men without jobs: Some correlates of age and length of unemployment. *Journal of Occupational Psychology, 57,* pp. 77–85.

Weber, M. (1905). *The Protestant ethic and the spirit of capitalism.* New York: Scribner.

Wilensky, H.L. (1966). Work as a social problem. In H.S. Becker (ed.), *Social problems: A modern approach.* New York: Wiley and Sons, pp. 117–66.

Williams, J.M. (1933). *Human aspects of unemployment and relief.* Chapel Hill, NC: University of North Carolina Press.

Zawadski, B., and Lazarsfeld, P.F. (1935). The psychological consequences of unemployment. *Journal of Social Psychology, 6,* pp. 224–51.

9

On the Reciprocal Relationship between the Meaning of Work and Political Economy

Walter R. Nord
Arthur P. Brief

*P*olitical economy refers to the complex set of processes that determines the production and allocation of a society's resources. While many of the components of this process are commonly treated under the heading of *economics,* political economy is more comprehensive. Whereas economics emphasizes the role of markets, the study of political economy also considers how ideology, religion, social processes, and government (in addition to market forces) influence production and resource allocation. This chapter considers the interaction between the objective and subjective meanings of work and political economy.

We argue that the study of the meaning of work is incomplete without consideration of macro-level factors that constitute a society's political economy. We propose that the meanings individual members of society give to work in general and to their own jobs in particular, are partially shaped by these political economic factors. However, we also argue that the meaning of work has influenced and continues to influence the political economy in significant ways. In short, the meaning of work and the nature of the political economy are dynamically interrelated. Since the argument is long and its elements are interwoven, a brief overview may be useful at the outset.

Overview

While work and political economy may be interrelated in many ways, in this chapter the core of the relationship is consumption. Recall, we have defined work as what people do to make a living. In important ways, *a living* is another term for an individual's consumption. Also, a key part of our defini-

The insightful comments of Elizabeth Doherty on several drafts of this chapter, and those of Jay Chandran on the final draft, are gratefully acknowledged.

tion of political economy referred to how society allocates its resources; it goes without saying that the character of consumption is an expression of this allocation process. Consequently, factors that affect consumption are apt to affect the meaning of work. Moreover, how people relate to work is likely to influence the other key part of our definition of political economy—namely, how productive a society is. In addition, a wide variety of social forces (e.g., values) influence how people define a living and, hence, affect the meaning of work and the pressures that influence how society uses its resources. In this chapter, we explore these interrelationships.

We begin by discussing the basis for positing these interrelationships in more detail and by noting a few caveats. We then focus on the joint evolution of work and consumption. We see immediately that work is related to economic growth and hence to aggregate consumption and to the distribution of wealth. We then review how these relationships changed over time and how these changes were related to political economic processes. We are especially concerned with: a) revisions in the meaning of work as society moved from extreme economic scarcity into the so-called consumer society, b) how changes in work contributed to the consumer society, and c) how the consumer society altered objective and subjective dimensions of work. We also explore how these developments were related to legal and other macro-level social changes.

We then shift our focus from the meaning of work to the individual to its meaning for the collectivity as a whole. This focus highlights several other aspects of the interrelationship between work and the political economy. Here, we see the meaning of work as serving two partially conflicting functions—on the one hand, beliefs about work can support effective cooperative activity; on the other, beliefs about work can serve parochial interests. Thus, while society can benefit from beliefs about work that increase effective cooperation, individuals have incentives to develop and promote beliefs about work in general and about their work in particular that favor their special interests. In other words, the meaning of work is one dimension of ideologies that serve as political tools. We trace the changing content of work ideologies as Western society evolved. We conclude by exploring: how work ideologies appear to have changed over time, what we believe to be a prominent modern ideology, and the implications of this analysis for students of work.

The Impact of Political Economic Factors on the Meaning of Work

Assumptions and Caveats

Assumptions. The chapter rests on two assumptions about how political economic forces affect the meaning of work. First, we assume that these forces help to shape the objective or tangible properties of work, including: what people work on, how hard they work, the technologies they use, and what they receive in exchange for their efforts. While such effects may be driven more directly by economic forces (i.e., markets) in some societies and more by political decisions in others, the general point holds—in most societies some combination of political and economic forces have a major impact on the objective properties of work.

Second, we assume that the interpretation of the objective or tangible characteristics of work is a social process. Following Berger and Luckmann (1966) and Weick (1979), we believe that, in important ways, the meanings of stimuli in human societies are products of social construction. Specifically, we assume that the meaning of work is determined by social construction processes operating at various levels in the social system.[1] For example, events in a particular locality (e.g., a neighborhood or workplace) may impact what work means to people in that immediate setting. Then, over time, these meanings may spread more widely. At the other extreme, the state of society as a whole can affect the meaning of work. For instance, work is likely to have a very different meaning to people when their society is fighting for its survival (such as during a war) than at other, less stressful times.

Caveats. Two caveats before we begin. First, in order to consider a wide spectrum of time in a very brief space, we are painting with a very broad brush. Accordingly, although we draw heavily on history, we do not offer a grounded historical account. We present only the framework for some new ways of thinking about the development and possible effects of meanings of work.

Second, the elements we are considering are interwoven with each other in complex ways. Consequently, our point of departure is somewhat arbitrary. We decided to begin at a point where our thinking about the meaning of work changed significantly. In applying our definition of work—namely, what people do to make "a living"—we realized that we needed to define *a living*. It became clear that, other things being equal, as the meaning of a living changes, so must the meaning of work. Therefore, to understand the meaning of work we realized it was important to define a living, and to consider how what constitutes "a living" changes over time.

"A Living," Political Economy, and the Meaning of Work

What is "a living"? Two of the definitions of *a living* listed in *Webster's New World Dictionary* (1986) are: "the means of sustaining life," and "the manner of existence." These definitions suggest that a living (and hence by definition the meaning of work) is a function of the quality and quantity of consumption society affords its members—that is, their standard of living. The standard of living a society affords its members is one of the most important expressions of how a society uses and allocates its resources—that is, its political economy. We have reasoned as follows. First, the meaning of work, by definition, is a function of the meaning of *a living*. Second, a living depends on the level of consumption. Third, the level of consumption is an expression of the political economy. Consequently, the meaning of work is, in part, a function of political economy. In this reasoning, a living is what links the meaning of work and the political economy; therefore, analysis of levels of consumption—both absolute and relative—is important. Two of the most salient factors affecting absolute and relative consumption are aggregate wealth and the distribution of wealth, respectively.

Work and Wealth

Influence of Work on Aggregate Wealth and Consumption. There is a reciprocal relationship between work and aggregate wealth. On the one hand, because the meaning people give to work is apt to influence how hard and how well members of society work, it helps to determine aggregate wealth. On the other hand, aggregate wealth affects the meaning of work because it influences "a living"—that is, the level of consumption people expect and/or envision. Our focus at this point is mainly on the latter—the effects of consumption on work. We postulate that, other things being equal, the greater the aggregate wealth, the higher the standard of living that people are apt to perceive as possible.

Aggregate wealth may be defined as the quantity of available goods and services. Of course, quantity by itself is a crude index; some consideration must be given to the quality and the character of goods and services in order to understand the effects of wealth on the human experience.

The quality of goods and services can be said to increase with the introduction of improvements in existing goods and services and with new goods and services that serve functions that previous ones did not. Admittedly there is room for debate as to whether such developments really make people better off, but we ignore these issues here.

As new and/or improved goods and services become available for consumption, what constitutes "a living," changes. For example, it is common for the luxuries of one era to become the necessities of another. Consider, for example, Rainwater's (1974) discussion of Ornati's (1956) description of two "subsistence budgets"—one for a family in Fall River, Massachusetts in 1908 and a second for a comparable family in New York City in 1960. In comparison to 1908, the subsistence budget of 1960 included dramatically higher levels of high protein food and more living space. Moreover, electricity which was not included in 1908 was defined as a necessity in 1960; in 1908, a full bathroom was not defined as part of subsistence; by 1960 it was. In short, the nature of a living changes as the quantity and quality of goods and services available for consumption change. Therefore, the meaning of work changes as well.

"A Living" and the Distribution of Wealth. In addition to aggregate wealth, the standard of living of any particular individual is also a function of the distribution of that wealth. Here again we see a solid link to political economy because key topics detailed in the study of political economy (e.g., rights, laws, and the "market mechanism") describe factors that determine how the distribution of wealth takes place and is legitimized. The meaning of work is not only a function of this distribution but is also a factor in legitimating it.

For a stable social system to exist, some means for allocating scarce resources to individuals must be devised and legitimated. One condition for social stability is the perception of some degree of correspondence between individuals' outcomes (i.e., their standard of living) and what they think they are entitled to (i.e., their acceptable standard of living).

What determines how people evaluate the degree of correspondence? Following Adams (1965), Homans (1974), and others, we suggest that, in general, individuals evaluate the fairness of the distribution of wealth by comparing themselves with others. Specifically, people compare the ratio of their outcomes (in this case, their consumption) to their contribution (inputs) with the corresponding ratios of other people. In some societies, including our own, work plays a central role in judgments about inputs. In other words, one's work can serve as an index of one's relative contributions and, thereby, become a criterion for assessing the relative level of benefits perceived to be equitable. At least in our society, work appears to be one of the most significant bases for judging one's inputs.

What factors affect judgments about the value of one's work? We suggest that a multilevel political economic process is involved. Obviously, economic factors that determine the demand for certain products and hence for the knowledge, skills, and abilities that produce them are important. However, as we will show, economics itself provides only a partial account because the demand for economic goods is shaped by a wide array of social institutions, including: education, class relationships, norms and laws, and other actions of governments. Consequently, then, the value which society gives to a particular type of work and, hence, to the legitimacy of one's level of consumption, requires a political economic account.

Other Social Influences on a Living. What is taken to constitute a living is influenced by other social factors. Values are particularly important because social values influence aggregate consumption. For instance, prevailing values sometimes foster high propensities to consume; in other cases, religious teachings or secular admonitions (e.g., conservation) encourage a frugal subsistence. Moreover, values about the normative character of society (e.g., about equality) affect the distribution of wealth.

Further, since a living is defined through social perception, a number of forces that influence perception must be considered. For example, different criteria for judgment can influence what people take to be an acceptable level of consumption. Ornati's (1956) discussion demonstrates this fact. Ornati distinguished three distinct anchoring points that might be used to judge what constitutes a living: subsistence, adequacy, and comfort. In his calculations, when defined as comfort, an adequate living required nearly twice as many resources as when defined as subsistence.

Social perception can also influence what one takes to be an acceptable living by affecting one's own feeling of worth. As Barrington Moore (1978) observed:

> Through certain social and psychological mechanisms . . . human beings can teach each other, and more significantly teach themselves, to put a low value on their own worth, to accept pain and degradation as morally justified, even in some cases to choose pain and suffering. Whole societies can at times teach themselves an ethic of submission. (p. 48)

Della Fave's (1980) discussion of how the unequal distribution of resources is sustained by self-perceptions of low self-worth by members of lower strata, and Ryan's (1982) argument that inequality "is to a large extent dependent on the prevailing belief system" (p. 38) suggest similar processes which can help to maintain inequalities in the distribution of wealth. Similarly, Sennett and Cobb (1973) reported that class-related socialization processes help to develop in members of the underclass an acceptance of their lower social and economic status. Among other things, people learn what a person "like myself" deserves and the criteria on which such a judgment should be made. We will show that political and economic forces are involved in these perceptions.

Summary. The meaning of work is a function of what constitutes "a living." Since the nature of a living is affected by how society uses and allocates its resources, the economic, political, and social forces that produce wealth and shape its distribution and consumption must be included in our understanding of the meaning of work. These forces and their interrelationships with work and consumption have a long history in Western society. Attention to this history reveals these interrelationships and serves to support our view of the need to understand the meaning of work as both a product and a determinant of political economy.

Work and Consumption: A Brief Review

For well over a century, social scientists have studied intensively the relationships among creation of wealth, levels of consumption, and development of the modern political economic system. The scenario of economic growth provided by liberal economists [see Samuelson (1970) for the best known summary] has had a major influence on contemporary thought.

Ignoring exogenous sources of resources (e.g., acquiring them through the conquest of other societies), three propositions are central to this account. First, for growth to occur, production (output) must increase at a rate faster than consumption. Second, future growth in output is a function of current investment in capital. Third, channeling resources into capital investment often requires constraints on current consumption. In short, the resources for capital investment that are needed for economic growth must come from some combination of decreased consumption and/or increased production (i.e., savings) of current output.

Both constrained consumption and increased production require sacrifice by someone; someone must produce more and/or someone must consume less. Various components of political economy (e.g., markets, governments, families, etc.) often play a major role in determining who sacrifices how much—that is, who consumes how much less and who produces how much more.

Constraining Consumption

At various times in the development of modern Western economies, a number of factors appear to have reduced the level of consumption that people viewed as constituting an acceptable living. Here, we consider five that appear to have been most important.[2]

We have noted that values can affect the definition of a living. Historically, values advanced by religious teachings appear likely to have limited how much people consumed. For example, consider how Christian teachings such as St. Paul's famous statement to Timothy—"Having food and raiment, let us be therewith content. For the love of money is the root of all evil"—encouraged limiting consumption. Tawney (1962) has suggested that this teaching served as a fundamental maxim of Christian ethics on the evils of economic appetites.

Secular injunctions of a moral nature also appear likely to have limited consumption. The principles of frugality and savings advanced by Benjamin Franklin are perhaps the best known illustration.

Governments affect consumption such as when they limit the production of consumer goods and/or reduce consumer spending power through taxation and inflation. Alternatively, governments can provide special incentives to people who can afford to reduce their consumption voluntarily. A recent example is the Individual Retirement Account (IRA) which gave tax reductions to individuals for participating in certain long-term savings programs.

Fourth, people have been, at various times, encouraged to save through ideological commitments. For example, patriotism has stimulated people to save to advance some national objective. Campaigns to sell war bonds to finance a military effort are prime examples.

Finally, of course, individuals save voluntarily. For one thing saving can be motivated by one's own self-interest. These interests include reducing one's vulnerability to financial disaster in the future and accumulating wealth through investment. Since the propensity to save may increase with wealth, savings can be increased by redistributing income to the more affluent groups. Also, sometimes savings may accrue from individual rigidities. For example, there may be a short-run tendency for consumption to increase at a slower rate than overall wealth because it takes individuals some time to "learn" to consume their newfound wealth (Duesenberry, 1952). To the extent that these processes operate, increased investment may be made possible without any deliberate constraints on consumption.

By reducing the amount of resources needed for a living, all five of these constraints on consumption have helped to provide the raw materials needed for economic growth at various times. However, constraining consumption is not the only means to garner these resources' investment.

Increasing Production (while Constraining Consumption)

Aggregate savings can also be generated by increasing output more rapidly than consumption. Among other things, improvements in technology and methods of production, harder work and longer hours, and increased education can contribute to a more productive work force. Of course, if gains in output were consumed immediately, no increase in investment would be possible. A variety of accounts for how increased production and constrained consumption have combined to achieve economic growth have been advanced.

Some accounts make it appear that both of these developments occurred due to voluntary actions of individuals (Linder, 1977). Such a laissez faire process is a key theme of much of modern economics, which, at least in the United States, seems to be the most widely accepted account for economic development. Economists who advance this view (see Samuelson, 1970) emphasize the role of individual choice and free markets in decisions concerning saving versus consuming and, hence, in the process of economic growth. While not challenging the central point that aggregate output must exceed consumption if growth is to occur, a number of influential writers (e.g.,

Marx) have provided a less voluntary account by pointing to factors other than market processes and free choice which explain both increased output and constrained consumption. These accounts have stressed coercive forces emanating from social and political processes and institutions. Work is one of the institutions that has figured prominently in several of the most well known of these alternative accounts.

One of these, advanced by Marx, centered on the material and coercive conditions of capitalism. A second, associated most frequently with Weber (and to a lesser degree with R.H. Tawney), stressed the role of religious thought. These accounts reveal the interrelationship between the meaning of work, a living, and coercive components of political economy.

Coercive, Materialist Perspective. Marx (1967) provided the most famous example of the coercive, materialist perspective. Under capitalism, Marx argued, the accumulation of capital was made possible by increasing the intensity of labor (i.e., forcing workers to work harder, while simultaneously driving their consumption to the level of subsistence) and the number of hours worked.

Cipolla (1980) provided support for Marx's view that capitalism increased the intensity of labor. Cipolla observed that in some preindustrial settings (e.g., the manors of the tenth and eleventh centuries), even though life was far from easy, in comparison to modern standards, work was relaxed. The large number of religious holidays and idleness caused by weather resulted in a good deal of leisure time—far more than would be the case for factory workers during and even after the industrial revolution. Moreover, while some individuals in the preindustrial workshops did work more hours than did factory workers during the industrial revolution, they were subject to far less discipline. In short, the industrial revolution and the rise of capitalism increased how long and how hard most people worked.

Moreover, Marx (1967) also held that the quest for profit that stimulated economic growth changed how humans who worked were viewed and altered the social relations surrounding work. Labor was now a commodity. Workers, collectively, were simply another factor of production to be used by the capitalist who employed them, with efficiency defined in terms of profitability for the capitalist. To maximize their returns, the capitalists introduced new sources of control and discipline in the factories. (We will discuss these developments in more depth below, in the section on the effects of the consumer society on work.)

Changes in social relationships surrounding work were not confined to the workplace. Marx also observed a fundamental alteration in the relationships between worker and consumer. Prior to capitalism, individuals' products were consumed by themselves, their families, and/or by people who knew them personally. Consequently, according to Marx, work spawned an organic social bonding. In contrast, when one's products were exchanged through an impersonal market these bonds were severed. Work lost an important source of meaning and society lost an important source of interpersonal bonding. As a result, Marx argued, work ceased to be a meaningful social expression of oneself.

Marx's coercive perspective on the evolution of work also attributed a key role to government. To begin with, Marx (1967) observed that in fifteenth and sixteenth century England, the process of enclosure (the fencing off of common lands or feudal manors) began to deprive the peasants of access to arable land. By the eighteenth century, via the Acts for Enclosures of Commons, government (i.e., Parliament) had become the instrument for driving peasants off the land and into the factories.

Other coercive acts of government also fostered industrial capitalism in its early stages. One reason that production increased was that people worked harder and longer and more predictably because, in part, they were subject to new sources of discipline and punitive measures. The threat of poverty and beatings, jail, and execution for vagrancy provided incentives for people to take whatever employment might be available. In this and other ways, government became part of the process that forged the industrial order. As Braudel (1982) observed, the state often played a major role in maintaining order on behalf of the upper classes. In his words: "When the state intervened *against* someone it was inevitably the masses who had to be contained and returned to the path of duty—that is, to work" (p. 516).

Economic pressures also forced people to tolerate the strains of factory life. Marx (1967) personified these pressures as the "industrial reserve army of the unemployed" (p. 487) waiting outside the factory gates to be hired. The presence of the reserve army reduced the propensity of workers to push for higher wages and to resist the demands of their employers.[3]

Finally, Marx made it clear that, at least under capitalism (and we suspect under most if not all political economic systems), the accumulation of wealth was furthered by constraints on consumption as well as by pressures to increase production. Specifically, greater aggregate saving was made possible by limiting consumption through the exigencies of competition which forced employers to pay wages that allowed workers to subsist, but no more.

Thus, the new economic and social order emerging from the industrial revolution changed what people did for a living and what constituted a living. These changes resulted from a long political economic process. Many of the coercive components of this process are often understated in liberal economics and other conventional accounts for the development of work.

Ideologies, Consumption, and Work.

Weber and Protestantism. The other major scenario for relating increases in production and constrained consumption to the development of modern work is best exemplified by the writings of Weber (1958) on the Protestant ethic and the rise of capitalism. Weber's account stressed the role of values and beliefs—especially those of Protestantism.

In chapter 2, we summarized Weber's analysis of how the Protestant ethic—with its asceticism and the belief that work and faithful labor, even at low wages, was pleasing to God—called forth hard work. This ethic did more than stimulate hard work; it *fused* the concept of a calling to work with an emphasis on self-control, prohibitions on consumption, and a justification of economic inequality. In addition, Weber maintained that these values furthered the accumulation of capital by *restricting passions, and, thereby, preparing the work force to accept specialized and rationalized work*—the form of work that was necessary for large-scale factory production. In essence, the same ethic that called forth hard work also constrained consumption and molded workers for the rational bureaucratic organization.

We reintroduce Weber's analysis here to emphasize the coherent pattern of relationships between macro-level institutions and the meaning of work his analysis contains. The Protestant ethic, as Weber portrayed it, provided the motivation for and justification of a wide set of behaviors and economic and social structures that affected the nature of work, the social relations surrounding work, and the nature of a living under capitalism. (As we will see shortly, it also may help to account for the development of the consumer society.)

Maoism as Another Example. While particulars of the development of capitalism in the West may well be unique, if we take religion as a special case of ideology, the types of relationships Weber described appear to be more general. Consider, for instance, the more recent attempt at economic development in the People's Republic of China under Mao.

Under Mao, a pervasive ideology inducing work and constraining consumption existed, although its content was quite different than the ideology described by Weber. In contrast to the otherworldly foundation of Protestant ethic, the attempt by the Chinese to limit consumption and increase work was secular. According to Whyte (1973), people were asked to work hard or to do unpleasant work to advance the goals of communism. As Whyte reported, workers were to:

> be convinced that their most mundane daily activities have some ultimate impact on the future of socialism and communism, and this realization is supposed to promote high quality work and diligence in avoiding waste and inefficiency. The method used is somewhat different, but the rationale is similar to that of Western advocates of job enlargement and enrichment: if a man finds more meaning in his work, he will work better. (p. 152)

The rationale for work was political and the means of managing the workplace (e.g., emphasis on political purity, and participatory leadership and discussion of decisions) were consistent with broader political images and objectives of communism. In this spirit, differential rewards for performance were narrowed and de-emphasized (although not eliminated). At the same time, according to Riskin (1974), consumerism was discredited—the government attempted to attenuate consumption through education and restrictions on the availability of luxury goods.

Not only did the basis for and content of the Maoist ideology differ from the case of the West described by Weber, but so did its implementation. Maoist China reflected a conscious effort on the part of a political elite to impose a meaning on work, whereas the case of the Western world appears to have been more ad hoc—the historical period was much longer, more nation states were involved, and no one central government can be pointed to as formally advancing the agenda.[4]

Summary. Our central theme is that the meaning of work derives, in part, from macro-level forces which, among other things, affect the propensity to work and the propensity to consume. The evidence that ideologies and social institutions have contributed to economic development by influencing components of the meaning of work such as orientations toward work and toward a living (consumption) supports this view.

So far, however, we have only considered the role of political economic forces operating in the early phases of economic development. Our argument would be much stronger if such forces also interacted with the meaning of work at more advanced stages. In the remainder of the chapter we show that, in fact, they have. We begin by considering their role in the growth of the so-called consumer society. The evolution of the consumer society reveals that as wealth accumulates and economic institutions evolve, the definition of a living and its role in economic activity changes. Further, these changes are associated with new objective conditions and subjective views about work.

Toward the Consumer Society—A "Case Study"

So far, we have focused on how the definition of *a living* served economic growth by restricting consumption. Curbing the propensity to consume, however, may not always be seen as the major requirement for a viable economy. In fact, sometimes *overproduction* rather than scarcity is viewed as the problem, whose solution lies in *increasing consumption*. The best known expression of this view was advanced by Keynes (1936) who argued that a sufficient level of aggregate consumer demand is a condition for drawing forth the investment needed to sustain economic growth.

Whether or not the Keynesians are right or wrong is less important for us here than the fact that a perspective suggesting that *overproduction* was a major problem once existed *and* was (and in some quarters still is) widely accepted. That such a problem could even be imagined reflects the gains in aggregate wealth (and shifts in attitudes toward consumption) of the last few centuries. These gains altered what constituted a living and thereby indirectly affected the meaning of work. As we will see, the changes in what constituted a living increased aggregate demand and altered its composition. Consequently, not only was the level of production altered but so was *what* was produced and therefore so was work. In short, as society became more affluent, the nature of consumption changed dramatically and with it, so did objective and subjective aspects of work.

If increases in aggregate wealth continued to alter the nature of work and a living even after society had attained considerable affluence, and if these changes were associated with ideologies, norms, values, and government policies that were different from those existing when economic scarcity was a more serious problem, then we could conclude that the interrelationships we have been discussing are not limited to the early stages of economic development. Consequently, we need to go beyond the theories of Marx and Weber.

New Rules for Consumption and Changes in "a Living"

It is an indisputable fact that over the last several centuries, consumption (by almost any measure) in the Western world has grown dramatically. As a result of this growth, modern society has been labeled the *consumer society*. [See, for example, McKendrick, Brewer, and Plumb's (1982) *Birth of a Consumer Society*.] What is less well recognized is the interplay among values, changing needs, ideologies, and government policies involved in this process.

Much of our knowledge about the emergence of consumerism is based on European and American history. Generalizing from one "case" to other eras and societies would, of course, be hazardous; fortunately, however, such generalization is not our major purpose. Here, we are interested in exploring the relationship of the meaning of work to macro-level social, political, and economic patterns in the Western experience. This "case study" simply illustrates how the meaning of work can be affected by changes in what defines *a living* and the evolution of political economy.

The nature of a living was altered dramatically as Europe passed through the Middle Ages and into the modern era. The absolute poverty that had characterized the lives of most inhabitants of preindustrial Europe abated. According to Cipolla (1980), before the fifteenth century, members of society's lower strata were chronically undernourished and threatened by starvation. Clothing also was scarce. Cipolla wrote: "In preindustrial Europe, the purchase of a garment or of the cloth for a garment remained a luxury the common people could only afford a few times in their lives" (p. 31). The meager possessions people had, tended to be inherited rather than purchased. In fact, a major concern of hospitals was to ensure that the clothes of the deceased were passed on to the rightful heirs. While the wealthy had it better, the level of consumption of the masses barely crossed the requirements for physical survival.

The next several centuries witnessed a remarkable transition. McKendrick (1982) observed that by 1800, the world's first consumer society had developed in England. New wants and desires for possessions arose. Fashion and social emulation through consumption (especially of clothes) become important *and* widespread. It had become accepted that "man was a consuming animal with boundless appetites to follow fashion, to emulate his betters, to seek social advance through spending, [and] to achieve vertical social mobility through possessions. To enjoy the act of purchase was no longer seen as the prerogative of the rich" (p. 25).

Clearly, what constituted a living was different. Terrail (1985b) went so far as to suggest that new consumption practices had altered the nature of human needs. What accounted for these changes? To what degree was the process ad hoc? To what degree were the seeds for the consumer society planted and nurtured through conscious efforts to influence tastes and values? While the answers to these questions are far from clear, exploration of them reveals some important links between the growth in emphasis on consumption and the evolution of work, the system of production, and the political economy. Several perspectives can be combined to reveal a probable explanation. In many of these accounts, the growth of the consumer society was a byproduct of changes in the workplace.

One perspective views the seeds of the consumer society as being planted during the industrial revolution by employers who were seeking productive and reliable employees. To control their employees, employers tried to shape them to respond to the incentives they had to offer. As Sidney Pollard (1963) observed: "Men who were nonaccumulative, nonaquisitive, [and who were] accustomed to work for subsistence, not for maximization of income, had to be made obedient to the cash stimulus, and obedient in such a way as to react precisely to the stimuli provided" (p. 254). According to Pollard, to instill these orientations, employers became concerned with educating workers and shaping their moral character—namely by indoctrinating them with bourgeois values. Initially, at least, these efforts seemed directed at curbing idleness, extravagance, waste, and bad language. In Pollard's view, these actions were important because they were directed to making the workmen wish to become respectable and this desire was necessary if the incentives employers had to offer (e.g., pay for performance) were to be effective.[5]

A second explanation of the origins of the consumer society, offered by Weber (1958), also was rooted in work. Toward the end of *The Protestant Ethic and the Spirit of Capitalism*, Weber noted how capitalism had fostered new motives. At least in retrospect, one of these motives reflects Weber's anticipation of the consumer society. Weber observed that with industrialization, the influence of religion in secular affairs had diminished and the economy and work had become organized in new ways. Consequently, the motivation to work was different—consumption was much more important. He wrote:

> Material goods have gained an increasing and finally an inexorable power over the lives of men. . . . Today the spirit of religious asceticism . . . has escaped from the cage. But victorious capitalism, since it rests on mechanical foundations, needs its support no longer. . . . The idea of duty in one's calling prowls about in our lives like the ghost of dead religious beliefs. (pp. 181–2)

As work became routinized, individuals could no longer fulfill their calling through work, Weber argued; in fact, they no longer attempted to justify work at all and "the pursuit of wealth, stripped of its religious and ethical meaning tended to become associated with purely mundane passions" (p. 182). And, whereas the promoters of the Protestant ethic such as Baxter had maintained that the interest in external goods should rest on one's shoulders like a light cloak which could easily be thrown aside, now "fate decreed that the cloak should become an iron cage" (p. 181). The desire for material goods—consumption—replaced the religious calling as the imperative for working. If so, then, clearly the meaning of work was different; consumption had replaced the service of God as a reason for working.

A third account of the origins of the consumer society can be found in Tawney's (1962) analysis of the growth of unconstrained self-interest. Writing primarily about England, Tawney observed that whereas before 1600, the medieval view of the law of nature was invoked as a moral restraint on self-interest, by the seventeenth century human appetites and natural rights were used to justify giving self-interest free play. He noted that while economic egotism and appetite for gain were common to every age: "What is significant is the change of standards which converted a natural frailty into a resounding virtue" (p. 247). Once the Christian life came to emphasize the zealous pursuit of private interests, the notion of social obligation faded. In short, the pursuit of self-interests was advanced and a secular and religious dualism evolved.

Like Weber, Tawney described the basis of a new relationship between work and consumption—one in which consumption was glorified and work was viewed as a means to support increasingly higher levels of consumption. However, Tawney called attention to a particular dimension of the new order: the glorification of self-indulgence. Clearly, if it occurred, such a development would have been a major change in what was meant by *a living*.

Additional Consequences of the Consumer Society

These accounts of the origins of the consumer society complement and reinforce each other. The processes they describe were, of course, only parts of a sweeping economic and social revolution which included enormous economic growth, new technologies, a more complex division of labor, new means of organizing work, an astounding increase in the quantity and variety of things to consume, and new processes of exchange.

The new processes of exchange may have been especially important. Recall in our discussion of Marx's coercive perspective, we noted that prior to industrialization, people had produced primarily for their own and their families' consumption, but with industrialization production increasingly became regulated by impersonal exchanges in the marketplace. Marx postulated that this change spawned qualitatively new economic and social relationships. Boldly stated, whereas people used to produce to satisfy their biological needs, now consumption (and hence production) was directed by acquired needs and the desire to accumulate wealth. This development was of great consequence because it *removed immediate biological limits to human wants and needs as constraints on production.* In principle, consumption and the desire to accumulate wealth became infinite. In response to seemingly infinite demand, producers could be expected to think and behave in new ways. Of course they did, and in so doing, further altered work and the political economy. Their responses and their effects can be viewed under two headings: the creation of new "needs," and the altered micro-level relationships of producers with their sources of capital and labor.

Incentives to Create New Needs

McKendrick (1982) observed that as early as 1690 it began to be recognized that consumer demand was more elastic than previously thought. In a society where there was a strong concern about moving upward in the social order, possessions (clothes in particular) symbolized success. As a result, domestic spending, driven by "envy, emulation, love of luxury, vanity, and vaulting ambition" (p. 14), could stimulate almost unlimited demand for goods.

The combination of the seemingly insatiable social needs and the attachment of greater importance to the accumulation of wealth, provided incentives to producers to serve mass markets and to create desires for new goods. McKendrick, Brewer, and Plumb (1982) described this process well in their discussion of the commercialization of fashion. They wrote:

> By the end of the eighteenth century the competitive, socially emulative aspect of fashion was being consciously manipulated by commerce in pursuit of increased consumption. This fashion world was one in which entrepreneurs were trying deliberately to induce fashionable change, to make it rapidly available to as many as possible and yet keep it so firmly under their control that the consuming public could be sufficiently influenced to buy at the dictate of *their* fashion decisions, at the convenience of *their* production lines. These fashion decisions were increasingly based on economic grounds rather than aesthetic ones, on the basis of what the factories could produce. (p. 43)

In a related development, as Plumb (1982) observed, the nature of leisure also changed considerably in the eighteenth century. Printing had increased the opportunity for advertising. The growth of advertising, in turn, by making it possible to disseminate information about scheduling, increased the feasibility of mass leisure in the form of theater, horse racing, cricket matches, and so forth. With these developments, even more new opportunities for consumption emerged and leisure itself became increasingly commercialized. These new ways of consuming, of course, impacted work.

In one of the most intricate treatments of the interrelated changes in consumption and work, Terrail (1985a and b) described how the nature of work and production affected consumption directly by determining what was available to consume and indirectly through its effects on social organization. According to Terrail, these developments were so profound that they can be viewed as changes in human *needs*.

To begin, Terrail observed the dual effects of production—production influences what is available to consume (and hence desired), and helps to define social relationships. For example, modes of production determine the relative importance of attributes such as physical strength and, thereby, affect the distribution of labor between men and women. Differences in the distribution of labor between the sexes affect the nature of the family and, among other things, what the family consumes. Moreover, the modes of production influence where people live and thus, who they live near and with whom they interact. Ultimately, these patterns determine one's reference group and class identification. Reference groups and class identifications influence what one believes he/she should consume and even what one does consume. In short, the nature of production spawns social relations which affect what people define as *a living*.

Further, Terrail argued that the modes of production influenced what people had to consume in order to be employable. First, any given mode of production requires particular skills, knowledge, credentials, and abilities. Consequently, it influences what individuals will buy in order to prepare themselves for work (e.g., the amount and type of education that people seek). Moreover, the demand for transportation services is a function of the modes of production. For example, the greater distance between home and work associated with modern production systems in comparison to cottage industries increased the consumption of transportation. Finally, Terrail argued that because the new methods increased the pace of work, they "entailed an accelerated wearing out of the labour force" (p. 107). This "wearing out" "is expressed in a variety of symptoms: accidents at work, physical exhaustion, as well as nervous and mental illness and a breakdown in health" (p. 107). These symptoms represent new needs that are expressed in demands for better working conditions, including more time off from work (e.g., holidays and weekend rest) in order to alleviate fatigue, greater expenditures on health care, and the desire for early retirement. Although evidence concerning the linkages outlined by Terrail is needed before we are willing to fully accept the validity of his position, his creative ideas illustrate some of the possible inter-relationships among the nature of work, consumption, and the macro-level social patterns we have labeled as *political economy*.

In sum, as the consumer society began to emerge, the actions of producers created new needs. Some of these seemed to be the result of rather conscious efforts whereas others were latent consequences of the efforts to satisfy the increased demands for consumption. With the development of the consumer society came new roles for consumption. As numerous writers, including Veblen (1953), Packard (1957), and Galbraith (1960) observed, in modern affluent societies, consumption, in addition to allowing physical survival, has come to serve ego and social needs (e.g., demonstrating to others one's prow-ess or "good" taste). In fact, as Scitovsky (1976) put it, consumption itself has become glorified.

New Micro-Level Relationships with Capital and Labor

The actions of producers in response to the advent of the consumer society were associated with a second set of processes that resulted in a restructuring of the relations between producers and those who supplied capital and labor. Two of these changes will be considered here. First, relationships became less personalized. Second, new forms and qualities of social relationships and con-trol emerged; labor became a resource—a factor of production.

Depersonalization. With industrialization the relations between producers and consumers changed. In a word, major components of exchange relation-ships were depersonalized. Previously, we noted how social bonds among human beings were altered as impersonal markets replaced personal relation-ships in mediating the flow between production and consumption; and how the relationships between employers and employees changed as labor became viewed as a "factor of production." Here, we add one other source of deper-sonalization.

The relationships between production and those who financed it became less personal as market forces replaced the control exercised by the aristoc-racy. Brewer (1982) observed that the first step was the breakdown of the client economy in which tradesmen had been highly dependent on aristocratic patronage. Increasingly, clubs and lodges became important means for reg-ularizing credit and served as sources of political influence for reducing the dependence of entrepreneurs on the aristocracy. Over time, control of eco-nomic activities became increasingly exercised through the open market. The environment in which work organizations existed became far less personal. We speculate that this depersonalization made bureaucratization both more necessary and more possible.

Changes in the Nature of Control of Work. In response to increased demands for consumption and the associated possibilities of achieving economies from scale, the modern bureaucratic organization gradually emerged, bringing new forms of discipline and control to the workplace. These developments were associated with new systems of incentives, management, and property rights.

One fundamental change concerned who had incentives to reduce the degree to which people shirked or "consumed" at work by choosing leisure over work. If an individual is self-employed and opts not to work hard, the person and his/her dependents bear the costs. However, when a worker is employed by someone else, if the worker opts to work less, the employer bears considerable costs. The employer's costs are apt to be greatest when workers are compensated on the basis of time, but the employer also incurs costs when pay is based on performance and employees do not work hard, because the employer's capital is not utilized fully.

The shift in the burden of *consumption at work* was particularly troublesome because it was accompanied by an increase in the scale of production (to serve mass markets). While shirking was undoubtedly present in preindustrial workshops, their smaller size quite probably permitted personal control to be exercised. However, as the numbers of people employed increased, new modes of less personalized control were needed inside the workplace to limit the ability of workers to "consume" on the job (Edwards, 1979). In short, the combination of the motives of employers to reduce shirking and the need to do so on a large scale helped to produce radically different work places—punishment-centered bureaucracies as we now call them.

Bureaucracies were also associated with increases in specialization, work pace, pressures to work, and sanctions for not working hard, as well as changes in conditions under which people worked and the distribution of what they produced. For the most part this transformation of the workplace is well known (see Edwards, 1979; Nelson, 1975). Nevertheless, in order to illustrate the linkage between these changes in work and political economic processes, we will review one case—the approach of one of the leading figures in the history of the transformation, Josiah Wedgewood.

In describing Wedgewood's efforts, Langton (1984) observed:

> Wedgewood began his firm with employees whose customs and attitudes were all, from a bureaucratic and capitalistic perspective, egregious vices. These workers were used to drinking on the job; they were used to working on a wide variety of different tasks, more or less at their own discretion and without regard to overall coordination; and they were used to flexible working hours and taking time off for "St. Monday" and every wake and fair. (p. 343)

Through rewards and punishments, rules, and firing leaders of recalcitrant activity, and with the help of religious leaders who preached sobriety, punctuality, and "responsible" behavior, Wedgewood produced a group of workers who were responsive to the requirements and controls of bureaucratic structures. Langton also argued that Wedgewood's success in introducing changes at the micro-level was aided by a number of macro-level developments, including: a rising standard of living, increased economic competition, improvements in communication and transportation, the bureaucratization of other industries, and the increased mobility of labor stemming from the enclosure movement. Langton concluded that all of these forces helped introduce a bureaucratic structure that enabled Wedgewood to increase "the efficiency and effectiveness of his firm" and enhance "his capacity to extract surplus value from his staff" (p. 346).

The case of Wedgewood provides only one example of how the process of bureaucratization of work in England was supported by macro-level developments. Braverman (1974), Edwards (1979), Jacoby (1985), Marglin (1974), Nelson (1975), Noble (1984), Stone (1974), and Gutman (1977) are only a small number of the scholars who have described how political economic variables (e.g., government actions, unemployment, immigration, and ideology) helped transform the nature of work in the United States in similar ways. The transformation entailed the principles of scientific management, modern personnel management, a number of automated technologies, job grades, the "drive" system and later its demise, human relations principles, and so forth.

Few, if any, individuals experienced the full sweep of these changes in their lifetimes. The new factory system emerged gradually and was "the product of many simultaneous developments that occurred in hundreds and in some cases thousands of individual factories" (Nelson, 1975, p. 164). Moreover, the pattern was very uneven (Jacoby, 1985) and not everyone was affected. At every point in time (including today), a number of small scale and nonbureaucratized jobs have remained. Thus, it is difficult to say how the full sweep of increased routinization and bureaucratization was experienced.

Nevertheless, it is hard to imagine that these objective changes produced anything less than enormous changes in the nature of the activities that a majority of individuals did to make a living and in how they interpreted them. The violence workers directed against the new forms of work described by Thompson (1963) and Braudel (1982) reveal how aversive the developments were to many.[6] For present purposes, however, we are less concerned with the content of these changes in the lives of individuals than we are with exploring how the origins, contents, and implementation of these changes were linked to the larger political economy.

Summary

We have sketched how consumption took on new meanings as Western Europe moved through the Middle Ages and the industrial revolution. Working and consuming changed radically. In addition to satisfying subsistence needs, production and exchange increasingly became the means to accumulate wealth; biological limits to consumption were superseded by social motivations. Because these developments affected what constituted *a living,* by definition, they changed the meaning of work.

We have also suggested throughout this sketch that these developments directly impacted the nature of work, particularly as they contributed to the development of mass markets and the organization of production to meet the demands of such markets. The consequences were far-reaching. Among other things, they altered the relationships between members of society. Production and other economic activities became directed by market exchanges and characterized by increasingly complex and impersonal social relationships. In addition, we have seen glimpses of the fact that these changes were associated with new roles for government (e.g., supporting the interests of capital) and other institutions (e.g., religion). In the remainder of the chapter we examine in more depth some of the consequences of these developments on work. As we do, new aspects of the relationship between political economy and the meaning of work are revealed.

To explore these aspects we must move to a different level of analysis. Throughout most of the book, attention has been devoted to the meaning of work for individuals and the effects on small social units (e.g., the family). Here, we shift to a more macro-level or sociological meaning of work—its meaning for the collectivity as a whole. At this level the meaning of work plays a political role.

The Meaning of Work for the Collectivity

From the perspective of society as a whole, work is the process by which the collectivity transforms matter and energy into consumable form so that its members can exist. To carry out this transformation, members of the collectivity must orchestrate their actions in an effective manner. Other things being equal, the wealth of the collectivity depends upon how effectively this transformation process is managed. The wealth of individual members depends upon the collectivity's wealth *and* the ability of individuals to channel the production and distribution of that wealth in their favor. The overall well-being of each individual is a function of his/her individual wealth, but more is involved.

The self-perceived welfare of individuals is a function of the relationship between their belief systems and *the ways* that the transformation and allocation processes are conducted. Assuming that at least a moderate amount of consistency among the beliefs, values, and actions contributes to perceived well-being, we make the following prediction. All else being equal, the greater the congruity between the noneconomic beliefs and values of members of the collectivity and the means used to orchestrate the transformation process, the greater the self-perceived well-being of members of the collectivity. In short, the characteristics of the collective transformation *process*—that is, the work of the society—affect the real and the perceived welfare of members of the collectivity.

In this context, the meaning of work can be seen as helping the collectivity to manage two fundamental political economic matters. First, one criterion for evaluating the nature of work in a society is its effectiveness in carrying out the transformation process. Second, in many societies, work functions as a mechanism for allocating costs and benefits among members of the collectivity in ways that members of society find acceptable—for legitimating the distribution of wealth and of burden. In other words, institutional arrangements surrounding work help to answer some fundamental and practical political economic questions about the distributions of effort, of wealth, and of power, including: Who should consume and how much? Who should work and how much and how hard should each person work? Who should control the work process? How should these decisions be made and their results legitimated? How should people be socialized?

Political Economic Changes Supporting Bureaucracy— Property Rights

We have described how a number of elements of political economy made these new types of work and organization possible. There is one other very important development that deserves mentioning—the system of property rights that made it profitable for owners to make long-term investments in developing bureaucracies.

The way in which a society answers many of the above questions is heavily influenced by how it allocates property rights. North (1981) has argued persuasively that one of the most important developments supporting economic growth, was the political and ideological support of property rights that increased the incentives for entrepreneurs to invest in capital and in organizing activities. Property rights define who has the control over a resource and the ability to exclude others from using it. Systems of property rights that protect the interests of entrepreneurs (e.g., those that give them control over the economic returns of their enterprises) are more conducive to economic growth than are others. Since the ultimate enforcer of property rights is often the government, we see once again the tight linkage between the nature of work and work organizations and the larger political economy.

Two words in the previous paragraph—*enforcer* and *exclude*—are very important in the present context. Both words suggest the presence of conflict over the use of resources. *Enforce* suggests that power will be used to advance certain people's interests relative to others. *Exclude* suggests that some people will be denied access to certain resources. Enforcing and excluding entail costs. Other things being equal, political economic systems that efficiently enforce property rights (i.e., at low cost) will have advantages over the other systems that less efficiently enforce property rights. North suggested that ideology is often an efficient means to enhance property rights—it may be far less costly, for example, than violence. If people believe that a given allocation of rights is appropriate, then enforcement costs can be quite low. While ideologies may occur "naturally," they also can be deliberately created and disseminated. Of course, this creation and dissemination has costs, but they may be low relative to other approaches—for example, the use of violence.

Effective and efficient legitimation of property rights is an important problem for a political economic system to solve. Often, resolution of this problem also preserves or contributes to a particular distribution of wealth. In addition, rights over property (e.g., the means of production) contribute to the development of particular forms of work and social relations surrounding work. For example, the processes of control and bureaucratization described by Braverman (1974), Edwards (1979), and Nelson (1975) can be attributed, in part, to the fact that the capitalist was the residual claimant.[7] However, the relationship between the legitimation of property rights and the distribution of wealth and work is two-way. We assert that the meaning of work can be an efficient means for *legitimating* property rights and the distribution of wealth. In this sense, *the meaning of work itself plays a political economic role*. The remainder of this chapter is concerned with this role.

Political Uses of the Meaning of Work

The fact that institutions surrounding work affect both the creation and distribution of wealth poses a major dilemma. On the one hand, there are institutional arrangements that, under particular circumstances, are likely to handle the transformation function best—that is, to be most efficient in increasing aggregate wealth. For example, a system that allocates property rights to inventors may foster innovation more than one that does not. On the other hand, because the institutions surrounding work help to determine the allocation of wealth and the costs of producing it, individuals operating in their own self-interests have incentives to introduce structures, rules, ideologies, and so forth about work that are favorable to themselves. In short, attempts both to improve the collectivity's transformation process (i.e., work) and to bias the allocation process towards parochial interests can be expected.

Under these conditions arriving at the optimal means to distribute effort and benefits is no easy matter. For one thing, it is difficult to distinguish arrangements that will be superior for a given community from those that are proposed as distributional ploys. Moreover, the collectivity benefits, to a degree, from *any* stable arrangement. Even if aggregate wealth is less than it could be under other arrangements, if the arrangements are perceived as legitimate and sufficiently satisfy the interests of enough members of society, the resulting social continuity can be a very desirable outcome. Under these conditions, it can be expected that any set of prevailing rules and structures will: 1) favor the interests of some groups (we refer to these favored groups as *elites*) over others; 2) serve the collective interests to some degree; 3) appear to be good for the collectivity and/or couched in a way so as to be consistent with some widely shared ideology or values; and 4) be less good for the collective interest than it appears to be to most members of the society.

To be most successful in institutionalizing work relationships that benefit its members at the expense of the collectivity as a whole and/or some members of the collectivity, an elite must find low-cost ways to induce other members of society to contribute more effort (i.e., work harder) and/or to accept lesser shares (i.e., a lower standard of living). Such acceptance may be advanced by a number of factors including perceptions by the "less well-off" that: the allocation process is legitimate, their own interests are satisfied at an acceptable level, and the particular arrangements (e.g., free enterprise) achieve some collective goal (e.g., economic growth) better than alternative arrangements (e.g., government regulation) could.

Also, elites (or any group) may benefit by appealing to certain emotions. People may be conditioned to enjoy working hard. Also, people may simply feel better about their well-being at any given level of wealth, if they fail to recognize that the arrangements are less than optimal and/or they perceive the arrangements as being consistent with their basic values, and therefore legitimate. (Ignorance is bliss.) For example, if an elite employs an ideology or social construction that helps members of the collectivity feel good about themselves and/or their society, even though the real conditions of the majority are far worse than they should be, the majority may still feel good about things.[8]

However, internal harmony and perceived well-being are not the only criteria and, under some circumstances, may not be the most significant criteria on which to base the transformation decisions. When, for example, a collectivity comes into competition with a second one whose social construction is equally successful in achieving internal order, but is more effective in the transformation process, the first collectivity is apt to be at a disadvantage. For instance, if at a given point in time cooperative relationships between owners and workers generate higher performance than do adversarial relationships, collectivities whose work ideologies promote the former are apt to have a competitive advantage.

Ideologies about work are one possible source of support for arrangements that advance and/or appear to advance collective well-being. Like all other such vehicles, however, individuals have incentives to advance work-related ideologies (e.g., acceptance of efficiency, with efficiency defined in narrow managerial terms) that only appear to be good for the collectivity.

If the meaning of work has been used as such a political tool, that fact would add further support to our thesis that the meaning of work must be understood in a political economic context. We demonstrate that political role of the meaning of work by exploring the interrelationship of the meaning of work and political economic processes in history, with special focus on developments in the United States.

The Meaning of Work and Work Ideology as Political Weapons in the United States

To understand the political economic role that work-related ideologies have played in modern society, it is useful to begin by recognizing several historical trends. First, the ways of evaluating the contributions of one's work and the process that mediates the relationship between work and consumption have changed radically over time.

Individual skills and outputs are less clearly measured and comparable to those of others. These and other changes provide the conditions for social construction to play a larger role in judging one's contributions. To illustrate, consider how the process may have existed in some preindustrial societies. In a stereotypical hunter-gatherer society one's consumption seems likely to be a function of how hard and how skillfully one hunts and gathers. Homans (1950) observed, for instance, this was the case in the primitive society of Tikopia: "The man who catches the fish eats it" (p. 275). Similarly in agrarian societies, the amount of resources one has available to consume (or provide to others for them to consume) is apt to be positively correlated with one's effort and competence in farming. Of course, due to all sorts of things that we often label as *luck* or *acts of nature* the correlation is often far less than +1.0.

Even in these stereotypic "simple" societies, however, social processes affected what one got to consume. For example, in advanced hunter-gatherer societies, territorial rights limiting where one could hunt or cultivate existed as a result of force and/or social customs (Watson and Watson, 1969). Also, in groups within preindustrial societies, force and social norms (e.g., kinship relations) influenced the distribution of the fruits of labor. In modern industrialized societies, force and social norms continue to influence and legitimate the distribution of consumption, but force appears to be less prevalent and the social processes more complex and abstract than those in preindustrial systems.[9]

In less industrialized societies, the data used in legitimation are apt to be *grounded in events that are close to the immediate experiences* of the individuals (e.g., kinship and personal relationships). The individual in a hunter-gatherer society, for instance, is apt to be able to see (or at least construct through attributions to luck, skill, or some supernatural force) a clear relationship between his/her actions and outcomes relative to those of others. Likewise, members of a face-to-face work group who produce and divide their product through direct social interaction are apt to have a clear idea of why benefits are allocated in a particular way. Even if the allocation is made on the basis of brute force, little in the way of social norms or ideologies are needed to legitimate the distribution. As long as technology and the division of labor do not change, one might expect the immediate experiences of people to provide much of the "raw material" from which people can construct an account that explains to themselves what they get to consume relative to others.

In contrast, many of today's economies feature a qualitatively different specialization of labor. Specialization is so great that people's direct experiences provide little basis for evaluating the skills or inputs of others. Because people do work that is quite different from one another's, they have little knowledge of each other's work. Consequently, it is difficult for an individual to judge how hard someone else is working. Moreover, the growth of large organizations and the scope of enterprise have contributed to making firsthand observation less possible by increasing the different types of work people do and separating people from each other. In addition, whereas in an earlier era, one's hard work could be easily recognized (e.g., "by the sweat on one's brow") or one's skill could be recognized by the size of one's crop or one's catch, mechanization and automation have made visible physical effort, even if people were proximate enough to observe others work, a less useful index of hard or productive work. The performance of managerial tasks and the contribution of ideas, which have become more important ways to make a living, are particularly difficult to evaluate.

Moreover, the rapid growth of nonproduction jobs has had similar effects. Insights into the magnitude and dynamics of this process have been described by Randall Collins. Collins (1979) argued that the twentieth century has witnessed the rapid growth of the tertiary sector (transportation, trade, finance, services, and government) in the United States. In fact the entire decline in the percentage of the labor force in agriculture (from 37 percent in 1900 to 5 percent in 1970) was absorbed by the tertiary sector. Evaluating contributions in this sector is problematic; Collins wrote: "Being remote from the sectors in which actual material production takes place, outputs in this sector have only arbitrary criteria by which they can be measured" (p. 88).

The tertiary sector achieves legitimation for its activities through what Collins (1979) termed the *ethos of technocracy,* which makes credentials (e.g., professional and technical degrees) the requirements for employment—even when the educational activities are not closely related to the actual jobs. Under these conditions, legitimation of a given distribution of income (i.e., rights to consume) is apt to take a more abstract form because the *basis for the distribution is remote from the direct experiences of individuals at work.*[10] In short, the nature of what many people do to make a living has become increasingly divorced from tangible outputs. In the tertiary sector and in managerial jobs, social processes—especially membership in groups which one achieves through educational credentials—become key elements in legitimating one's contribution and, hence, at least in our culture, one's rights to consume.

A second and related historical trend has been the growth in the amount and complexity of interdependence of people engaged in productive activity. As a result, the social relationships surrounding work have become more vital in performing the transformation process. Individuals are more affected by the work of other people and, therefore, have greater interest in what others do. The transformation process now requires the coordination of a large number of individuals and organizations operating within larger structures whose parts are highly interdependent. Employers' profits (which determine their "living") are dependent upon the work of others—their employees. Moreover, the profits of employers and the jobs of employees (their means to a "living") are a function of the consumption of others.

A third trend has been the embedding of work relationships in more complex networks. The interests of various groups in enhancing profits, jobs, and consumption have become interwoven with governments and other organizations. In fact, the entire process through which most people make their living is embedded in a complex set of political, economic, and social relationships. Included in this set are economic variables (e.g., levels of unemployment and the type of skills demanded), ideological factors (e.g., social beliefs about the nature of appropriate relations between capital and labor), and social variables (e.g., education and socialization).

These historical trends—the reduction in the directness of judging the value of one's work, the growth in interdependency, and the growing influence of more complex social networks—all have combined to increase the room for social construction to play a role in determining the living one deserves. Consequently, the potential to obtain benefits through using ideologies about work as political tools has increased substantially.

The Traditional Work Ethic as a Political Tool

Perhaps the most explicit recognition of the political use of the traditional meaning of work—the work ethic—can be found in Rodgers (1978). We have drawn heavily on Rodgers at other points in the book, but two of his themes are especially important for the current section. First, Rodgers shows how the work ethic was used in the mid-nineteenth century to justify inequalities in wealth. As Rodgers observed, property was asserted to be evidence of labor and conversely, "poverty was proof of idle viciousness" (p. 233). In other words, the existing distributions of wealth and power were legitimate because they reflected how hard people had worked. As described by Rodgers, the work ethic served to legitimate the existing distribution of "a living," at least in the minds of some, by papering over contradictions in society. Like the traditional Protestant ethic, a major theme was that one's outcomes (i.e., wealth and social standing) were evidence of one's inputs (i.e., hard work).

Second, the work ethic became more abstract as the real conditions of work changed. In Rodgers' words: "The rhetoric worked at all only by virtue of the very abstraction and conventionality of its premises" (p. 180). Moreover, the political power of the work ethic was, in some measure, due to its role in obscuring reality. Rodgers observed "how readily the rhetoric of the work ethic, muddying distinctions and obscuring meanings, could become a tyrannizing commonplace" (p. 209). The obfuscation was important in Rodgers' view because he argued that the work ethic, at least since the mid-nineteenth century, did not really fit the experiences of most people. For example, as large factories and organizations became the places where a sizable percentage of the population worked, there was less and less chance that people who entered the work force at menial jobs could work their way up the job and social economic ladder, no matter how hard one worked. Consequently, in order to serve as a legtimating ideology, the work ethic had to become increasingly *abstract*. Those who attempted to use and preserve the work ethic increasingly relied on fiction and generalized rhetoric that was far removed from real conditions.

Rodgers demonstrated the political role of work-related ideologies up until 1920. In addition, however, his focus on the role of abstraction provides us with a clue to more recent developments along the same line. We believe that work-related ideologies continue to play an important role in shaping and legitimating the existing social order, but they too are more abstract, more complex, and further removed from the workplace. They are embedded in more encompassing beliefs about the social order—the notions of economic choice and individual merit.

We have noted that the idea of free choice and voluntary action are central components of the liberal economic ideology that played a major role in interpreting and legitimating political economic relationships in the United States. Although the premises of the model of rational choice have been questioned (March, 1976), ideologies involving choice continue to be influential in thinking about the design of social systems. Generally, the more it can be shown that a system permits choice and/or that a given system resulted from a process where individuals exercised "free" choice in bringing it about, the more legitimacy that system is apt to be accorded.

Needless to say, choice and the perception of choice about work-related matters have important consequences for the meaning of work. The degree of actual and perceived choice relating to work are affected (and can affect) events at the level of political economy. The rhetoric of choice—in this case choices about work and work-related affairs—becomes an important tool in political discourse. Consequently, it is useful to explore some of the relations among choice, the meaning of work, and the operation of components of the political economic structure.

Choice, the Meaning of Work, and the Political Economy

Choices affecting the meaning of work are a function of at least two sets of political economic factors. One set includes processes that impact the nature of "a living" through the goods that are available for consumption. The second set of political economic relationships affecting the meaning of work through its impact on choice, encompasses elements that influence the alternative possibilities of work people can choose from. We will focus on that set of factors in depth, after briefly reviewing the influence of consumption on the meaning of work.

Choices in Consumption. We have already observed how, over the last several centuries, the quantity and quality of goods and services available for consumption increased dramatically. To the degree that the meaning of work is a function of consumption, changes in what is available to consume give work different meanings. In other words, we are hypothesizing that work is, at least in part, an instrumental activity and the meaning of an instrumental activity is given in part by the nature of the goal it helps to attain. As economic growth and other social changes have taken place, what one works for (one's goals and aspiration levels) have changed and hence, so have meanings of work.

Perceptions of Choices about Work. A second class of choices that affects the meaning of work consists of the alternative ways available for a person to make a living and the conditions prevailing that influence the exercise of choice. Consider the following conditions in which choice is possible. Under some conditions, almost any individual has the opportunity to choose, at almost any time during his/her working life, among a wide variety of diverse and attractive jobs that he/she can perform effectively. Moreover, the choice can be exercised at very low cost to the individual.[11] Under other conditions, a person may have no legitimate choices at all and the costs of asserting one's desires may be enormous. (This state of affairs appears to describe the conditions of slavery.) It is also possible to envision a case where individuals have no alternatives to a particular job but, since many other people have no jobs at all, feel fortunate to have a job—any job at all. Clearly, other conditions can be conceived, but these should illustrate the fact that one's perception of choice and the importance one gives to the exercise of choice are likely to be influenced by a host of political economic factors.

Both common intuition and any number of psychological theories (e.g., reactance theory, cognitive dissonance, or illusion of control) would predict that the nature of the experiences under these contrasting conditions would be very different. To illustrate, Snyder and Ickes (1985) found that individuals can and do attempt to select social situations that are self-confirming and dispositionally congruent. In all probability, the more opportunities from which to choose (other things such as the cost of choice being equal), the more likely the job one does will be self-confirming and dispositionally congruent. Likewise, Schneider's (1983) discussion of interactional psychology supports the view that people are proactive in choosing among environments that are compatible with their own behavioral tendencies. Similarly, Culbert and McDonough (1985) have discussed the quest of individuals to align their own core identities with the tasks that they perform.

Although people do socially construct the meanings of situations after they enter them, it seems clear that the meanings will be affected by the nature of the alternatives that they had to choose from and the process of choosing. With respect to work, it is reasonable to predict that the larger the variety of attractive opportunities people have to choose from, the greater the information they have to make informed choice; and the lower the costs involved in exercising the choice, the more likely they will be able to match their work with their inclinations.

In addition to increasing the opportunity for successful matching, the availability of alternatives aids the alignment process in another way. If an employer perceives an employee to be valuable and difficult to replace, then, other things being equal, the employee can exercise power over the employer. Under such conditions, the employee can, for example, win concessions in the workplace by threatening to "exit" (Hirschman, 1970). Similarly, the availability of alternative jobs provides incentives for employers to cater more to the preferences of potential employees in order to attract them. In short, knowledge of the availability of easily accessible, alternative employment opportunities affects the meaning of work by increasing the perception of autonomy and by increasing the chances of a "good" match.

One of the most important ways that choice affects the meaning of work operates through the perceived opportunity for job mobility. A number of factors affect the perception of and the availability of job choice. One's perceived mobility is determined by some combination of external (e.g., low unemployment) and internal (e.g., high self-esteem) factors. We hypothesize that the perception of being mobile will affect the meaning one gives to his/her current work. Some evidence supports this view. Both Chinoy (1955) and Jackall (1978) have reported evidence that perceptions of mobility do influence the meaning of one's work. For example, Jackall found that some individuals perceived their current job as a sidetrack. When, for instance, a wife was working to support her husband's education, she was apt to view the present job as a sacrifice for her mate. It is important to note, particularly in Chinoy's research, that the belief of auto workers that they could leave and start their own businesses, even though it was not realistic, affected how they related to their current jobs. As Chinoy put it, talk about leaving the job acted as a "safety valve" to relieve job-related tensions and as a way of eliciting respect from fellow workers by linking oneself to highly valued cultural beliefs of achievement.

While the perception of mobility appears to affect the meaning of one's work, whether the effect is positive or negative, is unclear. On the one hand, following the psychological theories of reactance (Brehm, 1966) and self-control (Langer, 1983), one might expect that perceptions of low mobility would lead to negative reactions to one's work. On the other hand, cognitive dissonance theory (Festinger, 1957) and other balance theories might lead us to expect perceptions of low mobility to be associated with positive feelings toward unpleasant jobs. Similarly, due to "approach-approach" conflicts, too many attractive options might induce frustration. In fact, in advancing their social information processing approach, Salancik and Pfeffer (1978) predicted that the greater the number of options, the less satisfied individuals would be with their current jobs. Despite this ambiguity, however, it is generally assumed that promoting choices concerning work is desirable. This assumption adds to the linkages between work and the political economy, through efforts to influence factors that increase the exercise and/or the appearance of the exercise of choices about work.

Political Economic Determinants of Effective Choice about Work. A great deal of effort (e.g., training and pressures for "full" employment) is devoted to increasing the options people have. Also, a great deal of ideological effort is directed at fostering the belief that people actually do determine their destinies by exercising choice (Lindblom, 1977). As a result, issues affecting real and perceived job choice (and, therefore, the meaning of work) are at the center of political discussions and economic policy. Being able to convince others that one's preferences increase mobility and the exercise of choice in the labor market can be an important source of political advantage. Consequently, the meaning of work is influenced by a host of political economic decisions and processes, including: government actions that regulate the nature of jobs; levels of unemployment; heterogeneity of jobs; educational activities (that distribute the knowledge and skills influencing how much individuals are valued in the labor market and thus, their abilities to exercise informed choice); and social ideologies.

Government Actions. In modern society, legislation and other actions by governments actually define important aspects of work. Laws which define the rights of employees and employers, regulate the workplace (e.g., safety procedures), directly impact wage levels, and deal with matters such as unemployment insurance, all affect the nature of jobs from which individuals can choose.

Levels of Employment. The rate of unemployment affects choice and power. High levels of unemployment are apt to give employers more employees to choose from and, hence, give them greater power relative to labor. Conversely, high levels of employment are associated with a greater number of choices for employees and, as a result, give a greater advantage to labor. It is not surprising then that the level of unemployment is often an important political issue. By raising or lowering the level of employment, a wide variety of laws and political decisions influence the number of choices each group has available, and thereby, will affect who will be favored in any exchange or contract. Decisions about such matters as immigration policies and foreign trade help to determine the effective supply of labor. Consequently, they have important consequences on whose interests get priority in the workplace.

In addition, unemployment levels, as well as many of the other factors affecting choice, also contribute to the wage levels. Of course, wage levels are in large measure another way of discussing the distribution of wealth. In essence, the factors that determine whose interests get priority are expressions of the power relationships in the social system. The ability to exercise choice is both a means to and an expression of power.

Heterogeneity of Jobs. If all jobs were exactly the same, even though there were many of them, the net effect would be to eliminate the opportunity to exercise real choice. Indeed, Braverman (1974) observed that one of the major consequences of scientific management was to make so many jobs virtually the same, that workers cannot exercise effective choice. While Braverman's assertion that "all alternatives" were destroyed (p. 149) overstates the case, his basic premise is sound—the existence of a variety of alternatives is a necessary condition for a labor market to be free in a real sense. (If there are no available alternatives to choose from, the theory that posits that "free" labor markets facilitate alignments fails in practice.) In addition to variations in job content, effective choice in the labor market is a function of such factors as permitting people to select: where they work (e.g., at home), how intensely they work, and how long they work (per day or per week and when to retire). Other things being equal, the more jobs an economy offers that vary on dimensions that are salient to people who work, the greater the choice it permits.

The heterogeneity of jobs also depends upon consumption patterns. At least in an economy where production is responsive to consumer preferences, what members of society, taken together, consider to be the package of goods and services that constitute a living shapes aggregate demand—that is, how much of what goods and services consumers wish to purchase. Consumer wishes affect what businesses produce, what technologies they use, and, in turn, the nature of the work they hire people to perform. As Mintzberg (1979) observed, an important reason why so many people in modern society have routine jobs in bureaucratic organizations is that consumers have a strong penchant for a high volume of mass-produced goods. The objective nature of work is, in part, a function of consumer preferences.

Education and Socialization. The content and processes entailed in how society educates and socializes its members also influences the exercise of choice. Education and socialization in almost all societies prepare individuals for work by providing skills and knowledge as well as values, attitudes, and expectations concerning work. Even though, as Collins (1979) argued persuasively, the actual contribution of education to a person's ability to perform most jobs is often overestimated, such training does play an important role (by giving one the "credentials") in determining what job opportunities a person has access to. Moreover, educational experiences appear to affect the criteria which people are apt to use in evaluating work (see Sennett and Cobb, 1973). With respect to the theme of this section, among the things people learn are orientations and skills relating to choice behavior.

Education and socialization affect the choices people make about work in at least three ways. First, they provide a set of attributes that are more or less valued in the labor market. The more valued the attributes that a person possesses, the more likely he/she will be able to have alternative employment opportunities to choose from. Second, education and socialization can help people to make choices in more informed ways, such as by stimulating them to seek and find out information about alternatives and by enabling them to effectively evaluate the information. Other things being equal, these capabilities seem likely to increase the chances for people to achieve effective alignments. Third, education and socialization shape expectations about which issues people should exercise choice. These expectations influence how much power people seek to exercise in a variety of social settings, including work, and how they will respond when their expectations about influence are violated.

While education is generally assumed to promote the ability to exercise choice, it is possible that education may not always lead to effective choice making. In fact, there is a "darker side" of the process of socializing the work force and shaping expectations about work—namely, the possibility that individuals and groups will attempt to use education as a political tool to advance their own interests by indoctrinating others toward passivity. As we will discuss in more detail shortly, many writers (e.g., Bowles and Gintis, 1976; Callahan, 1962; Sennett and Cobb, 1973) have asserted that because the U.S. educational system carries such messages, it constrains the exercise of choices about work and other social institutions.

Others have suggested that religions have had a similar pacifying effect. Rodgers (1978) argued that the Protestant work ethic blunted the efforts of members of society who offered alternatives to the prevailing work system. In addition, there is Liston Pope's (1942) classic study of how, early in the 1900s, mill owners in Gaston County, North Carolina, used churches to help shape a disciplined work force. Niebuhr's (1957) discussion of how the various sects of Christianity serve class interests can be interpreted as making a related point.[12]

Overall then, education and socialization can have mixed effects on the exercise of effective choice. Often they do contribute information, orientations, and competencies that aid informed choice. On the other hand, they can be used by various groups to advance their own parochial interests—by indoctrinating rather than informing, and by teaching people to be pawns rather than *origins* [see deCharms, 1976].

Social Ideologies. Many components of social ideologies function to legitimate certain economic activity, inequality of wealth and power, and the organization of work and the economy. Because ideologies can influence people without their being fully conscious of the reasons that underlie their actions, ideologies reify existing relations and, thereby, reduce deliberate choice.

Following North (1981), it is clear that ideologies do affect the general nature of economic organization by reifying existing distributions of property rights. In other words, ideologies induce people to accept particular arrangements as not subject to choice. That these reified relations affect choices about the nature of work can be deduced from the writings of Lindblom (1977), who showed how ideologies induce individuals and the collectivity as a whole to take a particular set of economic relationships as given—not really subject to choice. He argued that the interests of business in the United States have been advanced through a system of ideas that grant these interests substantial priority. The resulting hegemony of business has given the perspective of managers a great deal of influence in political economic debates on matters affecting objective conditions of work such as: physical conditions, requirements about health and safety, hours and wages, and the distribution of rights and power in and around the workplace.

Summary. We have noted a number of ways in which social institutions and processes related to the ways the collectivity transforms raw materials into consumable goods and services affect the meaning of work to individuals. We have seen how many of these processes affect work and its meaning by their effects on the exercise of choice. The opportunity to exercise choice, in general, can have a major impact on one's perceptions of many things. Specifically, exercising choice about one's work is likely to affect the meaning one gives to his/her work. In addition, the aggregate choices of people about what to consume and what type of work they are willing to do influence what type of work will be available in society. In short, choice affects the real or objective conditions. Third, the ability to exercise effective choice about work is a function of many factors, including education and socialization, and ideology. Taken together, these themes make it quite clear that the meaning of work, the workings of the larger political economy, and the realities and rhetoric of choice are all dynamically interrelated. Of particular interest is the fact that, because allocation of resources is affected by political economic processes, individuals have incentives to use work and rhetoric about choice to their advantage. They have incentives to constrain the choices of others and expand their own. In this context, work and its meaning are affected by the resulting political struggle. Further, the work-related social institutions and ideologies that contribute to perceived and actual choice can also serve as weapons to be used in the struggle.

In the final section of this chapter, we show how this process may be operating to legitimate the existing allocation of resources at the present time. We suggest that a work-related rationale has emerged which a) fits the abstract nature of the account required to evaluate the worth of one's work and b) preserves the voluntary and individualistic dimensions of our society's traditional ideology. This rationale, which we term the *updated work ethic,* legitimates high levels of consumption and centers on merit.

An Updated Work Ethic: The Ideology of "Merit"

Today, success at work still serves to legitimate inequalities in economic and social standing. However, the rationale has changed. As we suggested earlier, the religious value of work has been overwhelmed by secular concerns. Moreover, the nature of the ideology has changed in response to changes in the nature of work and the type of accounts for inequalities in wealth it permits. Here, we suggest a few trends in the ideologies, although we warn the reader that these are very speculative.

Legitimating Pleasure. One change we sense has been to make an explicit link between hard work and one's right to pleasure; pleasure through consumption is the reward for good or hard work. Consider a recent advertising campaign for a leading beer. The ads show various individuals working hard on their jobs and then, after work, the same people are shown drinking beer to the refrains of "For all you do, this Bud's for you." This pairing of consumption as a reward for hard work is an intriguing resolution of the tension between two valued, yet somewhat contradictory needs—the need for hard work and the desires for pleasure and leisure. Too strong an emphasis on pleasure could siphon off energy from work, whereas too strong an emphasis on work could limit the time needed to consume, including purchasing goods and services. By stressing that one *earns* pleasure by hard work, a possible contradiction can be resolved.[13]

A second change stems from differences in the process of judging what constitutes *valued* work. We suggested that technological developments over the last several centuries have made the information that is available for accounting for rewards from work more abstract and less precise. We still value "hard" work, but, as we have noted, advances in specialization and the division of labor make it difficult to compare how "hard" people are working. Moreover, the final product appears less directly related to the efforts of any individual.

We hypothesize that the greater difficulty in precise social comparisons introduced by the growing heterogeneity of work is associated with more abstract attributions and social construction playing an increasingly larger role. Claims over wealth are more likely to be made and actualized through social processes, including: rules, norms, power relationships, social traditions, and status systems. Work continues to affect how a given level of aggregate wealth is distributed, but the process is regulated in more abstract ways than when the nature of work was less specialized.

We further suggest that an ideology is needed that is congruent with the more abstract information on which judgments are based. The ideology that has emerged centers on *merit* (and related terms). The basic notion is that some members of the collectivity have privileged positions because they possess certain attributes that enable them to contribute more to the collectivity than their less privileged counterparts. Merit implies no particular attribute. The term is abstract enough to encompass a wide array of quite different attributes, including both inputs and outputs. Here, we consider only a few of these attributes.

Merit and the Meaning of Work

Merit and Economic Thought. One of the most abstract set of concepts currently used to operationalize merit is the economic concept known as *marginal product*. Basically, the position states that people make differential contributions to social welfare by working to produce things that others wish to consume. People are paid according to the value of their contribution to the demands of others as expressed through the market. In a phrase, they are paid an amount equal to the value of their marginal product.

On the face of it, this seems to be an objective and ethical way to determine the distribution of the results of work. With a few qualifications (e.g., provisions concerning inherited wealth) this view leads to the conclusion that as long as the conditions of free markets hold, any existing distribution of wealth rewards individuals equitably—that is, according to their merit (e.g., hard work and competencies) as judged by the collectivity through the workings of the market.

However, the value of one's marginal product is a function of more than just the merit of the individual. As Lester Thurow (1975) has argued, the value of one's marginal product depends on the structure of the market demand for goods and services, which in turn depends on the distribution of income. In Thurow's words: "The distribution of marginal products is a direct function of the initial distribution of money incomes" (p. 44). Similarly, as we have argued above, the demand for one's product is a function of some prior distribution of political power, that people (individually and/or collectively) exercise on behalf of their economic interests. Therefore, like the work ethic, the marginal productivity view, when used by itself, obscures existing social relationships and is an inadequate philosophical criterion for allocating rights to consume. Still, in the minds of economists, politicians, managers, and others, it functions as an important criterion of merit for legitimating the existing distribution.

Moreover, because this argument requires a level of economic literacy, its value as an ideology is problematic; it is only partially effective in providing an account that guides the attributions of many people. Perhaps, like the work ethic which served and was perpetuated primarily by the middle and upper classes (Rodgers, 1978), the marginal productivity view provides an account that is lost on the lower classes. Also, as with the work ethic, one would expect that the upper classes would seek to translate this view in ways that would help it to guide the attributions of the lower classes.[14]

In any case, the marginal productivity view is a prime example of an abstract account linking one's merit and one's wealth. Accordingly, it potentially could serve as an important ideological support for legitimating any given distribution of wealth. But other explanations that are closer to the direct experiences of people may be even more important in providing for attributions that help make sense of things for individuals and logics that help to legitimate social orders at macro-levels. Although religion may still be influential, we suspect that in the modern secular world, education and other features of secular socialization have become more so.

Education, Socialization, Merit, and Making a Living. Many writers have charged that a major function served by the U.S. educational system is the development of individuals who are willing to submit to the discipline of modern organizations.[15] Bowles and Gintis (1977) and Bowles, Gintis, and Meyer (1975–1976) are among the best known proponents of this view. In Bowles and Gintis' (1977) words:

> Major aspects of the structure of schooling can be understood in terms of the systemic needs for producing reserve armies of skilled labor, legitimating

the technocratic-meritocratic perspective, reinforcing the fragmentation of groups of workers into stratified status groups, and accustoming youth to the social relationships of dominance and subordinancy in the economic system. (p. 56)

While their polemic covers many dimensions, our concern here is limited to the notion of merit.

Central to Bowles and Gintis' argument is that competitive grading, standardized tests, and the emphasis on IQ as an indicator of potential, all serve to legitimate inequality. Arguing that IQ has little if any relationship to economic success, they asserted that emphasis on IQ functions "to legitimate an authoritarian, hierarchical, stratified, and unequal economic system, and to reconcile individuals to their objective position within this system" (p. 116). In other words, the students learn to accept inequality as based on merit.

Other writers have made similar points. Sennett and Cobb (1973) concluded that the means of control used in schools have a latent function. They teach people to accept education as an indicator of merit and superior ability. Therefore, they help to legitimate the exercise of control by people with more years of schooling. In addition, Sennett and Cobb argue that teachers act as impassive judges, making the child the only one who could appear responsible for his/her failures. Therefore, those who do not succeed are provided with an explanation for their condition—they lack the merits of the more successful.

Ryan's (1982) observations of schools led him to a similar conclusion. Like Sennett and Cobb, Ryan concluded that the mechanisms of control (e.g., those used to deal with tardiness) serve to "artificially enhance the egos of the children of the well-to-do and brutally assault the egos of the children of workers and poor people" (p. 136). Other writers including Brookover and Erickson (1975) and Brookover, Shailer, and Paterson (1964) also have shown how students' views of their own abilities are influenced by the evaluation process in school. Della Fave (1980) concluded that differential self-evaluation is produced through the evaluation process; as a result, individuals develop a conception of where they stand in the larger society. These conceptions are carried over to and reinforced in the workplace. Education and other socializing vehicles influence what people expect work should be, what type of work it is "reasonable" for people like themselves to do, and how people like themselves should behave with respect to work. In short, people learn to accept inequalities that appear to be based on merit and to accept the notion of merit as an appropriate criterion for evaluation.

While all of this may be true, it is important to note that the arguments of the critics can be overstated easily, so as to suggest that differences in personal outcomes have little or no relationship to abilities. Clearly, conclusions from Hunter's (1986) review of the research on the relationship between cognitive ability and job performance suggests otherwise. Hunter concluded:

"This paper has reviewed the evidence of hundreds of studies showing that general cognitive ability has high validity in predicting performance ratings and training success in all jobs" (p. 359). Why should this be so? Hunter argued it is because cognitive abilities predict learning the job—the key to job performance.

On the other hand, investigators such as Jencks (1979) might argue that since cognitive skills are a function of family background, even if they are viewed as equivalent to merit (which Jencks doubts), they do not provide a suitable moral basis for inequalities of wealth. Moreover, Hunter's conclusions stem from comparisons within jobs. In order to extrapolate from them to maintain that differences in compensation between jobs are justified, it would be necessary to show that the higher paid jobs do in fact require higher levels of the particular skills in question. In fact, they might—*we just do not know.*

However, we do know that the judgment of merit frequently is centered in and around work. We are also confident, following Thurow (1975), Ryan (1981), and others that perceptions of merit play an important role in the minds of people as they attempt to understand, to justify, and to alter their positions in the socioeconomic order. The less grounded these accounts are in data from the immediate experiences of individuals, the more important social construction processes may become in providing accounts. As a result, a person has much to gain from developing scenarios that support the view that particular abilities one has qualify as merit (i.e., those abilities related to achivement of socially valued outcomes) and from convincing others that one indeed has these abilities. We suggest such efforts to increase the perceptions of one's merit in the eyes of others is a key part of the political economic process of the modern social order. Many of these efforts center on perceptions of what people do to make a living.

These perceptions often go hand in hand with the establishment of institutional arrangements that reinforce the claims. While the political economic consequences of this process are hard to assess precisely, Collins (1979) has argued that the "credentialling" process played an important role in "an income revolution" which, during the twentieth century, shifted income from the upper classes to professionals and to the upper working class. The former have used the rhetoric of professionalism and educational requirements to gain power. The latter have used apprenticeship and licensing procedures to gain control entry into their domain. Again, we see the important political uses that can be made of beliefs about work and the growth, over time, in the role social construction plays in the process.

Merit, Work, and Organizational Interests. The merit attributed to people who work for an organization can also advance the political interests of an entire organization. This point has been argued convincingly by Meyer and

Rowan (1977), DiMaggio and Powell (1983), and other institutional theorists. Meyer and Rowan noted that, as organizational environments have become more institutionalized (what DiMaggio and Powell called *structurated*), myths and appearances of using appropriate methods and personnel become increasingly important to organizational success relative to more traditional concerns of efficiency. Part of these appearances stem from employing people who have the appropriate training—the credentials. Meyer and Rowan (1977) observed that U.S. schools have changed "from producing rather specific training that was evaluated according to strict criteria of efficiency to producing ambiguously defined services that are evaluated according to criteria of certification" (p. 354). Increasingly, credentials have become a badge of merit as the requirements for successful organizations have become less tied to concrete measures of efficiency. The attributions that people make about the work of others legitimate political economic relationships among organizations and other economic units, not just among individuals.

Summary. In this section we have argued that the meaning of work continues to play an important role in legitimating the social order at both micro- and macro-levels. In comparison with the past, however, the process involves more abstract attributions and scenarios. Hard work may still be important, but perceived merit (of which hard work may be a part) seems to have grown in importance.[16] To a large degree, merit is demonstrated in the workplace. Because it is abstract, the idea of merit may leave much more room for actors to help socially construct reality in their own favor than was the case in the more concrete worlds people experienced in the past.[17]

Conclusion

We have seen that, at least in the modern Western world, important components of the meaning of work and political economy evolved together in a mutually supportive fashion. Comprehension of this evolution can help us to understand the meaning of work today and some of the tensions surrounding it.

As we see it, contemporary students of work focus on two major themes—work is an instrumental activity and work is (or should be) a psychologically or even morally fulfilling experience. In examining the evolution of work and its meaning, we have seen that not only is this duality rooted in the history of our society, but that the emphasis given to each theme varies by stages of political economic evolution. In this context, statements about any absolute, universal, or historical meaning of work seem of little value.

Moreover, we have seen how different meanings are advanced to support special interests of individuals and groups. Various actors attempt to advance and institutionalize criteria that put their claims for resources ahead of those of others'. The particular claims and the rhetoric used to support them, of course, are expressions of a particular time and place. In today's society, they become manifest in the workplace as struggles over such issues as job rights, the role of seniority, social responsibility, and so forth. On the national level, they appear in debates about welfare versus workfare, plant closing legislation, minimum wages, unemployment, employee rights, equal employment opportunity, immigration policies, and so on. The rhetoric the debaters employ often links work and matters of political economy—the work ethic, human dignity, human rights, property rights, just wages, economic growth, and merit—to advance their positions.

These debates have both short- and long-term consequences. In the short run, they influence whose interests are given priority. In the longer run, the rhetoric (especially the "winning" rhetoric) contributes to the social construction of the meaning of work, thereby shaping what people expect from work and the meanings they give to their own work and to work more generally. Moreover, both the short- and long-run effects influence the real conditions of work and society—what people do, the relative distribution of power of actors, and the distribution of rewards for the work. As these conflicts run their courses, the objective and subjective nature of work continues to evolve, affected by and in turn affecting the evolution of the political economy. In these contests, often the meaning of work itself is a resource for one or more of the parties seeking to advance their particular interests.

We believe that greater awareness of the social, political, and economic aspects of the meaning of work we have sketched in this chapter is important to contemporary students of work. At the very least, it will reduce the chances that they mistake a historically specific manifestation for a universal phenomenon. More ambitiously, this awareness may help them to see the subject in a richer way, leading them to better scientific investigation and increased awareness of the forces that shape the objective and subjective experience of this central human activity. Finally, it may help them to realize that their own work contributes to constructing the meaning of work, to the process through which political economic conflicts are expressed, and even to the outcomes of these conflicts.

Notes

1. By noting these two ways, we in no way mean to imply that the "real" and the socially constructed interpretations are unrelated to each other. In fact, we assume there usually is a relationship, but that the degree and kind are problematic.

2. All of the mechanisms we describe here can also be used to increase consumption. We will see examples of this reversal later in this chapter.

3. It is worth noting that the same process is part of the liberal economic account, but is viewed in far less pejorative terms. In contrast to the coercive metaphors of

Marx, liberal economists have emphasized the role of rational choice and free will through which individuals decide how to allocate their time and effort. People's preferences are expressed in the trade offs they make between income for leisure, the decisions about what work to do, and how much to save or to consume.

Undoubtedly, both sets of metaphors inform us about what actually happened. However, in order to explain how the consumption of people whose standard of living was at or near the requirements for physical survival could be limited and how people (e.g., factory workers during the industrial revolution), who already worked long and hard, were induced to work even longer and harder, the coercion metaphor seems to deserve more emphasis than it has been given in many statements of the liberal economic view.

4. It should be noted, however, that historians such as Sidney Pollard (1963) have suggested that even the decentralized case of Western Europe included conscious action by elites to manipulate social institutions to help them solve the problems of recalcitrant workers. Pollard concluded that employers acted collectively to alter the preferences and orientations of workers through schools, churches, and other institutions, so as to make the workers more responsive to the types of incentives that employers had to offer through their factories. We will return to Pollard's notions shortly.

5. Taussig (1977) reported that, even in the 1970s, managers of plantations in the Cauca Valley of Colombia had difficulty motivating workers through financial means because when they had earned enough money for the day, workers left work.

6. Perhaps some appreciation for the magnitude of the effects these changes had on the meaning of work can be obtained by looking at some modern research dealing with differences in performing work. Consider, for example, differences between the nature of the work experience associated with working under the various classes of technology described by Woodward (1965). While Woodward's own discussion of how mass production technologies create conditions for social conflict is revealing, Reeves and Turner's (1972) comparison of the nature of work and social relationships in batch and mass production settings adds new insights. They reported clear differences in the amount of uncertainty experienced, the degree of consensus and understanding of the whole, and types of work flow controls, to name a few. Similarly, Hulin and Roznowski (1985) contrasted the nature of tasks and the social relationships surrounding complex and less complex technologies. Among other things, different types of tasks and technologies are associated with different organizational climates, job characteristics, and communication and leadership patterns. These differences are associated with different job perceptions and job affect. Finally, Barley's (1986) study of how the same objective technology could be associated with substantial differences in the nature of the work experiences of members of two radiology departments revealed how differences in the assumptions individuals made about each other could produce dramatically different work experiences.

If such seemingly small differences within a short period of time can produce such dramatic contrasts in the experience of work, it seems safe to conclude that the historical changes we have been describing were associated with even greater changes in meaning.

7. Bureaucracies, of course, exist in noncapitalist systems. Here we are merely suggesting that the impetus to "bureaucratize" in the case of capitalism was related to

the particular distribution of benefits. There can be many other sources of such impetus in other societies.

8. An extreme of this method would be an ideology praising the virtues of relative poverty—"It is easier for a camel to pass through the eye of a needle than for a rich man to enter the kingdom of heaven."

9. While force appears to be less important, its role in resolving distributional conflicts in modern society cannot be ignored. Force, as we have seen, played an important part in establishing contemporary forms of work and organizations. Recall Marx's description of how the Enclosure Acts forced the peasants off the land and into the cities and the industrial world. More recently, Gutman (1977) described the struggle of nineteenth century industrialists to gain sufficient political power to enable them to establish the systems of work that favored their interests. Force was important. Gutman observed that, at first, the resistance at local levels was so strong that industrialists could not rely on local police to protect their property. Instead, they had to hire their own police and their early successes depended on the use of state militia because the state government were more remote from local pressures. In a related vein, Green (1980) reported that in the late 1800s industrialists (e.g., Andrew Carnegie) were able to exercise control at local levels in so-called company towns and elsewhere with the aid of private guards, state militia, and federal troops, in settling labor disputes. In short, force played a key role in creating the modern work system in Europe and in the United States.

10. Of course, luck, nature, God or gods, and so forth could and perhaps still do play a role. On the other hand, the seemingly more predictable world and growth of a belief in science and secular control seem to reduce the need for such accounts.

11. A qualitatively different or perhaps more extreme case would be that people do not need to work at all if they do not want to. In an objective sense, at least, this may be true for a few individuals in any society. Presumably, the meaning of work to this privileged group would be different than it is for most other people. However, we do not deal with this possibility here.

12. It is important to note that these writers are generally critical of the role of social institutions being used by the upper classes to promote their agendas. Implicit in many of these critiques is some idea that the interests of the members of the working classes deserved better treatment. While we suspect that there is considerable truth to their position, it is by no means clear that the interests of the groups the critics favor were more consistent with those of the larger collectivity than were the interests of the elites.

13. It is interesting to note that the value of one's work—at least as measured in economic terms—may affect the quality as well as the quantity of one's leisure. As Becker (1976) observed, as the economic value of a person's work increases, so does the opportunity cost of leisure. In other words, other things being equal, the cost of taking an hour of leisure to people who can sell their labor for $100/hour is much greater than to people whose labor only commands a price of $5/hour.

14. Clearly, we are speculating here; the issue of a correlation between the acceptance of the marginal productivity argument and social class is an empirical one. We do not know of empirical evidence concerning the matter, but by pointing it out, we hope that we might stimulate such investigation or have someone bring existing data to our attention.

15. Most discussions of the role of education in legitimating the current order have been developed by social critics who wish it were otherwise. Consequently, our discussion draws primarily from critical writers, even though there is room for considerable debate over many of their points. It is noteworthy, however, that while these changes are often considered to be products of modern radicals, the basic idea was shared in 1776, albeit in less pejorative terms, by Adam Smith (1904) in *The Wealth of Nations*. Smith advocated, contrary to his normal laissez-faire position, that the state provide public education as a means for preserving the established order. Smith argued that education made individuals "more likely to obtain the respect of their lawful superiors, and . . . therefore more disposed to respect those superiors" (p. 273).

16. Paradoxically, hard work may even be viewed as a negative, One may be seen as more worthy if one "works smart." If one is working too hard, one's "smartness" may come into question.

17. The work of Burawoy (1979) is a related but quite different perspective on the social construction processes that achieve acceptance of existing work (and societal) relationships. Burawoy argued that the consent is generated through the process of work "on the shop floor." Burawoy does not deal directly with the specific matter of accepting a given distribution of income, but rather with the failure of people to recognize major conflicts because their attention becomes focused on the microprocesses—especially the game of "making out"—at work. In a sense, his argument represents a potential challenge to the macro-focus of the latter portion of this chapter. On the other hand, we feel Burawoy did not fully consider the viability of possible macro-processes that might contribute to games in general or "making out" in particular. Overall, we tend to see Burawoy as describing an important complementary process to those we have described. In any case, his major thesis is consistent with the central ideas of this chapter—the nature of work and the social construction generated around it have important political and economic consequences.

References

Adams, J.S. (1965). Inequity in social exchange. In L. Berkowitz, (ed.), *Advances in Experimental Social Psychology*, vol. 2. New York: Academic Press, pp. 267–99.

Barley, S.R. (1986). Technology as an occasion for structuring: Evidence from observation of CT scanners and the social order of radiology departments. *Administrative Science Quarterly, 31*, pp. 78–107.

Barling, J., and Rosenbaum, A. (1986). "Work stressors and wife abuse." *Journal of Applied Psychology, 71*, pp. 346–8.

Bartolome, F., and Evans, P.A.L. (Spring 1979). *Organizational Dynamics*, 7(4), pp. 2–30.

Becker, G.S. (1976). *The economic approach to human behavior*. Chicago: University of Chicago Press.

Berger, P.L., and Luckmann, T. (1966). *The social construction of reality*. Garden City, NY: Anchor Books.

Bowles, S., and Gintis, H. (1977). *Schooling in capitalist America*. New York: Basic Books.

Bowles, S., Gintis, H., and Meyer, P. (1975–1976). Education, IQ, and the legitimation of the social division of labor. *Berkeley Journal of Sociology, 20*, pp. 223–64.

Braudel, F. (1982). The wheels of commerce. *Civilization capitalism, fifteenth to eighteenth centuries,* vol.2. New York: Harper and Row.

Braverman, H. (1974). *Labor and monopoly capital.* New York: Monthly Review Press.

Brehm, J.S. (1966). *A theory of psychological reactance.* New York: Academic Press.

Brewer, J. (1982). "Commercialization and politics." In N. McKendrick, J. Brewer, and J.H. Plumb (eds.), *The birth of a consumer society: The commercialization of eighteenth-century England.* Bloomington, IN: Indiana University Press, pp. 195–262.

Brookover, W.B., and Erickson, E.L. (1975). *Sociology of education,* rev. ed. Homewood, IL: Dorsey.

Brookover, W.B., Shailer, T., and Paterson, A. (1964). Self-concept of ability and school achievement. *Sociology of Education, 37,* pp. 271–8.

Burawoy, M. (1979). *Manufacturing consent. Changes in the labor process under monopoly capitalism.* Chicago: University of Chicago Press.

Callanhan, R.E. (1962). *Education and the cult of efficiency.* Chicago: University of Chicago Press.

Carse, J.P. (1986). *Finite and infinite games.* New York: Free Press.

Chinoy, E. (1955). *Automobile workers and the American dream.* New York: Doubleday.

Cipolla, C.M. (1980). *Before the industrial revolution. European society and the economy, 1000–1700.* 2nd ed. New York: W.W. Norton.

Collins, R. (1979). *The credential society. An historical sociology of education and stratification.* New York: Academic Press.

Culbert, S., and McDonough, J.J. (1985). *Radical management: Power struggles, power politics, and the pursuit of trust.* New York: Free Press.

deCharms, R. (1976). *Enhancing motivation. Change in the classroom.* New York: Ervington.

Della Fave, L.R. (1980). The meek shall not inherit the earth: Self-evaluation and the legitimacy of stratification. *American Sociological Review, 45,* pp. 955–71.

DiMaggio, P.J., and Powell, W.W. (1983). Institutional isomorphism. *American Sociological Review, 48,* pp. 147–60.

Duesenberry, J.S. (1952). *Income, saving, and the theory of consumer behavior.* Cambridge: Harvard University Press.

Edwards, R. (1979). *Contested terrain. The transformation of the workplace in the twentieth century.* New York: Basic Books.

Festinger, L.A. (1957). A theory of cognitive dissonance. Stanford, CA: Stanford University Press.

Galbraith, J.K. (1960). *The affluent society.* Boston: Houghton Mifflin.

Green, J.R. (1980). *The world of the worker. Labor in twentieth-century America.* New York: Hill and Wang.

Gutman, H.G. (1977). *Work, culture, and society in industrializing America.* New York: Vintage.

Halle, D. (1984). *America's working man.* Chicago: University of Chicago Press.

Hirschman, A.O. (1970). *Exit, voice and loyalty.* Cambridge: Harvard University Press.

———. (1977). *The passions and the interests.* Princeton, NJ: Princeton University Press.

Hoffman, L.W. (1986). "Work, family and the child." In M.S. Pallak and R.O. Perloff (eds.), *Psychology and work: Productivity, change and employment.* Washington, DC: American Psychological Association, pp. 173–220.

Homans, G.C. (1950). *The human group.* New York: Harcourt, Brace, and World.

———. (1974). *Social behavior: Its elementary forms.* rev. ed. New York: Harcourt Brace Jovanovich.

Hulin, C.L., and Roznowski, M. (1985). Organizational technologies: Effect on organizations' characteristics and individuals' responses. In L.L. Cummings and B.M. Staw (eds.), *Research in organizational behavior, 7.* Greenwich, CT: JAI Press, pp. 39–85.

Hunter, J.E. (1986). Cognitive ability, cognitive aptitudes, job knowledge, and job performance. *Journal of Vocational Behavior, 29,* pp. 340–62.

Jackall, R. (1978). *Workers in a labyrinth. Jobs and survival in a bank bureaucracy.* Montclair, NJ: Allanheld, Osmun Co.

Jacoby, S.M. (1985). *Employing bureaucracy. Managers, unions, and the transformation of work in American industry, 1900–1945.* New York: Columbia University Press.

Jencks, C. (1979). *Who gets ahead? The determinants of economic success in America.* New York: Basic Books.

Kelley, H.H. (1973). The processes of causal attribution. *American Psychologist, 28,* pp. 107–28.

Kemper, T.D., and Reichler, M.L. (1976). Work integration, marital satisfaction, and conjugal power." *Human Relations, 29,* pp. 929–44.

Keynes, J.M. (1936). *The general theory of employment, interest, and money.* New York: Harcourt Brace Jovanovich.

Kolko, G. (1963). *The triumph of conservatism.* New York: Free Press.

Langer, E.J. (1983). *The psychology of control.* Beverly Hills, CA: Sage Publications.

Langton, J. (1984). The ecological theory of bureaucracy: The case of Josiah Wedgewood and the British pottery industry. *Administrative Science Quarterly, 29,* pp. 330–54.

Lindblom, C.E. (1977). *Politics and markets.* New York: Basic Books.

Linder, M. (1977). *Anti-Samuelson.* Vol. 1. New York: Urizen Books.

March, J.G. (1976). The technology of foolishness. In J.G. March and J.P. Olsen (eds.), *Ambiguity and choice in organizations.* Bergen, Norway: Universitets forlaget, pp. 69–81.

Marglin, S.A. (1974). What do bosses do? The origins and functions of hierarchy in capitalist production. *Review of Radical Political Economics, 6,* pp. 60–112.

Marx, K. (1967). *Capital: A critique of political economy.* Vol. 1. New York: International Publishers.

McKendrick, N. (1982). "Commercialization and the Economy." In N. McKendrick, J. Brewer, and J.H. Plumb. *The birth of a consumer society. The commercialization of eighteenth-century England.* Bloomington, IN: Indiana University Press.

Meyer, J.W., and Rowan, B. (1977). Institutionalized organizations: Formal structure as myth and ceremony. *American Journal of Sociology, 83,* pp. 340–63.

Mintzberg, H. (1979). *The structuring of organizations.* Englewood Cliffs, NJ: Prentice Hall.

Moore, B., Jr. (1978). *Injustice: The social bases of obedience and revolt.* White Plains, NY: M.E. Sharpe.

Nelson, D. (1975). *Managers and workers. Origins of the new factory system in the United States, 1880–1920*. Madison, WI: University of Wisconsin Press.

Niebuhr, H.R. (1957). *The social sources of denominationalism*. New York: Meridian Books.

Noble, D.F. (1984). *Forces of production*. New York: Alfred A. Knopf.

North, D.C. (1981). *Structure and change in economic history*. New York: W.W. Norton.

Ornati, O. (1956). *Poverty amid affluence*. New York: Twentieth Century Fund.

Packard, V. (1957). *The hidden persuaders*. New York: David McKay.

Plumb, J.H. (1982). Commercialization and society. In N. McKendrick, J. Brewer, and J.H. Plumb (eds.), *The birth of a consumer society: The commercialization of eighteenth century England*. Bloomington: Indiana University Press, pp. 263–334.

Pollard S. (1963). Factory discipline in the industrial revolution, *Economic History Review, 16*, pp. 254–71.

Pope, L. (1942). *Millhands and preachers. A study of Gastonia*. New Haven: Yale University Press.

Rainwater, L. (1974). *What money buys. Inequality and the social meanings of income*. New York: Basic Books.

Reeves, T.K., and Turner, B.A. (1972). A theory of organization behavior in batch production factories. *Administrative Science Quarterly, 17*, pp. 81–98.

Riskin, C. (1974). Incentive systems and work motivations: The experience in China. *Working Papers for a New Society, 1*(4), pp. 27–31, 77–92.

Rodgers, D.T. (1978). *The work ethic in industrial America, 1850–1920*. Chicago: University of Chicago Press.

Ross, L. (1977). The intuitive psychologists and his shortcomings: Distortions in the attribution process. In L. Berkowitz (ed.), *Advances in experimental social psychology*. vol. 10. New York: Academic Press.

Ryan, W. (1982). *Equality*. New York: Vintage Books.

Salancik, G.R., and Pfeffer, J. (1978). A social information processing approach to job attitudes and task design. *Administrative Science Quarterly, 23*, pp. 224–53.

Samuelson, P.A. (1970). *Economics*, 8th ed. New York: McGraw-Hill.

Schaef, A.W., and D. Fassel. (1988). *The addictive organization*. San Francisco: Harper and Row.

Schneider, B. (1983). Interactional organizational psychology. In L.L. Cummings and B.M. Staw (eds.), *Research in organizational behavior*. vol. 5. Greenwich, CT: JAI Press, pp. 1–31.

Scitovsky, T. (1976). *The joyless economy*. New York: Oxford University Press.

Sennett, R., and Cobb, J. (1973). *The hidden injuries of class*. New York: Vintage Books.

Smith, A. (1904). *An inquiry into the nature and causes of the wealth of nations*. vol. 2 New York: G.P. Putnam's Sons.

Snyder, M., and Ickes W. (1985). "Personality and social behavior." In G. Lindzey and E. Aronson (eds.), *Handbook of social psychology*. vol. 2, 3rd ed. New York: Random House, pp. 883–947.

Stone, K. (1974). The origins of job structures in the steel industry. *Review of Radical Political Economics, 6*, pp. 113–73.

Taussig, M. (1977). "The genesis of capitalism amongst a South American peasantry:

Devil's labor and the baptism of money." *Comparative Studies in Society and Economic History,* vol. 19, pp. 130–55.

Tawney, R.H. (1962) *Religion and the rise of capitalism.* Gloucester, England: Peter Smith.

Terrail, J.P. (1985a). Commodity fetishism and the ideal of needs. In E. Preteceille and J.P. Terrail (eds.), *Capitalism, consumption, and needs.* Oxford, UK: Basil Blackwell, pp. 6–36.

———. (1985b). The Historical and Social Nature of Needs. In E. Preteceille and J.P. Terrail (eds.), *Capitalism, consumption, and needs.* Oxford, UK: Basil Blackwell, pp. 37–81.

Thompson, E.P. (1963). *The making of the English working class.* New York: Random House.

Thurow, L.C. (1975). *Generating inequality mechanisms of distribution in the U.S. economy.* New York: Basic Books.

Veblen, T. (1953). *The theory of the leisure class.* New York: Mentor Books.

Watson, R.A., and Watson, P.J. (1969). *Man and nature. An anthropological essay in human ecology.* New York: Harcourt, Brace, and World.

Weber, M. (1958). *The Protestant ethic and the spirit of capitalism.* New York: Charles Scribner's Sons.

Weick, K.E. (1979). *The social psychology of organizing.* 2nd ed. Reading, MA: Addison-Wesley.

Weinstein, J. (1968). *The corporate ideal in the liberal state: 1900–1918.* Boston: Beacon Press.

Whyte, M.K. (1973). Bureaucracy and modernization in China: The Maoist critique. *American Sociological Review, 38,* pp. 149–63.

Woodward, J. (1965). *Industrial organization: Theory and practice.* London: Oxford University Press.

Young, M., and Willmott, P. (1973). *The symmetrical family.* New York: Pantheon Books.

Epilogue

Arthur P. Brief
Walter R. Nord

After spending many years preparing to write this book and then the better part of three years actually writing the early drafts of the essays, the task of finalizing the chapters evoked some sharply contrasting feelings. On the one hand, we were pleased by what we learned and, albeit to a lesser extent, what we were able to put on paper so that others might benefit from our efforts. On the other hand, we became even more sharply aware of what had not been accomplished.

In this concluding chapter, we highlight both our accomplishments and failures. In discussing what we hope to have contributed, we try to make it very clear that most of what we did was simply view, in a slightly different way, what others had contributed. In discussing what we were unable to do, we comfort ourselves (to some degree) by suggesting that recognizing our failures may help others to focus on areas where effort is needed. We are aware that such self-comforting can easily turn into rather mindless rationalizing, but we tried to be as objective as possible.

Perhaps the most significant learning that we experienced was one of humility. If we can successfully communicate this learning to our fellow social scientists, we think the value of our efforts may go well beyond anything we have said about work *per se*. As was indicated in the first chapter, despite numerous attempts, we never were able to come up with a fully satisfactory definition of *work*. In attempting to understand why these efforts were so unsatisfactory, we believe we came in touch with some issues that plague modern social science as it is currently practiced. Below, we review our efforts under three headings: contributions to our understanding of the meaning of work, gaps in our knowledge, and implications for social science more generally.

Contributions to the Study of Work

Our review of the literature produced two themes that we see as important contributions to the study of the meaning of work. First, the nature and meaning of work are best understood as being very relative to special contexts. Second, in the contemporary context, an extremely important component of what work means to individuals is its financial outcomes.

Relativistic View of Work

Throughout the book, it has been clear that the objective characteristics of work (e.g., type and amount of effort, physical setting, and compensation) vary widely as a function of time, space, and one's position in the social strata. Different countries and geographic settings spawn markedly contrasting kinds of work. Moreover, over time the nature and settings of work have changed dramatically. Finally, at any given point in time, what constitutes work differs across hierarchical levels, even within a narrow geographic region—even, in fact, within a unit as small as an office. Without judging whether their work is any better or any worse, it is safe to say that the nature of the tasks performed by people at the highest levels of most organizations is very different from those performed by individuals at the lowest levels.

Under these circumstances, it is unrealistic to expect that there will be any meaning to work that is common to all circumstances. Consequently, serious efforts to comprehend what work means to people are unlikely to find a great deal of commonality. Therefore, theories about the meaning of work must be rich enough to take into account variations across times, places, and jobs. Moreover, at the level of the individual, the meaning of work arises out of a process through which people translate and integrate stimuli and the context in which the stimuli appear with their own states of being to arrive at some subjective experience. Since the meaning of work is affected by differences in the subjective experiences of individuals, data collection must include characteristics of individuals that influence their interpretations of various stimuli. In addition, given that a person may change his/her view of even the same stimulus over time, the meaning of work is not constant even across an individual's lifetime. In short, theories about the meaning of work should rest on data that reflect the dynamic interaction of various and changing individuals in various and changing contexts.

We also have noted that in addition to the meaning of work for individuals, work can be said to have meaning for the social collectivity. Here, the meaning of work is more concerned with processes that affect the way a "society as a whole" views what work is and/or should be. Clearly, the subjective experiences of individuals who are working are part of society's view, but so are ideological statements and social structures that summarize and institutionalize these subjective understandings. The fact that various institutional patterns can serve special interests introduces the possibility that the social meaning of work can be manipulated (consciously or unconsciously) to give advantages to some people over others.

The relativistic theme has two major implications. First, as we have stated often, it means that one is unlikely to discover any universal meaning of work. Work must be understood in context. The second implication flows from the first—study of the meaning of work must be grounded in understandings of history and political economy. Cross sectional studies of what people want from work or reports as to the effects of work on people's lives are apt to be of very limited value unless they also include ways to link the findings to the "events" of the particular time and place in which they are conducted. These events may be economic, political, and/or social in nature, sharing only in the characteristic that they condition how people interpret their work. General understanding of the meaning of work requires analysis of the interaction among individuals, time, places, and jobs.

The Financial Component

A second contribution to studies of the meaning of work is the theme that emerged far more powerfully than we had expected—the important weight that economic outcomes appear to have in what work means to people. To some degree this should come as no surprise given the definition of *work* as what people do to make a living. This raises the question: Why should we, as social scientists who have spent a good deal of our lives studying work, have been surprised at all by this pattern?

Perhaps we have misread or only partially read the literature. Certainly this could be. However, we believe that at least equal weight needs to be given to the possibility that the more recent literature, particularly in the organizational sciences, has underestimated the role of economic outcomes to contemporary workers. Brief and Aldag (in press), Fein (1976), and Goldthorpe et al. (1969) have emphatically made this point.

These observations raise a second question: Why have the monetary aspects of work received less attention than they might deserve? Perhaps, drawing on Weick (1980), students of work have been "blinded by spotting." In other words, we have found (i.e., *spotted*) so many novel or unexpected aspects of work (e.g., variety, autonomy, feedback, etc.) to be important that we have been blinded to even more fundamental concerns. Additionally, part of our surprise might stem from the lingering influence of the work ethic that keeps one focused on the nonmaterial aspects of work. Perhaps, as Nord (1977) noted, we have underemphasized the importance of money owing to biases introduced by the quest for finding non-zero sum solutions to conflicts between management and workers rather than zero sum solutions such as higher wages. Whatever the reason, it seems the importance of economic outcomes to the meaning of work is seriously underrepresented in the modern social sciences—with the obvious and important exception of economics (where the case probably is overstated).

Major Shortcomings

There are several important deficiencies in our collection of essays that we recognize. First, with the exception of those chapters that were commissioned, we opted for breadth rather than depth. The major symptom of this shortcoming was that we often used the research literature to illustrate possibilities rather than analyze particular studies in depth and based our conclusions on interpretations of the total pattern. As a result, the chapters we wrote and, therefore, the book as a whole are best interpreted as pointing out possible relationships and calling for deeper inquiry into the available literature as well as for additional empirical work. Our only defense for this deficiency is that we were overwhelmed, to some degree, by the magnitude of the phenomenon. Nevertheless, we decided that it would be useful to publish the results of our efforts to date in order to stimulate others. Hopefully, other investigators will probe more deeply without losing sight of the fundamental intellectual problem we encountered—namely, the breadth of the meaning of work.

Second, we, along with other students of work, remain trapped by the current uses of words. We were never able to define *work* and other salient terms (such as *leisure, family* and *retirement*) in fully satisfactory ways. In this sense, we may have done a disservice—continuing to use words that are so imprecise may only reify them further. In our defense, we did show the inadequacy of some of the words we used and thereby challenged others to employ them in more circumspect fashion.

Third, the chapters remain loosely integrated. Basically, all we did was show the number of dimensions that have been considered and that need further development if the meaning of work is to be better comprehended. We have not provided any meaningful framework for reducing the complexity to a more tractable form. In essence, we have complicated things when our initial desire was to put them in better order.

These are all serious limitations. Nevertheless, we are hopeful they are outweighed by the positive contributions outlined above and, even if not, by their value to stimulate others to overcome our shortcomings.

Contributions to Organizational Science

The organizational sciences are plagued by inconsistent empirical results. As a result, theory construction is extremely difficult. The problems we had in defining precisely words such as work and the relativistic theme that emerged from our research may be instructive for organizational scientists in their attempts to build more viable theories.

Entropy from Everyday Language. Applied social scientists tend to derive their concepts and problems from the language of everyday life. This source, of course, has the advantage of increasing the likelihood that their research will be viewed as applicable. There is, however, a major disadvantage in mining this source for our constructs.

Everyday words are often far too general and dynamic to serve science. The problem is analogous to stimulus generalization where a perceiver assigns the same label to a wide variety of stimuli that have basic commonality but differ in some particulars. However, the particulars may make an enormous difference in how the concrete experiences of social reality are experienced at any given point in time. As a result, words like *work* are too coarse to be useful as constructs in building nomological networks.

The problem of overgeneralization increases with time. The usefulness of measures that may have been highly valid indicators of constructs (i.e., that reflected social reality) at a given point in time, will decay as that reality changes. If, for example, the nature of and the roles played by the family change over time, the stimuli that a family provides to its members and the interpretations they tie to it also will change. As a result, *family* simply can not serve as a useful construct over time. Moreover, as we have shown throughout, neither can *retirement* nor *leisure* nor, most significantly, *work* itself. Undoubtedly, the same can be said for many other social categories— *education, religion, organization, foreman,* and so forth.

Responding to the Problems of Complexity and Word Entropy. What can be done? We have several interrelated suggestions. First, *recognize the problem.* The changing nature of social reality must be recognized by social scientists; and, they must actively wrestle with the implications of this recognition in their research and theory development. [See Gergen (1982) on this point.] In some sense, this is very easy—we can simply teach ourselves and our students about the evolution in the meaning of words and social categories. Using this awareness, on the other hand, is more difficult. Conventional social categories provide such attractive starting points for inquiry. To require that empirical inquiries directed at particular topics also incorporate ways to detect changes in meaning is to impose an extremely demanding burden on our field.

Second, *describe contexts.* This suggestion might be one means of reducing the formidable task implied by our first. We suggest that research be conducted in ways that allows the context in which it occurs to be more fully comprehended by future investigators. This means going beyond simply describing the methodology. It means "thickly" describing, for instance, the time and place in which the study took place. While exactly what information will be needed cannot be anticipated a priori, the starting point is clear.

Topics such as work must be viewed in context and the dimensions of context that are important for specific topics must be uncovered over time. Clearly, the dimensionalization of context is required at both the micro- and macro-levels. At the micro-level, one would want to be concerned with how components of context affect the thoughts, feelings, and behaviors of individuals. At the macro-level, frameworks are needed for examining how, for example, demographic, economic, cultural, and political forces shape the social institutions in which individuals are embedded. Over time, these two levels probably can and should be intergrated; but we anticipate the task will not be an easy one.

Third, *go back to the basics.* In some ways, this suggestion really is a synthesis of the first two. Basically, research must be developed that will permit us to define the nature of the stimuli that work, family, and other social institutions present to people. Further, research should permit us to understand those factors that influence what people attend to at work and what interpretations they give to those things. In other words, we postulate that there are principles of human behavior that operate in work settings and for individuals across their life spans. These may be psychological, physiological, sociological, or whatever. If useful theories are to be built, they will emerge from our understanding of the interrelationships among these perspectives. If our research is so grounded, we should be able to understand better how the human experience changes over time as institutions change.

If we are to understand the meaning of work (or other human experiences), we must recognize that due to what we call *word entropy,* it can not be assumed that the complex set of stimuli and processes that are described by a particular social label (e.g., *work, family,* or *career*) at one time will exist in the same configuration the next time the label is applied. Consequently, we must organize our research around *basic* processes of human behavior *and* human institutions. For example, at the individual level, Weick's (1979) view that we ought to study general processes such as selection, enactment, and retention is in this direction. At the institutional level, rather than focusing on "the family" we might be better advised to focus on how and with whom people allocate their time to get certain needs met and on the dimensions of the social context in which they learn and maintain themselves and others who might be dependent on them. The major relevance of the family in this sense is its role as a dimension of the social context that provides a source of normative grounding on which people make comparisons and judgments about appropriateness of their actions. However, the focus is on the generic phenomena of standards of comparison, handling of dependency, learning, and maintenance, not the family *per se.*

Research guided by these more generic phenomena will be, in the long run, best able to help us comprehend a specific topic such as work. Moreover, it will be useful in answering more questions about how human institutions and people change over time. Perhaps the basic theories to turn to remain to be discovered, but we suspect they will emerge from the fundamental disciplines, such as psychology and sociology.

Conclusions

In short, we suggest that work and other terms used to describe everyday human experiences are best understood through analyzing them in reference to concepts used to describe human behavior more generally. Investigations grounded in these "basic" categories will be more useful in developing theories and understanding the phenomena than have been the conventional categories, the meanings of which are themselves changing constantly. A side benefit of such theoretically grounded research is that it may yield information that contributes to the advancement of basic theory itself. Of course, what we have crudely depicted is an aspiration, one which currently is not within our grasp.

In any case, the message of this book is that work *cannot* be isolated— either practically or theoretically—from the rest of human experience. The sooner we begin to incorporate fundamental theories and constructs about human behavior *and* social institutions into our study of the meaning of work, the better for all concerned.

References

Brief, A.P., and Aldag, R.J. (N.d.). The economic functions of work. In K.M. Rowland and G.R. Ferris (eds.), *Research in Personnel and Human Resources Management.* Greenwich, CT: JAI Press. In press.

Fein, M. (1976). Motivation for work. In R. Dubin (ed.), *Handbook of work, organization, and society.* Chicago: Rand McNally, pp. 465–530.

Gergen, K.J. (1982). *Toward transformation in social knowledge.* New York: Springer-Verlag.

Goldthorpe, J.H., Lockwood, D., Bechhofer, F., and Platt, J. (1969). *The affluent worker in the class structure.* Cambridge: Cambridge University Press.

Nord, W.R. (1977). Job satisfaction reconsidered. *American Psychologist, 32,* pp. 1026–35.

Weick, K.E. (1980). Blind spots in organizational theorizing. *Group and Organization Studies, 5,* pp. 178–88.

Index

About the Contributors

Elizabeth M. Doherty is assistant professor of management at the University of Nevada/Reno. She received her Ph.D. in organizational behavior from Washington University in 1988. Her research focuses on organizational work-life issues, the application of behavior modification to organizations, and the sociopolitical context of organizations. Underlying these themes is an interest in improving the quality of life at work. Professor Doherty is currently engaged in several studies on rewards and reward systems. In particular, she is investigating the effects of reinforcement schedules on cognitive processes in an effort to advance an integrated behavioral-cognitive perspective to organizational behavior, and is studying the implementation of a gain-sharing system in a not-for-profit agency.

George W. England is director of the Meaning of Work Research Program and professor emeritus of management in the College of Business Administration at the University of Oklahoma. Professor England is author or co-author of several books on organizational psychology and management including *The Manager and the Man, Organizational Functioning in a Cross-Cultural Perspective, The Functioning of Complex Organizations,* and *The Meaning of Working.*

Jennifer M. George received her Ph.D. in management and organizational behavior from New York University's Graduate School of Business Administration. She is currently an assistant professor in the management department at Texas A & M University. Her research interests include personality influences, affect/mood at work, work–life linkages, stress and well-being, values, prosocial organizational behavior, and customer service. She has published articles in the *Journal of Applied Psychology,* the *Journal of Personality and Social Psychology,* the *Journal of Organizational Behavior,* and *Personality and Individual Differences.*

Edwin A. Locke, Ph.D., is professor of business and management at the University of Maryland. He received his M.A. and Ph.D. degrees in industrial psychology from Cornell University. Dr. Locke is the coauthor with G. Latham of *Goal Setting: A Motivational Technique that Works* (Prentice Hall 1984) and *A Theory of Goal Setting and Task Performance* (Prentice Hall 1990), and is the author of *Generalizing from Laboratory to Field Settings* (Lexington Books 1986). He is an internationally known behavioral scientist whose work is included in leading textbooks and acknowledged in other works on the history of management. Dr. Locke is a fellow of the American Psychological Association and of the Academy of Management.

Loriann Roberson received her doctorate in psychology in 1984 from the University of Minnesota. In 1985, she received the S. Rains Wallace Dissertation Award from the Society for Industrial and Organizational Psychology. She is currently an assistant professor in the industrial and organizational psychology program at New York University.

M. Susan Taylor is associate professor of management and organizations at the College of Business and Management, University of Maryland at College Park, and has taught on the faculties at the Graduate School of Business, University of Wisconsin at Madison, and the Amos Tuck School, Dartmouth College. She holds a doctorate in industrial/organizational psychology from Perdue University. Taylor currently serves on the executive committee of the Personnel/Human Resources Division. She is a member of the Personnel Human Resource Research Group, the Society of Industrial/Organizational Psychology, and Division 14 of the American Psychological Association and serves on the editorial boards of the *Academy of Management Review* (1985 to 1990), and the *Journal of Applied Psychology* (1988 to 1991). Dr. Taylor has written more than thirty journal articles and book chapters on organizational recruitment, individual career development, and performance feedback, with her work appearing in the *Academy of Management Journal, JAI Press Research in Personnel/Human Resource Management,* the *Journal of Applied Psychology, Organizational Behavior and Human Decision Processes, Personnel Psychology, Personnel Administrator,* and *Public Personnel Management.* She recently co-authored an exercise series that uses cognitive, behavioral modeling and experiential approaches to develop human-resource skills required by the manager's role (*Human Resource Management Skills Modules,* Southwestern 1989). Her current research examines the intersection of executive career development and business strategies, the mechanisms used to integrate individual's work and life roles, and the design of organizational-feedback systems.

William T. Whitely is associate professor of human resource management in the College of Business at the University of Oklahoma. He was a member of the international research team that gathered the data on which his chapter with Professor England is based. He is currently a member of a ten-country team conducting a longitudinal study of work-role development in youth who are entering the labor force for the first time. His other current research interests include the early career development of managers and professionals, and a longitudinal study of strategic human-resource management practices in banks that have undergone growth, decline, turnaround, or reorganization in their performance. He is a member of the Academy of Management and the American Psychological Association, and is an American Brands International Scholar in comparative management.

About the Editors

Arthur P. Brief received his Ph.D. from the University of Wisconsin at Madison in 1974 and is currently professor of organizational behavior at Tulane's A.B. Freeman School of Business and, by courtesy, professor of psychology. Prior to his move to Tulane in 1989, Professor Brief was on the faculties at several schools including, most recently, the Stern School of Business at New York University. In addition to lecturing throughout the United States, he has taught organizational behavior in the People's Republic of China. Professor Brief has authored dozens of articles and chapters on his studies of employee attitudes and behaviors and has written six books including *Task Design and Employee Motivation, Managing Job Stress,* and *Productivity Research in the Behavioral and Social Sciences.* He is co-editor with Benjamin Schneider of the Lexington Books series entitled "Issues in Organizational Management" and editor of a series of ancestral books in administrative science for Garland Publishing Company. He has served on the editorial boards of the *Academy of Management Review,* the *Academy of Management Journal,* and other learned journals and is currently on the board of the *Journal of Applied Psychology.* Professor Brief is a fellow of the American Psychological Association and the American Psychological Society as well as past president of the Midwest Academy of Management. He is also founding co-chairperson of the Academy of Management's Public Sector Division and a member of the American Sociological Association and the Society for Human Resource Management. In addition to being an educator, Professor Brief is an active advisor to management in the human-resources area, serving as a consultant to a variety of industries including health care, commercial banking, legal services, insurance, manufacturing, retailing, and publishing.

Walter R. Nord, Ph.D., is professor of management at the University of South Florida/Tampa. His current research interests center on critical political economics of organizations, organizational innovation, and organizational conflict. He holds a doctorate in social psychology from Washington University, an M.S. from Cornell University, and a B.A. from Williams College. Dr.

Nord's most recent publications include a chapter with Arthur Brief, Jennifer Atieh, and Elizabeth Doherty entitled "Work Values and the Conduct of Organizational Behavior" for *Research in Organizational Behavior,* a chapter entitled "OD's Unfulfilled Visions: Some Lessons from Economics" for *Research in Organizational Change in Development,* and *Implementing Routine and Radical Innovations* with S. Tucker.